The Earthscan Reader on Risk

The Earthscan Reader on Risk

Edited by

Ragnar E. Löfstedt and Åsa Boholm

earthscan
from Routledge

First published by Earthscan in the UK and USA in 2009

For a full list of publications please contact:
Earthscan
2 Park Square, Milton Park, Abingdon, Oxon OX14 4RN
711 Third Avenue, New York, NY 10017

Earthscan is an imprint of the Taylor & Francis Group, an informa business

Notices
Practitioners and researchers must always rely on their own experience and knowledge in evaluating and using any information, methods, compounds, or experiments described herein. In using such information or methods they should be mindful of their own safety and the safety of others, including parties for whom they have a professional responsibility.

Product or corporate names may be trademarks or registered trademarks, and are used only for identification and explanation without intent to infringe.

ISBN: 978-1-84407-686-4   hardback
      978-1-84407-687-1   paperback

Typeset by Domex e-Data, India
Cover design by Andrew Corbett

A catalogue record for this book is available from the British Library

Library of Congress Cataloging-in-Publication Data has been applied for

Contents

Part I – The Concept of Risk

Part II – Risk Perception

Part III – Communication about Risk

Part IV – Trust and Post-Trust

Part V – Policy and Regulation

List of Figures and Tables

Figures

Tables

Preface

In 1998, when Lynn Frewer and I published our first *Earthscan Reader in Risk and Modern Society*, it was chiefly to provide an updated account of what had been happening in the risk research field in the 1990s. Many of the theoretical questions raised in that reader still apply today, including those pertaining to the social amplification of risk and trust. That reader was published 10 years ago, however, and much has happened since. A number of new journals have entered the scene, most notably *Health Risk and Society, Risk Management* and *Regulation and Governance*. Some of the more established journals are now published more frequently: *Risk Analysis* now comes out six times a year and carries as many as 25 articles per issue, while *Journal of Risk Research*, first published in 1998, is now published eight times a year. The volume of risk research has grown exponentially over the 10-year period.

The world is also a changed place. In the late 1990s, risk researchers did not give the field of terrorism much thought. The 11 September 2001 terrorist attacks in the US, along with the bombings in Madrid (March 2004) and London (July 2005) changed all that. Similarly, researchers are now becoming increasingly concerned about new and emergent risks posed by nanotechnology, something that was not discussed in the 1990s. Many of the salient topics in risk research 10 years ago when the first reader was published, however, remain pertinent. What we see today is perhaps a stronger focus on regulation and policy processes, growing interest in organizational responses to risk and risk management, and concern about the role of uncertainty in the whole chain of risk-related undertakings, from assessment to regulation and communication. What is just as urgent now as when the field was new is debate on the very concept of risk, to answer questions about the nature of risk itself and how it can be conceptualized in philosophical and sociological terms.

This new *Earthscan Reader on Risk* is therefore intended not to replace the 1998 *Reader in Risk and Modern Society*, but rather to both complement and build on its foundations. All the articles featured in the present volume are new. The introduction has also been completely rewritten, highlighting some of the conceptual advances in the field over the past decade and focusing on some underlying philosophical underpinnings of the research area. The responsibility for writing the introduction and selecting the articles for this volume has been shared with my new co-editor, Åsa Boholm. Many of the articles selected for this volume and ideas expressed in the introduction reflect our numerous discussions over the last 15 years as research collaborators.

Ragnar E. Löfstedt
November 2008

List of Sources

Chapter 1 Löfstedt, R. E. and Boholm, Å. (2009) 'The study of risk in the 21st century', previously unpublished
Copyright © Ragnar E. Löfstedt, 2009

Chapter 2 Bradbury, J. A. (1989) 'The policy implications of differing concepts of risk', *Science, Technology and Human Values*, vol 14, no 4 (Autumn), pp380–399
Copyright © Sage Publications, Inc., 1989

Chapter 3 Hansson, S. O. (1999) 'A philosophical perspective on risk', *Ambio*, vol 28, no 6 (September), pp 539–542
Copyright © Royal Swedish Academy of Sciences, 1999

Chapter 4 Reith, G. (2004) 'Uncertain times: The notion of "risk" and the development of modernity', *Time and Society*, vol 13, no 2–3, pp383–402
Copyright © Sage Publications, Inc., 2004

Chapter 5 Finucane, M. L. Slovic, P., Mertz, C. K., Flynn, J. and Satterfield, T. A. (2000) 'Gender, race and perceived risk: The "white male" effect', *Health, Risk and Society*, vol 2, no 2, pp159–172
Copyright © Taylor & Francis Ltd, 2000

Chapter 6 Fischhoff, B., Slovic, P., Lichtenstein, S., Read, S. and Combs, B. (1978) 'How safe is safe enough? A psychometric study of attitudes towards technological risks and benefits', *Policy Sciences*, no 9, pp127–152
Copyright © Elsevier Scientific Publishing Company, 1978

Chapter 7 Loewenstein, G. F., Weber, E. U., Hsee, C. K. and Welch, N. (2001) 'Risk as feelings', *Psychological Bulletin*, vol 127, no 2, pp267–286
Copyright © 2001 American Psychological Association, Inc., 2001

List of Acronyms and Abbreviations

BPR	blame prevention re-engineering
CFI	comparative fit index
DoE	US Department of Energy
EC	European Commission
ECJ	European Court of Justice
EP	European Parliament
EPA	US Environmental Protection Agency
EU	expected utility; *also* European Union
FSA	UK Food Standards Agency
GM	genetically modified
J/DM	judgement and decision-making
MANOVA	multivariate analysis of variance
ML	maximum likelihood
NIMBY	not in my backyard
NRC	Nuclear Regulatory Commission
PCA	principal-components analysis
PRA	probabilistic risk assessment
RRR	risk regulation regime
SPS	sanitary and phytosanitary
SVS	salient value similarity
WTO	World Trade Organization

The Study of Risk in the 21st Century

Ragnar E. Löfstedt and Åsa Boholm

It is unclear when exactly the field of risk analysis came into being. Some researchers argue that risk analysis may predate Greek and Roman times (Covello and Mumpower, 1985). Others argue that risk analysis in some sense has been with us since the invention of gambling more than 5000 years ago (Bernstein, 1996). That said, risk analysis did not grow in prominence before the advent of complicated engineering systems, including chemical factories, nuclear power plants and space rockets/stations (e.g. Farmer, 1967, 1977). For example, when the first nuclear power plants were built in the UK in the 1950s, there were no quantitative safety criteria for the reactors, and the only guidance available came from the International Commission for Radiological Protection and from engineers in the chemical industry (Chicken, 1982). The standards then established were extremely vague and could not realistically be considered regulations, leading to problems for nuclear plant manufacturers, as they were unsure of what safety criteria to adopt. In the UK, for example, risk analysis per se did not appear until 1967, when Professor F. Farmer, then head of the UK Atomic Energy Authority's Safety and Reliability Directorate, proposed a whole new set of safety criteria for the nuclear sector, based on statistical probabilities and reliability techniques from the aerospace sector. These techniques, now referred to as probabilistic risk assessment (PRA), comprising fault and event trees, changed risk management profoundly (Farmer, 1967, 1977; Chicken, 1982; O'Riordan, 1987).

In the social science area of risk, aside from the very important mid-1940s work on natural hazards of Gilbert White, a geographer at the University of Chicago, relevant research did not arguably begin until the late 1960s (for a discussion of this, see Löfstedt and Frewer, 1998). There were two primary instigators of this research at that time, namely, researcher curiosity and increased research funding in the area. In 1969, Chauncey Starr published a seminal article in *Science* entitled 'Social benefit versus technological risk'. In it, Starr used historical analysis to gain an understanding of the degree of acceptance of the risks posed by different hazards. His research was driven by a need to understand society's previous responses to risk. A critical issue was whether or not particular risk exposures were considered voluntary or involuntary, and whether the voluntary nature of an exposure was significantly correlated with the extent to which a hazard was accepted by the public (Starr, 1969). At the same time, Paul Slovic, a psychologist who had been working with Ward Edwards at the University of Michigan on experimental studies of risk-taking and decision-making, met Gilbert White. White was curious to find out if Slovic's work on decision-making under risk could provide insight into how the public perceive natural hazards. The laboratory research done by Slovic and his colleagues was unable to address White's questions, as it was too narrowly focused on choice (see Slovic, 2000, for a detailed discussion). Eventually, however, Slovic and others were able to address them (e.g. Slovic et al, 1974) with the assistance of the latest developments in cognitive psychology, in particular, those regarding heuristics and biases (Tversky and Kahneman, 1974; for an excellent updated discussion, see Gilovich et al, 2002). The Starr article also led Slovic and his colleagues Sarah Lichtenstein and Baruch Fischhoff to replicate its findings via research in the area of cognitive processes and attitudes to risk-taking (Fischhoff et al, 1978; reprinted as Chapter 6 in this volume). This initial research led to the formation of the psychometric paradigm, arguably one of the main building blocks of the social science risk research field (Fischhoff et al, 1978).

At about the same time as this research began, mainly in the US, funding started to become available from research councils (e.g. National Science Foundation), government departments (the US Department of Energy and US Environmental Protection Agency) and industry (mainly the chemical and nuclear power industries) (Golding, 1992). Much of this funding was driven by public outcry against certain modern technologies. In the wake of the Love Canal, Times Beach and other technological mishaps, the public in many cases no longer trusted the regulators or risk-imposers (i.e. industry), making it increasingly difficult to site and build everything from chemical to nuclear power plants. Traditional top-down risk communication no longer appeared to work. Hence, regulators and industry were interested in funding research aimed at a better understanding of why the public was so opposed to certain new technologies (Golding, 1992), both to develop proactive risk communication strategies to address public concern and to shape technologies to make them more acceptable to the general public.

Over the years, the risk research field has been heavily dominated by US-based researchers. Most early work on simulations, gaming and straightforward risk analysis came out of North American research institutions. Similarly, most of the early social science work was dominated by American researchers. Baruch Fischhoff, Paul Slovic, Chauncey Starr and Gilbert White and the cognitive psychologists Daniel Kahneman and Amos Tversky were all based in the US. In current social science risk research, however, US dominance is diminishing. If one looks at the leading risk research journals (e.g. *Journal of Risk Research*, *Risk Analysis* and *Risk and Uncertainty*), increasingly over half of the social science articles are by European-based researchers. The shift is even more marked in areas such as trust, uncertainty and social theory. The phenomenon is recent (no more than 10–15 years old), reflecting the changing funding environment in Europe, particularly with increased research monies being available from European Commission DG Research Framework Programmes (e.g. Framework Programmes 6 and 7) and with interest in the area on the part of the research councils of certain nations, most notably, The Netherlands, Sweden, Switzerland and the UK. This second volume features some of the most noteworthy social science articles in the risk research field, and the reader will note that, unlike in the first volume, approximately half the new selections are by European scholars.[1]

In the remainder of this introduction, we will summarize some of the changes occurring in the risk research field over the past ten years or so, as we see them.

The Concept of Risk

The field of risk research is broad and interdisciplinary, comprising a variety of theoretical approaches, disciplinary backgrounds and meta-theoretical and philosophical inclinations. The concept of risk implicates a range of classical philosophical problems and issues (see Chapter 3). In risk research there is no ruling regime of any specific philosophy of science doctrine, and the field encompasses approaches based on realism, idealism, rationalism, empiricism, methodological individualism and holism (see Bunge, 1998, for a discussion of philosophical paradigms in the social sciences). The variety of perspectives and positions reflects both the disciplinary diversity of the field and its status as a 'post-normal' science addressing problems that actualize system uncertainties in combination with high decision stakes, where scientific considerations intertwine with policy matters, democratic values and public trust (Funtowicz and Ravetz, 1993; Ravetz, 1999). From a sociological perspective, the representation of risk can be understood as a by-product of modern society (Chapter 4; Luhmann, 1993). The notion of contingency is fundamental to the modern project, through the ideas that the world could always be otherwise, that humans influence their fate by their own decisions, that the future is in the hands of human beings and is not designed by some non-human agency (Chapter 4; Bernstein, 1996).

> The revolutionary idea that defines the boundary between modern times and the past is the mastery of risk: the notion that the future is more than a whim of the gods and that men and women are not passive before nature. (Bernstein, 1996, p1)

The concept of risk is abstract and multidimensional, relating to decision-making and foresight under conditions of contingency (see Kunreuther and Slovic, 1996; Hansson, 2007; see also Hamilton et al, 2007 regarding the linguistic use and meanings of the word 'risk' in contemporary written and spoken English). Approaching phenomena in terms of risk arguably demands a cognitive effort to weigh evidence, consider alternatives and assess likelihood and uncertainty regarding adverse prospects (see Chapter 3; Hansson, 2007).

An influential distinction in the philosophical and economic literature on risk is that between risk and uncertainty. 'Risk' usually refers to future random adverse occurrences that can be statistically calculated according to their probability. 'Uncertainty', in contrast, refers to a situation in which random events cannot be predicted on the basis of probabilistic outcomes (Knight, 1921). This distinction between risk and uncertainty identifies probability as the key element. Risk, as the economist Maynard Keynes has argued, is characterized in terms of probability, while uncertainty cannot be reduced to knowledge of probability.

> By 'uncertain' knowledge, let me explain, I do not mean merely to distinguish what is known for certain from what is only probable. The game of roulette is not subject, in this sense, to uncertainty... The sense in which I am using the term is that in which the prospect of a European war is

> uncertain, or the price of copper and the rate of interest twenty years hence... About these matters there is no scientific basis on which to form any calculable probability whatever. We simply do not know. (Keynes, 1937, p210–211)

This distinction between risk and uncertainty opens itself up to classic philosophical questioning. Do our concepts refer to the world as such, or to the world as we know it? Do our concepts reflect an objective reality, human knowledge of reality or reality as subjectively perceived? The debate in risk research between objective and subjective risk (see Shrader-Frechette, 1991; Pidgeon et al, 1992; Lupton, 1999) can be seen as a weaker and less-articulate version of the 1920s debate in Cambridge that engaged philosophers and micro-economists on the issue of objective versus subjective probability. While Keynes (1921) argued that probabilities are real and objective features of the outside world, the philosopher Frank Ramsey (1926) argued that probability is an epistemological concept referring to our subjective knowledge of the world. In economics and economic anthropology (Cancian, 1972), probability usually refers to subjective probability – that is to say, the beliefs and knowledge people have about probabilities (which are not necessarily 'true') that guide decisions and actions. Uncertainty then refers to a lack of knowledge of the world, together with – or without – recognition that knowledge is itself insufficient (Cancian, 1972).

In risk research, the debate about real versus perceived risk reflects philosophical arguments about the relationship between knowledge and perception, on the one hand, and the real objective world, on the other (see Shrader-Frechette, 1991; Lupton, 1999). The distinction between objective and subjective risk – or in philosophical terms, between realism and idealism – has served as a conceptual divide in much research into risk. A positivistic perspective on risk acknowledges facts and causality in a natural world where science identifies sources of potential harm, detects measurable correlations and assesses the probabilities of harm. The notion of subjective risk (Douglas, 1985, 1992; Kunreuther and Slovic, 1996), in contrast, acknowledges that risks are perceived and understood and more or less 'stamped' by beliefs, opinions and values. An argument against the positivistic notion of risk is that the categorization of something as a 'risk' presupposes values (Rosa, 1998). The concept of risk therefore, by definition, arguably integrates descriptive – factual and normative – evaluative components (see Shrader-Frechette, 1991; Renn, 1998).

The last 15 years of discussion of whether risks are real/objective or perceived/subjective has not produced a commonly accepted answer in risk research generally. The question is not simply 'academic', as which risk concept is adopted has consequences for regulatory policies (Chapter 2). Natural scientists, technical scientists and many regulators, however, continue to regard risk as a matter of fact constituted as a calculable product of adverse effects and probabilities. From this techno-mathematical perspective, the discussion circles around issues of definition, operationalization and measurement. How can adverse effects be defined and measured? And how can probabilities be estimated and calculated so as to allow accurate risk assessments? Such questions take the material world very much for granted as a universe of meanings. What is identified as problematic are causal and factual properties and how such properties can be empirically described and statistically calculated. From a regulatory point of view, the idea of a universal risk management programme that could be applied to all risks in the same standardized way according to a single formula continues to be an attractive goal (see Viscusi, 1996). Such ideas have been criticized by philosophers such as Hansson (2005), who argues that due to the idiosyncrasies of risk – one risk is not like another – deriving from differences in the nature of the underlying hazard, the distribution of adverse effects and benefits, the responsibility and intentionality of actors, and the varied relationships between risk-takers and risk-bearers, such universal rationality is a utopian dream rather than a realistic goal (Hansson, 2005). Ethical dimensions pertaining to risk issues and inherent in risk management were highlighted by Shrader-Frechette as early as 1991. Reducing risk to scientific facts does not solve ethical dilemmas concerning fairness and morally acceptable action. The matter of risk actualizes a number of problematic ethical issues. Have we a right to expose others to risk even if its probability is low and there is 'good cause' for doing so? Under what conditions and on what grounds can actions that put other people at risk be ethically justified? A complication is that the potential harms and benefits of a certain course of action might be unequally distributed among potential victims, or that those making the decisions do not have to bear their consequences (Hermansson and Hansson, 2007).

A dominant view in sociology and anthropology is that risk is a conceptual construction relative to social, historical and cultural conditions (for an overview, see Lupton, 1999). Although it is agreed that risk is constructed, opinions diverge as to how this construction should be theoretically conceived, depending on meta-theoretical ideas and assumptions as to the nature of human society, human interaction and communication. Reflexive modernity theory in sociology (Beck, 1992), discursive approaches (Strydom, 2002), governmentality theory (Ewald, 1991; Dean, 1999) and cultural theory (see Douglas and Wildawsky, 1982; Douglas, 1985, 1992) all have different answers to fundamental questions in social theory (e.g. regarding agency, determination, structure, cohesion, meaning and power) and hence also approach the concept of risk quite differently. A common viewpoint, however, is that risk is recognized to exist because someone identifies something as posing a risk *to* somebody or something. For a social scientist, the statement that red meat can cause cancer is not a question of dose–response relationships and carcinogenic processes in body biochemistry; it is a question of how groups and organizations in society frame an issue, how meaning is created, how arguments are made, how action is mobilized, and how social, political and administrative processes emerge and develop as driven by scientific facts and their interpretations. To focus on risk as a social construction, however, does not imply philosophical idealism, a refutation of the belief that there exists a world outside us and independent of our senses (Searle, 1995; Hacking, 1999). The social scientist approaches risk from the assumption that risks can be differently assessed and understood by people depending on their knowledge and experience, worldviews, cultural intuitions, trust in those communicating risk messages, and roles played in a risk issue (i.e., whether they are stakeholders or policymakers) (Luhmann, 1989, 1993; Douglas, 1992; Lupton, 1999; Boholm, 2003; Mairal Buil, 2003; Stoffle and Arnold, 2003; Sjölander-Lindqvist, 2004).

In what follows, we will discuss the field of risk research focusing thematically on risk perception, risk communication, the role of trust, and policy and regulatory issues. These thematic fields, as we see it, are central to the field today and will be so tomorrow.

Risk Perception

The purpose of the psychometric paradigm was to measure individual perceptions of risk and the judgements associated with different risk-related options. Slovic, Fischhoff and Lichtenstein's original work, first published in the 1970s, remains highly relevant today (Slovic et al, 1976). All publics, no matter whether European, North American, Asian or Australian, remain more concerned about involuntary risks than voluntary ones, more worried about risks that are unfamiliar than familiar, and risks that they cannot control. The initial studies of the Decision Research team have been replicated in many nations around the world, and the results come out more or less the same as the those of the original Decision Research sample (for a summary, see Slovic, 2000; see also Boholm, 1998; Renn and Rohrmann, 2000).

Over the last decade, however, the risk perception field has broadened both its theoretical perspective and area of focus, moving forward in two distinct directions, namely, the development of risk as feelings (Chapter 7), incorporating research into the affect heuristic and emotions, and the influence of social background and gender. Affect is a form of emotion, distinguishable as positive or negative feelings toward an external stimulus. These positive and negative feelings arise quickly and affect how the public perceives risks. Early work on the affect heuristic indicated that negative views of nuclear power influenced perceptions of the technology (Peters and Slovic, 1996; Slovic et al, 2004). Along similar lines, Lerner et al have explored the role of emotions in perceptions of risks and benefits. This research group's numerous findings include that pessimistic and optimistic judgements are influenced by fear and anger, respectively (Lerner and Keltner, 2000, 2001; Lerner et al 2003). Although the affect heuristic has been criticized by Sjöberg, who notes that the term is confusing and that the causal link is between emotion and risk perception (Sjöberg, 2006), the existence of the heuristic has been widely accepted (e.g. see Finucane et al, 2000; Finucane and Holup, 2006; Townsend, 2006; Wardman, 2006).

Over the past 30 years of risk perception research, findings indicate that females are more concerned about risks than males (e.g. Slovic, 2000). More recently, however, researchers began uncovering that not only women were more concerned about risks, but also that non-whites (at least in the US), be they male or female, were more concerned about risks (Chapter 5; Flynn et al, 1994). There have been several explanations of the so-called white male effect, the most commonly accepted of which is well paraphrased by Slovic when he notes:

> White males may perceive less risk than others because they are more involved in creating, managing, controlling and benefiting from technology and other activities that are hazardous. Women and non-white men may perceive greater risk because they tend to have less control over these activities and benefit less from them. Indeed, risk perceptions seem to be related to individuals' power to influence decisions about the use of hazards. (Slovic, 2000, pxxxiv)

It would be interesting to see whether the 'white male effect' only applies in the US, or whether it will prove to be like the psychometric paradigm and have general applicability.

Finally, the risk perception area has broadened its area focus. Initially, risk perception researchers were primarily interested in risks pertaining to nuclear power, the environment (e.g. hazards posed by chemicals, oil and waste) and the food sector (e.g. Otway et al, 1978; Krimsky and Plough, 1988; Kunreuther et al, 1990; Slovic et al, 1991; Flynn et al, 1992, 1993; Petts, 1995; Frewer et al, 1997). However, over the past 10 years the focus has shifted markedly toward new and emerging hazards. In the wake of the 9-11 terrorist attacks on the US, there has been growing interest on both sides of the Atlantic in the perception of terrorism risks (see the special issue of *Journal of Risk Analysis* vol 27, no 3, 2007; Lerner et al, 2003; Fischhoff et al, 2003a, 2003b, 2005; Sjoberg, 2005b; Bier and von Winterfeldt, 2007). This research has produced several significant findings. Fischhoff et al (2005), for example, found that two months after the 9-11 attacks, Americans perceived greater personal risk from terrorism if they lived within 100 miles of the World Trade Center than if they lived farther away. There were no noticeable differences between individuals within this 100-mile radius, men and women viewing terrorism risks more or less equally (Fischhoff et al, 2003b). Similarly, research into terrorism has demonstrated that fear is an effective determinant of perceived public risk (Lerner and Keltner, 2001; Lerner et al, 2003).

Another sector that has attracted the attention of social science risk researchers is nanotechnology. To date, most interviewed members of the public do not know what nanotechnology is. A 2004 Royal Society and Royal Academy of Engineering poll indicated that only 29 per cent of the UK public had heard of nanotechnology and only 19 per cent could offer a definition of it (BMRB, 2004; see also the 2005 investigation by UK Department of Industry, Barnett et al, 2006b). In the US, nationwide polls indicate that more than 82 per cent of the public have heard little or nothing about nanotechnology (Cobb and Macoubrie, 2004). Due to this lack of knowledge of nanotechnology, leading research institutions such as the US National Science Foundation believe it is necessary to involve risk researchers early on in the communication process (Roco and Bainbridge, 2001; Renn and Roco, 2006), something that the academics themselves agree with (e.g. Barnett et al, 2006b; Pidgeon and Rogers-Hayden, 2007; Rogers-Hayden and Pidgeon, 2006, 2008).

Risk Communication

Development in the risk communication, as opposed to risk perception, field, however, has been arguably more limited (for reviews, see Bostrom and Löfstedt, 2003; McComas, 2006; Breakwell, 2007). Compared with the situation in 1990, when there was considerable conceptual work in the area, notably regarding the social amplification of risk and mental models areas, the last decade has been rather quiet. For example, the research that was highlighted in the first edition of the *Earthscan Reader in Risk and Modern Society*, into matters such as mental model techniques and the social amplification of risk, has moved forward. Mental models are now an accepted and much-used tool, ranging from developing proactive communication strategies regarding breast cancer and sexually transmitted diseases, to understanding how users of paint stripper can best avoid methylene chloride exposure (Riley et al, 2000; Byram et al, 2008).

In 2002, the Carnegie Mellon team published a 'how-to' book on how best to use mental model techniques in developing proactive risk communication (Morgan et al, 2002), as is now being done in both North America and Europe (e.g. Breakwell, 2001; Cox et al, 2003; Niewohner et al, 2004; Hagemann and Scholderer, 2007). Finally, several consulting firms have adopted the mental model approach as a main tool in promoting proactive risk communication, the firm arguably closest to adopting the Carnegie Mellon University model being Decision Partners.

Similarly, the research area of the social amplification of risk, originally developed in 1988 (Kasperson et al, 1988), has matured. Although the model was somewhat criticized for lack of practical applicability when first reported (Rayner, 1988; Rip, 1988; Svenson, 1988), and later for theoretical weakness (Wahlberg, 2001), it has become a widely accepted risk communication metaphor applied and used by researchers on both sides of the Atlantic (e.g. Hill, 2001; Löfstedt, 2003, 2008; Bakir, 2005). The popularity of the framework is related to its comprehensive aim, or as Kasperson et al argue:

> The framework does ... help to clarify phenomena, such as the key role of the mass media in risk communication and the influence of culture on risk processing, providing a template for integrating partial theories and research, and to encourage more interactive and holistic interpretations. (Kasperson et al, 2003, p38)

Over the past 10 years, the seminal work in the area has been the 2003 Pidgeon et al volume, *The Social Amplification of Risk* (Pidgeon et al, 2003), which both built a conceptual foundation for the field and demonstrated how the model is relevant to public policy. Interestingly, the book itself grew out of a British multi-department government funding effort involving the Cabinet Office, Civil Aviation Authority, Environment Agency, Food Standards Agency, and UK Health and Safety Executive – among many others. This research and other similar work at the time (e.g. UK Strategy Unit, 2002) was driven by the need of the British government to better respond (and communicate) to the public in the wake of the government's mishandling of the BSE 'mad cow' crisis (Lord Phillips et al, 2000). Since the Pidgeon et al volume was published, there have been several case studies of social amplification (e.g. Bakir, 2005).

That the social context of risk communication includes political, economic, ideological and historical circumstances was already noted by Johnson in 1987 (see Chapter 8). One area of risk communication that was discussed a great deal in the 1990s was cultural theory. The theory of cultural bias, it is argued, predicts personal dispositions in the assessment of technological risks (for a discussion, see Löfstedt and Frewer 1998). The theory quickly caught on among industrialists and regulators who saw that it might help them better predict how members of the public perceive risk, based on their individual cultural biases. In 1996, one study found that individuals who perceived themselves as egalitarian were more concerned about a wider range of certain risks, such as nuclear power, than were other individuals (Peters and Slovic, 1996). Peters and Slovic (1996) and other cultural theory researchers were criticized by Sjöberg (1997), who noted that the correlations were weak and hence not as predictive as they could have been. Following Sjöberg's criticism, a number of viewpoints and counter-viewpoints were voiced regarding the usefulness of cultural theory as a predictive tool and the merits of using qualitative and quantitative research methods to support cultural theory (Sjöberg, 2003, 2004, 2005a; Tansey, 2004a, 2004b). Another criticism is that cultural theory, by virtue of its holistic assumption that there is a given (pre-defined) functionality of ideas, behaviours and social organization in society, paradoxically fails to describe the social and cultural processes that produce risk, both as a cognitive mode (a way of thinking) and as a praxis (a way of acting and organizing) (see Boholm, 1996, 2003).

An area of risk communication that has received considerable attention in recent decades is the role of public deliberation in the policymaking process (Petts, 2004). The need for public dialogue and reciprocal risk communication was recognized in earnest in the late 1980s, when contemporary studies indicated that the most common form of risk communication, 'top-down', was not successful in alleviating public concerns (National Research Council, 1989, 1996). The main reasons identified for this failure were poor risk communication among the experts themselves, and their contemptuous response to public opposition. The development of dialogue-based risk communication techniques was welcomed among regulators and industry. Industry and local and federal government regulators, frustrated by the difficulty of siting plants and dumping and burning wastes, were keen to learn how to increase public trust via more active engagement, and to gain information on affected citizens' preferences by involving them directly in the policymaking process. In Europe, in particular, there was a rush by industry to establish deliberative risk communication techniques following such crises as the disposal of the Brent Spar oil storage buoy (1995), the regulatory scandals associated with BSE, tainted blood in France and dioxin in Belgian chickens (Chapter 9; House of Lords, 2000). Although deliberation involving the public and stakeholders can lead to public trust, it should not be treated as a panacea (Barber, 1983; Fiorino, 1989; Wynne, 1989, 1996; Chess et al, 1995; Petts, 1995, 2001; Rowe and Frewer, 2000).

The issue of whether and how deliberation may or may not be adequate should be critically evaluated. For example, in many cases the public distrusts regulators, policymakers and/or industry for reasons other than fairness. Perceived lack of competence and lack of efficiency can also be important factors contributing to public distrust (Löfstedt, 2005) that cannot be addressed by deliberation. Furthermore, it is difficult to ensure the representativeness of those participating in deliberative processes. There is often a self-selection problem, as most members of the public refuse to give their opinions when asked for them (Löfstedt, 1999), meaning that identified 'public opinion' does not represent that of the population as a whole (see Pidgeon et al, 2005; Rowe et al, 2005; Horlick-Jones et al, 2007). These and related issues, however, are being dealt with by the so-called IRGC model (Renn and Walker, 2008).[2] The authors of the IRGC model argue, for example, that deliberation should not be used in all cases but only in cases of so-called ambiguous risks, where fundamental differences exist among the actors with respect to the interpretation of information or values associated with particular outcomes (Renn and Walker, 2008). The initial model was first reported in 2006, and since then it has been tested in a number of case studies of matters ranging from acrylamide (Bonneck, 2008) to genetically modified crops (Tait, 2008) and nanotechnology (Renn and Roco, 2006).

Trust and Post-Trust

Trust has attracted considerable attention from risk researchers over the past decade. Arguably, much of the relevant research of the past 10 years builds on three seminal studies of trust published in the 1990s, those of Slovic (1993), demonstrating that trust is an important element in understanding perceived risk, Renn and Levine (1991), examining the various components of trust, and Earle and Cvetkovich (1995), discussing value similarities as an important dimension of trust. Following the publication of these and related articles (e.g. Cvetkovich and Löfstedt, 1999; Earle, 2004), much research has focused on identifying further dimensions of trust, or proving (or disproving) the importance of the social trust dimension.

For example, Pidgeon et al (2007) identified the concept of critical trust as a new dimension:

> Critical trust lies on a continuum between outright scepticism (rejection) and uncritical emotional acceptance. Such a concept attempts to reconcile the actual reliance by the public on institutions, while simultaneously possessing a critical attitude towards the effectiveness, motivations, or independence of the agency in question. (Pidgeon et al, 2007)

Pidgeon et al (2007) tested this concept via a number of large quantitative surveys in the UK and found the concept validated (Chapter 10; Poortinga and Pidgeon, 2003a, 2005, 2006; Walls et al, 2004). In a sense, these findings indicate that distrust is not in itself necessarily undesired (for an excellent discussion of this point, see O'Neill, 2002). Critical distrust can in effect be healthy for society, as the public may have become more knowledgeable and competent over time and hence be able to make up their own minds (Barber, 1983). The question remains, however, if this is always and everywhere the case, or whether the situation is unique to the UK, a country that has been plagued by regulatory scandals and hence distrust for many years (Chapter 9; UK Strategy Unit, 2002). Arguably, in countries such as Sweden, where there has been much greater trust in regulators for many years (Löfstedt, 2005), critical trust would be seen by the establishment as unhealthy and worrying.

Other research indicates that openness (transparency) and honesty increase trust while secrecy destroys it (Peters et al, 1997). Schutz and Wiedemann (2000), for example, demonstrated that chemical companies that offered more information about their operations were more trusted than those that did not. Similarly, Matsumoto et al (2005) found that corporations providing balanced information on nuclear power, discussing both its risks and benefits, were more trusted than those providing only positive communications. Finally, research into organizations indicates that institutional trust can be built over time if these organizations show the public what they are doing in terms of health and safety, as indicated by the successful siting of a biosafety level 4 (BSL-4) facility in Winnipeg, Canada (Löfstedt, 2002). It should be clarified, however, that although transparency and openness promote trust, their implementation is not unproblematic. For example, they encourage members of the public, both directly and indirectly, to make their own decisions about risks, for example, regarding what food to eat or not, or whether to have their children vaccinated and the like, rather than relying on the regulators to decide for them. Similarly, greater transparency leads to the development of policy vacuums (Powell and Leiss, 1997); these are quickly filled by the most efficient communicators, which are not always the regulators but rather non-governmental organizations (Chapter 9).

Clearly, the concept of trust is multidimensional (Fischhoff, 1999), and several definitions of it have been proposed (e.g. see Renn and Levine, 1991; Kasperson et al, 1992; Löfstedt, 2005). The components of trust include competence, fairness and efficiency, a formulation that has been repeatedly tested over the past 10 years. There has yet to emerge a clear consensus as to whether these dimensions are truly correct, but Frewer et al (1996) and Pidgeon et al (2007) do provide empirical support for them. By far the most important finding to date is the correlation between high levels of public trust and low levels of public-perceived risk and vice versa (Kunreuther et al, 1990; Slovic, 1993; Löfstedt, 1996; Siegrist and Cvetkovich, 2000; Siegrist et al, 2005). That said, other academics have attempted to disprove the importance of social trust. Sjöberg, for example, notes that the correlations between perceived risk and social trust are weak (Sjöberg, 1999), a finding in turn questioned by Siegrist et al (Chapter 11) who found strong rather than weak correlations between these variables. More recently, however, Sjöberg put forward new data indicating that the perceived 'antagonism' (hostile intent) of the risk producers was a higher predictor of public-perceived risk than was social trust (Sjöberg, 2008). It is doubtful that this will be the last word on the topic. Social trust has more or less been universally accepted as the most important predictor of public-perceived risk (Slovic, 1993; Siegrist et al, 2007), leading some regulatory agencies and industrial organizations in Europe and North America to revamp their communication efforts regarding how best to win back public trust (Löfstedt, 2005).

Policy and Regulation

Risk management has today become a moral imperative for organizations – both businesses and government agencies – which have to demonstrate their capacity to deal with risk, by means of risk assessment and risk management plans (Power, 2007). Not only does the complexity of risk and of the decisions called for, together with the awareness of such complexity, increase with the sheer expansion of technology and scientific knowledge; in addition, the numerous risk issues that reach the political agenda all become matters for potential regulation by a growing number of authorities. The pressure on organizations to account for how they manage risk and uncertainty in their operations or administration creates the possibility of a variety of organizational responses (Hutter and Power, 2005; Power, 2007). Many risk decisions in the public domain involve both private and public actors in multi-purpose interactions, unfolding over time in arenas characterized by multi-level governance and concerning intertwined multi-sectorial issues. For example, as found by research into infrastructure facility siting and land-use planning (Boholm and Löfstedt, 2004), many stakeholder groups, organizations and authorities are involved, having divergent ways of organizing value hierarchies. Whereas some privilege economic growth, others prefer to secure historical heritage or promote sustainable development or biodiversity. Such divergent priorities are often manifested in planning procedures on municipal, regional and state levels.

The proliferation of 'risk regulation regimes', as has been shown by Hood et al (2001), produces a multitude of frames of reference and procedures for assessing risk, costs, benefits, values at stake and the roles of scientific, administrative and political considerations. To develop integrated risk management with regard to complex issues (e.g. food, transportation infrastructure, climate change and pandemics) in which a variety of values (e.g. biodiversity, safety and security, public health or economic growth) must be included and prioritized, various specialized segments of government, the public sector, the private sector and civil society must coordinate and align their activities (European food safety regulation serves as a telling example, see Vos and Wendler, 2006).

Over the past decade, risk researchers have become increasingly interested in analysing policy and regulatory issues. This has long been a preserve of political science and law (e.g. Vogel 1986, 2003; Kagan and Axelrad 2000; Sunstein 2002, 2005, 2007; Wiener 2002; Wiener and Rogers 2002), but, increasingly, a wide range of social science disciplines have entered the area as well. This recent work originates in the early 1990s, in the wake of numerous regulatory scandals engulfing a number of nations in Europe and elsewhere, when a new industry developed to advise policymakers and industry on how to manage risks better, and how to avoid controversy and conflict with the public regarding risk issues. Increasingly, the research basis of this work is emerging from within academia, implying the direct transfer of research skills from risk communication and management theory to regulation and risk policy practice. In so doing, the field of risk has become much more applied and policy relevant.

The precautionary principle has arguably attracted the most attention from risk researchers, so it is of interest to define what exactly it entails. To date, researchers have uncovered multiple definitions of the concept (Sandin, 1999), some arguing that these multiple definitions could be justified depending on the policy context in which the principle is being applied (Chapter 12; Löfstedt et al, 2002). Other academics have tried to defend the principle against the onslaught of risk analysts (e.g. European Environment Agency, 2001; Sandin et al, 2002), arguing, for example, that the principle has a long history (Karlsson, 2006). There has also been substantial discussion of the traditions and ideals in risk regulation in Europe versus the US. There is no real consensus here. Some say that the Europeans today are considerably more precautionary than their American counterparts (Kempton and Craig, 1993; Sunstein, 2005), while others state there has merely been a recent flip-flop: Americans were more precautionary historically, but today the Europeans have taken that lead (Chapter 14; Lynch and Vogel, 2000; Löfstedt and Vogel, 2001; Vogel, 2003). Another group of researchers argues that it depends: sometimes the Europeans are more precautionary than Americans are, and sometimes not (Wiener, 2002; Wiener and Rogers, 2002; Hammit et al, 2005). Others have analysed how the precautionary principle has been invoked in past legal cases (Forrester and Hanekamp, 2006; van Asselt and Vos, 2006) and how the principle has been communicated in official European documents (Graham and Hsia, 2002).

One area within the precautionary principle field that has garnered considerable attention is the link between issuing precautionary principle-type regulations or advice and social trust. Earlier research findings have implied that tough regulations lead to high levels of public trust, as the public takes the view that the regulators are acting in their best interests. The converse is that weak regulations lead to lower levels of public trust, as the public sees the regulators as more or less 'in the pockets' of industry (Löfstedt, 2005). One could therefore hypothesize that regulators who issue precautionary advice, acting in the public's best interest, would gain increased public trust (see Chapter 11, for a discussion). However, research into this topic has not succeeded in verifying this hypothesis: putting forward precautionary measures does not necessarily increase public trust in the regulator in question; rather, it can actually lead to public distrust (Wiedemann and Schutz, 2005; Wiedemann et al, 2006). To complicate matters still further, having regulators take precautionary measures and issue precautionary advice regarding a certain matter (e.g. mobile phone electromagnetic fields) can lead to increased public concern (Wiedemann et al, 2003, 2006; Wiedemann and Schutz, 2005; Barnett et al, 2006a; Timotijevic and Barnett, 2006).

One of the most important books on regulation is the volume edited by John Graham and Jonathan Wiener, *Risk vs. Risk* (Graham and Wiener, 1995). The book aims to explore the fact that trade-offs arise in the making of regulations. The main thrust of their argument is 'that efforts to combat a target risk can unintentionally foster increases in countervailing risks' (Graham and Wiener, 1995, pp1–2). Countervailing risks can range from unintended consequences of public policy to medical side-effects. To reduce the chances of risk–risk trade-offs, decision-makers need to consider all aspects of any regulatory policy. Proponents of risk–risk trade-offs note that public-driven regulatory agendas in many cases ignore the risk–risk trade-off. The last few years have seen significant debate on the importance of these trade-offs. One of the better-known risk–risk trade-offs is the issue of water chlorination. Following risk studies in the US that classified chlorine as carcinogenic, Peru stopped chlorinating the water in Lima in 1991, resulting in an outbreak of cholera that killed 7000 people and affected nearly 800,000 others (Anderson, 1991). Recently, advocates of the precautionary principle have dismissed this analysis and argued that the epidemic was caused by an inadequate public health infrastructure unable to cope with the microbial contamination (Tickner and Gouveia-Vigeant, 2005). Similarly, in 2007 Hansen et al argued that the precautionary principle was a better regulatory tool than the risk versus risk paradigm, noting that in an examination of 88 cases, only 4 fit the definition of what constitutes a false positive. In the other cases, using the precautionary principle helped to improve the environment and public health (Hansen et al, 2007a), something that has been questioned by Cox (2007) and defended by Hansen et al, (2007b).

Research in the risk policy and governance area is likely to continue to grow with time. From an organizational perspective, responsiveness to risk – and uncertainty – is an important area for future research (see Hutter and Power, 2005; Power, 2007). In our daily lives, we are exposed to any number of known risks for which we are prepared by means of strategies of prevention, mitigation and management. There are, however, situations introducing new risks (emerging from new technology, new scientific findings, new regulatory measures and new media alarms) that are not associated with clear and effective risk management strategies or that might even seem unmanageable. What Klinke and Renn have denoted as 'systemic risks' characterized by high complexity, uncertainty, ambiguity and, in addition, uncertain high-consequence ripple effects, present a veritable challenge for policymakers and regulators (Klinke and Renn, 2006).

Conclusions

It will be interesting to see in what directions the risk perception, communication and management fields move over the next decade. What issues will we highlight in 2019? Although we are both terrible soothsayers, we propose several hypotheses as to what the lead topics will be.

In the field of risk perception, the focus will shift toward new subject areas rather than the development of new heuristics per se. We project that the next decade will see exponential growth of such research in the areas of nanotechnology, terrorism, climate change and public health (e.g. obesity). In addition, there will be considerable research into the food scare topic of the moment, be it cattle cloning or yet another artificial sweetener crisis.

Conceptual advances in the risk communication area have arguably peaked. Mental models and social amplification research has matured. Rather than uncovering new and innovative tools in these areas, we hypothesize that academics in the risk communication area will be examining the importance of social trust as a variable of public perception. We hope to see more studies drawing theoretical inspiration from disciplines in communication research (e.g. linguistics, pragmatics, media studies or marketing). More knowledge is needed of how risk messages are produced and interpreted in real life, and of how understandings are influenced by communication context, assumptions, knowledge, social roles and expectations and, not least, social and interpersonal trust.

Compared with the other areas highlighted in this risk reader, we hypothesize that the real growth area is that of risk management and policy and the whole topic of communicating uncertainty. Of interest here is the continued evaluation of precautionary messages/advice vis-à-vis non-precautionary ones, how regulators can better communicate uncertainty in what we see as a post-trust society, and what type of communication messages are needed to regain public trust. Is greater transparency and openness the key to solving the post-trust conundrum (European Commission, 2001; UK Strategy Unit, 2002) or is it highly overrated (O'Neill, 2002; Hood and Heald, 2006)?

Acknowledgements

We are grateful to the following individuals who have either provided us with information or commented on earlier drafts of this introductory chapter: Frederic Bouder, Hervé Corvellec, Baruch Fischhoff, Ortwin Renn and Jamie Wardman. This work has been funded by research grants from the Swedish Research Council, the Swedish Rescue Services Agency, the Emergency Management Agency, the Swedish Governmental Agency for Innovation Systems, the Swedish Road Administration and the Swedish Maritime Administration.

Notes

1   There is growing interest in risk analysis in other parts of the world as well. Japan has a Society for Risk Analysis and there are a number of Asian risk journals. However, the amount of growth in the social science risk area in Asia has not been as great as in Europe over the last ten years.
2   The IRGC stands for the International Risk Governance Council, which was established in 2003 in Geneva, Switzerland. The IRGC is a global organization for scientists, policymakers and industry funded by government boards, research councils and companies.

References

Anderson, C. (1991) 'Cholera epidemic tied to risk miscalculation', *Nature*, vol 354, 28 November, p255

Bakir, V. (2005) 'Greenpeace vs. Shell: Media exploitation and the social amplification of risk framework (SARF)', *Journal of Risk Research*, vol 8, pp679–691

Barber, B. (1983) *The Logic and Limits of Trust*, New Brunswick: Rutgers University Press

Barnett, J., Timotijevic, L., Shepherd, R. and Senior, V. (2006a) 'Public responses to precautionary information from the Department of Health (UK) about possible health risks from mobile phones', *Health Policy*, vol 82, no 2, pp240–250

Barnett, J., Carr, A. and Clift, R. (2006b) 'Going public: Risk, trust and public understandings of nanotechnology', in G. Hunt and M. Mehta (eds), *Nanotechnology: Risk, ethics and law*, London: Earthscan

Beck, U. (1992) *Risk Society*, London: Sage

Bernstein, P. (1996) *Against the Gods: The remarkable story of risk*, New York: John Wiley and Sons

Bier, V. M. and von Winterfeldt, D. (2007) 'Meeting the challenges of terrorism risk analysis', *Risk Analysis*, vol 27, pp503–504

BMRB (2004) *Nanotechnology: Views of the general public*, London: BMRB International Ltd

Boholm, Å. (1996) 'The cultural theory of risk: An anthropological critique', *Ethnos*, vol 61, pp64–84

Boholm, Å. (1998) 'Comparative studies of risk perception: A review of twenty years of research', *Journal of Risk Research*, vol 1, pp135–161

Boholm, Å. (2003) 'The cultural nature of risk: Can there be an anthropology of uncertainty?', *Ethnos*, vol 68, pp159–178

Boholm, Å. and Löfstedt, R. (eds) (2004) *Facility Siting: Risk, power and identity in land-use planning*, London: Earthscan

Bonneck, S. (2008) 'Acrylamide risk governance in Germany', in O. Renn and K. Walker (eds), *Global Risk Governance: Concept and practice using the IRGC framework*, Dordrecht: Springer.

Bostrom, A. and Löfstedt, R. E. (2003) 'Communicating risk: Wireless and hardwired', *Risk Analysis*, vol 23, pp241–248

Breakwell, G. M. (2001) 'Mental models and social representations of hazards: The significance of identity processes', *Journal of Risk Research*, vol 4, pp341–351

Breakwell, G. M. (2007) *The Psychology of Risk,* Cambridge: Cambridge University Press

Bunge, M. (1998) *Social Science Under Debate*, Toronto: University of Toronto Press

Byram, S. J., Schwartz, L. M., Woloshin, S. and Fischhoff, B. (2008) 'Women's beliefs about breast cancer risk factors: A mental models approach', in J. Krueger (ed), *Rationality and*

Social Responsibility: Essays in honour of Robyn Mason Davis, Mahwah, NJ: Lawrence Erlbaum Associates, pp245–274

Cancian, F. (1972) *Change and Uncertainty in a Peasant Economy: The Maya corn farmers of Zinacantan*, Stanford: Stanford University Press.

Chess, C., Salomone, K. L., Hance, B. J. and Saville, A. (1995) 'Results of a national symposium on risk communication: Next steps for government agencies', *Risk Analysis*, vol 15, pp115–125

Chicken, J. C. (1982) *Nuclear Power Hazard Control Policy*, Oxford: Pergamon Press.

Cobb, M. D. and Macoubrie, J. (2004) 'Public perceptions about nanotechnology: Risk, benefits and trust', *Journal of Nanoparticle Research*, vol 6, pp395–405

Covello, V. and Mumpower, J. (1985) 'Risk analysis and risk management: An historical perspective', *Risk Analysis*, vol 5, pp103–120

Cox, L. A. (2007) 'Regulatory false positives: True, false or uncertain?', *Risk Analysis*, vol 27, pp1083–1086

Cox, P., Niewohner, J., Pidgeon, N., Gerrard, S., Fischhoff, B. and Riley, D. (2003) 'The use of mental models in chemical risk perception: Developing a generic workplace methodology', *Risk Analysis*, vol 23, pp311–324

Cvetkovich, G. and Löfstedt, R. E. (eds) (1999) *Social Trust and the Management of Risk*, London: Earthscan

Dean, M. (1999) *Governmentality: Power and rule in modern society*, London: Sage

Douglas, M. (1985) *Risk Acceptability According to the Social Sciences*, New York: Russell Sage Foundation

Douglas, M. (1992) *Risk and Blame: Essays in cultural theory*, London: Routledge

Douglas, M. and Wildavsky, A. (1982) *Risk and Culture: An essay on the selection of technological and environmental dangers*, Berkeley, California: University of California Press

Earle, T. (2004) 'Thinking aloud about trust: A protocol analysis of trust in risk management', *Risk Analysis*, vol 24, pp169–183

Earle, T. C. and Cvetkovich, G. (1995) *Trust: Toward a Cosmopolitan Society*, Westport, CT: Praeger

European Commission (2001) *European Governance: A white paper*, COM 2001 Final. Brussels: European Commission

European Environment Agency (2001) *Late Lessons from Early Warnings: The precautionary principle 1896–2000*, Copenhagen: European Environment Agency

Ewald, F. (1991) 'Insurance and risk', in G. Burchell, C. Gordon and P. Miller (eds), *The Foucault Effect: Studies in governmentality*, Chicago: University of Chicago Press

Farmer, F. R. (1967) 'Siting criteria – a new approach', in International Atomic Energy Agency (eds), *Containment and Siting Nuclear Power Plants*, Vienna: International Atomic Energy Agency, pp303–329

Farmer, F. R. (ed) (1977) *Nuclear Reactor Safety*, New York: Academic Press

Finucane, M. L. and Holup, J. L. (2006) 'Risk as value: Combining affect and analysis in risk judgments', *Journal of Risk Research*, vol 9, pp141–164

Finucane, M. L., Alhakami, A. S., Slovic, P. and Johnson, S. M. (2000) 'The affect heuristic in judgments of risk and benefits', *Journal of Behavioral Decision Making*, vol 13, pp1–17

Fiorino, D. (1989) 'Environmental risk and democratic process: A critical review', *Columbia Journal of Environmental Law*, vol 14, pp501–547

Fischhoff, B. (1999) 'If trust is so good, why isn't there more of it?', in G. Cvetkovich and R. E. Löfstedt (eds), *Social Trust and the Management of Risk*, London: Earthscan, ppviii–x.

Fischhoff, B., Gonzalez, R. M., Small, D. A. and Lerner, J. S. (2003a) 'Evaluating the success of terror risk communications', *Biosecurity and Bioterrorism: Biodefence strategy, practice and science*, vol 1, pp255–258

Fischhoff, B., Gonzalez, R. M., Small, D. A. and Lerner, J. S. (2003b) 'Judged terror risk and proximity to the World Trade Center', *Journal of Risk and Uncertainty*, vol 26, pp137–151

Fischhoff, B., Gonzalez, R. M., Lerner, J. S. and Small, D. A. (2005) 'Evolving judgments of terror risks: Foresight, hindsight and emotion', *Journal of Applied Experimental Psychology*, vol 11, pp124–139

Flynn, J., Burns, W., Mertz, C. K. and Slovic, P. (1992) 'Trust as a determinant of opposition to a high-level radioactive waste repository: Analysis of a structual model', *Risk Analysis*, vol 12, pp417–430

Flynn, J., Slovic, P. and Mertz, C. K. (1993) 'The Nevada Initiative: A risk communication fiasco', *Risk Analysis*, vol 13, pp497–502

Flynn, J., Slovic, P. and Mertz, C. K. (1994) 'Gender, race, and perception of environmental health risks', *Risk Analysis*, vol 14, pp1101–1108

Forrester, I. and Hanekamp, J. C. (2006) 'Precaution, science and jurisprudence: A test case', *Journal of Risk Research*, vol 9, pp297–311

Frewer, L. J., Howard, C., Hedderly, D. and Shepherd, R. (1996) 'What determines trust in information about food related risk?', *Risk Analysis*, vol 16, pp473–486

Frewer, L. J., Howard, C., Hedderly, D. and Shepherd, R. (1997) 'Public concerns about general and specific applications of genetic engineering: Risk, benefit and ethics', *Science, Technology and Human Values*, vol 22, pp98–124

Funtowicz, S. and Ravetz, J. (1993) 'Science for the post-normal age', *Futures*, vol 25, pp735–755

Gilovich, T., Griffin, D. and Kahneman, D. (2002) *Heuristics and Biases: The psychology of intuitive judgment*, Cambridge: Cambridge University Press

Golding, D. (1992) 'A social and programmatic history of risk research', in S. Krimsky and D. Golding (eds), *Social Theories of Risk*, Westport, CT: Praeger

Graham, J. D. and Hsia, S. (2002) 'Europe's precautionary principle: Promise and pitfalls', *Journal of Risk Research*, vol 5, pp371–390

Graham, J. D. and Wiener, J. B. (eds), (1995) *Risk vs. Risk Tradeoffs in Protecting Public Health and the Environment*, Cambridge, MA: Harvard University Press.

Hacking, I. (1999) *The Social Construction of What?* Harvard: Harvard University Press

Hagemann, K. S. and Scholderer, J. (2007) 'Consumer versus expert hazard identification: A mental models study of mutation-bred rice', *Journal of Risk Research*, vol 10, pp449–464

Hamilton, C., Adolphs, S. and Nerlich, B. (2007) 'The meaning of "risk": A view from corpus linguistics', *Discourse and Society*, vol 18, no 2, pp163–181

Hammit, J. K., Wiener, J. B., Swedlow, B., Kall, D. and Zhou, Z. (2005) 'Precautionary regulation in Europe and the United States: A quantitative comparison', *Risk Analysis*, vol 25, pp1215–1228

Hansen, S. F., Krayer von Kraus, M. P. and Tickner, J. A. (2007a) 'Categorizing mistaken false positives in regulation of human and environmental health', *Risk Analysis*, vol 27, pp255–269

Hansen, S. F., Krayer von Krauss, M. P. and Tickner, J. A. (2007b) 'Response to "regulatory false positives": True, false, or uncertain?', *Risk Analysis*, vol 27, pp1087–1089

Hansson, S. O. (2005) 'Seven myths of risk', *Risk Management*, vol 7, pp7–17

Hansson, S. O. (2007) 'Risk', *Stanford Encyclopedia of Philosophy*, http://plato.stanford.edu/entries/risk (accessed 11 January 2008)

Hermansson, H. and Hansson, S. O. (2007) 'A three party model tool for ethical risk analysis', *Risk Management*, vol 9, pp129–144

Hill, A. (2001) 'Media risks: The social amplification of risk and the media debate', *Journal of Risk Research*, vol 4, pp209–226

Hood, C. and Heald, D. (eds), (2006) *Transparency: The key to better governance?* Oxford: Oxford University Press.

Hood, C., Rothstein, H. and Baldwin, R. (2001) *The Government of Risk: Understanding risk regulation regimes*, Oxford: Oxford University Press.

Horlick-Jones, T., Walls, J., Rowe, G., Pidgeon, N. F., Poortinga, W., Murdock, G. and O'Riordan, T. (2007) *The GM Debate: Risk, politics and public deliberation*, London: Routledge

House of Lords (2000) *Select Committee on Science and Technology: Science and Society*, London: Stationery Office

Hutter, B. and Power, M. (2005) *Organizational Encounters with Risk*, Cambridge: Cambridge University Press

Kagan, R. A. and Axelrad, L. (2000) *Regulatory Encounters: Multinational corporations and American adversarial legalism*, Berkeley: University California Press

Karlsson, M. (2006) 'The precautionary principle, Swedish chemicals policy and sustainable development', *Journal of Risk Research*, vol 9, pp337–360

Kasperson, J. X., Kasperson, R. E., Pidgeon, N. and Slovic, P. (2003) 'The social amplification of risk: Assessing fifteen years of research and theory', in N. Pidgeon, R. E. Kasperson and P. Slovic (eds), *The Social Amplification of Risk*, Cambridge: Cambridge University Press

Kasperson, R. E., Renn, O., and Slovic, P. et al (1988) 'The social amplification of risk: A conceptual framework', *Risk Analysis*, vol 8, pp177–187

Kasperson, R. E., Golding, D. and Tuler, S. (1992) 'Social distrust as a factor in siting hazardous facilities and communicating risks', *Journal of Social Issues*, vol 48, pp161–187

Kempton, W. and Craig, P. P. (1993) 'European perspectives on climate change', *Environment Magazine*, April, pp16–20, 41–45

Keynes, J. M. (1921 [1921] 1973) 'A treatise on probability', in *The Collected Writings of J. M. Keynes*, Vol. VIII, London: Macmillan for the Royal Economic Society

Keynes, J. M. (1937) 'The general theory of employment', *Quarterly Journal of Economics*, vol 51, pp209–223

Klinke, A. and Renn, O. (2006) 'Systemic risks as challenge for policy making in risk governance', *Forum Qualitative Sozialforschung /Forum: Qualitative Social Research* (on-line journal), vol 7, no 1, Art. 33. www.qualitative-research.net/fqs-texte/1-06/06-1-33-e.htm (accessed 20 February 2008)

Knight, F. H. (1921) *Risk, Uncertainty, and Profit*, Hart, Schaffner, and Marx Prize Essays, no. 31, Boston and New York: Houghton Mifflin

Krimsky, S. and Plough, A. (1988) *Environmental Hazards: Communicating risks as a social process*, Dover, MA: Auburn House

Kunreuther, H. and Slovic, P. (1996) 'Science, values, and risk', *American Academy of Political and Social Science*, vol 545, pp116–125

Kunreuther, H., Easterling, D., Desvousges, W. and Slovic, P. (1990) 'Public attitudes toward siting a high-level nuclear waste repository in Nevada', *Risk Analysis*, vol 10, pp469–484

Lerner, J. S. and Keltner, D. (2000) 'Beyond valence: Toward a model of emotion-specific influences on judgment and choice', *Cognition and Emotion*, vol 14, pp473–493

Lerner, J. S. and Keltner, D. (2001) 'Fear, anger, and risk', *Journal of Personality and Social Psychology*, vol 81, pp146–159

Lerner, J. S., Gonzalez, R. M., Small, D. A. and Fischhoff, B. (2003) 'Emotion and perceived risks of terrorism: A national field experiment', *Psychological Science*, vol 14, pp144–150

Löfstedt, R. E. (1996) 'Risk communication: The Barseback nuclear plant case', *Energy Policy*, vol 24, pp689–696

Löfstedt, R. E. (1999) 'The role of trust in the North Black Forest: An evaluation of a citizen panel project', *Risk, Health Safety and Environment*, vol 10, pp10–30

Löfstedt, R. E. (2002) 'Good and bad examples of siting and building biosafety level 4 laboratories: A study of Winnipeg, Galveston and Etobicoke', *Journal of Hazardous Materials*, vol 93, pp47–66

Löfstedt, R. E. (2003) 'Science communication and the Swedish acrylamide "alarm"', *Journal of Health Communication*, vol 8, pp407–430

Löfstedt, R. E. (2005) *Risk Management in Post Trust Societies*, Basingstoke: Palgrave/Macmillan

Löfstedt, R. E. (2008) 'Risk communication, media amplification, and the aspartame scare', forthcoming in *Risk Management*

Löfstedt, R. E. and Frewer, L. (eds) (1998) *The Earthscan Reader in Risk and Modern Society*, London: Earthscan

Löfstedt, R. E. and Vogel, D. (2001) 'The changing character of regulation: A comparison of Europe and the United States', *Risk Analysis*, vol 21, pp399–406

Löfstedt, R. E., Fischhoff, B. and Fischhoff, I. (2002) 'Precautionary principles: General definitions and specific applications to genetically manipulated organisms (GMOs)', *Journal of Policy Analysis and Management*, vol 21, pp381–407

Luhmann, N. (1989) *Ecological Communication*, Chicago: The University of Chicago Press

Luhmann, N. (1993) *Risk: A sociological theory*, New York: Aldine de Gruyter

Lupton, D. (1999) *Risk*, London and New York: Routledge

Lynch, D. and Vogel, D. (2000) 'Apples and oranges: Comparing the regulation of genetically modified food in Europe and the United States'. Paper prepared for the American Political Science Association annual meeting, 31 August–3 September

McComas, K. (2006) 'Defining moments in risk communication research: 1996–2005', *Journal of Health Communication*, vol 11, pp75–91

Mairal Buil, G. (2003) 'A risk shadow in Spain', *Ethnos*, vol 68, pp179–191

Matsumoto, T., Shiomi, T. and Nakayachi, L. (2005) 'Evaluation of risk communication from the perspective of the information source: Focusing on public relation officers for nuclear power generation', *Japanese Journal of Social Psychology*, vol 20, pp201–207

Morgan, M. G., Fischhoff, B., Bostrom, A. and Altman, C. J. (2002) *Risk Communication: A mental models approach*, New York: Cambridge University Press

National Research Council (1989) *Improving Risk Communication*, Washington DC: National Academy Press

National Research Council (1996) *Understanding Risk*, Washington DC: National Academy Press

Niewohner, J., Cox, P., Gerrard, S. and Pidgeon, N. F. (2004) 'Evaluating the efficacy of a mental models approach for improving occupational chemical risk perception', *Risk Analysis*, vol 24, pp349–361

O'Neill, O. (2002) *A Question of Trust*, Cambridge: Cambridge University Press

O'Riordan, T. (1987) 'Assessing and managing nuclear risk in the United Kingdom', in R. E. Kasperson (ed), *Nuclear Risk Policy*, Boston: Allen and Unwin, pp197–218

Otway, H. J., Maurer, D. and Thomas, J. (1978) 'Nuclear power: The question of public acceptance', *Futures*, vol 10, pp109–118

Peters, E. and Slovic, P. (1996) 'The role of affect and worldviews as orienting dispositions in the perception and acceptance of nuclear power', *Journal of Applied Psychology*, vol 26, pp1427–1453

Peters, R. G., Covello, V. T. and McCallum, D. B. (1997) 'The determinants of trust and credibility in environmental risk communication: An empirical study', *Risk Analysis*, vol 17, pp43–54

Petts, J. (1995) 'Waste management strategy development: A case study of community involvement and consensus-building in Hampshire', *Journal of Environmental Planning and Management*, vol 38, pp519–536

Petts, J. (2001) 'Evaluating the effectiveness of deliberative processes: Waste management case studies', *Journal of Environmental Planning and Management*, vol 44, pp207–226

Petts, J. (2004) 'Barriers to participation and deliberation in risk decisions: Evidence from waste management', *Journal of Risk Research*, vol 7, pp115–133

Phillips, Lord, Bridgeman, J. and Ferguson-Smith, M. (2000) *The Report of the Inquiry into BSE and Variant CJD in the UK*, London: The Stationery Office.

Pidgeon, N. F. and Rogers-Hayden, T. (2007) 'Opening up nanotechnology dialogue with the publics: Risk communication or "upstream engagement"?' *Health, Risk and Society*, vol 9, pp191–210

Pidgeon, N., Hood, C., Jones, D., Turner, B. and Gibson, R. (1992) 'Risk perception', in *Risk: Analysis, Perception and Management*, London: The Royal Society, pp89–134

Pidgeon, N. F., Kasperson, R. E. and Slovic, P. (2003) *The Social Amplification of Risk*, Cambridge: Cambridge University Press

Pidgeon, N. F., Porrtinga, W., Rowe, G., Horlick-Jones, T., Walls, J. and O'Riordan, T. (2005) 'Using surveys in public participation processes for risk decision-making: The case of the 2003 British GM Nation? Public debate', *Risk Analysis*, vol 25, pp467–480

Pidgeon, N. F., Porrtinga, W. and Walls, J. (2007) 'Scepticism, reliance and risk management institutions: Towards a conceptual model of critical trust', in M. Siegrist, T. C. Earle and H. Gutscher (eds), *Trust in Cooperative Risk Management: Uncertainty and scepticism in the public mind*, London: Earthscan, pp117–142

Poortinga, W. and Pidgeon, N. F. (2003a) *Public Perceptions of Risk, Science and Governance: Main findings of a British survey on five risk cases*, Norwich, UK: University of East Anglia, Centre for Environmental Risk

Poortinga, W. and Pidgeon, N. F. (2005) 'Trust in risk regulation: Cause or consequence of the acceptability of GM food?' *Risk Analysis*, vol 25, pp199–209

Poortinga, W. and Pidgeon, N. F. (2006) 'Prior attitudes, salient value similarity, and dimensionality: Toward an integrative model of trust in risk regulation', *Journal of Applied Social Psychology*, vol 36, pp1674–1700

Powell, M. and Leiss, W. (1997) *Mad Cows and Mother's Milk*, Montreal: McGill-Queen's University Press

Power, M. (2007) *Organized Uncertainty: Designing a world of risk management*, Oxford: Oxford University Press

Ramsey, F. (1926) 'Truth and probability', in F. Ramsey, (1931), *The Foundations of Mathematics and Other Logical Essays*, ed R. B. Braithwaite, London: Kegan Paul, pp156–184

Ravetz, J. R. (1999) 'What is post-normal science', *Futures*, vol 31, pp647–653

Rayner, S. (1988) 'Muddling through metaphors to maturity: A commentary on Kasperson et al "The social amplification of risk"', *Risk Analysis*, vol 8, pp201–204

Renn, O. (1998) 'Three decades of risk research: Accomplishments and new challenges', *Journal of Risk Research*, vol 1, pp49–71

Renn, O. and Levine, D. (1991) 'Credibility and trust in risk communication', in R. E. Kasperson and P. J. Stallen (eds), *Communicating Risks to the Public: International dimensions*, Dordrecht: Kluwer.

Renn, O. and Roco, M. (2006) *Nanotechnology Risk Governance*, Geneva: International Risk Governance Council

Renn, O. and Rohrmann, B. (eds) (2000) *Cross-Cultural Risk Perception Research*, Dordrecht: Kluwer.

Renn, O. and Walker, K. (eds) (2008) *Global Risk Governance: Concept and practice using the IRGC framework*, Dordrecht: Springer

Riley, D. M., Small, M. J. and Fischhoff, B. (2000) 'Modeling methylene chloride exposure-reduction options for home paint-stripper users', *Journal of Exposure Analysis and Environmental Epidemiology*, vol 10, pp240–250

Rip, A. (1988) 'Should social amplification of risk be counteracted?', *Risk Analysis*, vol 8, pp193–197

Roco, M. C. and Bainbridge, W. (2001) *Social Implications of NanoScience and Nanotechnology*, Dordrecht: Kluwer

Rogers-Hayden, T. and Pidgeon, N. F. (2006) 'Reflecting upon the UK citizens' jury on nanotechnologies: Nano Jury UK', *Nanotechnology Law and Business*, vol 2, pp167–178

Rogers-Hayden, T. and Pidgeon, N. F. (2008) 'Developments in nanotechnology public engagement in the UK: "Upstream" toward sustainability', forthcoming in *Journal of Cleaner Production*

Rosa, E. A. (1998) 'Metatheoretical foundations for post-normal risk', *Journal of Risk Research*, vol 1, pp14–44

Rowe, G. and Frewer, L. (2000) 'Public participation methods: A framework for evaluation', *Science, Technology and Human Values*, vol 225, pp3–29

Rowe, G., Horlick-Jones, T., Walls, J. and Pidgeon, N. F. (2005) 'Difficulties in evaluating public engagement initiatives: Reflections on an evaluation of the UK GM Nation? Public debate about transgenic crops', *Public Understanding of Science*, vol 14, pp331–352

Sandin, P. (1999) 'Dimensions of the precautionary principle', *Human and Ecological Risk Assessment*, vol 5, pp889–907

Sandin, P., Peterson, M., Hanson, S. O., Ruden, C. and Juthe, A. (2002) 'Five charges against the precautionary principle', *Journal of Risk Research*, vol 5, pp287–299

Schutz, H. and Wiedemann, P. M. (2000) 'Hazardous incident information for the public: Is it useful?' *Australasian Journal of Disaster and Trauma Studies*, vol 2

Searle, J. R. (1995) *The Construction of Social Reality*, New York: The Free Press

Shrader-Frechette, K. S. (1991) *Risk and rationality: Philosophical foundations for populist reforms*, Berkeley CA: University of California Press.

Siegrist, M. and Cvetkovich, G. (2000) 'Perception of hazards: The role of social trust and knowledge', *Risk Analysis*, vol 20, pp713–719

Siegrist M., Gutscher, H. and Earle, T. C. (2005) 'Perception of risk: The influence of general trust and general confidence', *Journal of Risk Research*, vol 8, pp145–156

Siegrist, M., Earle, T. C. and Gutscher, H. (eds) (2007) *Trust in Cooperative Risk Management: Uncertainty and scepticism in the public mind*, London: Earthcan

Sjöberg, L. (1997) 'Explaining risk perception: An empirical and quantitative evaluation of cultural theory', *Risk, Decision and Policy*, vol 2, pp113–130

Sjöberg, L. (1999) 'Perceived competence and motivation in industry and government as factors in risk perception', in G. Cvetkovich and R. E. Löfstedt (eds), *Social Trust and the Management of Risk*, London: Earthscan

Sjöberg, L. (2003) 'Distal factors in risk perception', *Journal of Risk Research*, vol 6, pp187–212

Sjöberg, L. (2004) 'Explaining individual risk perception: The case of nuclear waste', *Risk Management*, vol 6, pp51–64

Sjöberg, L. (2005a) 'The importance of respect for empirical findings: Response to Tansey', *Journal of Risk Research*, vol 8, pp713–715

Sjöberg, L. (2005b) 'The perceived risk of terrorism', *Risk Management*, vol 7, pp43–61

Sjöberg, L. (2006) 'Will the real meaning of affect please stand up?' *Journal of Risk Research*, vol 9, pp101–108

Sjöberg, L. (2008) 'Antagonism, trust and perceived risk', *Risk Management*, vol 10, pp32–55

Sjölander-Lindqvist, A. (2004) 'Local environment at stake: The Hallandsås railway tunnel in a social and cultural context', Lund: Lund dissertations in human ecology, Lund University

Slovic, P. (1993) 'Perceived risk, trust and democracy', *Risk Analysis*, vol 13, pp675–682

Slovic, P. (2000) *The Perception of Risk*, London: Earthscan

Slovic, P., Kunreuther, H. and White, G. (1974) 'Decision processes, rationality and adjustment to natural hazards', in G. F. White (ed), *Natural Hazards: Local, national, global*, New York: Oxford University Press, pp187–205

Slovic, P., Fischhoff, B. and Lichtenstein, S. (1976) 'Cognitive processes and societal risk taking', in J. S. Carroll and J. W. Wayne (eds), *Cognition and Social Behavior*, Potoma, MD: Erlbaum, pp165–184

Slovic, P., Layman, M. and Flynn, J. (1991) 'Risk perception, trust, and nuclear waste: Lessons from Yucca Mountain', *Environment*, vol 33, pp6–11, 28–30

Slovic, P., Finucane, M., Peters, E. and MacGregor, D. G. (2004) 'Risk as analysis and risk as feelings: Some thoughts about affect, reason, risk and rationality', *Risk Analysis*, vol 24, pp311–322

Starr, C. (1969) 'Social benefit versus technological risk', *Science*, vol 165, pp1232–1238

Stoffle, R. W. and Arnold, R. (2003) 'Confronting the angry rock: American Indians' situated risk from radioactivity', *Ethnos*, vol 68, no 3, pp230–248

Strydom, P. (2002) *Risk, Environment and Society*, Buckingham: Open University Press

Sunstein, C. R. (2002) *Risk and Reason: Safety, law and the environment*, Cambridge: Cambridge University Press

Sunstein, C. R. (2005) *Laws of Fear: Beyond the precautionary principle*, Cambridge: Cambridge University Press

Sunstein, C. R. (2007) *Worst-Case Scenarios*, Cambridge, MA: Harvard University Press

Svenson, O. (1988) 'Mental models of risk communication and action: Reflections on social amplification of risk', *Risk Analysis*, vol 8, pp199–200

Tait, J. (2008) 'Risk governance of genetically modified crops: European and American perspectives', in O. Renn and K. Walker (eds), *Global Risk Governance: Concept and practice using the IRGC framework*, Dordrecht: Springer

Tansey, J. (2004a) 'If all you have is a hammer ... a response to Sjoberg', *Journal of Risk Research*, vol 7, pp361–363

Tansey, J. (2004b) 'Risk as politics, culture as power', *Journal of Risk Research*, vol 7, pp17–32

Tickner, J. and Gouveia-Vigeant, T. (2005) 'The 1991 cholera epidemic in Peru: Not a case of precaution gone awry', *Risk Analysis*, vol 25, pp495–502

Timotijevic, L. and Barnett, J. (2006) 'Managing the possible health risks of mobile telecommunications: Public understandings of precautionary action and advice', *Health, Risk and Society*, vol 8, pp143–164

Townsend, E. (2006) 'Affective influences on risk perceptions of, and attitudes toward, genetically modified food', *Journal of Risk Research*, vol 9, pp125–139

Tversky, A. and Kahneman, D. (1974) 'Judgment under uncertainty: Heuristics and biases', *Science*, vol 185, pp1124–1131

UK Strategy Unit (2002) *Risk: Improving government's capacity to handle risk and uncertainty*, London: Cabinet Office, Strategy Unit

Van Asselt, M. B. A. and Vos, E. (2006) 'The precautionary principle and the uncertainty paradox', *Journal of Risk Research*, vol 9, pp313–336

Viscusi, K. (1996) *Rational Risk Policy: The 1996 Arne Ryde Memorial Lectures*, Oxford: Oxford University Press

Vogel, D. (1986) *National Styles of Regulation: Environmental policy in Great Britain and the United States*, Ithaca, NY: Cornell University Press

Vogel, D. (2003) 'The hare and the tortoise revisited: The new politics of consumer and environmental regulation in Europe', *British Journal of Political Science*, vol 33, pp557–580

Vos, B. and Wendler, F. (2006) *Food Safety Regulation in Europe: A comparative approach*, Antewerpen, Oxford: Intersentia

Wahlberg, A. E. (2001) 'The theoretical features of some current approaches to risk perception', *Journal of Risk Research*, vol 4, pp237–250

Walls, J., Pidgeon, N. F., Weyman, A. and Horlick-Jones, T. (2004) 'Critical trust: Understanding lay perceptions of health and safety risk regulation', *Health, Risk and Society*, vol 6, pp133–150

Wardman, J. K. (2006) 'Commentary: Toward a critical discourse on affect and risk perception', *Journal of Risk Research*, vol 9, pp109–124

Wiedemann, P. and Schutz, H. (2005) 'The precautionary principle and risk perception: Experimental studies in the EMF area', *Environmental Health Perspectives*, vol 113, pp402–405

Wiedemann, P. M., Schutz, H. and Thalman, A. T. (2003) *Mobilfunk und Gesundheit: Risikobewertung im wissenschaftlichen Dialog*, Juelich: Research Center Juelich

Wiedemann, P. M., Thalmann, A. T., Grutsch, M. A. and Schutz, H. (2006) 'The impacts of precautionary measures and the disclosure of scientific uncertainty on EMF risk perception and trust', *Journal of Risk Research*, vol 9, pp361–372

Wiener, J. B. (2002) 'Precaution in a multi-risk world', in D. Paustenbach (ed), *Human and Ecological Risk Assessment: Theory and practice*, New York: Wiley and Sons, pp1509–1531

Wiener, J. B. and Rogers, M. (2002) 'Comparing precaution in the US and Europe', *Journal of Risk Research*, vol 5, pp317–349

Wynne, B. (1989) 'Sheep farming after Chernobyl: A case study in communicating scientific information', *Environment*, vol 31, pp10–15, 33–39

Wynne, B. (1996) 'May the sheep safely graze?' in S. Lash, B. Szersynski, and B. Wynne (eds), *Risk, Environment and Modernity: Toward a new ecology*, London: Sage Publications

Part I

The Concept of Risk

2

The Policy Implications of Differing Concepts of Risk

Judith A. Bradbury

A neglected area in the field of risk analysis is the implications for policy of differing conceptual approaches to risk. The purpose of this chapter is to draw on the policy analysis literature to delineate the linkage between conceptualization of risk and the formulation and proposed solution of risk-related policy problems.

An insight from the literature that is of particular relevance to the current debate about risk is the emphasis on problem structuring as the most crucial task in policy development (Dunn, 1981). If a policy problem is not structured appropriately, that is, if it does not take into account all of the dimensions of the problem, policy failures are likely to result. In effect, attempts will have been made to solve the wrong problem (Ackoff, 1974).

This discussion examines three broad groups of studies and the concept of risk that underlies the way they formulate risk management and risk communication policy problems. I identify two concepts of risk. One concept reflects a view of scientific knowledge as composed of objective facts: these facts provide the basis for decisions. A second concept reflects the view that facts cannot be separated from values in policy-related science contexts. My argument is that this latter concept, which addresses key dimensions of the problems, provides a firm theoretical basis for the design of policy. The argument is based on a social constructivist perspective that views the discussion of risk as involving a more fundamental discussion about the nature and role of science in modern, industrialized society).[1]

In this discussion, *risk assessment* is defined (following Kates and Kasperson, 1984, p7029) as including the processes of identification, estimation, and evaluation. *Risk management* is defined broadly as 'the process by which decisions about risk are made' (adapted from Zimmerman, 1986, p436). This latter definition differs from some common usages in which the term refers more narrowly to the process of regulation or to the selection and implementation of a strategy for control of a specific risk. I approach the discussion from the standpoint of my interest in nuclear waste policy.

Two Concepts of Risk

Otway and Thomas (1982) have pointed to a fundamental difference in views toward, and use of, the risk concept. The two risk concepts represent ideal types, which are frequently blurred in practice. However, each is linked to and implicitly underlies a particular formulation of risk management and communication policy problems.

One approach conceives of risk as a physically given attribute of hazardous technologies: objective facts, which can be explained, predicted and controlled by science, are separated from subjective values. A second approach conceives of risk as a socially constructed attribute, rather than as a physical entity that exists independently of the humans who assess and experience its effects. This latter viewpoint emphasizes that the processes of risk identification and risk estimation can never be value-free, that the scientist's judgement involves the balancing of conflicting evidence, and that "factual" empirical evidence alone does not lead to any conclusions' (Wynne, 1980, p182). Consequently, the so-called objective activities of risk identification and estimation need to be integrated with, rather than separated from, the subjective process of evaluation.

The Concept of Risk as a Physically Given Attribute

A view of risk as a physically given attribute of hazardous technologies underlies the approach of two different groups of studies: the traditional, technical approach to risk assessment and the psychometric, social science approach of Slovic and associates.

The technical approach

The traditional, technical approach defines risk as the product of the probability and consequences (magnitude and severity) of an adverse event (Hadden, 1984). This concept, which until recently dominated the risk analysis literature, reflects the influence of engineering safety studies on the emergence of modern risk analysis (Otway and Thomas, 1982; Kates and Kasperson, 1984). Probabilistic risk assessment (PRA) of nuclear reactor risks, which developed into a 'multi-billion dollar activity' after its first major application in the WASH-1400 report (US Nuclear Regulatory Commission, 1975), has been applied to a variety of non-nuclear situations (Vesely, 1984, p154).

Most PRA practitioners would agree that their estimates, which incorporate the analyst's judgments at many critical points,[2] cannot be viewed as value-free or so-called objective reality. This is particularly the situation, for example, for technological developments such as high-level waste repositories, where there is no base of accumulated experience against which the analyst's calculations can be validated and where the timeframe for predicting and preventing risk extends thousands of years into the future. Moreover, as Spangler has emphasized, value-laden, 'nitty-gritty, everyday decisions' are made routinely by scientists and engineers employed by government and regulatory bodies (Spangler, 1985, p920). Nevertheless, the policy implications of this inevitable element of human judgment frequently are obscured or overlooked: among approaches that start from the phenomenon of risk rather than from the perceiver of risk, an implicit reification of risk may be discerned. That is, risk is treated as an objective fact.

The implicit reification of risk can be seen in continued attempts to make a distinction between fact and value, between the activities of identification and estimation on the one hand and the activity of evaluation on the other.[3] This distinction may be useful as an analytical tool; it is misleading when it assumes that risk identification and estimation represent value-neutral activities and that evaluation can be undertaken as a separate step (Conrad, 1980, p248; see also, Wynne, 1980; Hadden, 1984).

Reification also can be seen in approaches to risk management that incorporate an unexamined assumption that technical analyses represent absolute, rather than relative, truth. Logically, such an assumption leads to the view that risk management decisions are rational to the extent that they are based on the realist, non-personal factors (mortality statistics, economic efficiency) of technical analysis.[4] From this viewpoint, the public's failure to make risk decisions on a similar basis is seen as economically inefficient and as evidence of irrationality or lack of knowledge and understanding.

Although the technical approach to risk may be entirely appropriate for purely engineering decisions, it is inappropriate when used as the basis for societal decisions.[5] Structuring the risk management problem solely in terms of technical and economic rationality fails to recognize that societal rationality has additional dimensions. Two key dimensions omitted are:

- the political dimension – how to proceed in a democracy when there is a discrepancy between 'what the experts deem most important and what the public demands from its government' (Plough and Krimsky, 1987, p7); and
- the ethical dimension – how to surface and address questions of values that inherently are embedded in the judgments of the analyst.

The omission of key dimensions leads to attempts to apply inappropriate solutions, that is, attempts to solve the wrong policy problem.

The unexamined assumption that technical analyses represent absolute, rather than relative truth also leads, logically, to a structuring of the risk communication problem in terms of lack of public understanding and knowledge. Equally logically, the proposed solution is to convince or educate the public about the real risk. Structuring the communication task this way requires the skills of the social scientist for implementation. However, as Rayner has emphasized, when risk managers turn to behavioural scientists for advice, they meet 'apparent theoretical disarray' (Rayner, 1988, p201). The theoretical disarray has significant practical implications.

The psychometric approach

Social science studies of risk include both the pioneering psychometric, risk perception studies of Slovic and associates and a large body of attitudinal research. The research has examined a wide range of factors, including underlying beliefs and values, that are incorporated into an individual's assessment of risk. In this section, I focus on the contributions of Slovic and associates, which have received prominent treatment in the literature.

These psychometric studies have found differences between expert and lay risk judgments, and they point to a concept of risk that is multidimensional and considerably more complex than the statistical or actuarial concepts of the technical analyst. But as in the technical approach, Slovic and associates start from the technical concept of risk, rather than starting from the person who is perceiving the risk or the broader, social implications of technology. In examining the individual's response to risk, this research provides a subjectivist interpretation within a realist paradigm. Psychometric research thus straddles technical and social paradigms uneasily.

Because of ambiguity in its initial concept of risk, the psychometric school is unable to develop a truly social critique that would assist in solving problems left unsolved by the technical approach. The ambiguity is epitomized in its common use of the term *perceived* risk. The term connotes that natural sciences study reality, while the factors discovered by the social sciences represent 'mere perceptions' (Thompson and Parkinson, 1984, p557). Such a distinction is misleading: experts' and laypersons' assessments of risk both constitute judgments and both are subject to bias (Kates and Kasperson, 1984; Earle and Cvetovich, 1985). The ambiguity of the term is particularly evident in conflicting statements that appear in the work of Slovic and Fischhoff, two prominent researchers from the psychometric school. Some statements specifically deny the possibility of absolute, real risk; others clearly suggest that the experts' definition of risk is the real, correct one. Thus it is possible to interpret the psychometric research findings in different ways:

- as a demonstration of the diversity of risk judgments, that is, that the difference between expert and layperson represents a legitimate difference in viewpoint; or
- as implying that there is a standard of real risk (the technical definition of risk) against which lay perceptions may be judged to be more or less accurate.

In the latter case, the difference between expert and layperson is attributed to a lack of public understanding. From a policy standpoint, the difference between interpretations is significant.

Fischhoff's work provides examples of the first interpretation and the related policy approach. In an early article, he emphasizes the element of values in risk decisions and the potential for bias in technical expert as well as lay judgments (Fischhoff, 1979). In a more recent publication, Fischhoff and his co-authors (1983) provide a detailed discussion of underlying reasons for disagreements between experts and laypersons, including situations (e.g. the Alaska pipeline) in which laypersons have information the experts lack. Here, Fischhoff starts from the premise that attributing disagreements to public misperceptions is 'often factually wrong' and 'from a societal perspective corrosive by encouraging disrespect among the parties involved... Although there are actual risks, nobody knows what they are. All that anyone does know about risks can be classified as perceptions' (Fischhoff et al, 1983, pp236, 237; see also Fischhoff et al, 1981, pxii).

The policy approach linked to this premise is clearly different from the technical approach, in which the management problem is structured in terms of economic and technical rationality and the communication problem is seen to be informing or educating the public about risk as defined by the technical expert. For Fischhoff, risk management involves seeking citizen participation in risk decisions (Fischhoff, 1979); education of the public is only one of a number of possible policy solutions. Management requires careful thought and research 'to clarify just what it is that the various parties know and believe'; only after this clarification can the underlying problem and its associated solution – 'scientific, educational, semantic, or political' – be diagnosed (Fischhoff et al, 1983, p247). Although Fischhoff does not specifically address the issue of risk communication, his general orientation toward the communication task involves the structuring of a two-way rather than one-way process of communication. Such a process enhances mutual learning and respect between public and experts. 'That respect may be one of society's greatest assets' (Fischhoff et al., 1983, p247).

Examples of the second interpretation of psychometric research findings are more evident in publications authored by Slovic as sole or lead author (although Fischhoff is a contributing author to a number of these joint publications). The assumption of a standard or real risk as defined by the expert can be discerned in many areas, for example: (1) the early, well-known article, 'Rating the risks', which opens with the statement: 'People respond to the hazards they perceive. If their perceptions are *faulty*, efforts at public and environmental protection are likely to be misdirected' (Slovic et al, 1979, p14, emphasis added); (2) comparison of ratings of experts, who 'have statistical evidence on hand', with those of laypersons who 'in most cases ... must make inferences based on what they remember hearing or observing' (Slovic et al, 1981, p17); and (3) the use in a variety of articles, of terms such as *perceived risk, misperceptions, inaccurate views*, or *when people err* and even the use of a title such as 'Facts and fears: Understanding perceived risk' (Slovic et al, 1980a). Despite acknowledging that expert judgments are also subject to bias (Slovic et al, 1977, 1984), Slovic tends to focus on 'biased newspaper coverage and biased judgments of the public' (Slovic et al, 1981, p19) rather than on the implications of expert biases.

Significantly, the policy applications Slovic discusses are based on a technical concept of risk. His management focus is the lack of public understanding and knowledge exacerbated by the media. The proposed solution is to inform and educate the public: 'The fact that perceptions of risk are often inaccurate points to the need for warnings and educational programs' (Slovic, 1986, p405; see also, Slovic et al, 1980b). Elsewhere, he singles out two policy applications of psychometric research: the need for education of the public and the need to understand and forecast public response to technologies (Slovic et al, 1981). The need to involve people with differing perspectives in making societal decisions is not elaborated.

Among psychometric researchers, Slovic has been a foremost contributor to the recent discussion of risk communication policy. Here, the underlying conceptual confusion evident in earlier work is compounded by his adoption of the terminology and focus of linear, one-way communication models. The result, which may be unintended, is an implicitly technocentric approach to risk communication. Two examples of this approach can be cited: the manual for plant managers, published by the Chemical Manufacturers' Association (Covello et al, 1988), and a conference discussion on risk communication, subsequently published by the Conservation Foundation (Covello et al, 1987).

The manual for plant managers begins with the seven cardinal rules of risk communication, which have been published as a handout by the Environmental Protection Agency (Covello and Allen, 1988). The first rule acknowledges that in a democratic society, citizens have a right to participate in decisions that affect their lives; the goal of risk communication should not be to diffuse public concerns and avoid action. Significantly, however, the goal of risk communication is 'to produce an informed public that is involved, interested, reasonable, thoughtful, solution-oriented, and collaborative' (Covello et al, 1988, p2). This focus on the public is an almost-classic example of what Rogers and Kincaid (1981, p39) cite as the 'individual-blame' bias of linear communication models. The manual acknowledges but does not stress ways that the provision of information to managers from and about the public might also enhance the communication process. It does not suggest enhancing communication as a two-way process among participants who have equal, though differing, contributions to make. Nor does it discuss ways the public might be involved in making decisions about risk, rather than being passive recipients – the 'target audience' (Covello et al, 1988, p9) – for technical spokespersons' messages. Rather, the manual focuses on risk communication as an act rather than a process and stresses ways to enhance the technical manager's presentation of probabilistic risk concepts. Effective communication is conceived in the limited sense of the manager's ability to explain risk concepts clearly.

The manual is based on an earlier publication by Covello, von Winterfeldt and Slovic (1987). In this earlier discussion of four tasks of risk communication, the theoretical underpinnings of the authors' approach to risk communication are revealed. Communication is restricted to the 'act' (Covello et al, 1987, p112) rather than the process of communication. Throughout, the discussion uses the terminology of linear models of communication, which posit transmission of a message, via a channel, from a source to a receiver. Over the past decade, one-way transmission models, which were accepted during the 1950s and 1960s, have been subjected to severe criticism.[6] Essentially, the goal of the message-source-channel-receiver model is persuasion rather than information sharing: the focus is the effect of communication on a passive receiver rather than the context in which communication occurs and the relationship between senders and receivers as joint participants in the mutual generation of meaning.

Adopting linear model terminology leads Slovic and his co-authors to particular problems in reconciling practice with theory in their fourth task of risk communication, namely, joint problem solving and conflict resolution. While recognizing elsewhere that 'the heart of effective communication is negotiation and coalition building not manipulation' (Covello, 1987, p65) and that 'risk communication efforts are bound to fail unless they are structured as a two-way process' (Slovic, 1986, p410), Covello and Slovic fail to structure risk communication accordingly. Rather, they reinforce a structuring of the policy decision in technical terms: government and industry officials (the source) send messages to individual citizens (receivers). The authors are thus unable to present a firmly grounded case for a two-way process of communication and negotiation.

The one-way feature of the communication model of Covello et al. has been criticized, and suggestions have been made for an alternative, two-way model that explicitly recognizes the role of all parties as communicators (Leiss and Krewski, 1987). But such criticism stops short of identifying the fundamental cause of the problem. The problem stems from the initial concept of risk. The very selection of linear model terminology is only symptomatic of a continuing failure to recognize the philosophical contradictions of both the model and the authors' underlying concept of risk. Ambivalence over the risk concept reinforces the role of the experts as the sole possessors of the accurate facts: there is no logical alternative but to place the experts in the role of communicators *to* rather than *with* the public. The technical approach to risk communication follows inevitably.

In sum, therefore, the theoretical confusion evident in the work of the two most prominent authors from the psychometric school has serious policy implications. Nowhere do the authors explicitly acknowledge a difference in viewpoint or specifically address the implications of their initial concepts of risk. However, in starting from the phenomenon of risk rather than from the perceiver of risk, they cannot provide a theoretical basis adequate to support an unambiguous interpretation of their findings. As a result, there is no consistent, firmly grounded basis for structuring the policy problem.

The ambiguity is additionally significant in that policy decisions about risk typically are made by technical managers rather than by social scientists. In this context, the insights of the literature on knowledge utilization are particularly relevant. That literature emphasizes that knowledge, as opposed to the physical symbols of a body of knowledge, does not have an independent existence: the products of knowledge are interpreted differently by various users according to their frames of reference. Frames of reference constitute the underlying structure of assumptions, expectations, and decision rules or criteria for assessing knowledge claims, structuring enquiry, and constructing meanings (Dunn et al, 1985; Dunn and Holzner, 1988). They form the 'unreflected basis for structuring inquiry' (Holzner and Fisher, 1979, p231). By virtue of their frames of reference, technical managers are predisposed to adopt technical approaches to risk management. The information/education solution is more likely to be congruent with their pre-existing structuring of risk management in technical terms and their structuring of the communication problem in terms of a lack of public understanding of science. Although psychometric researchers might protest that the breadth of their studies does not support a narrowly technocentric view and that the value of the studies lies in their display of the rich and wide diversity of views about risk that need to be incorporated into risk decisions, technical managers may not perceive these features.[7]

Thus, perhaps against their best intentions, authors from the psychometric school have contributed to a formulation of risk management and risk communication on the technical analyst's terms. The management approach in effect permits the technical manager to pursue the technical aspects of technology development in isolation from its social implications, that is, to adopt what Wynne has termed a *tool concept* of technology. The participation of, and communication with, other affected groups becomes a separate activity, an adjunct rather than an integral part of management decision-making. In the process, social science knowledge comes to be viewed in purely instrumental terms: the social scientist is reduced to the subordinate role of change-agent. Such a role subtly undermines the autonomy of the public whose attitudes are deemed to be in need of change and also causes ethical problems for the social scientist.[8]

The Concept of Risk and Technology as Social Processes

Cultural scholars start from the premise that risk and technology are social processes rather than physical entities that exist independently of the humans who assess and experience them. This alternative concept, which explicitly addresses the value-embedded nature of all knowledge claims about risk, leads to a formulation of the management and communication policy problems different from that of the technical approach. The discussion changes from a focus on probabilities to a focus on the risk perceiver – expert as well as layperson – and hence to a focus on social institutions and the social and cultural context in which risk is assessed and managed.

The viewpoint that risk is socially constructed rather than a physically given attribute is most succinctly expressed by Otway and Thomas (1982, p70):

> It is clear that truths do not exist independently of *people*, whether taken to be individuals, significant social groups in the general public, professional or political/industrial groups. It is *people*, and not independent facts, who constrain the way concepts are framed, questions posed, and research goals set. And it is people who design event and fault trees, close options, choose attribute sets, fund data collection, interpret and publish findings. Once the criterion of an absolute truth is abandoned, then surely no one can avoid the inference *that people see the world differently* and that these differences emerge from different experiences of differently constructed social worlds.

Among cultural theories, the grid/group framework of Douglas and Wildavsky (1982) illuminates the social processes that affect the tendency to take or avoid different types of risk. These authors emphasize that ideas about the world, including perceptions of risk, come from human experience, but experience differs among groups. Different forms of social organization thus influence the way we take or avoid risks. Differences in views of risk can therefore best be understood by analysing different forms of social organization and underlying value systems. Moreover, as Plough and Krimsky succinctly point out, 'There is a social context of expertise and officialdom as well as of lay communities. Bias, irrational action, and narrow interest group behaviour intrude into both these contexts' (1987, p9).

Wynne (1980, 1983) examines the issue of technological risk in terms of its relationship to an underlying view of the social relations of expertise and the nature and effects of technology. His distinction between what he terms a tool concept of technology and technology as a way of life highlights the need for participation as an essential, rather than simply a desirable, part of the societal decision-making process on technology and risk. Each of the two viewpoints on technology is associated with a distinct view of the role of risk assessment and of public participation. Wynne is critical of the narrow focus of the tool concept, which adopts a view of technology as a neutral phenomenon and risk as a reified concept. This latter viewpoint seeks to identify, predict and control physical impacts, and insulates physical risks and effects of technology from broader social effects. Participation is restricted in scope because it is viewed as a factor external to technology – as an inefficient process that may delay the technology's deployment.

The alternative view of technology as a way of life recognizes that technology is not a neutral phenomenon but is social in origin, character and effects. From this viewpoint, the implications of technological development are the social relationships involved in innovation and implementation rather than its physical consequences. The key uncertainties in risk-related problems stem not so much from technical uncertainties, as addressed in technical risk analysis, as from uncertainties over potential social changes. Face-to-face interaction among groups and participants from a range of socio-cultural perspectives is a prerequisite in the development of socially viable technologies. The societal question is 'not whether and how to let the so-called "outsiders" in, but of whether it is sane and feasible to keep the "insiders" (the risk-bearers) out' (Wynne, 1983, p19).

The major contribution of the social and cultural literature on risk and technology is the insight it provides into problem unsolving and into an appropriate reformulation of the risk management and risk communication problems. Although cultural theorists have been accused of embracing a radical, social reductionist stance (see especially Funtowicz and Ravetz, 1985), it can be argued that their insights have pinpointed and provided a firm theoretical foundation for an appropriate design of policy.

In the notion of *problem unsolving*, the social and cultural approaches explicitly recognize that decisions based on statistical probabilities are too narrow to be used as the basis for social acceptability. Such decisions seem to solve problems, but leave their deeper dimensions unsolved. The cultural approaches do not deny the importance of technical, economic analyses in informing the risk decision. Their criticism is that technical and economic analyses are being used alone to drive decisions (Hadden, 1984). Improved technical analyses are not the key to improved risk management decisions. Decisions that involve trans-scientific, rather than scientific, questions cannot be answered by science (Weinberg, 1972). Since societal risk management decisions on the level, acceptability and distribution of risk involve questions of values, and since differing values are held by those affected, risk management decisions must take into account the political, social and ethical, as well as the technical, aspects of the policy problem.

Moreover, the cultural approach provides an *appropriate formulation of the policy problem* by starting from the risk perceiver, from different perspectives on risk and the inherently value-laden nature of risk decisions, and by emphasizing the essential role of participation by a range of perspectives in societal decisions about risk. The management approach implied in the cultural view is premised on a belief in the rationality of differing values and differing risk claims – where rationality is defined, in the words of Dunn (1981, p225), as a 'self-conscious process of using reasoned argument to make and defend advocative claims'. Once it is explicitly acknowledged that 'truths do not exist independently of people' (Otway and Thomas, 1982, p70), the policy problems are structured in terms of negotiating among the 'alternative cultural perspectives' (Rayner, 1984, p160) of all socio-cultural groups – the technical analyst, the policymaker, and the various groups involved in, and affected by, policy implementation. Managers need to understand the basis of their own and of other groups' perspectives on risk and to initiate the development of institutional means for accommodation.[9]

From this viewpoint, acceptance and acceptability of risk cannot be analytically determined but must be negotiated, that is, socially constructed. This is essentially a question of policy analysis rather than science (Clark, 1980), in which a priority is placed on the consent of the governed to the process by which decisions are made.[10] The solution is not – and indeed cannot be – a definitive one. Rather, it requires putting in place a process that, in Clark's words, will permit learning from error and that provides for the negotiation of mutually acceptable solutions in the dialogue among those involved. The key questions to be addressed are how to compare critically the competing claims as to what constitutes risk and how to reach societal decisions concerning the control of risk and technology when a diversity of values exists. Some key insights on the need for and nature of this dialogue are provided by Funtowicz and Ravetz, and by Dunn.

Funtowicz and Ravetz address the need for a 'civilized dialogue of risks' (1985, p841) in their differentiation of three types of policy-related research, each of which calls for a qualitatively different approach or method for solution. Their discussion may be viewed in the context of Ravetz's search for a 'new appropriate sort of science' (1987, p89) to replace our inherited conception of science as the facts – a conception that is inadequate to meet the challenge posed by policy-related science issues, characterized by uncertain facts, disputed values, high stakes and a need for urgent decisions. Funtowicz and Ravetz (1985) distinguish a factual and a valuative dimension (systems uncertainty and decision stakes) in such problems; the dimensions may be assigned low, medium, or high values. Where both dimensions are low, a traditional, technical approach is appropriate. In these situations, disputes are likely to be settled easily, either because a substantial body of data has accumulated or because disputes between scientists are not seen to involve critical social issues. This traditional approach is inappropriate, however, for policy issues such as high-level waste management where both dimensions are high, that is, where the data base is not well established and where important values are at stake. Here the approach (termed *total environmental assessment*) takes the form of a dialogue, even on technical issues. Although these types of problem seem, initially, to be a 'clash between incommensurable world views', over time they 'tend to stimulate the production of relevant facts and value-commitments', thus enabling resolution by 'political debate rather than civil war' (Funtowicz and Ravetz, 1985, p844).

Dunn (1982, 1988) provides specific guidance on the nature of the dialogue in his advocacy of the Toulmin model of argumentation (Toulmin, 1958; Toulmin et al, 1979) as the conceptual framework for structuring practical, policy discourse. (The term *practical* is used in Aristotle's sense, namely, providing guidance about what is right and just.) The model, which recognizes the need for ethical, valuative analysis, is thus broader in application than Campbell's (1987) call for a sociology of scientific validity. A primary advantage of the Toulmin model is that it provides a systematic approach to appraising and critically testing the various grounds for assertions or claims. It thus accommodates the range of knowledge claims (e.g. ethical arguments, arguments based on scientific knowledge, or arguments based on experience) that typically are encountered in policy debates. In effect, the dialogue is a process of 'reasoned argument and debate' (Dunn 1982, p302) or critical social transactions among stakeholders with different reference frames who 'engage in the competitive reconstruction of knowledge claims' (Dunn 1982, p304). In this process, each stakeholder's underlying assumptions and standards of assessment (both implicit and explicit) surface for cross-examination: knowledge is socially constructed on the basis of competing knowledge claims and the expansion of learning over time.

From this viewpoint, risk communication is an integral part of the critical dialogue – a process of negotiation among alternative cultural perspectives. The viewpoint is consistent with recent convergence theories of communication that see communication as a process of knowledge transaction among participants and the negotiation of shared meanings over time (Rogers and Kincaid, 1981; Rogers, 1986). Such a concept has several important policy implications.

First, this concept views communication as a two-way process of knowledge sharing and negotiation and for eliminating the blame-the-public orientation of linear model terminology. The priority for management is not the publication of information products but the development of processes of interaction. The various publics affected by policy may need information; equally important, managers also need information about these publics. Information, however, is a means to improve the quality of the process and the relationship among participants rather than an end in itself.

Second, this concept views communication as an integral part of decision-making. It is linked to a view of technology as a social system, or way of life, in which the assessment of physical risks is only one part of the societal decision-making process and participation is an essential part of that process. Communication is seen as an integral part of the management function of actively seeking dialogue with those who hold alternative cultural perspectives – with the various groups of experts, laypersons and organizations that act as filters for and express the public's views.[11]

Third, this concept highlights the relational aspects of communication and the context in which communication occurs. It includes both the interpersonal, explicit exchange of information (which is the sense of the term typically employed in the literature) and the implicit meaning conferred by participants' actions.[12] Communication conceived as a process of developing shared understanding and generating mutual meaning is thus linked to the broader process of participation in its Aristotelian sense. This is the concept of political action as a mode of existence – as a common enterprise in which humans create values and the nature of social reality.[13]

Fourth, this concept provides a role for the use of social science knowledge in policymaking that extends beyond the instrumental role to which it so frequently is assigned. Here, rationality is constitutive, not instrumental; social scientists are freed from their subordinate role. Thus the cultural approach opens the door to the use of social science knowledge for practical and critical as well as for technical (instrumental) purposes.[14] Used for practical purposes, social science knowledge can help facilitate the development of creative solutions to policy problems by the parties concerned. Used for critical purposes, social science knowledge can contribute to defining the nature of the policy problem itself.

Finally, this concept links the current discussion on risk communication to the more fundamental discussion of the appropriateness of older concepts of science to address the problems we currently face. Risk is not a topic to be discussed in isolation from the more fundamental issue raised by Ravetz: can science and scientists remain credible if they try to design policy on risk as if 'they face simple policy questions determined by simple factual inputs' (Ravetz, 1987, p90)?

Conclusion

Social and cultural approaches, which explicitly deny the possibility of a standard of absolute risk, provide a firm theoretical foundation for an appropriate formulation of the policy problem of risk and a framework for solution. Improved technical analyses are not the key to improved risk management and risk communication decisions. The risk management problem requires the development of institutional procedures for structuring a critical dialogue among different perspectives and societal groups. In addressing the question of how to evaluate socially constructed knowledge claims and in pointing to the need for citizen consent and participation, prominent authors from this school have suggested a framework within which the dialogue can take place. The communication problem is formulated as an integral part of this critical dialogue. Communication is seen as a convergence process of knowledge transactions among participants who have equal, if different, contributions to make to societal decisions.

This concept places the risk discussion firmly within a social constructivist framework. Thus the entire discussion of risk – of perception, management and communication – is conceptually linked to the larger societal debate on the nature and role of science in our modern, industrialized civilization.

Notes

1   The discussion, throughout, draws heavily on the insights of Ravetz (1973, 1987), whom Campbell regards as the founder of the social constructivist movement (Campbell, 1987, p391). In his 1987 publication, 'Usable knowledge, usable ignorance: Incomplete science with policy implications', Ravetz argues that our 'one-sided experience of science as the facts', which is 'deeply embedded in our image of science' (p92) has not prepared us for dealing with many of the policy-related science issues we currently face. These issues, resulting largely from the interactions of technology with the environment, raise novel questions of control. Here, we are confronted with pervasive scientific ignorance and the impossibility of separating facts and values. From this viewpoint, the risk discussion is about how we replace our inherited, simplistic conception of science with a 'new appropriate sort of science' (p89).

2   As Vesely (1984, p155) has noted, 'The dominant risk contributors found in a PRA are often those which are most subjective and have the largest uncertainties: examples are human error and dependent failure contributions.' Experts in the field recognize that the value of such assessments lies primarily in the systematic, disciplined thinking that they impose on the assessors.

3   For example, Lowrance's (1976) two-stage model of risk assessment reappears as a recommendation for a 'clear distinction' to be made between assessment and evaluation in the 1983 report by the National Research Council, *Risk Assessment in the Federal Government: Managing the Process.*

4   For examples of such approaches, see Wilson's (1979) incremental risk approach, which evaluated the introduction of new risks with already existing risks in terms of life expectancy rates, and Cohen's (1980) comparison of societal activities in terms of dollars spent per averted fatality and the cost per 20 years of added life expectancy.

5   Both the theoretical and the applied literature support this conclusion. For example, Shrader-Frechette (1986) points to specific flaws in the equity and rationality arguments underlying the commensurability presupposition on which proponents of the technical approach rely. Nelkin's (1979) compilation and discussion of a range of cases of technological controversy demonstrates the limitations of technical competence.

6   Particular criticisms of the linear model made by Rogers (1986) and Rogers and Kincaid (1981) are (1) the concept of information as a physical entity to be transmitted like a material object and the associated lack of recognition of the interpretive element in the communication process; (2) the psychological, 'individual-blame' bias in which the focus becomes the effect of communication on the individual receiver rather than the context in which communication occurs and the relationship between senders and receivers as joint participants in the process; and (3) the underlying theory of mechanistic causation.

7   The author's research on the use of social science knowledge in implementing the Nuclear Waste Policy Act confirmed that technical managers were more likely to interpret psychometric studies as a difference between real and perceived risk. Moreover, the overwhelming majority of all agency personnel who were interviewed conceived of communication as a one-way provision of technical information to the public, rather than a two-way process of convergence among different perspectives (Bradbury, 1989).

8   Otway notes an alternative solution for those reluctant to adopt the education/information approach: risk-related social science research can provide decision-makers with 'a better understanding of social phenomena'. However, as he succinctly points out, 'the problem is that nobody really knows what to do with the results' (1980, p134).

9   The findings of social science research conducted in applied settings (and frequently independently of the traditional risk perception field) provide confirmation of many of the key theoretical insights of the cultural approach to risk. For example, the research of Elliott (1984, 1988), conducted from the perspective of mediated dispute resolution, is in striking agreement with Rayner (1984, 1987). Fundamentally, the approach of both lines of research is premised on a belief in the legitimacy of and the need to accommodate differing values and perceptions of risk.

Elliott (1988) emphasizes that 'the debate about rational analysis has been misplaced' and refocuses the discussion of rationality in terms of the essential rationality of different forms of coping with risk. He points out that, from the viewpoint of risk management, a key difference between groups lies not so much in their perceptions of risk, but in preferred ways of coping with risk and uncertainty. These preferences stem from the importance placed by each group on different characteristics of risk.

By working with the practical implications of differences in perceptions, by trying to manage risks as perceived by the affected groups rather than vainly trying to alter perceptions or educate a seemingly uninformed, irrational public. Elliott has reformulated the risk management task in a way that points to the possibility of effective solution.

10 See especially, MacLean (1986), who argues that citizen consent to the *process* by which decisions are made is the key to acceptability. He advances two reasons for the crucial role of consent and outlines three models of consent that represent a continuum from direct to indirect. Because individuals and groups may have different preferences for one or another form of consent and the associated method for making decisions about risk, the decision process as well as the decision outcome becomes an important expression of our values. Rayner and Cantor (1987) similarly emphasize the importance of citizen consent. As epitomized in the title of their article, the question is not 'How safe is safe enough?' but 'How fair is safe enough?'

11 See Mitchell (1987), who emphasizes communicating via the already existing frameworks of the receivers (i.e., people interpret new information according to these frameworks). The links between the experts and the public are political organizations and ideologies that have arisen to express, and act as filters for the expression of, the views of different segments of the public. Communication (and bargaining) with and among these organizations is a key, though frequently ignored, aspect of the communication problem.

12 Lievrouw (1988) points out that communication consists of more than 'micro-scale personal encounters'. In addition to meanings that are created interpersonally, participants in the knowledge-sharing process attribute meanings to the artefacts, social structures, and institutions created by other participants. Therefore, it is impossible to separate the interpersonal aspects of communication from other aspects of management activities.

13 For a succinct discussion of the implications of differing conceptions of participation, see Keim (1975).

14 This discussion of the technical, practical, and critical purposes of social science knowledge draws on the distinctions made by Habermas (1971).

References

Ackoff, R. L. 1974. *Redesigning the future: A systems approach to societal problems.* New York: John Wiley.

Bradbury, J. A. 1989. The use of social science knowledge in implementing the Nuclear Waste Policy Act. PhD diss., Graduate School of Public and International Affairs, University of Pittsburgh.

Campbell, D. T. 1987. Guidelines for monitoring the scientific competence of preventive intervention research centers: An exercise in the sociology of scientific validity. *Knowledge* 8: 389–430.

Clark, W. C. 1980. Witches, floods, and wonder drugs: Historical perspectives on risk management. In *Societal risk assessment: How safe is safe enough?*, ed. R. C. Schwing and W. A. Albers, 287–313. New York: Plenum.

Cohen, B. L. 1980. Society's valuation of life saving in radiation protection and other contexts. *Health Physics* 38: 33–51.

Conrad, J. 1980. Society and risk assessment: An attempt at interpretation. In *Society, technology and risk assessment*, ed. J. Conrad, 241–76. New York. Academic Press.

Covello, V. T. 1987. Case studies of risk communication: Introduction. In *Risk communication: Proceedings of the National Conference on Risk Communication held in Washington, DC, January 1986*, ed. J. C. Davies, V. T. Covello, and F. W. Allen. 63–65. Washington, DC: Conservation Foundation.

Covello, V. T., D. von Winterfeldt, and P. Slovic. 1987. Communicating scientific information about health and environmental risks. In *Risk communication: Proceedings of the National Conference on Risk Communication held in Washington, DC, January 1986.* ed. J. C. Davies, V. T. Covello, and F. W. Allen, 109–34. Washington, DC: Conservation Foundation.

Covello, V. T., and F. Allen. 1988. *Seven cardinal rules of risk communication.* Washington, DC: US Environmental Protection Agency. Office of Policy Analysis.

Covello, V. T., P. M. Sandman, and P. Slovic. 1988. *Risk communication, risk statistics, and risk comparisons: A manual for plant managers.* Washington, DC: Chemical manufacturers Association.

Douglas, M., and A. Wildavsky. 1982. *Risk and culture.* Berkeley: Univ. of California Press.

Dunn, W. N. 1981. *Public policy analysis: An introduction.* Englewood Cliffs, NJ: Prentice-Hall.

Dunn, W. N. 1982. Reforms as arguments. *Knowledge: Creation, diffusion, utilization* 3(3): 293–326.

Dunn, W. N. 1988. Reconstructing policy inquiry: The logics of public discourse. *Evaluation and Program Planning.*

Dunn, W. N., and B. Holzner. 1988. Anatomy of an emergent field. *Knowledge in Society: The International Journal of Knowledge Transfer* 1(1): 3–26.

Dunn, W. N., B. Holzner, and G. Zaltman. 1985. Knowledge utilization. In *The international encyclopedia of education*, ed. T. Husen and T. N. Postlethwaite, 2831–39. Oxford: Pergamon.

Earle, T. C., and G. Cvetovich. 1985. Risk judgment and the communication of hazard information. In *Environmental impact assessment, technology assessment, and risk analysis*, ed. V. T. Covello, J. L. Mumpower, P. J. M. Stallen, and V. R. R. Uppuluri, 257–312. New York: Springer-Verlag.

Elliott, M. L. P. 1984. Improving community acceptance of hazardous waste facilities through alternative systems for mitigating and managing risk. *Hazardous Waste* 1: 397–410.

Elliott, M. L. P. 1988. The effect of differing assessments of risk in hazardous waste facility siting negotiations. In *Negotiating hazardous waste facility siting and permitting agreements*, ed. G. Bingham and T. Mealey. Washington, DC: Conservation Foundation.

Fischhoff, B. 1979. Informed consent in societal risk-benefit decisions. *Technological Forecasting and Social Change* 13: 347–57.

Fischhoff, B., S. Lichtenstein, P. Slovic, S. L. Derby, and R. L. Keeney. 1981. *Acceptable risk.* New York: Cambridge Univ. Press.

Fischhoff, B., P. Slovic, and S. Lichtenstein. 1983. The public vs. 'the experts'. In *The analysis of actual vs. perceived risks*, ed. V. T. Covello, W. G. Flamm, J. V. Rodricks, and R. G. Tardiff, 235–49. New York: Plenum.

Funtowicz, S. O., and J. R. Ravetz. 1985. Three types of risk assessment: A methodological analysis. In *Environmental impact assessment, technology assessment, and risk analysis*, ed. V. T. Covello, J. L. Mumpower, P. J. M. Stallen, and V. R. R. Uppuluri, 831–48. New York: Springer-Verlag.

Habermas, J. 1971. *Knowledge and human interests.* Boston: Beacon.

Hadden, S. G. 1984. Introduction: Risk policy in American institutions. In *Risk analysis, institutions, and public policy*, ed. S. G. Hadden, 3–17. Port Washington, NY: Associated Faculty Press.

Holzner, B., and E. Fisher. 1979. Knowledge in use. *Knowledge* 1: 219–43.

Kates, R., and J. X. Kasperson. 1984. Comparative risk analysis of technological hazards (a review). CENTED Reprint no. 46. Worcester, MA: Clark Technology Center for Technology, Environment, and Development.

Keim, D. W. 1975. Participation in contemporary democratic theories. In *Participation in politics*, ed. J. R. Pennock, 1–38. New York: Liber-Atherton.

Leiss, W., and D. Krewski. 1987. Risk communication processes: A review of some conceptual models and some current practices. Department of Communication, Simon Fraser University, British Columbia.

Lievrouw, L. A. 1988. Four programs of research in scientific communication. *Knowledge in Society: The International Journal of Knowledge Transfer* 1(2): 6–22.

Lowrance, W. 1976. *Of acceptable risk: Science and the determination of safety.* Los Altos, CA: William Kaufman.

MacLean, D. 1986. Risk and consent: Philosophical issues for centralized decisions. In *Values at risk*, ed. D. MacLean, 17–30. Totowa, NJ: Rowman and Allenheld.

Mitchell, R. C. 1987. Nuclear and other energy sources. In *Risk Communication: Proceedings of the National Conference on Risk Communication held in Washington DC, January 1986*, ed. J. C. Davies, V. T. Covello, and F. W. Allen, 77–81. Washington, DC. Conservation Foundation.

National Research Council, Commission on Life Sciences, Committee on the Institutional Means for Assessment of Risks to Public Health. 1983. *Risk assessment in the federal government: Managing the process.* Washington, DC: National Academy Press.

Nelkin, D., ed. 1979. *Controversy: Politics of technical decisions.* Beverly Hills, CA: Sage.

Otway, H. J. 1980. Discussion paper on A. Mazur. In *Society, technology and risk assessment*, ed. J. Conrad, 163–64. New York: Academic Press.

Otway, H. J., and K. Thomas. 1982. Reflections on risk perception and policy. *Risk Analysis* 2: 69–82.

Plough, A., and S. Krimsky. 1987. The emergence of risk communication studies: Social and political context. *Science, Technology, and Human Values* 12 (Summer/Fall): 4–10.

Ravetz, J. R. 1973. *Scientific knowledge and its social problems.* New York: Oxford Univ. Press.

Ravetz, J. R. 1987. Usable knowledge, usable ignorance: Incomplete science with policy implications. *Knowledge* 9: 87–116.

Rayner, S. 1984. Disagreeing about risk: The institutional cultures of risk management. In *Risk analysis, institutions, and public policy*, ed. S. G. Hadden, 150–68. Port Washington, NY: Associated Faculty Press.

Rayner, S. 1987. Risk and relativism in science for policy. In *The social and cultural construction of risk*, ed. B. B. Johnson and V. T. Covello, 5–23. Norwell, MA: Reidel.

Rayner, S. 1988. Muddling through metaphors to maturity: A commentary on Kasperson et al., 'The social amplification of risk'. *Risk Analysis* 8: 201–4.

Rayner, S., and R. Cantor. 1987. How fair is safe enough? The cultural approach to societal technology choice. *Risk Analysis* 7: 3–9.

Rogers, E. M. 1986. *Communication technology*. New York: Free Press.

Rogers, E. M., and D. L. Kincaid. 1981. *Communication networks: Toward a new paradigm for research*. New York: Free Press.

Shrader-Frechette, K. 1986. Risk-cost-benefit methodology and equal protection. In *Risk evaluation and management*, ed. V. T. Covello, J. Menkes, and J. Mumpower, 275–96. New York: Plenum.

Slovic, P. 1986. Informing and educating the public about risk. *Risk Analysis* 6: 403–15.

Slovic, P., B. Fischhoff, and S. Lichtenstein. 1977. Behavioral decision theory. *Annual Review of Psychology* 28: 1–39.

Slovic, P., B. Fischhoff and S. Lichtenstein. 1979. Rating the risks. *Environment* 21 (3): 14–39.

Slovic, P., B. Fischhoff and S. Lichtenstein. 1980a. Facts and fears: Understanding perceived risk. In *Societal risk assessment: How safe is safe enough?*, ed. R. Schwing and W. A. Albers, 181–213. New York: Plenum.

Slovic, P., B. Fischhoff and S. Lichtenstein. 1980b. Informing people about risk. In *Product labeling and health risks*, ed. L. Morris, M. Mazis, and B. Barofsky, 165–80. Banbury Report 6. New York: Cold Spring Harbor Laboratory.

Slovic, P., B. Fischhoff, and S. Lichtenstein 1981. Perceived risk: Psychological factors and social implications. In *The assessment and perception of risk*, ed. F. Warner and D. Slater, 17–34. London: Royal Society.

Slovic, P., B. Fischhoff and S. Lichtenstein. 1984. Perceptions and acceptability of risk from energy systems. In *Public reactions to nuclear power*, ed. W. Freudenburg and E. Rosa, 115–35. Boulder, CO: Westview Press.

Spangler, M. B. 1985. Heuristic opinion and reference evaluation for assessing technological options – a user's view. In *Environmental impact assessment, technology assessment, and risk analysis*, ed. V. T. Covello, J. L. Mumpower, P. J. M. Stallen, and V. R. R. Uppuluri, 917–52. New York: Springer-Verlag.

Thompson, P. B., and W. J. Parkinson. 1984. Distinguishing between HC/LP and LC/HP risk. In *Low probability high consequence risk analysis*, ed. R. A. Walker and V. T. Covello, 551–67. New York: Plenum.

Toulmin, S. 1958. *The uses of argument*. Cambridge: Cambridge Univ. Press.

Toulmin, S., R. Rieke, and A. Janik. 1979. *An introduction to reasoning*. New York: Macmillan.

US Nuclear Regulatory Commission. 1975. *Reactor safety study: An assessment of accident risks in U.S. commercial nuclear powerplants*. WASH 1400. Washington, DC: US Nuclear Regulatory Commission.

Vesely, W. E. 1984. Robust risk analysis: The need for it in nuclear probability risk evaluations. In *Low probability high consequence risk analysis*, ed. R. A. Walker and V. T. Covello, 153–60. New York: Plenum.

Weinberg, A. 1972. Science and trans-science. *Minerva* 10: 209–22.

Wilson, R. 1979. Analyzing the daily risks of life. *Technology Review* (February): 40–46.

Wynne, B. 1980. Technology, risk and participation. In *Society, technology and risk assessment*, ed. J. Conrad, 173–208. New York: Academic Press.

Wynne, B. 1983. Redefining the issue of risk and public acceptance. *Futures* 15 (February): 13–32.

Zimmerman, R. 1986. The management of risk. In *Risk evaluation and management*, ed. V. T. Covello, J. Menkes, and J. Mumpower, 435–60. New York: Plenum.

3

A Philosophical Perspective on Risk

Sven Ove Hansson

The Word 'Risk'

The meanings of many everyday words have been transformed by science. Contrary to what was the case a century or two ago, we do not call the whale a fish, and we call the sun a star but not Venus. There are other words that scientists – or at least some scientists – have tried to appropriate and redefine, but which still have their original meaning in non-scientific contexts. 'Risk' is one of these words.

In non-technical contexts, 'risk' refers, often rather vaguely, to situations in which it is possible, but not certain, that some undesirable event will occur. In technical uses, 'risk' refers to something quantifiable. In decision theory, 'decision under risk' means decision with known probabilities. In risk analysis, 'risk' often denotes a numerical representation of severity that is obtained by multiplying the probability of an unwanted event with a measure of its disvalue (negative value).

Do the technical meanings, and the quantifications, of risk, really help us to understand the problems of risk? Or can they instead distract us from the concerns that should be central in our endeavours? This, I believe, is one of the more important issues in risk research that philosophers can contribute to answering. It will reappear in several guises in this brief overview of some central philosophical problems in connection with risk. The overview will be to some extent iconoclastic; I will focus on the failures and the limitations of models and assumptions that are commonly used in risk studies.

Risk and Uncertainty

In decision theory, lack of knowledge is divided into two major categories, that are commonly labelled 'risk' and 'uncertainty'.[1-3] In decision-making under risk, it is known what the possible outcomes are and what their probabilities of occurring are.[4] In decision-making under uncertainty, probabilities are either not known at all or are only known with insufficient precision.[5]

The distinction between risk and epistemic (knowledge-related) uncertainty is practically useful, but from a more theoretical point of view it is not at all clear how to draw it in a principled way. Consider, for instance, the question whether or not it will rain tomorrow in Stockholm. The meteorological prediction says that there is a 50 per cent probability of rain, given what we know at this moment. If you are a meteorologist who fully believes in the underlying assumptions of this prognosis, then this is a case of risk (known probabilities). But if you are less confident about the reliability of the probability estimate, then it is a case of (epistemic) uncertainty.

Similarly, if you are absolutely certain that current estimates of the effects of low-dose radiation are accurate, then decision-making referring to such exposure may be decision-making under risk. If you are less than fully convinced, then this too is a case of decision-making under uncertainty. Experts are known to have made mistakes, and a rational decision-maker should take into account the possibility that this may happen again. Experts often do not realize that for the non-expert, the possibility of the experts being wrong may very well be a dominant part of the risk – in the informal sense of the word – involved, e.g. in the use of a complex technology. When there is a wide divergence between the views of experts and those of the public, this is certainly a sign of failure in the social system for division of intellectual labour, but it does not necessarily follow that this failure is located within the minds of the non-experts who distrust the experts. It cannot be a criterion of rationality that one takes experts for infallible.

Only very rarely are probabilities known with certainty. Strictly speaking, the only clear-cut cases of 'risk' (known probabilities) seem to be idealized textbook cases that refer to devices such as dice or coins that are supposed to be known with certainty to be fair. More typical real-life cases are characterized by (epistemic) uncertainty that does not, primarily, come with exact probabilities. Hence, almost all decisions are decisions 'under uncertainty'. To the extent that we make decisions 'under risk', this does not mean that these decisions are made under conditions of completely known probabilities. Rather, it means that we have chosen to simplify our description of these decision problems by treating them as cases of known probabilities.

The Reduction of Uncertainty

In everyday reasoning, only a small proportion of our uncertainties are associated with a quantitative representation such as probability. One important issue in normative decision theory is: to what extent may, or should, a rational agent assign (exact numerical) probabilities to her uncertain beliefs? To what extent should uncertainty be reduced to probability? A related issue is: to what extent may, or should, a rational agent reduce uncertainties all the way to full, i.e. non-probabilistic, beliefs?[6]

A radical and immensely influential answer to this question is provided by Bayesian decision theory. According to the Bayesian ideal of rationality, a rational agent must assign a definite probability value to each and every statement about the world that can be made in the language. Non-logical propositions should never be fully believed, i.e. they should not be assigned probability 1 (only high probabilities close to 1). Hence, the Bayesian undertakes a complete reduction of uncertainty to probability, but never to full belief. The resulting belief system is a complex web of interconnected probability statements.[7]

In my view, it is a crucial drawback of Bayesianism that it does not take into account the cognitive limitations of actual human beings. Of course, we may reflect on how a rational being with unlimited cognitive capabilities should behave, but these are speculations with only limited relevance for actual human beings. A much more constructive approach is to discuss how a rational being with limited cognitive capabilities can make rational use of these capabilities.

In practice, the degree of uncertainty reduction achieved by Bayesianism is insufficient to achieve a manageable belief system. Bayesianism simply does not go far enough in reducing the uncertainties that we have to cope with. We cannot handle the mass of unsettled issues, interconnected in complex ways, that will emerge when probabilities are assigned to each and every sentence about the world. In order to grasp complex situations, we need to reduce the prevailing epistemic uncertainty not only to probabilities but also to full beliefs.[8] In other words, we must hold many contingent statements about the world to be true or false, not just assign probability values to them. This process of uncertainty-reduction, or 'fixation of belief',[9] helps us to achieve a cognitively manageable representation of the world and, thus, increases our competence and efficiency as decision-makers. Such reductions will have to be temporary, so that we can revert from full belief to probability or even to uncertainty, when there are reasons to do this. A theory of rational changes in full beliefs has recently been developed.[10–12]

There are important lessons for risk research to draw from this. In risk analysis, it is mostly taken for granted that a rational individual's attitude to uncertain possibilities should be representable in terms of probability assignments. Due to our cognitive limitations, this assumption is not always correct. In many instances, more crude attitudes such as 'This will not happen' or 'It is possible that this may happen' may be more serviceable. Transitions between such, non-probabilistic attitudes to risk seem to be worth careful investigations, both from an empirical and a normative point of view.

The process of uncertainty reduction is not a value-free or purely epistemic process. We are less reluctant to ignore remote or improbable alternatives when the stakes are high. Suppose that when searching for mislaid ammunition, I open and carefully check a revolver, concluding that it is empty. I may then say that I know that the revolver is unloaded. However, if somebody then points the revolver at my head asking: 'May I then pull the trigger?', it would not be unreasonable or inconsistent of me to say 'No', and to use the language of probability or uncertainty when explaining why. In this case, we revert from full belief to uncertainty when the stakes involved are changed.

Given our limited cognitive capabilities, this behaviour appears to be quite rational. We have to reduce much of the prevailing uncertainty to (provisional) full beliefs. In order to minimize the negative consequences of these reductions, considerations of practical value must have a large influence on the reduction process.

Science

Thus far, I have discussed the reduction process in everyday life. In science, as well, cognitive limitations make a reduction process necessary. The corpus of scientific knowledge consists of those standpoints that we take, in science, for provisionally certain. However, there is one important difference between the scientific reduction process and that of everyday life: Science programmatically ignores considerations of practical value. More precisely, contrary to everyday reasoning, the scientific process of uncertainty-reduction is bound by rules that – at least ideally – restrict the grounds for accepting or rejecting a proposition to considerations unrelated to practical consequences. There are good reasons for this restriction. As decision-makers and cognitive agents with limited capacity, we could hardly do without a general-purpose, intersubjective, and continually updated corpus of beliefs that can for most purposes be taken to be the outcome of reasonable reductions of uncertainty.

There are also good reasons for the scientific reduction process to be based on fairly strict standards of proof. When determining whether or not a scientific hypothesis should be accepted for the time being, the onus of proof falls squarely on its adherents. Similarly, those who claim the existence of an as yet unproven phenomenon have the burden of proof. These proof standards prevent scientific progress from being blocked by the pursuit of all sorts of blind alleys. They also ensure that the scientific corpus is reliable enough to be useful for (most) extra-scientific applications.

Nevertheless, the proof standards of science are apt to cause problems whenever science is applied to practical problems that require standards of proof other than those of science. Examples of this are readily found in risk-related decision-making. The application of toxicology to regulatory decisions is a case in point. It would not seem rational – let alone morally defensible – for a decision-maker to ignore all preliminary indications of toxicity that do not amount to full scientific proof. Therefore, such decisions have to be based on scientific knowledge, but yet apply proof standards that differ from those of science.[13–16] This combination is difficult to cope with both for scientists and decision-makers. It also seems to require new tools for extracting decision-relevant information from scientific data.[17]

Unknown Possibilities

Up to now, I have talked about uncertainty in the conventional sense: uncertainty prevails when we do not know which among a certain set of given alternatives will actually materialize. However, there is also a more profound type of uncertainty, namely that of *unknown possibilities*.[18] On some occasions we do not have a complete list of the alternatives or of the consequences that should be taken into account when evaluating them. Let me give a historical example:

The constructors of the first nuclear bomb worried that the bomb might trigger an uncontrolled reaction that would propagate throughout the entire atmosphere. Theoretical calculations convinced them that this possibility could be neglected.[19] The group might equally well have worried about the possibility that the bomb could have some other, not thought-of, catastrophic consequences in addition to its – most certainly catastrophic – intended effect. The calculations just mentioned could not have laid such apprehensions to rest, and arguably no other scientific argument could have done so either. The decision would have been much more difficult if unknown possibilities had been taken into account.

The problem of unknown possibilities is difficult to come to grips with. On one hand, there are cases in which it would seem unduly risky to entirely dismiss unknown possibilities. Suppose, for instance, that someone proposes the introduction of a genetically altered species of earthworm that will displace the common earthworm and that will aerate the soil more efficiently. It would not be unreasonable to take into account the risk that this may have unforeseen negative consequences. For the sake of argument we may assume that all concrete worries can be neutralized. The new species can be shown not to induce more soil erosion, not to be more susceptible to diseases, etc. Still, it would not be irrational to say: 'Yes, but there may be other negative effects that we have not been able to think of. Therefore, the new species should not be introduced.' Similarly, if someone proposed to eject a chemical substance into the stratosphere for some good purpose or other, it would not be irrational to oppose this proposal solely on the ground that it may have unforeseeable negative consequences, and this even if all specified worries can be neutralized.[20]

On the other hand, there are cases in which it seems to be sensible enough to ignore unknown possibilities. An illustrative example is offered by the debate on the polywater hypothesis, according to which water could exist in an as yet unknown polymeric form. In 1969, *Nature* printed a letter that warned against producing polywater. The substance might 'grow at the expense of normal water under any conditions found in the environment', thus replacing all natural water on Earth and destroying all life on this planet.[21] The author might equally well have referred to other possible disasters, or mentioned the problem of unknown possibilities. Soon afterwards, it was shown that polywater is a non-existent entity. If the warning had been heeded, then no attempts would have been made to replicate the polywater experiments, and we might still not have known that polywater does not exist.

In a sense, any decision may have unforeseen catastrophic consequences. If nothing else, in the last resort, any action whatsoever might invoke the wrath of evil spirits that *might* exist, thus drawing misfortune upon all of us. If such possibilities are taken into account, then selected appeals to unknown possibilities may stop investigations, foster superstition and hence depreciate our general competence as decision-makers.

The choice when to take unknown possibilities into account and when to ignore them is one of the more difficult issues in uncertainty-reduction. Factors that may be relevant include:

- *Novelty.* New and untested phenomena should be treated with special care.
- *Spatial and temporal limitations.* Cautiousness is particularly important with respect to global changes and to disruptions that have unlimited or very long duration.
- *Complex systems.* Ecosystems and the atmospheric system are known to have reached some type of balance, which may be impossible to restore after a major disturbance.[18]

Decision Theory

There are two philosophical sub-disciplines that try to answer the question 'What should we do?', namely decision theory and moral theory. According to the received view, these are distinct disciplines with clearly demarcated subject areas. Decision theory is assumed to take values for given and to add no new values. It is therefore, in a sense, seen as morally neutral. In issues of risk, decision theory takes value assignments for deterministic cases for given, and derives from them instructions for rational behaviour in an uncertain, unpredictable, and indeterministic world. Another way to express this is that, given preferences over deterministic alternatives, decision theory derives preferences over indeterministic alternatives.

Suppose, for instance, that moral considerations have led us to attach certain values to two outcomes X and Y. Then decision theory provides us with a value to be attached to mixed options such as 50 per cent chance of X and 50 per cent chance of Y. The crucial assumption is that, given well-determined probabilities, and well-determined values of the basic, non-probabilistic alternatives X and Y, the values of mixed options can be *derived*. In other words, probabilities and the values of non-probabilistic alternatives are assumed to completely determine the value of probabilistic alternatives. This is the conventional wisdom, so conventional that it is seldom stated explicitly. I believe it to be grossly misleading.

It is clear that we assign values to (or have preferences over) both deterministic and indeterministic objects of value. It is also reasonable to expect that there be correlations and connections between these two types of preferences. However, I have found no good reasons to believe that our intuitions on deterministic objects are always more reliable than our intuitions on indeterministic objects. To the contrary, we have in many contexts more experience from uncertain than from certain objects of value. It does not then seem reasonable to disregard all our intuitions on the former category from our deliberations, and reconstruct value assignments to them that are based only on our intuitions on the latter type of objects.

Clearly, our evaluations of non-probabilistic and probabilistic objects should cohere. However, it does not follow that the demands of coherence should be so strict that our evaluations of probabilistic objects should be unequivocally derivable from our evaluations of non-probabilistic objects. Although not all combinations of deterministic and non-deterministic preferences are acceptable, a given set of deterministic preferences may be compatible with different, and mutually incompatible, sets of non-deterministic preferences.

In this perspective, the deductive reasoning of conventional decision theory should be replaced by *consolidative* reasoning.[22] Consolidation refers to the process of adjusting parts of a mental state in order to reduce its internal tensions. Consolidative reasoning may or may not lead to an end-point in the form of a reflective equilibrium.[23, 24] In real life, new tensions arise continuously in response to changes in the outer world, so that a reflective equilibrium may be as illusive as the end of the rainbow. Needless to say, this does not make the consolidative process less important.

In this perspective, moral philosophy and decision theory are not two distinct disciplines with separable subject matters, one of which should be treated prior to the other. Instead, the two disciplines have developed different approaches to one and the same problem – two approaches that stand in need for integration rather than separation.

The Causal Dilution Problem

Throughout the history of moral philosophy, moral theorizing has for the most part referred to a deterministic world in which the morally relevant properties of human actions are both well-determined and knowable. Consequently, mainstream ethical theories cannot be effectively applied to problems involving risk and uncertainty, unless they are generalized to a non-deterministic setting. The problem of how to perform this generalization can be specified in terms of *the causal dilution problem:* Given that a certain moral theory prohibits a certain action because it has the property *P*, under what conditions should a generalized version of the same theory prohibit an action because it possibly, but not certainly, has the property *P*?[6]

For utilitarian theories (theories maximizing total value), a standard answer is provided by expected utility theory. Under the assumption that probabilities are available for all uncertain outcomes, expected utility maximization serves as a both operative and convenient extension of utilitarianism. It has indeed been almost universally accepted in modern literature on risk analysis and risk management. However, it does not follow from utilitarianism that a utilitarian must choose this solution to the causal dilution problem. In particular, utilitarianism is compatible with more cautious or risk-aversive decision rules, that give priority to the avoidance of catastrophic outcomes.

Expected utility theory also has another, more deeply disturbing problem: it tries to reach a definite conclusion from insufficient information. As indicated above, a risky situation is not exhaustively characterized by the probabilities and the utilities of corresponding non-probabilistic events. To the contrary, the morally relevant aspects of situations of risk and uncertainty go far beyond the impersonal, free-floating sets of consequences that expected utility theory operates on. Risks are taken, run, or imposed.[25] It makes a difference if it is my own life or that of somebody else that I risk in order to earn a fortune for myself, even if the probabilities and the severities of the outcomes are the same. A moral analysis of risk that includes considerations of agency and responsibility will have to be an analysis more in terms of the verb (to) 'risk' than of the noun (a) 'risk'. Probabilities and utilities may be important aspects, but they are not all the aspects that we need to know in order to evaluate a risky situation.

Major policy debates on risks have in part been clashes between the 'noun' and the 'verb' approach to risk. Proponents of nuclear energy emphasize how small *the risks* are, whereas opponents question the very act of *risking* improbable but potentially calamitous accidents.

Non-utilitarian Moral Theories

For an account of the ethics of risking, it would seem natural to abandon utilitarianism, and turn instead to deontological (duty-based) or rights-based theories. Unfortunately, these theories have their own causal dilution problems that do not seem to be easier to solve. The relevant question, with respect to rights-based theories, was asked by Robert Nozick: 'Imposing how slight a probability of a harm that violates someone's rights also violates his rights?'[26, 27] Your right not to be killed by me implies that I am forbidden to perform certain acts that involve a risk of killing you, but it does not prohibit all such acts. (I am allowed to drive a car in the town where you live, although this increases the risk of being killed by me.) Perhaps the most obvious solution is to require that each right be associated with a probability limit, below which risking is allowed and above which it is prohibited. However, as Nozick observed, such a solution is not credible since probability limits 'cannot be utilized by a tradition which holds that stealing a penny or a pin or anything from someone violates his rights. That tradition does *not* select a threshold measure of harm as a lower limit ...'.[26] Furthermore, no rights-based method for the determination of such probability limits seems to be available, so that they would have to be external to the rights-based theory. No other credible solution to the causal dilution problem for rights-based theories seems to be available.

For deontological theories, the picture is very much the same: The problems are analogous, and no solution – in particular no internal solution – seems to be available.

Contract theories may perhaps appear somewhat more promising. The criterion that they offer for the deterministic case, namely consent among all those involved, can also be applied to risky options. Unfortunately, this solution is far from unproblematic. Consent, as conceived in contract theories, is either actual or hypothetical. Actual consent does not seem to be a realistic criterion in a complex society in which everyone performs actions with marginal but additive effects on many people's lives. According to the criterion of actual consent, you have a veto against me or anyone else who wants to drive a car in the town where you live. Similarly, I have a veto against your use of coal to heat your house, since the emissions contribute to health risks that affect me. In this way we can all block each other, creating a society of stalemates. When all options in a decision are associated with risk, and all parties claim their rights to keep clear of the risks that others want to impose on them, the criterion of actual consent does not seem to be of much help.

We are left then with hypothetical consent. However, as the debate following Rawls's *Theory of Justice* has shown, there is no single decision-rule for risk and uncertainty that all participants in a hypothetical initial situation can be supposed to adhere to.[28] It remains to show, if this can at all be done, that a viable consensus on risk-impositions can be reached among participants who apply different decision-rules in situations of risk and uncertainty. If a unanimous decision will be reached due to the fact that everybody applies the same decision-rule, then the problem has not been solved primarily by contract theory but by the underlying theory for individual decision-making.

Much more could be said about the causal dilution problem, but to make a long story short, no solution to it seems to be available for any moral theory. One plausible reason for this has already been indicated: In order to solve the causal dilution problem we need to know much more than probabilities and utilities. We need to analyse who imposes what risks on whom and with what intentions. In other words, we need to develop a full analysis of *risking*. Doing this in a satisfactory manner may very well require a more fundamental renewal of moral thinking than mere additions to existing theories.

Conclusion

In summary, the problems of risk have a deep impact on philosophy. In order to give a reasonable account of risk we have to rethink the relationship between full belief and probabilistic belief. We have to reconsider the nature of the scientific corpus of knowledge, in particular with respect to its applicability in science-based decision-making. Perhaps most importantly, in order to deal with the normative issues related to risk we will have to break up the boundary between moral philosophy and decision theory and find new ways to combine the traditions of these two disciplines in answering the basic question 'What should I do?'. In the course of treating this and other basic issues about risk, I hope that the philosophy of risk will also improve its contributions to the general, interdisciplinary study of risk that is presently one of the most interesting new avenues of interdisciplinary research.

References and Notes

1   Knight, F.H. [1921] 1935. *Risk, Uncertainty and Profit.* Houghton Mifflin, Boston.
2   Duncan, L.R. and Raiffa, H. 1957. *Games and Decisions.* Wiley, New York.
3   Alexander, E.R. 1970. The limits of uncertainty: A note. *Theory Decision 6*, 363–370.
4   The special case when all the probabilities are either 0 or 1 coincides with decision-making under certainty.
5   The case when they are not known at all is also called 'decision-making under ignorance'.
6   Hansson, S.O. 1996. What is philosophy of risk? *Theoria 62*, 169–186.
7   Jeffrey, R.C. 1956. Valuation and acceptance of scientific hypotheses. *Philos. Sci. 23*, 237–249.
8   The word 'reduction' is used metaphorically. I do not wish to imply that all probability assignments or full beliefs have been preceded by more uncertainty-laden belief states, only that they can be seen as reductions in relation to an idealized belief state in which uncertainty is always fully recognized.
9   Peirce, C. 1934. The fixation of belief. In: *Collected Papers of Charles Sanders Peirce.* Hartshorne, C. and Weiss, P. (eds). Harvard University Press, vol. 5, pp. 223–247.
10 Alchourrón, C.E., Gärdenfors, P. and Makinson, D. 1985. On the logic of theory change: Partial meet contraction and revision functions. *J. Symbolic Logic 50*, 510–530.
11 Gärdenfors, P. 1988. *Knowledge in Flux. Modeling the Dynamics of Epistemic States.* The MIT Press, Cambridge, Massachusetts, 262 pp.
12 Hansson, S.O. 1999. *A Textbook of Belief Dynamics. Theory Change and Database Updating.* Kluwer. 398 pp.
13 Jellinek, S.D. 1981. On the inevitability of being wrong. *Ann. NY Acad. Sci. 363*, 43–47.
14 Crawford-Brown, D. and Pearce, N.E. 1988. Sufficient proof in the scientific justification of environmental actions. *Clio 18*, 153–167.
15 Hansson, S.O. 1997. Can we reverse the burden of proof? *Toxicol. Lett. 90*, 223–228.
16 Hansson, S.O. 1998. *Setting the Limit. Occupational Health Standards and the Limits of Science.* Oxford University Press. 166 pp.
17 Hansson, S.O. 1995. The detection level. *Regulatory Toxicol. Pharmacol. 22*, 103–109.
18 Hansson, S.O. 1994. Decision making under great uncertainty. *Philos. Soc. Sci. 26*, 369–386.
19 Oppenheimer, R. 1980. *Letters and Recollections.* Smith, A.K. and Weiner, C. (eds). Harvard University Press. 376 pp.
20 This is precautionary reasoning, and intuitively we would expect it to be supported by the precautionary principle. However, most formulations of that principle do not cover this type of cases, since they refer to threats for which there is some (but weak) scientific evidence. See Sandin, P. 1999. Dimensions of the Precautionary Principle. *Human Ecol. Risk Assess. 5*, 889–907.

21 Donahoe, F.D. 1969. Anomalous water. *Nature 224*, 198.
22 Hansson, S.O. 1999. The modes of value, manuscript.
23 Rawls, J. 1972. *A Theory of Justice.* Oxford University Press. 607 pp.
24 Tersman, F. 1993. *Reflective Equilibrium: An Essay in Moral Epistemology.* PhD thesis, Stockholm University, Stockholm, Sweden.
25 Thomson, J. 1985. Imposing risk. In: *To Breathe Freely.* Gibson, M. (ed.). Rowman and Allanheld, pp. 124–140.
26 Nozick, R. 1974. *Anarchy, State, and Utopia.* Basic Books. 367 pp.
27 McKerlie, D. 1986. Rights and risk. *Can. J. Philos. 16*, 239–251.
28 Hare, R.M. 1973. Rawls's theory of justice. *Am. Philos. Quart. 23*, 144–155, 241–252.

4

Uncertain Times: The Notion of 'Risk' and the Development of Modernity

Gerda Reith

Introduction: A Risk Society?

The state of uncertainty – of not knowing, and therefore being unable to control, the unfolding of the future and the state of the world – has preoccupied humanity for centuries. And, as Luhmann (1993) points out, the manner in which this state is explained is crucial for understanding how societies operate and organize themselves, and indeed, for revealing within those explanations the nature of entire worldviews.

In the modern world, such concerns tend to be increasingly couched in terms of 'risk', a concept which is both historically specific and grounded in a particular temporal orientation. It is the purpose of this chapter to examine the development of this concept, tracing its construction out of the interaction of grand temporal narratives with wider socio-economic relations. It starts by noting how medieval narratives of temporality explained away uncertainty as part of a cosmology in which the future was relatively determined and 'closed' to human intervention. It goes on to examine the erosion of this hierarchical system and the gradual 'colonization of the future' that was brought about by the advent of a system of global capitalism. Such socio-economic upheaval engendered new notions of temporality and human agency, expressed in the optimistic Enlightenment belief in the possibility of eliminating the uncertainties of the future through rational action in the present. This notion of the future as something open and amenable to transformation cleared a space for the emergence of the concept of risk as a means of calculating – and so controlling – the uncertainties of that future; a concept which gained increasing influence throughout the development of the modern period. More recently, its ability to quantify the contingencies of the future, and so provide a guide for action in the present, has given the concept of risk a central explanatory role in the indeterminate world of late modernity, and it is at this point that this chapter begins its analysis.

In the last 20 years or so, the notion of risk has become extremely popular in social science, influencing research in many areas of social enquiry, from social policy and theory to international relations and political science. Its effect is particularly marked in sociology, where, since the late 1980s a distinctive 'sociology of risk' has emerged. Lupton (1999a) has grouped this into three broad perspectives – the cultural-constructivist approach exemplified by Douglas (1986, 1992), the governmentality perspective influenced by Foucault and provided by writers such as Castel (1991), Ewald (1991), O'Malley (1996, 2000) and Dean (1999a, b), and lastly, perhaps the most influential perspective – the 'risk society' model advanced by Beck (1992) and also Giddens (1991). In all of these, the notion of risk is crucial in different ways: as a social construct, as a calculative discourse, and finally, as an integral feature of late modern societies. On a more subjective level, the recognition that we live in insecure times has given us a reflexive awareness of the risks we face in everyday life – through our consumption habits (Bauman, 1988; Ward, 1994), our leisure (Lyng, 1990; Parker et al, 1998), our work practices (Nelkin and Brown, 1984) and our attitudes to our bodies and our health (Gabe, 1995).

To paraphrase Beck (1992), at the beginning of the new millennium, it sometimes appears that we are living not so much in a risk *society*, as in a society saturated in risk *discourse*.

The reification of risk

However, this enthusiastic deployment that draws 'risk' into ever grander and more diverse theoretical and empirical fields frequently tends to overlook the limitations of the concept itself, disregarding its constructed, temporal nature and treating it as though it referred to some 'real' state of the world.

Running though much of the literature is an implicit acceptance of 'risk' as a real or quasi-real phenomenon, and an assumption that it exists as something that can be 'experienced', 'produced' or 'measured' as if it were an a priori reality. Such usage reifies potential danger as if it were a property of things (Levidow, 1994). This orientation may partly stem from the origins of the concept in the physical sciences, but, more recently, is surely at least encouraged by Beck's (1992) influential neo-realist depiction of 'risk' as an objective feature of post-industrial society. Although he does admit that risk is 'open to social definition and construction' (p23), implicit throughout his analysis is a realist assumption of a 'risk society' as a global phenomenon within processes of modernization, and an increased incidence of actual risk in the world. In this nomenclature, risks are 'goods to be avoided' (p34). Furthermore, they are incalculable, and it is this move to incalculablity that lies behind the transformation of society. The growth of technology generates risks whose effects are unlimited in time and space, with the potential to affect unborn generations across the globe; a feature that renders the legal and scientific calculation of risk obsolete (p22). As a result of this incalculability, modern 'risks' cannot be contained, anticipated or protected against, and a whole new social order comes into being around them.

The postulation of 'risk' as something that is both real and yet incalculable is based on a misapplication of the concept of risk itself. It is argued here that 'risk' is *not* real, but rather that it is a measure of calculation: a means of quantifying that reality. Both these strands of argument are developed throughout the remainder of this chapter, but before we turn to them, it is useful to briefly address some of the issues surrounding the status – 'real' or otherwise – of this notion of risk.

Firstly, it can be stated that the fundamental reflexivity of the social world means that 'risk' cannot exist as an objective phenomenon. There are no risks 'out there', as many commentators from broadly constructionist and governmental positions have pointed out (Adam, 1990, 1995; Ewald, 1991; Luhmann, 1993; Dean, 1999a). The world does not exist 'objective' and independent of human consciousness. By being in the world, we affect it, and by knowing it, we respond to it in ways that change it. Similarly with the case of risk, our perception of what might constitute a risk affects how we act, which in turn alters the nature of the 'objective' world in which the 'risk' is situated. So, as long as human actors who perceive and think and respond are involved in the probability equation, there can be no such thing as 'objective' risk. As Luhmann (1993) puts it: 'The outside world itself knows no risks, for it knows neither distinctions, nor expectations, nor evaluations, nor probabilities' (p6). There is no such thing as risk in the world, only dangers we construct in our head.

Furthermore, we cannot 'experience' risk, since the concept itself is essentially a temporal one, grounded in its relation to an unknown future. It is defined by and through temporality: the notion of 'risk' expresses not something that *has* happened or *is* happening, but something that *might* happen. Although its meanings have changed since its emergence in the 17th century, and although it is used in a variety of ways to describe different social situations today, the concept of risk can still be defined largely through its attempt to calculate and so manage the uncertainties of the future. It is an expression of the likelihood of some situation or event – usually negative – occurring, and so, when we are talking about risks, we are talking about the future: trying to work out what will happen next, and what we can do to avoid or expedite it. In this sense, it cannot be experienced directly – by definition, risk is the calculation of uncertainty in the future, and once something previously defined as a risk has occurred, it can no longer be a risk, but becomes a past event, an occurrence, a fact. Risk vanishes as soon as the anticipated event occurs. Strictly speaking, we should not really write of 'lived' risk or the 'experience' of risk at all, but only of 'risk calculation', since in Kantian terms, risk is fundamentally an epistemological category – it exists as a feature of *knowing*, not an aspect of *being*.

Having outlined these basic limitations, the remainder of this chapter seeks to show that the concept of risk is a means of dealing with uncertainty that rests on a particular temporal orientation. By tracing its historical development through certain key periods, it highlights how the emergence and evolution of the concept exists in dynamic interdependence with notions of temporality and uncertainty, that in turn are embedded in wider social, economic and epistemological formations.

'Sublime Recapitulation': Medieval Narratives of Temporality

There were no risks in pre-industrial societies. In cultures where technological control over the natural world was limited, the uncertainties of everyday life were expressed and managed through a range of religious and magical beliefs in concepts such as fate, providence and luck.

During the medieval period, such beliefs were part of a cosmology in which every earthly event and the fate of every individual was depicted as a symbolic representation of the will of God (Gurvitch, 1964). The doctrine of divine providence stipulated that everything happened for a purpose and so every event, however insignificant, was a predetermined part of a grand design, clues to which were to be found in apparently random or 'chance' events (Hacking, 1975).

Even time was subject to meaning in such worldviews. Since the categories of space and time were created by God, both were imbued with religious meaning, and were interdependent. They came together in the individual's position in the 'great chain of being' (Lovejoy, 1960) – the rigid social hierarchy that determined one's place in the world, as well as the unfolding of their destiny. Since the material world was regarded as a microcosm of a higher one, such a position was a literal, as well as a symbolic, depiction of the order of the universe. Such a position – established by God, continued by heredity, and backed by tradition – assured individuals of their place, their function and their role in the world, and was utterly inflexible. In this determined structure, 'time' was not a measure of earthly duration, but a symbolic representation of transcendental meaning, and as such was regarded as heterogeneous in nature, with different times possessing different values or properties (Gurvitch, 1964; Le Goff, 1980). Furthermore, it was assumed to unfold in a regular and predictable manner as it had done in the past, following the course set out by God in the ideal of what Umberto Eco (1995) called 'sublime recapitulation'.

However, even within such a relatively closed system, an alternative set of beliefs in magic and luck existed that allowed for the exercise of at least some degree of human intervention in matters of contingency.[1] Medieval life was surrounded by rituals that attempted to foresee and influence the future, with, for example, divination utilized to forecast the weather and determine the most propitious times to harvest, charms and blessings used to encourage health and prosperity and ward off misfortune, and the notion of lucky times invoked to explain the vicissitudes of everyday life, and to decide a future course of action (Thomas, 1997).

Such a cosmology embodied a conception of time as a meaningful, symbolic entity that explained the apparent uncertainties of the future with reference to motive forces, whether providential designs or magical influences.[2] At the same time, however, within such an orientation, it was virtually impossible to conceive of the concept of randomness, far less ideas such as 'risk', for it did not allow for the conception of a world in which things happened for no reason, nor, crucially, for one in which the future was shaped by human, rather than transcendental, intervention.

The 'Colonization of the Future': The Emergence of Risk

From around the 17th century, dramatic developments in social, intellectual and economic life transformed ideas about uncertainty, the future and human agency, modifying the determinism of the Middle Ages and laying the groundwork for the creation of the notion of 'risk'. These momentous changes have been well documented elsewhere (Braudel, 1973; Holton, 1985; Freudenthal, 1986). Here, the focus is confined to specific aspects that paved the way for the emergence of the notion of risk and, in Hagerstrand's (1985) words, allowed for the 'colonization of the future'.

In economics, the growth of a system of mercantile capitalism, speculation, insurance and credit in an international marketplace undermined the traditional social hierarchy of the Middle Ages. This move has been described as a 'temporalizing of the great chain of being' (Lovejoy, 1960), and the agents of change were the dynamic new merchant class, whose trade-related concerns encouraged a more active engagement with the uncertainties of the future. The idea that fate or providence would oversee the unfolding of events could no longer provide sufficient assurance to those whose goods might be at stake in trading situations. The creation of profits depended on foresight and planning, which in turn demanded consideration of a future that was neither fixed nor beyond human control (Ewald, 1991). Now 'God's time' became 'merchants' time'[3] (Le Goff, 1980): a commodity to be used, saved or sold to create profits, rather than something that was simply doled out by the creator. Concern with issues such as rates of profit, interest and wages rationalized the heterogeneous time of the Middle Ages, and encouraged the conception of it as something homogeneous and universal instead. Its new location in the abstract institutions of commerce finally liberated it from the symbolic representation of higher meaning, and separated it from its interdependence with place (Weber, 1904/1989; Harvey, 1989).

This new conception of temporality dovetailed with the emergent trade-related focus on the future, and laid the groundwork for a way of reasoning about uncertainty that was based on long-term predictions and large-scale spatial units. This was articulated in the new mathematical fields of probability and statistics, in whose abstract, formal theorems the preoccupations of the era were reflected. This area of study, which Pascal (1656/1987) called 'the geometry of hazard', was based on a radical reorientation to the future. Up until then, the focus had been on individual, unconnected events in the present that were seen as signs of providential meaning. Now, attention shifted from the short term to the long term and from the individual case to the general rule. It was a case of casting the analytical net over a wide expanse: over time and across space to capture large groups of events or individuals over the long term, and of expanding the timeframe to a 'size which smoothed out local perturbations into an overall uniformity' (Daston, 1988, p115).[4] This approach demonstrated that, although singular events might appear random and unpredictable in the short term, over an extended period, they invariably fell into regular and predictable patterns. In other words, by gathering enough information over a sufficiently long period of time, informed estimates about the unfolding of the future could be made.

Although they transformed thinking about the future, the predictive capacity of probability and statistics was marred by one theoretical flaw, for although they were able to make generalizations about groups over time, they were unable to deal with small units in the present. The aggregate was greater than the sum of its parts, but it was not reducible to them, and so although probability could estimate, for example, the odds of red coming up at roulette at 50:50, it could never predict what the *specific* outcome of the *next* round would be (Reith, 1999a).

Still, the significance of these theorems lay elsewhere, for within their formulae lay a reconceptualization of the future that was expressed in the new concept of 'risk'.[5] From the Anglo-French *risqué*, the term was first used in the mid-17th century, and brought time and uncertainty into a quantifiable relation: quite simply, the *risk* of an event occurring was the *probability* of it happening over a stated period of time. The practice of insurance as a means of guarding against uncertainty developed almost simultaneously, and was an attempt to protect the individual from the threat of these newly predictable events (Hacking, 1975; Ewald, 1991).[6]

The notions of risk and insurance embodied a calculative, long-term approach to uncertainty that signalled a radical new way of thinking about temporality. Probability's emphasis on the importance of the long term for making predictions was indicative of a worldview in which the uncertainties of the future were no longer regarded as acts of Divine intention, but rather as events to be understood through the concept of risk and managed through the practice of insurance. The notion of risk itself embodied this new conception of an open future, signifying not something that *will* happen, but something that *might* happen. Together, these provided a formal guide for behaviour based on the premise of rational action in the present in order to ameliorate the uncertainty of the future. In the concept of risk, then, we can see the articulation of a new worldview, released from the strictures of tradition, in which the world is opened up to the influence of human agency. For the first time, individuals were free to determine their own trajectory and to shape their own destiny, in the expansive move, described eloquently by Alexander Koyré (1982), from 'the closed world to the infinite universe'.

Ironically, however, although the calculation of risk made a space for the exercise of human will, it was in fact a *limited* form of agency, for the very predictive power of probability and statistics themselves was founded on the basis of a strict determinism. This was part of the Enlightenment's scientific *episteme*, based on a Newtonian model of the universe as a machine bound by fixed relations of cause and effect. In it, events in the future were regarded as being caused by occurrences in the past, from which they proceeded in a straightforward linear progression. Probability theory was able to quantify potential risks because, in a world governed by causal relations, sufficient knowledge of relevant factors made the uncertainties of the future estimable. Moreover, such analysis – like all scientific endeavour – was regarded as part of the progressive advancement of knowledge which would uncover the 'truths' of the natural world and allow for ever-greater accuracy in prediction and, ultimately, control of an increasingly certain future. The determinism that underlined this orientation was supported by the concepts of absolute space and time as entities in their own right: as categories that were homogeneous, objective and everywhere true. In Newton's words: 'Absolute, true and mathematical time, of itself and from its own nature, flows equably, without regard for anything external' (in Koyré, 1982, p161). In other words, the laws that bound time, space and matter were fixed and immutable. Furthermore, they were also essentially *meaningful*, for although it was generally agreed that mechanical forces governed the universe, crucially, these were overseen by the prime mover, and as such, were an expression of providential, rather than secular, order (Hacking, 1975).

However, this would change. Even as it was being 'colonized' by human agency, the future was already coming under threat from technological and scientific developments that would undermine the basis of determinism and ultimately oversee the disappearance of the 'open' future of the early modern period.

The Loss of the Future: Indeterminism

The consolidation and advancement of increasingly sophisticated forms of capitalist production between the 19th and 21st centuries transformed notions of temporality, determinism and causation, and created new applications for the concept of risk. In particular, the development of scientific and technological innovations such as the telephone, wireless and aeroplane, shrunk and accelerated the world, overcoming physical distance as they created systems of communication between individuals and events around the globe. These effectively undermined absolutist perceptions of time and space in a period of what Harvey (1989) terms 'space-time compression'. At the same time, the French Revolution, widespread industrial unrest and political agitation shattered the Enlightenment ideal of the existence of universal standards of human rationality, while widespread certainties were eroded and long-held beliefs in the existence of God shaken, giving rise to the 'ontological insecurity' of the age (de Jong, 1975).

These changes – most notably, secularization and the undermining of absolutism – destroyed the basis of the providential determinism of previous centuries, and led to a growing awareness, throughout the physical and social sciences, that the world was not, in fact, deterministic (Hacking, 1975, 1990).[7]

This transformation was reflected most noticeably in physics, where indeterminism demolished the mechanistic, Newtonian model of the universe, replacing the certainty and predictability of solid matter and causal laws with uncertainties and probabilities – the building blocks of quantum reality (Zohar and Marshall, 1993). The work of Albert Einstein showed that time was relative and contextual: dependent on observers and their frames of measurement, rather than absolute and quantifiable. Heisenberg's Uncertainty Principle proved the impossibility of measuring both position and momentum simultaneously, showing that time and space were not constant and measurable, but could only, at best, ever be probable (Gigerenzer et al, 1989). While Niels Bohr demonstrated how electrons jumped from one state to another in unpredictable and discontinuous 'leaps', Brownian motion was revealed as an example of pure a-causal movement. Far from being guided by the hand of God or by regular scientific laws, the new science portrayed activity that was simply random; that followed no obvious pattern, and revealed no hidden meaning.

The undermining of determimism had dramatic implications for temporality. While Newtonian physics rested on the assumption of logical relations between events that are separate in time, the world of quantum reality postulated the principles of simultaneity, instantaneity and relativity, so halting the predictable march of linear time and undermining the basis of causation. In its place came a reality based on 'non-local connections and a-causal events; an indivisible, dynamic, patterned whole that resisted abstraction or sequencing' (Adam, 1990, pp57–58). It was now stochastic processes, not causal laws, that were regarded as the foundation of the natural world – and, gradually, extended to the social world too.[8]

During the period known variously as 'late', 'high', 'post' or 'reflexive' modernity (Giddens, 1991; Bauman, 1992; Beck, 1992; Baudrillard, 1998), the technological innovations that were so crucial in the development of modernity were intensified and reached an apogee in the creation of what has been described as a global present in which the future is virtually un-knowable (Adam, 1990, 1995; Giddens, 1991). In these 'disorganized' capitalist economies (Lash and Urry, 1994), the pace of life is accelerated, and its direction is increasingly unpredictable. Globally connected financial markets and advanced digital networks create instant communication, so that events and decisions can be transmitted around the world in nanoseconds.

Technologies such as interactive television, mobile phones and the Internet transform relations between individuals, overcoming separation in space and time by what Giddens (1990) describes as the processes of 'disembedding' – the removal of events from their local timeframe, and 'time–space distantiation': the reorganization of time and space in a way that 'connect[s] presence and absence' (p14). Such instantaneity renders causal relations meaningless since, as became apparent in the early 20th century, events must be separate from their causes in time to allow for the establishment of a predictable relationship. The speed of the modern world distorts such straightforward relations however, giving us 'the triumph of effect over cause, of instantaneity over time' (Baudrillard, 1988).

All of this works to effectively eliminate the future, replacing it instead with an endlessly extended present. As the distance between the 'now' and the future disappears, the latter ceases to have any forward projection, and collapses in on itself. Such a movement is described by Nowotny (1985), who writes that 'the category of the future is shrinking towards becoming a mere extension of the present because science and technology have successfully reduced the distance that is needed to accommodate their own products' (p15). Contemporary technology not only collapses the future into the present but also creates systems of such profound complexity that the prediction of future events is virtually impossible. These systems, known as 'chaotic', describe how a minor occurrence in one part of the world, whether, for example in financial markets or ecological systems, can multiply exponentially and create major, unpredictable events in another.

These kinds of simultaneity and non-linearity in physical, economic and social systems make prediction all but impossible; a state of affairs that has a significant impact on human action. While determinism allowed for the planning of the future based on knowledge of the past, in an indeterministic world, such prediction is impossible. With the undermining of the assumption that the future will follow the past, and with the very notion of the future itself becoming increasingly tenuous as it collapses into an extended present, the basis for planning, expectation and the forward movement of the self becomes difficult to sustain. As Bauman (1992) puts it, the postmodern condition 'is both *undetermined* and *undetermining*. It 'unbinds' time; weakens the constraining impact of the past and effectively prevents colonization of the future' (p190, emphasis in original). It has long been recognized that such a forward movement is crucial for human existence, and that the self is defined and maintained through its dynamic projection into the future (Bergson, 1911/1991; Minkowski, 1970).[9] Indeed, it has been shown that when this sense of forward movement into the future breaks down, for example through sickness (Charmaz, 1992), depression (Ellenberger, 1958), addiction (Reith, 1999b) or imprisonment (Brown, 1998), then certain distortions or 'pathologies' of the self can arise. Such issues are especially pressing in an age in which the future is more than ever the site of identity formation for the rational self-determining individual. Given that the 'reflexive project of the self' (Giddens, 1991) is an ongoing process of calculation that involves the individual moving forwards into the future, radical uncertainty about the nature of that future undermines the very nature of being, and gives rise to a state of heightened ontological insecurity. Such a problem is especially acute in the modern world where, to a greater extent than ever before, the structural conditions of late capitalism force the individual to confront the world alone. Traditional social institutions and practices, such as the family, work and religion, that once provided security and stability are becoming increasingly fluid, leaving the individual without solid footing in economic and social life (Bauman, 1988; Giddens, 1991).

The profound uncertainty generated within a globalized, indeterministic world erodes the basis for decision-making, freezes action, and ultimately blocks the possibility of forward movement into the future. Indeed, the future no longer exists as something that is open to 'colonization' by confident, rational action, but rather as a site of anxiety, full of unknowns, that is not amenable to human intervention. This creates a quandary, for although the future may be radically contingent and unknowable, the individual must still engage with it. The problem that now faces them is – how to act.

Back to the Future: The Utility of 'Risk'

It is here that the notion of risk has efficacy.

Given that the calculation of risk had originally been based on the assumption that the future was, to an extent, predictable, the state of indeterminism might be expected to render it obsolete as a form of knowledge. Far from it. If anything, its field of application expanded even further within an indeterminate universe as the notion of risk moved progressively through the social sciences, explaining uncertainty in a variety of disciplines.[10]

The postulation of indeterminism did not abolish the utility of risk calculation, for the latter was simply adapted to suit its modified subject. We have seen that the essence of risk assessment is the attempt, through the calculus of probability and statistics, to quantify and predict the future. By gathering relevant information over a sufficiently long period, an informed estimate regarding the unfolding of future occurrences can be made. However, these are never specific predictions about exact events, but only generalizations about likely ones. This was what was undertaken in the formulae of probability and statistics in the 17th century, when the world was thought to be predictable and absolute knowledge was thought to be possible. Even then, the project was not always successful, for, quite simply, the world was *not* always predictable, and perfect knowledge remained an ideal. Today, in the 21st century, the focus of probability and statistics is still long-term regularities, albeit within a world now deemed indeterminate. However, given that the type of knowledge produced by statistics and probability has only ever been – and *can* only ever be – generalized likelihoods, their 'predictive' power – always vague – is hardly compromised. Instead, only their claims to authority need be scaled back, and this is what has happened. Rather than aiming for certainty, around the mid-20th century the calculation of risk began to reflect the uncertainties of an indeterminate world instead.

At this point, statistics began to be used to represent fluctuations and probabilities, rather than to measure and quantify certainties. In other words, they were starting to show that knowledge was imperfect, uncertain and limited. This shift influenced the disciplines that used statistical techniques, and it was in economics that the concept of risk first expanded to provide a new form of knowledge based on uncertainty. Here, the ideal of perfect knowledge and prediction was replaced with partial knowledge and risk minimization. Writers such as Knight (1921), von Mises (1949) and von Neumann and Morgenstern (1953) constructed a model that moved away from the ideal of perfect knowledge in certain conditions, and replaced it with one based on partial knowledge and risk minimization. Since absolute certainty of future events was impossible, the best course of action was simply risk minimization, and this could be achieved by the rational calculation of relevant factors. In such models, the notion of risk represents an order of knowledge that has given up all hope of certainty, instead concerning itself with calculating degrees of probability and belief; hence Knight's (1921) classic description of it as 'determinate uncertainty' (p46). Contrary to the optimistic Enlightenment belief that greater knowledge brings greater certainty, this application of risk makes clear that the more knowledge we have, the *less* certain we become, and the ideal of certainty is replaced with an ongoing exercise in probability calculation. As Luhmann (1993) puts it, this is a form of knowledge in which 'nothing certain can be discerned ... only what is more or less probable or improbable' (pix)

It can be seen then, that the postulation of indeterminism does not in itself undermine the utility of risk calculation as a means of dealing with the future. Following on from this, the distinction between 'calculable' and 'incalculable' risk can be seen to be wrong. When, for example, Beck (1992) argues that certain dangers, such as nuclear and chemical hazards, abolish the calculus of risk because they are too vast to be estimated, he is mistaking their uninsurability (which is undoubtedly the case, and a feature of insurer's policies) with such supposed incalculability (p102).[11] In fact, there is nothing that cannot be assessed by risk analysis, since, by definition, the latter is based on the calculus of a variety of uncertain contingencies. The concept of risk is tailor-made for situations of indeterminacy, for there can be no such thing as an 'incalculable' risk. Whether it calculates these contingencies accurately is, of course, another matter entirely. However, the point being made here is that the utility of the notion of 'risk' lies not in its ability to correctly predict future outcomes (at which, on the level of the individual, it is not particularly successful), but rather in its ability to provide a basis for decision-making.

The utility of risk

The utility of such a role, in terms of the problem of human action, can perhaps be better seen through an examination of what O'Malley (1996, 2000) and Dean (1999a) describe as 'prudentialism' – an aspect of neo-liberal government based on the premise of rational individuals taking responsibility for their own welfare through the calculation of risk. Here, citizens have a duty to safeguard themselves against what are perceived to be risks by keeping themselves informed about potential dangers, weighing up probabilities and likelihoods, evaluating courses of action and ultimately, protecting themselves against harm (O'Malley, 1996; Dean, 1999a, b; Rose, 1999). Myriad practices and consumer products exist to make the management of these so-called risks a part of everyday life, from the fitness regimes, low-fat diets and private insurance that safeguard against ill-health and old age; to the burglar alarms, security devices and informed suspicion of dangerous areas and persons that protect against crime. Added to this, a plethora of official publications and specialist and lay organizations advise the individual on how to avoid, manage or cope with the contingencies of everyday life, from the British Medical Association's guide to *Living With Risk* (1987), to the formation of community groups such as Neighbourhood Watch. Such responses indicate that, despite the tendency for it to be individualized, the concept of risk may also act as a stimulus for the emergence of new social formations that coalesce around the shared rituals of calculation and avoidance (Dean, 1999b).

Although the focus of the discourse on prudentialism is on the technology of risk as a means of bio-power and control, the approach as a whole can be argued to have wider implications, and can illuminate the broad, pragmatic role of risk calculation as a guide for individual behaviour.

In this sense, the utility of the concept of risk derives from its essentially forward-looking orientation, and, from this, its ability to express uncertainty in calculable form. By taking a set of known factors in the present, the calculation of risk involves the expansion of the timeframe and the projection into the future until the appearance of regularities and patterns create a sense of predictability. It takes the lone individual and socializes them, by placing them in groups of their own kind; and it takes the collapsed present of late modernity and expands it into the future.

Such a strategy does not, of course, make the future any more certain, and the individual's movement into it is still a journey into new territory – what Giddens (1991) calls the realm of 'counterfactual possibility' (p111). However, in many ways the calculation of risk does something more important, for the active weighing up of the future in order to minimize loss and maximize gain provides individuals with a guide for rational action and confers a degree of control over uncertainty (Douglas, 1992). They may not know what the future holds, but by following expert advice, they know that they are 'doing the right thing': armed with the appropriate information, individuals can feel secure as they go about their business, knowing that they are taking active steps to protect their well-being and shape their future. It may be impossible to know 'what will happen', but at least if things *do* go wrong, they have the comfort of knowing that they acted 'correctly' in ways that are consonant with agreed principles of risk management. As Luhmann (1998) put it: 'If the impossible happens, one can defend oneself with the argument that one decided correctly, namely in risk-rational manner' (p72). In this way, risk calculation works to 'immunize decision-making against failure' (Luhmann, 1993, p13).[12] The calculation of risk cannot guarantee the avoidance of ill-results, and it cannot provide assurances about an uncertain future. But its role transcends this: independently of success or failure, it provides a justifiable guide for behaviour. Although it cannot make the future predictable or the world certain, it can create the means *for acting as though it were*.

Knowledge of the world in terms of risk embodies a particular view of the future: It 'brings the future into a calculative relation to the present' (Levitas, 2000, p201). It also embodies a particular view of the individual as an agent moving forwards into it; towards a specific vision of the self. In the 17th century, the concept of risk captured the sense of the future as something that was opening up, breaking free from the strictures of traditional society. Today, the particular calculative and temporal orientations that are involved in the calculation of risk are useful in a different way: Not as a *reflection* of an open future, but as an *image* of such a thing. Since the identification of something as 'a risk' refers to some knowledge – however partial – of future danger, its threat is located within the boundaries of human action. The temporal orientation involved in the calculation of risk brings the uncertain future into the domain of individual agency in the present, so creating the possibility of self-realization and control. Moreover, such a projection acts as a stimulus to the individual, whose forwards movement is animated by the awareness and negotiation of risks. This way of thinking and acting reanimates the 'blocked' future, allowing individuals to form their own trajectories, and can be seen as a 'means of seeking to stabilize outcomes, a mode of colonising the future' (Giddens, 1991, p133). In the world of late modernity, where the future has collapsed into a globalized, indeterminate present, the ongoing calculation of risk becomes a formal strategy for moving into the future, so that, as Luhmann (1998) puts it, today 'modern society experiences its future in the form of the risk of deciding' (pp70–71).

The Limitations of 'Risk'?

An important qualification should be mentioned at this point, for although it can be argued that the concept of risk has efficacy as a guide for action within an indeterminate present, in many ways this role is quite limited. This shortcoming does not stem from the fact that the world is indeterministic, however – it applies when its subject is determined too – but rather from the *type* of knowledge that the calculation of risk provides.

It is somewhat ironic that, although the management of risk is individualized in contemporary life, in reality, there is no such thing as an 'individual' risk. As we have seen, probability deals with aggregates over the long term, and so it is impossible for 'risk analysis' to make recommendations for individuals or for specific times. Because 'risk only becomes calculable when it is spread over a population' (Ewald, 1991, p203), it cannot tell the individual what will happen to them in the short term. It can provide plenty of information on, for example, the chances of motorists being involved in road accidents, but it cannot tell a particular motorist their chances of a crash at any specific time. The concept of 'risk' tells us everything and it tells us nothing. Anything can be the subject of risk analysis; nothing is 'incalculable', and probabilistic assessments can very effectively construct future scenarios that create a space for active human intervention. But they can never tell us about the individual case: how we fit in to this future scenario, or whether it is applicable to us at any particular moment in time. In this sense, the future is left opaque, and this is its shortcoming in providing us with a totally satisfactory guide for action in uncertainty.

Another point that should be made concerns the fact that, although many of the beliefs and practices relating to the management of risk are shared, many more are not. Indeed, there is often considerable disagreement over the calculation and application of the concept of risk across a variety of disciplines, from health and the environment to economics and finance. Furthermore, a considerable body of work exists on the disregard and/or misinterpretation of risk, on the existence of continued beliefs in notions such as luck and fate, on voluntary risk-taking in activities that are often dangerous and even life-threatening, and of the increasing scepticism of individuals towards forms of expert authority (Kahneman and Tversky, 1984; Lyng, 1990; Wynne, 1996). Further consideration of the place of such 'refusals' of risk rationality within late modern society are, unfortunately, outside the scope of this chapter. However, although they question its hegemony, their existence does not undermine the argument for a pragmatic role for risk calculation, if perhaps a limited one.

This pragmatic aspect does not undermine the argument for the essentially constructed nature of the notion of risk, as Mary Douglas (1992) demonstrates (albeit from a different perspective) when she notes the affinity of the idea as a 'forensic resource' with its wider cultural milieu. In *Risk and Blame* she writes admiringly of the idea of risk as the ideal discourse for our times, asserting that: '[It] could have been custom made. Its universalising terminology, its abstractness, its power of condensation, its scientificity, its connection with objective analysis, make it perfect. Above all, its forensic uses fit the tool to the task of building a culture that supports a modern industrial society' (p15). While Douglas is concerned with its specific function of signifying danger and attributing blame when things go wrong, here, a more general role is being suggested for the notion of risk: as a construct that not only reflects the preoccupations of the culture in which it is used, but which, by rearticulating the collapsed future of late modernity, also provides a framework for agency within it.

Perhaps, ultimately, the most significant aspect of the notion of risk in contemporary society is not to be found in its epistemological status at all, but rather in its pragmatic role – in its ability to provide a guide for action within the world – whatever the 'reality' of that world might be.

Notes

1   Although these were never accorded the same status as those of organized religion and eventually came to be regarded as evidence of superstition and paganism, their influence – especially among the peasantry – cannot be overlooked, and they remained a constant source of comfort in the face of material insecurity.
2   A considerable body of literature exists documenting the efficacy of magical and religious beliefs in making sense of uncertainty. See for example Dewey (1930), Evans-Pritchard (1991) and Reynolds White (1998).
3   This orientation was already being utilized by the merchant class in trading situations who, since the Reformation, had had a concept of time as something that, while still imbued with religious meaning, could also be utilized to shape the world in particular ways and so demonstrate success in a worldly calling (Weber, 1904/1989).
4   This was realized in two separate but related movements. In France, the analysis of chance in gambling games led to the creation of formulae for estimating the probability of outcomes based on new concepts such as odds and expectations, while in England, a focus on the apparently random fluctuations of the population in terms of births, marriages and deaths, revealed stable trends among what had appeared to be disparate groups of individuals (Reith, 1999a).
5   It has been argued that variations on the concept of risk existed prior to this, with Luhmann (1993) pointing out that a form of 'risk' appeared in German in the mid-16th century, and that the Latin *riscum* had been in use even before that. Ewald (1991) also suggests that a medieval understanding of risk designated the God-driven dangers that could be encountered during voyages at sea. However, such a conception of some kind of danger that was an act of God and excluded human action puts it closer to the notion of chance, and so it can reasonably be said, as Luhmann (1993, p9) later argues, that 'risk' was not actually regarded as a distinct category at this time.
6   A form of insurance known as 'bottomry contracts' – loans to ship owners whose repayment depended on the safe completion of a voyage – had existed since the fourth millennium BC.

In the 17th century, however, a more sophisticated form emerged that calculated the chances of a ship coming home against the chances of its being lost at sea, and in doing so, for the first time took account of the probability of marine losses and gains (Daston, 1988).

7   See Hacking (1990) on this process, related to what he calls 'the taming of chance' as secularization undermined basis of determinism.

8   Although the insights of quantum physics are far removed from the macro reality of the social world, discoveries in science both influence and are influenced by 'ways of seeing' the broader world around us (Kuhn, 1970), and it is in this sense that the new temporal and epistemological structures suggested by the quantum revolution are significant.

9   As well, of course, as a recognition of its location in the past, expressed through the continuities of memory and tradition.

10 All of these have their own different perspectives, with their own areas of study and their own distinct set of epistemological assumptions. The concern here is not with the particular arguments and discourses that have sprung up around the concept of risk, as these are numerous and have been dealt with extensively elsewhere. See for example Adam et al (2000), Caplan (2000) and Lupton (1999a, b). Rather, what is important here is simply the existence and extent of a widespread discourse on risk within the social sciences itself. The concern is with how it is possible that these perspectives have become meaningful – and popular – at all.

11 See Dean (1999b) on the confusion of the identification of 'risk' in general with the specific case of insurer's risks.

12 Luhmann (1993) also points out that the form of risk rationality 'serves to generate a paradox, namely the demonstration that a wrong decision is right' (p24).

References

Adam, B. (1990) *Time and Social Theory*. Cambridge: Polity Press.

Adam, B. (1995) *Timewatch: The Social Analysis of Time*. Cambridge: Polity Press.

Adam, B., Beck, U. and van Loon, J. (eds) (2000) *The Risk Society and Beyond: Critical Issues for Social Theory*. London: Sage.

Adams, J. (1995) *Risk*. London: UCL Press.

Baudrillard, J. (1988) *America*. London:Verso.

Baudrillard, J. (1998) *The Consumer Society: Myths and Structures*. London: Sage.

Bauman, Z. (1988) *Freedom*. Milton Keynes: Open University Press.

Bauman, Z. (1992) *Intimations of Postmodernity*. London: Routledge.

Beck, U. (1992) *Risk Society: Towards a New Modernity*. London: Sage.

Bergson, H. (1911/1991) *Matter and Memory*. London: Macmillan.

Braudel, F. (1973) *Capitalism and Material Life*. London: Weidenfield and Nicolson.

British Medical Association (1987) *Living With Risk*. Chichester: John Wiley.

Brown, A. (1998) '"Doing Time": The Extended Time of the Long Term Prisoner', *Time & Society* 7(1): 93–105.

Caplan, P. (ed.) (2000) *Risk Revisited*. London: Pluto Press.

Castel, R. (1991) 'From Dangerousness to Risk', in G. Burchell, C. Gordon and P. Miller (eds) *The Foucault Effect: Studies in Governmentality*, pp. 281–99. London: Harvester Wheatsheaf.

Charmaz, K. (1992) *Good Days, Bad Days: The Self in Chronic Illness and Time*. New Brunswick, NJ: Rutgers University Press.

Daston, L. (1988) *Classical Probability in the Enlightenment*. Princeton, NJ: Princeton University Press.

de Jong, A. (1975) *Dostoevsky and the Age of Intensity*. London: Secker and Warburg.

Dean, M. (1999a) *Risk and Reflexive Government: Power and Rule in Modern Society*. London: Sage.

Dean, M. (1999b) 'Risk, Calculable and Incalculable', in D. Lupton (ed.) *Risk and Socio-cultural Theory*, pp. 67–84. Cambridge: Cambridge University Press.

Dewey, J. (1930) *The Quest for Certainty: A Study of the Relation of Knowledge and Action*. London: Allen and Unwin.

Douglas, M. (1986) *Risk Acceptability According to the Social Sciences*. London: Routledge.

Douglas, M. (1992) *Risk and Blame: Essays in Cultural Theory*. London: Routledge.

Eco, U. (1995) *Travels in Hyper-reality*. London: Pan Books.

Ellenberger, H. (1958) 'A Clinical Introduction to Psychiatric Phenomenology and Existential Analysis', in R. May, E. Angel and H. Ellenberger (eds) *Existence: A New Dimension in Psychiatry*, pp. 203–65. New York: Simon & Schuster.

Evans-Pritchard, E. E. (1991) *Witchcraft, Magic and Oracles among the Azande*. Oxford: Clarendon Press.

Ewald, F. (1991) 'Insurance and Risk', in G. Burchell, C. Gordon and P. Miller (eds) *The Foucault Effect: Studies in Governmentality*, pp. 197–211. London: Harvester Wheatsheaf.

Freudenthal, G. (1986) *Atom and Individual in the Age of Newton: On the Genesis of the Mechanistic World View*. Dordrecht: Reidl.

Gabe, J. (ed.) (1995) *Medicine, Health and Risk: Sociological Approaches*. Oxford: Blackwell.

Giddens, A. (1990) *The Consequences of Modernity*. Cambridge: Polity.

Giddens, A. (1991) *Modernity and Self-Identity*. Cambridge: Polity.

Gigerenzer, G., Swijinck, Z., Porter, T., Daston, L., Beatty, J. and Kruger, L. (1989) *The Empire of Chance*. Cambridge: Cambridge University Press.

Gurvitch, G. (1964) *The Spectrum of Social Time*. Dordrecht: Reidl.

Hacking, I. (1975) *The Emergence of Probability*. Cambridge: Cambridge University Press.

Hacking, I. (1990) *The Taming of Chance*. Cambridge: Cambridge University Press.

Hagerstrand, T. (1985) 'Time and Culture', in G. Kirsch, P. Nijkamp and K. Zimmerman (eds) *Time Preferences: An Interdisciplinary Theoretical and Empirical Approach*, pp. 1–15. Berlin: Wissenschaftszentrum.

Harvey, D. (1989) *The Condition of Postmodernity: An Enquiry into the Origins of Cultural Change*. Oxford: Basil Blackwell.

Holton, R. (1985) *The Transition from Feudalism to Capitalism*. London: Macmillan.

Kahneman, D. and Tversky, A. (1984) 'Choices, Values and Frames', *American Psychologist* 39(4): 341–50.

Knight, F. (1921) *Risk, Uncertainty and Profit*. Cambridge: The Riverside Press.

Koyré, A. (1982) *From the Closed World to the Infinite Universe*. Baltimore, MD: Johns Hopkins University Press.

Kuhn, T. (1970) *The Structure of Scientific Revolutions*. Chicago: University of Chicago Press.

Lash, S. and Urry, J. (1994) *Economies of Signs and Space*. London: Sage.

Le Goff, J. (1980) *Time, Work and Culture in the Middle Ages*. Chicago: University of Chicago Press.

Levidow, L. (1994) 'De-reifying Risk', *Science as Culture* 4(3): 440–56.

Levitas, R. (2000) 'Discourses of Risk and Utopia', in B. Adam, U. Beck and J. van Loon (eds) *The Risk Society and Beyond: Critical Issues for Social Theory*, pp. 198–211. London: Sage.

Lovejoy, A. (1960) *The Great Chain of Being: A Study of the History of Ideas*. New York: Harper.

Luhmann, N. (1993) *Risk: A Sociological Theory*. Berlin: Walter De Gruyter.

Luhmann, N. (1998) *Observations on Modernity*. Stanford, CA: Stanford University Press.

Lupton, D. (ed.) (1999a) *Risk and Sociocultural Theory*. Cambridge: Cambridge University Press.

Lupton, D. (1999b) *Risk*. London: Routledge.

Lyng, S. (1990) 'Edgework: A Social Psychological Analysis of Voluntary Risk Taking', *American Journal of Sociology* 95(4): 851–86.

Minkowski, E. (1970) *Lived Time: Phenomenological and Psychopathological Studies*. Evanston, IL: Northwestern University Press.

Nelkin, D. and Brown, M. (1984) *Workers at Risk: Voices From the Workplace*. Chicago: University of Chicago Press.

Nowotny, H. (1985) 'From the Future to the Extended Present: Time in Social Systems', in G. Kirsch, P. Nijkamp and K. Zimmerman (eds) *Time Preferences: An Interdisciplinary Theoretical and Empirical Approach*, pp. 1–21. Berlin: Wissenschaftszentrum.

O'Malley, P. (1996) 'Risk and Responsibility', in A. Barry, T. Osborne and N. Rose (eds) *Foucault and Political Reason: Liberalism, Neo-Liberalism and Rationalities of Government*, pp. 189–207. London: UCL Press.

O'Malley, P. (2000) 'Uncertain Subjects: Risks, Liberalism and Contract', *Economy and Society* 29(4): 460–84.

Parker, H., Aldridge, J. and Measham, F. (1998) *Illegal Leisure: The Normalisation of Adolescent Recreational Drug Use*. London: Routledge.

Pascal, B. (1656/1987*) Pensées*. London: Penguin.

Reith, G. (1999a) *The Age of Chance: Gambling in Western Culture*. London: Routledge.

Reith, G. (1999b) 'In Search of Lost Time: Recall, Projection and the Phenomenology of Addiction', *Time and Society* 8(1): 99–117.

Reynolds White, S. (1998) *Questioning Misfortune: The Pragmatics of Uncertainty in Eastern Uganda*. Cambridge: Cambridge University Press.

Rose, N. (1999) *Governing the Soul: The Shaping of the Private Self*. London: Free Association Books.

Thomas, K. (1997) *Religion and the Decline of Magic: Studies in Popular Beliefs in Sixteenth and Seventeenth Century England*. London: Weidenfield and Nicolson.

von Mises, L. (1949) *Human Action*. New Haven, CT: Yale University Press.

von Neumann, J. and Morgenstern, O. (1953) *Theory of Games and Economic Behavior*. London: Hurst and Blackett.

Ward, A. (1994) 'Consumption, Identity Formation and Uncertainty', *Sociology* 28(4): 877–98.

Weber, M. (1904/1989) *The Protestant Ethic and the Spirit of Capitalism*. London: Unwin and Hyman.

Wynne, B. (1996) 'May the Sheep Safely Graze? A Reflexive View of the Expert-Lay Knowledge Divide', in S. Lash, B. Szerszynski and B. Wynne *Risk, Environment and Modernity*, pp. 44–83. London: Sage.

Zohar, D. and Marshall, I. (1993) *The Quantum Society*. London: Bloomsbury.

Part II

Risk Perception

5

Gender, Race and Perceived Risk: The 'White Male' Effect

Melissa L. Finucane, Paul Slovic, C.K. Mertz, James Flynn and Theresa A. Satterfield

Introduction

Risks tend to be judged as lower by men than by women (see, for example, Brody, 1984; Steger and Witt, 1989; Gwartney-Gibbs and Lach, 1991; Gutteling and Wiegman, 1993; Stern et al, 1993; Flynn et al, 1994). However, progress has been slow in explaining gender differences in perceived risk, and few studies have examined how differences are related to other characteristics of individuals, such as race. Flynn et al (1994) suggest that the role of gender or race in perceived risk may relate to socio-political factors. The main aim of this chapter is to examine how gender and race are related to a range of sociopolitical factors thought to influence risk perceptions. The study reported here was designed to oversample minority populations and address a range of sociopolitical issues. Data suggest that general attitudes toward the world and its social organization (which we shall refer to as worldviews and trust) and stigma are different for white males compared with other groups and that this effect is more complex than previously indicated by Flynn et al. We also note that gender and race are politically sensitive issues, and raising them in public discussions about risks (where there is often much at stake) can be emotionally intense and difficult. Therefore, a second aim of this chapter is to provide data about how people of different genders and races perceive risks.

Traditionally, one explanation for differences in risk perceptions is based on an assumption of differences in rationality and education. According to the 'irrationality' perspective, risk perceptions that deviate from estimates of fatality rates or other 'objective' indices are thought to arise from a lack of understanding of complex scientific and technical information (see Cohen, 1983; Cross, 1998). Some risk regulators and health risk communicators seem to believe that arming people with more information should reduce their scientific illiteracy and improve their decision-making. That is, risk perceptions would be more accurate if people used more complete information about product or technology attributes (Bettman et al, 1987). Others seem to believe that if people just listened to the facts, they would reach the same conclusions as experts (Wandersman and Hallman, 1993). However, extensive efforts to educate the public about risks and risk assessment, such as advertisement campaigns for nuclear power, have failed to move public opinion to coincide with the experts. When measured by expert views, the public overestimates some risks and underestimates others (Adler and Pittle, 1984; see also Svenson et al, 1985). Furthermore, addressing risk controversies with technical solutions may contribute to conflict (Kunreuther and Slovic, 1996).

Research on gender differences suggests that discrepancies in risk perceptions of men and women may not reflect differences in rationality or education (Gardner and Gould, 1989). For instance, Barke et al (1997) showed risk perception differences between men and women scientists. Thus, men and women with considerable technical understanding of risk and knowledge of risk assessment procedures still differ in their risk perceptions. Similar data were reported by Slovic et al (1997), who found that among members of the British Toxicology Society, females were far more likely than males to judge societal risks as moderate or high (see also Kraus et al, 1992; Slovic et al, 1995). Furthermore, biased risk judgements have been demonstrated within expert populations, suggesting even the most highly educated are influenced by the specific context of risk estimation questions. For example, McNeil et al (1982) showed that framing outcomes in terms of the probability of survival rather than the probability of death affected physicians' preferences for different lung cancer treatments, despite the survival and death probabilities being objectively equivalent.

Another common explanation for gender differences in risk perceptions is based on biological differences. However, recent research (for example, Flynn et al, 1994; and see also Slovic, 1997) has reduced the salience of a purely biological approach. Flynn, Slovic, and colleagues found that:

- non-white males and females are more similar in their perceptions of risk than are white males and females; and
- white males are different from everyone else in their perceptions and attitudes toward risk.

Biological explanations imply that the differences between men's and women's risk perceptions would transcend racial boundaries.

In the study by Flynn et al (1994), 1512 Americans were asked, for each of 25 hazard items, to indicate whether the hazard posed (1) *little or no risk*, (2) *slight risk*, (3) *moderate risk*, or (4) *high risk* to society. Results showed that the percentage of high-risk responses was greater for women than men on every item. Similar analyses showed that the percentage of high-risk responses was greater among people of colour than among white respondents for every item studied. The most striking result, however, is shown in Figure 5.1, which presents the mean risk ratings separately for white males, white females, non-white males, and non-white females. For all 25 hazards, white males' risk perception ratings were consistently much lower than the means of the other three groups.

This 'white male' effect seemed to be caused by about 30 per cent of the white male sample that judged risks to be extremely low. When these low-risk white males (LRWM) were compared with the rest of the respondents, they were found to be better educated, had higher household incomes, and were politically more conservative. They also held very different attitudes, characterized by trust in institutions and authorities and by anti-egalitarianism, including disinclination toward giving decision-making power to citizens in areas of risk management.

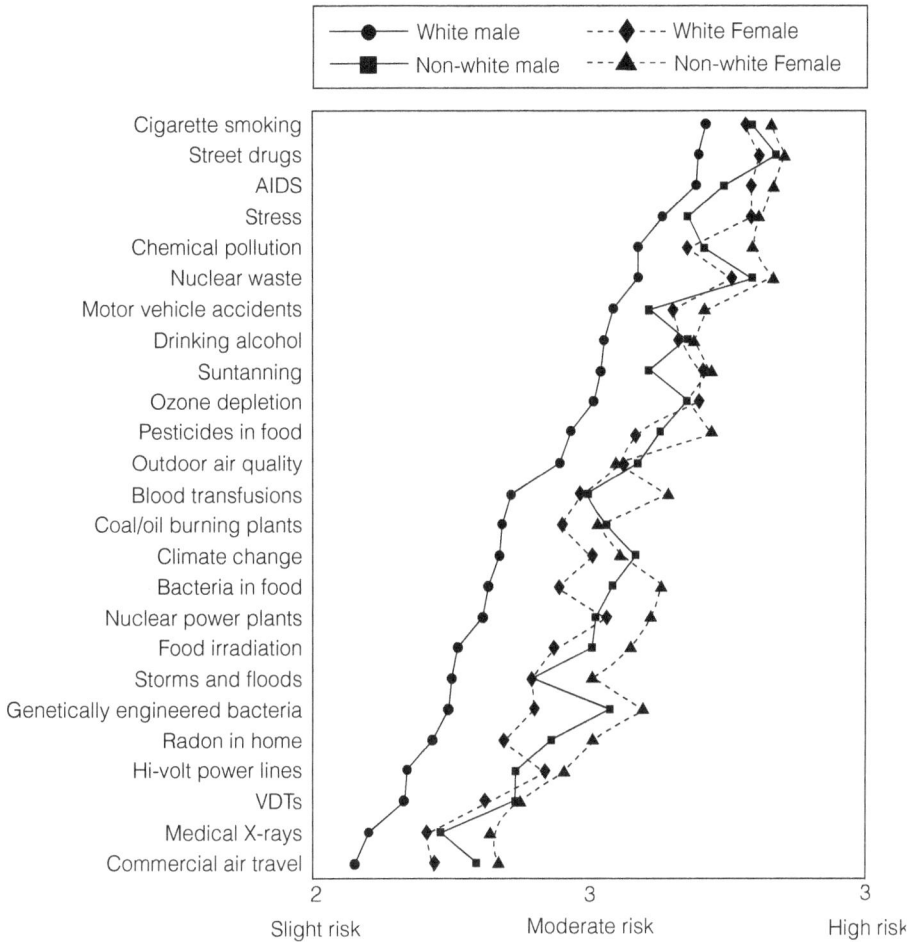

Figure 5.1 *Mean risk-perception ratings by race and gender*

Source: Flynn et al. (1994)

The role of socio-political factors: people vary in their worldviews, trust and control

The results described above led to the hypothesis that differences in worldviews, trust, control and other socio-political factors could be key determiners of gender and race differences in risk judgements, and that risk perceptions may reflect deep-seated values about technology and its impact on society (Barke et al, 1997). White males may perceive less risk than others because they are more involved in creating, managing, controlling and benefiting from technology. Women and non-white men may perceive greater risk because they tend to be more vulnerable, have less control, and benefit less. Indeed, some research suggests that risk perceptions are related to individuals' levels of decision power (for example, whether they have high or low ability to influence decisions about the use of hazards such as liquefied petroleum gas) and their interest in a hazard (for example, direct, indirect or adversarial) (see, for example, Kuyper and Vlek, 1984; Baird, 1986; Bord and O'Connor, 1997).

Understanding how socio-political factors differ by gender and race is important because it would help explain why attempts to impose the elite view of the world have often failed to improve public acceptance of risks. In the present research we expected to find that white males differ from others in that they have lower risk perceptions across a range of hazards and tend to endorse hierarchical and anti-egalitarian views.

Method

This chapter reports data collected as part of a national telephone survey designed to test hypotheses about risk perceptions over a range of hazards. The survey contained questions about worldviews, trust and a range of demographic variables. Also included were questions designed to assess the respondent's recognition of potential adverse effects from risk-induced stigmatization of places and products associated with transport of chemical and radioactive wastes (see, for example, Gregory et al, 1995).

Procedure

A stratified random sample of household members over 18 years of age in the United States was surveyed by telephone from 27 September 1997 to 3 February 1998. A total of 1204 completed interviews were obtained with an overall response rate of 46.8 per cent. Interviewing was conducted within a sample of US households and three racial/ethnic groups (African-American, Hispanic and Asian) were oversampled to permit reliable analyses of differences among these minorities. Race and ethnicity were combined in one question for the survey: 'What is your race or ethnic background? Do you consider yourself White, Hispanic, Black, Asian, American Indian, multiracial or multiethnic, or other?' This procedure relies on self-definition, which as Cooper (1994) points out is the 'only legal basis for racial classification' in the United States. The final survey database contains responses for 672 white Caucasians, 217 African-Americans, 180 Hispanics, 101 Asians, and 34 respondents of Native American, multiracial/ethnic or other origin. Interviews were conducted in English and Spanish. The mean age was 43.5 years and 45 per cent were males and 55 per cent were females. The average interview length was approximately 35 minutes. Data displays that include both race and gender characteristics are unweighted. All other uses of the data are weighted to the US census estimates of the 1997 US population in terms of race and gender, resulting in a weighted sample size of 859 respondents. The data are weighted so that individual ethnic/racial groups within the non-white group will be representative of the US non-white population.

Survey design

The survey contained questions on a wide variety of environmental and health hazards. Only the items relevant to this chapter are described here.

All respondents were asked to consider health and safety risks 'to you and your family' and to indicate whether there is *almost no risk, slight risk, moderate risk*, or *high risk* from each of 13 hazardous activities and technologies (for example, blood transfusions; motor vehicles; nuclear power plants; vaccines). We shall refer to these data as *perceived risk to individuals*, in contrast to the next series of questions in which all respondents were asked to indicate (on the same four-category scale) the level of health and safety risks from 19 hazards for 'the American public as a whole' (including most of the 13 hazards for which perceptions of risk to individuals and their families were elicited). A general risk perception index was calculated for each respondent by averaging ratings of risk to the public across the 19 hazards.

An additional eight items specifically about food hazards (for example, bacteria in food, hormones and antibiotics in meat, eating fatty foods) were rated for their risks to the public on the four-category scale described above.

Finally, all respondents were asked a series of questions regarding the effects of stigma, worldviews, trust and demographics (including gender and race).

Results

Risk perceptions

Gender differences

We found differences in the high-risk responses of males and females (see Figure 5.2a) with the percentage of high-risk responses greater for females on every item. A similar pattern was found for ratings of health risks to the American public, and ratings of the public risks of food hazards (see Figure 5.2b).

Racial differences

Likewise, examining the differences between the percentages of whites and non-whites who rate a hazard as a 'high risk' to individuals, the percentage of high-risk responses was greater for non-whites on every item (see Figure 5.3a). A similar pattern was found for ratings of health risks to the American public, and ratings of the public risks of food hazards (see Figure 5.3b).

The white male effect

Examining the differences between the percentages of white males and the rest of the sample who rated hazards as a 'high risk' to individuals and to the public, we found high-risk responses were lower for white males on every item (see Figures 5.4 and 5.5). That is, white males were always less likely to rate a hazard as posing a 'high risk.' This was particularly true for handguns, nuclear power plants, second-hand cigarette smoke, multiple sexual partners, and street drugs.

Similarly, white males differed from others in their ratings of perceived risks to individuals and the public. Mean ratings of risks to individuals were lower for white males than for white females, non-white males, and non-white females (see Figure 5.6a). A similar pattern was found when ratings of risks to individuals were considered separately

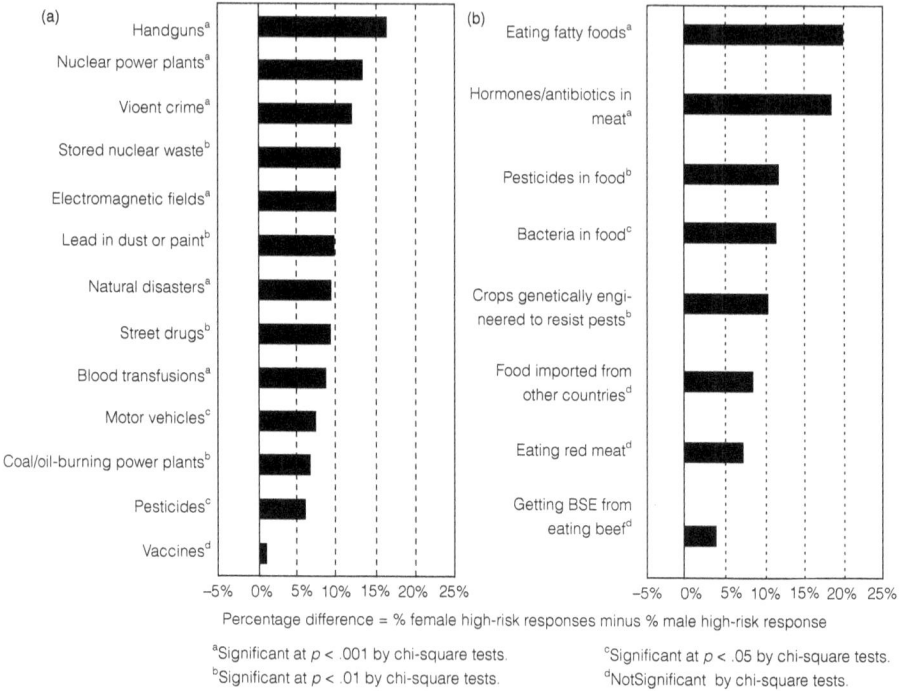

(a)

Handguns[a]
Nuclear power plants[a]
Vioent crime[a]
Stored nuclear waste[b]
Electromagnetic fields[a]
Lead in dust or paint[b]
Natural disasters[a]
Street drugs[b]
Blood transfusions[a]
Motor vehicles[c]
Coal/oil-burning power plants[b]
Pesticides[c]
Vaccines[d]

−5% 0% 5% 10% 15% 20% 25%

(b)

Eating fatty foods[a]
Hormones/antibiotics in meat[a]
Pesticides in food[b]
Bacteria in food[c]
Crops genetically engineered to resist pests[b]
Food imported from other countries[d]
Eating red meat[d]
Getting BSE from eating beef[d]

−5% 0% 5% 10% 15% 20% 25%

Percentage difference = % female high-risk responses minus % male high-risk response

[a]Significant at $p < .001$ by chi-square tests.
[b]Significant at $p < .01$ by chi-square tests.

[c]Significant at $p < .05$ by chi-square tests.
[d]NotSignificant by chi-square tests.

Figure 5.2 *Percentage difference in high-risk responses of males and females for (a) perceived health risks to individuals ('you and your family') and (b) perceived food risks to the American public*

Source: 1997 National Risk Survey, $N = 859$, data weighted for race and gender.

for males and females in each racial group (see Figure 5.6b), although the Asian males scored lower (2.68) than white males (2.80) in rating the risks of motor vehicles.

The mean ratings of risks to the American public showed that white males differed from white females, non-white males and non-white females (see Figure 5.7a). Non-white females show the highest risk estimates for several hazards (for example, lead in dust or paint, blood transfusions). When perceived public risk ratings are considered separately for males and females in each racial group (see Figure 5.7b), Asian males show similar or lower perceptions of public risks than white males for several hazards (for example, motor vehicles, tap water, vaccines, cellular phones). Some hazards (for example, pesticides) display greater variance in risk ratings across the groups than others (for example, motor vehicles).

Perceptions of risk to the American public from food hazards showed that, compared with white females and non-white males and females, white males had lower mean ratings for all items (see Figure 5.8a). Non-white females again show the highest risk estimates for several items (for example, bacteria and pesticides in food). When ratings from males and females were considered separately for each racial group, the

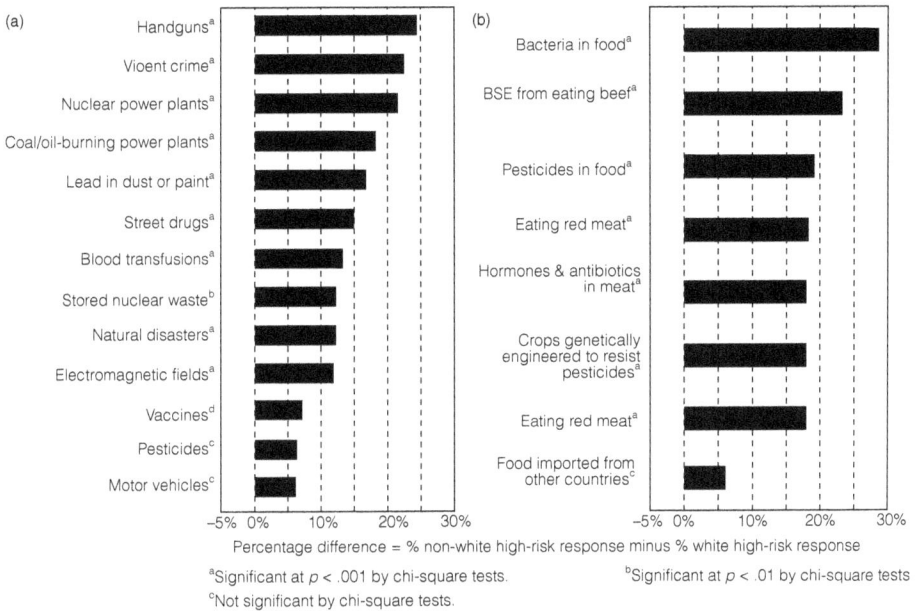

Figure 5.3 *Percentage difference in high-risk responses of whites and non-whites for (a) perceived health risks to individuals ('you and your family') and (b) perceived food risks to the American public*

Source: 1997 National Risk Survey, N = 859, data weighted for race and gender.

'white male' effect was less apparent. Asian males gave less risky ratings than white males did for several food hazards, such as imported food, eating red meat, and hormones/antibiotics in meat (see Figure 5.8b).

Behavioural intentions

Gender and racial differences were also evident on items measuring behavioural intentions about risky activities and technologies (administered to only half of the sample; weighted N = 426). For example, responses to the statement 'If I were hospitalized and my physician recommended a blood transfusion, I would accept blood from a blood bank' showed that a higher proportion of females than males disagreed or strongly disagreed that they would accept blood (44.3 per cent vs. 23.6 per cent, data weighted for race and gender, N = 426). Hispanic people disagreed or strongly disagreed more than whites (44.7 per cent for Hispanics vs. 30.5 per cent for whites); likewise African-American people disagreed or strongly disagreed more than whites (43.6 per cent for African-Americans vs. 30.5 per cent for whites; in these comparisons the data were weighted for gender only, N = 611). White males were less likely to disagree or strongly disagree than Asian females (23.0 per cent for white males vs. 42.9 per cent for Asian females) but more likely to disagree or strongly disagree than Asian males (17.6 per cent) (data unweighted). All differences were significant at p < 0.05 by chi-square tests, except for Asian males versus white males.

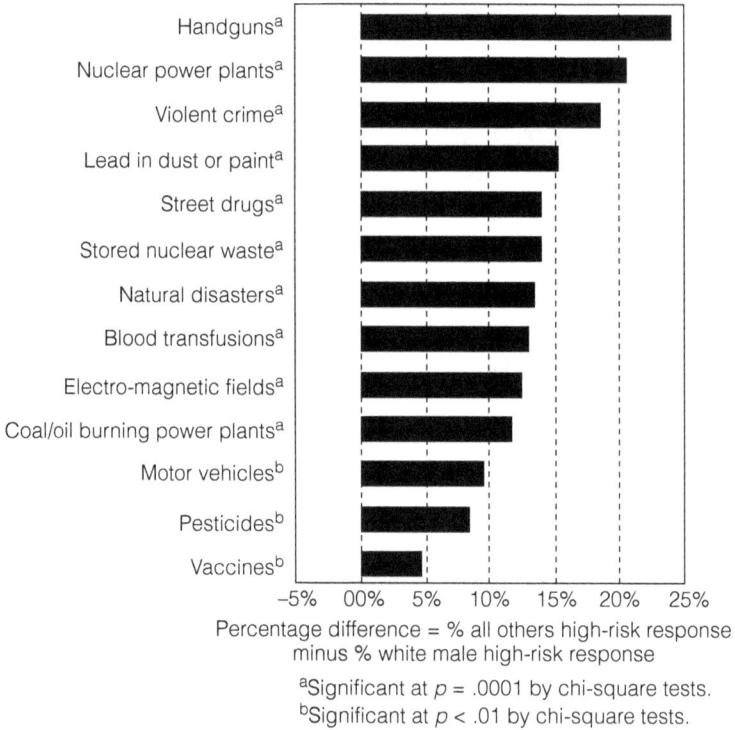

Figure 5.4 *Percentage difference in high-risk responses of white males and others: perceived health risks to individuals ('you and your family')*

Source: 1997 National Risk Survey, N = 859, data weighted for race and gender.

Socio-political factors

What differentiates white males from the rest of the sample? Turning to attitudes, we found that white males seemed to demonstrate different views from others on a range of questions about worldviews, trust, and potential for chemical and radioactive waste hazards to stigmatize places and products. (For the items below, all analyses used data weighted for race and gender to match the US population as a whole, *N* = 859. All differences are significant by chi-square tests at *p* < 0.05, with the exception of item (c) where *p* = 0.05.)

Worldviews

White males displayed more hierarchical and individualistic views and less fatalistic and egalitarian views. Fatalism is reflected in statement (a) below; hierarchical views by statements (b) and (c); egalitarianism by (d) and (e); individualistic views by (f) and (g). Specifically, when compared to all other respondents, white males were more likely to:

(a) disagree that 'I have very little control over risks to my health' (83.4 per cent vs. 76.3 per cent);
(b) disagree that 'I often feel discriminated against' (81.3 per cent vs. 67.6 per cent);

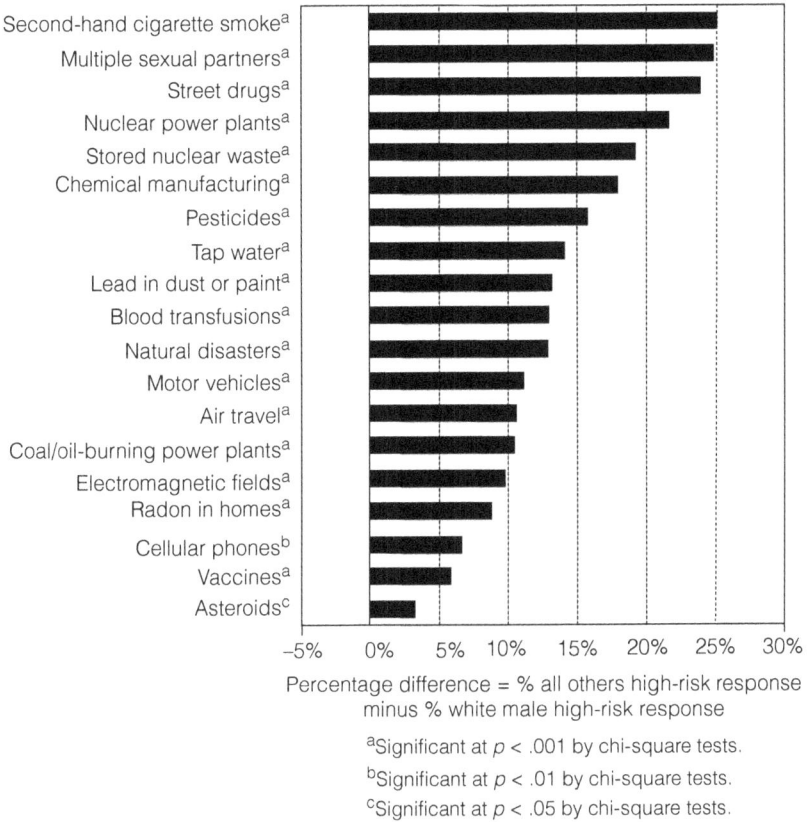

Figure 5.5 *Percentage difference in high-risk responses of white males and others: perceived health risks to the American public*

Source: 1997 National Risk Survey, *N* = 859, data weighted for race and gender.

(c) agree that when a risk is very small, it is OK for society to impose that risk on individuals without their consent (20.8 per cent vs. 15.6 per cent);

(d) disagree that the world needs more equal distribution of wealth (40.1 per cent vs. 23.3 per cent);

(e) agree that we have gone too far in pushing equal rights (49.8 per cent vs. 37.5 per cent);

(f) agree that people with more ability should earn more (88.9 per cent vs. 81.6 per cent); and

(g) disagree that the government should make rules about people's personal risk-taking activities (86.8 per cent vs. 74.6 per cent).

Trust

White males seemed more trusting of technological hazards and less trusting of government, possibly because they prefer to be in control of policy- and decision-making. They were more likely than the others to:

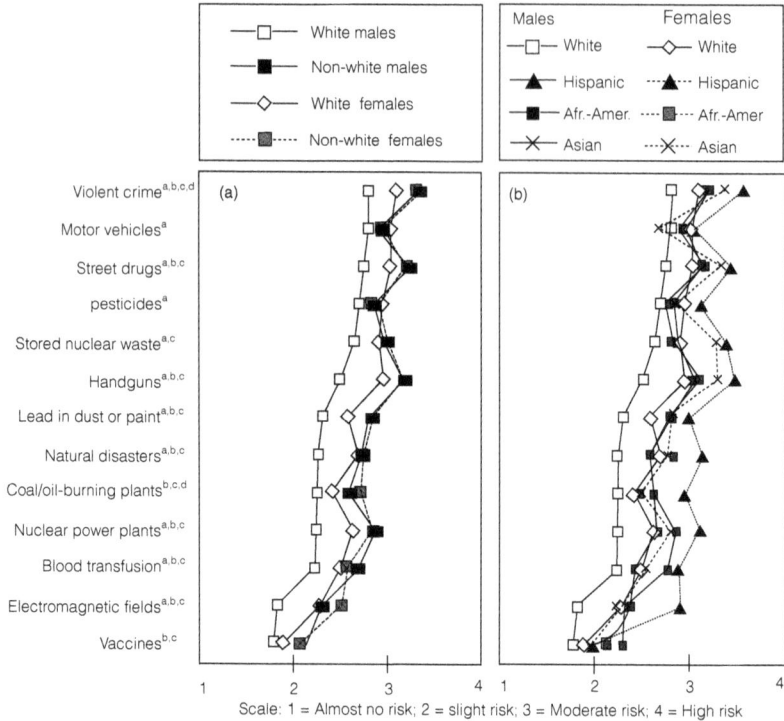

Figure 5.6 *Mean ratings of perceived risks to individuals and their families for (a) white and non-white males and females (data weighted for race and gender, N = 859) and (b) white, Hispanic, African-American and Asian males and females (data not weighted, N = 1170)*

Source: 1997 National Risk Survey.

(a) disagree that people living near a nuclear power plant should be able to vote and to close the plant if they think it is not being run safely (34.3 per cent vs. 12.9 per cent); and

(b) disagree that the federal government can be trusted to properly manage the risks from technology (74.7 per cent vs. 67.8 per cent).

Stigma

White males were far less worried about adverse public responses from risk exposure to chemical and radioactive waste hazards. They were more likely than the others to:

(a) disagree that the selection of an existing highway for future transportation of nuclear and chemical waste would lower the value of nearby homes (40.5 per cent vs. 16.4 per cent); and

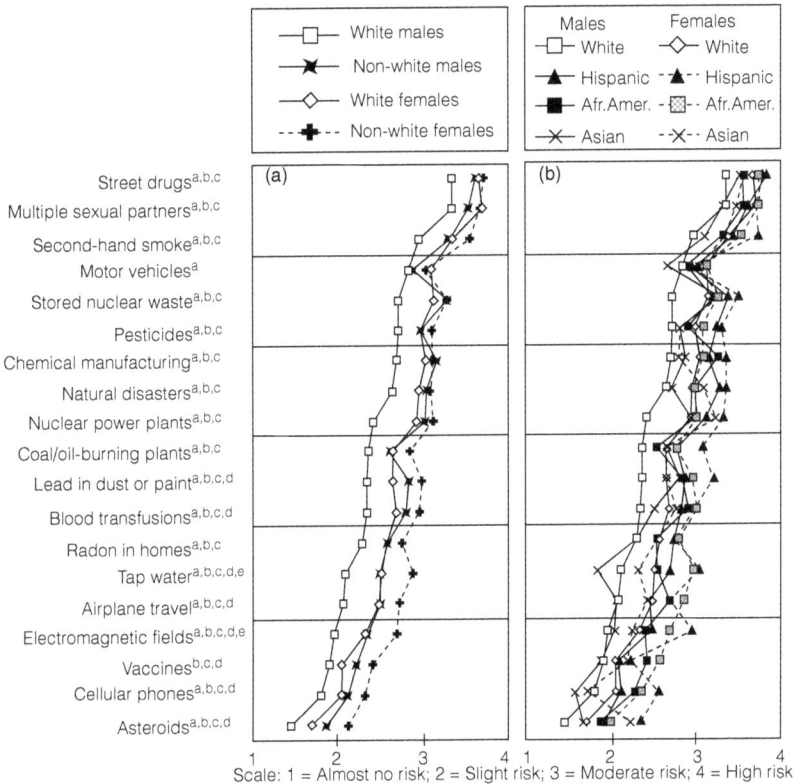

Figure 5.7 *Mean ratings of perceived risks to the American public for (a) white and non-white males and females (data weighted for race and gender, N = 859) and (b) white, Hispanic, African-American and Asian males and females (data not weighted, N = 1170)*

Source: 1997 National Risk Survey.

(b) disagree that farm products are less acceptable to the public when radioactive waste is transported past farms (59.9 vs. 32.0 per cent).

Other social and demographic variables

Since gender and race are correlated with other variables such as age, income, education and political orientation, we conducted regression analyses to see if gender and race were still significant predictors of overall risk perceptions after these other variables were

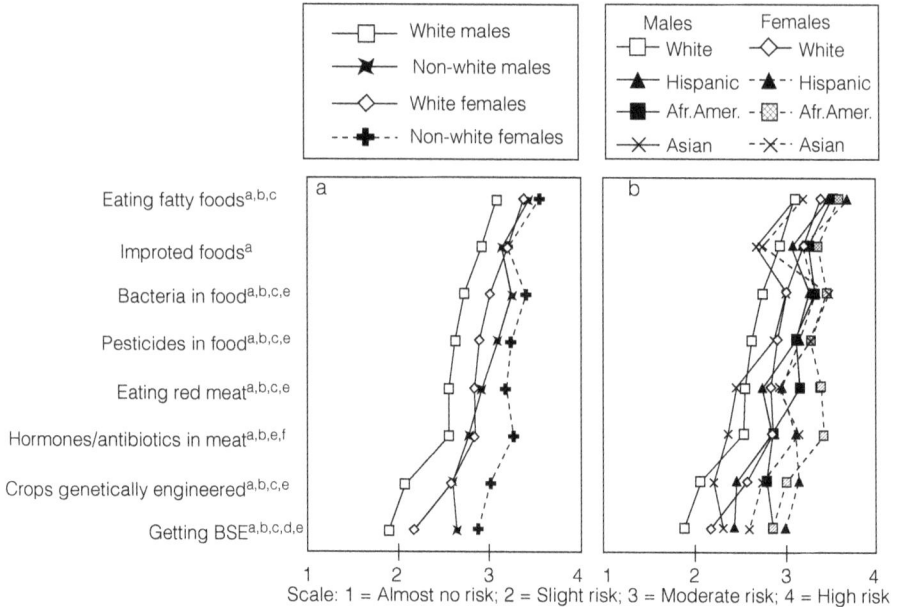

Figure 5.8 *Mean ratings of perceived risks to the American public for (a) white and non-white males and females (data weighted for race and gender, N = 859) and (b) white, Hispanic, African-American and Asian males and females (data not weighted, N = 1170)*

Source: 1997 National Risk Survey.

controlled statistically. The analyses showed that gender, race and 'white male' remained highly significant predictors of the hazard index, even when the other variables were controlled statistically.

Discussion

As expected, our survey revealed that men rate a wide range of hazards as lower in risk than do women. This result is consistent with gender differences found previously in many studies (for example, Brody, 1984; Steger and Witt, 1989; Gwartney-Gibbs and Lach, 1991; Gutteling and Wiegman, 1993; Stern et al, 1993; Flynn et al, 1994). Our survey also revealed that whites rate risks lower than do non-whites. Non-white females often gave the highest risk ratings. The group with the consistently lowest risk perceptions across a range of hazards was white males, a result replicating the earlier research by Flynn et al (1994). A few exceptions were found: compared with white males, Asian males gave lower risk ratings to six items (motor vehicles, tap water, cellular phones, imported food, eating red meat, and hormones/antibiotics in meat). Furthermore, we found sizeable differences between white males and other groups in socio-political attitudes. Compared with the rest of the sample, white males were more sympathetic with hierarchical, individualistic and anti-egalitarian views, more trusting of technology managers, less trusting of government, and less sensitive to potential stigmatization of communities from hazards. These positions suggest greater confidence in experts and less confidence in public-dominated social processes.

Our data support the view that differences cannot be explained entirely from a biological perspective. Explanations based on biological factors would require men and women to show discrepancies in their risk perceptions regardless of race. Clearly, this is not the case, at least for the environmental and health hazards studied here. Socio-political explanations are made more salient by our finding that compared with others, white males seem to promote individual achievement, initiative and self-regulation, trust in experts and risk proponents, and intolerance of community-based decision and regulation processes. As a consequence, we speculate that the world seems safer and hazardous activities seem more beneficial to white males than to other groups. For people who place less weight on the importance of individual achievement, and more weight on distributing wealth equitably and endorsing community-based regulation, many hazardous technologies and activities are viewed as posing great risks. Compared with white males, many females and non-white males tend to be in positions of less power and control, benefit less from many technologies and institutions, are more vulnerable to discrimination, and therefore see the world as more dangerous. Further investigation of the role of a broad array of socio-political factors in risk judgements is recommended to clarify gender and racial differences. It may be that the low-risk white males see different things at risk than do other citizens.

Although our data showed that white males stood apart from others, the data also revealed substantial heterogeneity in risk perceptions among the race and gender groups that comprised the 'other' category. That is, risk perceptions varied considerably across African-American, Asian and Hispanic males and females. The heterogeneity implies that risk perceptions depend importantly on the characteristics of the individuals facing the risk. Researchers should examine more closely the variation across individuals within these groups. Although resources did not permit finer analyses in the present study, Flynn et al (1994) found that about 30 per cent of their white males had extremely low risk perceptions. Their results suggest that race/gender groupings may be decomposed further into subgroups with particularly high or low risk perceptions.

Furthermore, while there is a tendency for gender and racial groups to align along social and political attitudes, it does not rule out the idea that socio-political attitudes also vary within groups. That is, perhaps some individuals are more prone than others to endorsing individualism or egalitarianism, regardless of gender or race. Some white males may be closer to typical Hispanic women in their views on the value of community-based regulation and equitable distribution of wealth. Some African-American women may be closer to typical white males in their endorsement of individual achievement and reward. Clearly, aligning particular socio-demographic groups with certain perspectives may overlook the possibility that there is variation across individuals regarding their socio-political attitudes and associated risk perceptions.

Viewing risk as a social construct dependent on characteristics of individuals raises important questions. What might be found in societies not dominated by white males?

Are women bigger risk-takers in matrilineal societies and are there some Asian or African countries where non-whites perceive lower risk than do whites? Furthermore, even within societies seemingly dominated by the white male perspective, there seem to be some hazardous activities for which women are willing to take the greatest risks (such as smoking). Can differences in worldviews, feelings of trust, and sensitivity to potential product and community stigmatization, explain risk perception differences across cultures and subcultures?

Furthermore, given that we found risk perceptions varied more for some hazards (for example, tap water, genetically engineered crops) than for other hazards (for example, stored nuclear waste, eating fatty foods), the type of hazard typically examined in risk perception research should be considered. Our findings of lower risk ratings by Asian males than by white males on several items suggested an interaction between characteristics of the hazard being rated and of the individual doing the rating. It seems possible that we may have found white women to have the lowest risk perceptions if household rather than technical risks were studied, for instance.

Research on the heterogeneity of risk perceptions across various sociocultural groups has important practical implications. Despite knowing very little about the risk perceptions and socio-political attitudes of minority groups, they are perhaps precisely the people who might be at greatest risk (and who might receive most benefit) from some activities or technologies. Without understanding the complex factors influencing perceptions, risk communicators and regulators cannot tailor their messages or policies appropriately to the target populations.

Overall, efforts to explain risk perception differences among people of different genders and races would be best addressed by incorporation of what we can learn about social roles, status differentiation, political values, and concepts of fairness. Attempts to realign risk perceptions according to the white male view of the world are likely to be unsuccessful. We expect that risk controversies can be better avoided and/or resolved when discussions and negotiations include the full spectrum of interested and affected parties. Some may fear such an approach may be more expensive because of the transaction costs. However, the current stalemates in managing numerous hazardous conditions from nuclear power to chemical contamination clean-ups show that social conflict has extremely high costs, economic and otherwise. Whether decision-sharing approaches that depend upon compromise and negotiation work as well or better than the current approaches is a question that can be answered with empirical research. Investigators should be careful, however, to pay close attention to the inevitability that just as risk perceptions are based on a wide range of value-laden judgements, views on how to define the economic and health benefits and costs will be disparate. Acknowledging the complexity of perspectives within an already diverse sample of US residents is the first step towards increasing the efficiency and effectiveness of social decision-making in general, and risk management and communication in particular.

Acknowledgements

This research was supported by a grant from the Annenberg Public Policy Center and the Annenberg School for Communication of the University of Pennsylvania and by the National

Science Foundation under Grant No. SBR-9631635. Our thanks to Kathleen Hall Jamieson of the Annenberg School for her support of this survey work, to Stephen Johnson and Professor Patricia Gwartney of the Oregon Survey Research Laboratory for assistance in design and administration of the survey reported here, and to Janet Douglas for her help with manuscript preparation.

References

Adler, R. and Pittle, D. (1984) Cajolery or command: are educated campaigns an adequate substitute for regulation?, *Yale Journal on Regulation*, 1, pp. 159–194.

Baird, B.N.R. (1986) Tolerance for environmental health risks: the influence of knowledge, benefits, voluntariness, and environmental attitudes, *Risk Analysis*, 6, pp. 425–435.

Barke, R.P., Jenkins-Smith, H. and Slovic, P. (1997) Risk perceptions of men and women scientists, *Social Science Quarterly*, 78, pp. 167–176.

Bettman, J.R., Payne, J.W. and Staelin, R. (1987) Cognitive considerations in designing effective labels for presenting risk information, in: K. Viscusi and W. Magat (Eds) *Learning about Risk: Evidence on the Economic Responses to Risk Information*, pp. 1–28 (Cambridge, MA, Harvard University Press).

Bord, R.J. and O'Connor, R.E. (1997) The gender gap in environmental attitudes: the case of perceived vulnerability to risk, *Social Science Quarterly*, 78, pp. 830–840.

Brody, C.J. (1984) Differences by sex in support for nuclear power, *Social Forces*, 63, pp. 209–228.

Cohen, B.L. (1983) *Before it's too Late: A Scientist's Case for Nuclear Energy* (New York, Plenum Press).

Cooper, R.S. (1994) A case study in the use of race and ethnicity in public health surveillance, *Public Health Reports*, 109, pp. 46–52.

Cross, F.B. (1998) Facts and values in risk assessment, *Reliability Engineering and System Safety*, 59, pp. 27–40.

Flynn, J., Slovic, P. and Mertz, C.K. (1994) Gender, race, and perception of environmental health risks, *Risk Analysis*, 14, pp. 1101–1108.

Gardner, G.T. and Gould, L.C. (1989) Public perceptions of the risks and benefits of technology, *Risk Analysis*, 9, pp. 225–242.

Gregory, R., Flynn, J. and Slovic, P. (1995) Technological stigma, *American Scientist*, 83, pp. 220–223.

Gutteling, J.M. and Wiegman, O. (1993) Gender-specific reactions to environmental hazards in The Netherlands, *Sex Roles*, 28, pp. 433–447.

Gwartney-Gibbs, P.A. and Lach, D.H. (1991) Sex differences in attitudes toward nuclear war, *Journal of Peace Research*, 28, pp. 161–176.

Kraus, N., Malmfors, T. and Slovic, P. (1992) Intuitive toxicology: expert and lay judgments of chemical risks, *Risk Analysis*, 12, pp. 215–232.

Kunreuther, H. and Slovic, P. (1996) Science, values, and risk, *The Annals of the American Academy of Political and Social Science*, 545, pp. 116–125.

Kuyper, H. and Vlek, C. (1984) Contrasting risk judgments among interest groups, *Acta Psychologica*, 56, pp. 205–218.

McNeil, B.J., Pauker, S.G., Sox, H.C., Jr. and Tversky, A. (1982) On the elicitation of preferences for alternative therapies, *The New England Journal of Medicine*, 306, pp. 1259–1262.

Slovic, P. (1997) Trust, emotion, sex, politics, and science: surveying the risk assessment battlefield, in: M.H. Bazerman, D.M. Messick, A.E. Tenbrunsel and K.A. Wade-Benzoni (Eds) *Environment, Ethics, and Behavior*, pp. 277–313 (San Francisco, New Lexington).

Slovic, P., Malmfors, T., Krewski, D., Mertz, C.K., Neil, N. and Bartlett, S. (1995) Intuitive toxicology. II. Expert and lay judgments of chemical risks in Canada, *Risk Analysis*, 15, pp. 661–675.

Slovic, P., Malmfors, T., Mertz, C.K., Neil, N. and Purchase, I.F.H. (1997) Evaluating chemical risks: results of a survey of the British Toxicology Society, *Human* and *Experimental Toxicology*, 16, pp. 289–304.

Steger, M.A. and Witt, S.L. (1989) Gender differences in environmental orientations: a comparison of publics and activists in Canada and the U.S., *The Western Political Quarterly*, 42, pp. 627–649.

Stern, P.C., Dietz, T. and Kalof, L. (1993) Value orientations, gender, and environmental concerns, *Environment and* Behavior, 24, pp. 322–348.

Svenson, O., Fischhoff, B. and MacGregor, D. (1985) Perceived driving safety and seatbelt usage, *Accident Analysis* and *Prevention*, 17, pp. 119–133.

Wandersman, A.H. and Hallman, W.K. (1993) Are people acting irrationally? Understanding public concerns about environmental threats, *American Psychologist*, 48, pp. 681–686.

6

How Safe is Safe Enough? A Psychometric Study of Attitudes towards Technological Risks and Benefits

Baruch Fischhoff, Paul Slovic, Sarah Lichtenstein, Stephen Read and Barbara Combs

Citizens of modern industrial societies are presently learning a harsh and discomforting lesson – that the benefits from technology must be paid for not only with money, but with lives. Whether it be ozone depletion and consequent skin cancer from the use of spray cans, birth defects induced by tranquilizing drugs, or radiation damage from nuclear energy, every technological advance carries some risks of adverse side-effects.

Reduction of risk typically entails reduction of benefit, thus posing serious dilemmas for society. With increasing frequency, policymakers are being required to 'weigh the benefits against the risks' when making decisions about technological enterprises. To do this, they have been turning to risk–benefit analysis, an offshoot of cost–benefit analysis that is still in its early stages of development, as the basic decision-making methodology for societal risk-taking (Fischhoff, 1977).

The basic question that risk–benefit analysis must answer is: Is this product (activity, technology) acceptably safe? Alternatively, how safe is safe enough?

There are, at present, two main approaches to answering these questions. One, the 'revealed preference' method advocated by Starr (1969), is based on the assumption that by trial and error society has arrived at an 'essentially optimum' balance between the risks and benefits associated with any activity. One may therefore use economic risk and benefit data from recent years to reveal patterns of acceptable risk–benefit trade-offs. Acceptable risk for a new technology is defined as that level of safety associated with ongoing activities having similar benefit to society. The present study investigates an alternative approach, called 'expressed preferences', which employs questionnaires to measure the public's attitudes towards the risks and benefits from various activities. Both approaches have their proponents and critics (e.g. Kates, 1975; Linnerooth, 1975; Otway and Cohen, 1975).

Starr (1969) illustrated the potential usefulness of revealed preferences by examining the relationship between risk and benefit across a number of common activities. His measure of risk for these hazardous activities was the statistical expectation of fatalities per hour of exposure to the activity. Benefit was assumed to be equal to the average amount of money spent on an activity by an individual participant, or alternatively, equal to the average contribution that the activity makes to a participant's annual income.

From this analysis, Starr derived what might be regarded as 'laws of acceptable risk'; namely, that:

- the acceptability of risk is roughly proportional to the third power (cube) of the benefits;
- the public seems willing to accept risks from voluntary activities (e.g. skiing) roughly 1000 times greater than it would tolerate from involuntary activities (e.g. food preservatives) that provide the same level of benefit;
- the acceptable level of risk is inversely related to the number of persons exposed to that risk; and
- the level of risk tolerated for voluntarily accepted hazards is quite similar to the level of risk from disease.

On the basis of this last observation, Starr (1969) conjectured that: 'The rate of death from disease appears to play, psychologically, a yardstick role in determining the acceptability of risk on a voluntary basis' (p1235). Figure 6.1 depicts the results of Starr's analysis in a *revealed preference* risk–benefit space.

Starr's approach has the advantage of dealing with public behaviour rather than with attitudes. It has, however, a number of serious drawbacks. First, it assumes that past behaviour is a valid indicator of present preferences. In Starr's words, 'The ... assumption is that historically revealed social preferences and costs are sufficiently enduring to permit their use for predictive purposes' (Starr, 1969, p1232). However, Starr and his colleagues have subsequently acknowledged that 'The societal value system

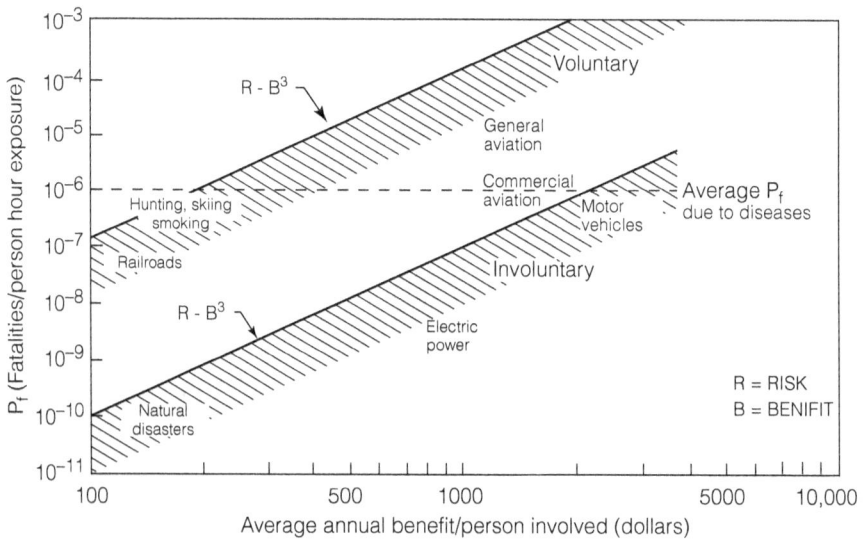

Figure 6.1 *Revealed risk–benefit relationships*

Source: taken from Starr, 1972

fluctuates with time, and the technological capability to follow fast-changing societal goals does not exist' (Starr et al, 1976, pp635–636). Second, Starr's approach 'does not serve to distinguish what is "best" for society from what is "traditionally acceptable" (Starr, 1969, p1232). What is accepted in the marketplace may not accurately reflect the public's safety preferences. Consider the automobile, for example. Unless the public really knows what is possible from a design standpoint and unless the automobile industry provides the public with a varied set of alternatives from which to choose, market behaviour may not indicate what 'a reflective individual would decide after thoughtful and intensive inquiry'. A revealed preference approach assumes that people not only have full information, but also can *use* that information optimally, an assumption which seems quite doubtful in the light of much research on the psychology of decision-making (Slovic et al, 1977). Finally, from a technical standpoint, Otway and Cohen (1975) have shown that the quantitative conclusions one derives from an analysis of the type Starr performed are extremely sensitive to the way in which measures of risk and benefit are computed from the historical data.

Although only a few questionnaire studies have specifically considered levels of acceptable risk (e.g. Maynard et al, 1976), or the value of a life at risk (Acton, 1973; Torrance, 1970), direct questioning procedures have been used to scale the perceived seriousness of a wide variety of natural and man-made hazards (see, for example, Wyler et al, 1968; Golant and Burton, 1969; Otway et al, 1975; Otway and Pahner, 1976; Lichtenstein et al, 1978).

Use of psychometric questionnaires has been criticized on the grounds that answers to hypothetical questions bear little relationship to actual behaviour.

> Time and time again, action has been found to contradict assertion. Since surveys always elicit some degree of strategic behaviour ('What do they want me to say?'), we would be better advised to observe what people choose under actual conditions (Rappaport, 1974, p4).

Such criticisms of psychometric studies appear to us to be overstated. Attitudes elicited in surveys often correlate highly with behaviour (Liska, 1975). Furthermore, they elicit present values rather than historical preferences.

The goal of the present study is to evaluate the usefulness of questionnaire techniques for investigating issues pertaining to risk–benefit trade-offs. Psychometric procedures were used to elicit quantitative judgements of perceived risk and benefit from various activities and technologies as well as judgements of acceptable risk levels. Participants in our experiment also judged the degree of voluntariness of each activity or technology. These judgements were used to determine whether people do, indeed, judge the acceptability of risks differently for voluntary and involuntary activities. The influence of other potential moderators of perceived and acceptable risk were also studied. These included familiarity with the risk, its perceived controllability, its potential for catastrophic (multiple-fatality) consequences, the immediacy of its consequences, and the extent of scientists' and the public's knowledge about its consequences. Various authors have speculated about the influence of these factors (e.g. Green, 1974; Otway, 1975; Lowrance, 1976; Otway and Pahner, 1976; Starr et al, 1976; Rowe, 1977), but little empirical data is available.

Method

Design

The participants in our study evaluated each of 30 different activities and technologies with regard to (1) its perceived benefit to society; (2) its perceived risk, (3) the acceptability of its current level of risk; and (4) its position on each of nine dimensions of risk. As tasks (1) and (2) were quite arduous and as we were interested in independent judgements of perceived risk and benefit, participants performed either tasks (1), (3) and (4) or tasks (2), (3) and (4). Which of the two combinations of tasks they faced was determined randomly. As part of their general instructions, participants were told, 'This is a difficult, if not impossible, task. Nevertheless, it is not unlike the task you face when you vote on legislation pertaining to nuclear power, handguns, or highway safety. One never has all the relevant information; ambiguities and uncertainties abound, yet some judgement must be made. The present task should be approached in the same spirit.'

Items

The 30 activities and technologies included the 8 items used by Starr (1969) and 22 others chosen to vary broadly in the quality and quantity of their associated risks and benefits. They appear in Table 6.1.

Tasks

Perceived benefit

People given this task were asked to 'consider all types of benefits: how many jobs are created, how much money is generated directly or indirectly (e.g., for swimming, consider the manufacture and sale of swimsuits), how much enjoyment is brought to people, how much of a contribution is made to the people's health and welfare, and so on'. Thus, they were told to give a global estimate of all benefits, both tangible and intangible. They were specifically told: 'Do not consider the costs of risks associated with these items. It is true, for example, that swimmers sometimes drown. But evaluating such risks and costs is not your present job. Your job is to assess the *gross benefits*, not the net benefits which remain after the costs and risks are subtracted out. Remember that a beneficial activity affecting few people will have less gross benefit than a beneficial activity affecting many people. If you need to think of a time period during which the benefits accrue, think of a whole year – the total value to society from each item during one year.'

In order to make the evaluation task as easy as possible, each activity appeared on a 3 × 5 inch card. Participants were told first to study the items individually, thinking of the benefits accruing from each; then to order them from least to most beneficial; and finally, to assign numerical benefit values by giving a rating of 10 to the least beneficial and making the other ratings accordingly. They were also given additional suggestions, clarifications and encouragement to do as accurate a job as possible. For example, they were told 'a rating of 12 indicates that the item is 1.2 times as beneficial as the least beneficial item (i.e., 20% more beneficial). A rating of 200 means that the item is 20 times as beneficial as the least beneficial item, to which you assigned a

10 ... Double-check your ratings to make certain that they are consistent. For example, if one activity is rated 50 and a second 100, the second item should seem twice as beneficial as the first. Adjust the numbers until you feel that they are right for you.'

Perceived risk

Participants in this task (who, it will be remembered, did not judge perceived benefit) were told to 'consider the risk of dying as a consequence of this activity or technology. For example, use of electricity carries the risk of electrocution. It also entails risk for miners who produce the coal that generates electricity. Motor vehicles entail risk for drivers, passengers, bicyclists and pedestrians, etc.' They were asked to order and rate these activities for risk with instructions that paralleled the instructions for the perceived benefit task, giving a rating of 10 to the least risky item and scaling the other items accordingly.

Note

These measures of risk and benefit differ from Starr's in several respects other than their source in attitudes rather than in behaviour. Our subjects were asked to evaluate total risk per year to participants, not risk per hour of exposure, the unit of measurement used by Starr (1969). Several considerations motivated this change of unit, the most important of which is that the definition of 'hour of exposure' is extremely equivocal for some items (e.g. handguns, pesticides). Excluding activities and technologies for which such measurement is problematic would introduce a systematic bias into our sample of items. Although the shape or magnitude of the relationship may vary with choice of measure, there is no a priori reason why people's historical risk–benefit trade-offs are best revealed with one particular measure of risk. Starr, himself (1972, p28), apparently believed that total risk per year was a more appropriate measure but rejected it because of measurement difficulties and because of his belief that 'the hour of exposure unit [is] more closely related to the individual's intuitive process in choosing an activity than a year of exposure would be'. In any case, he found that use of either unit 'gave substantially similar results'.

A second difference in unit is that we have considered *total* benefit and risk to society rather than *average* benefit and risk per person involved. For activities and technologies whose risks and/or benefits are shared by all members of society, this change is inconsequential. For the others, our risk and benefit measures should be weighted by the proportion of individuals participating in the activity in order to achieve strict comparability with Starr's measures.

A third difference from Starr is that relying on our participants' ability to consider all types of benefits relieved us of the restriction which Start imposed upon himself to consider only benefits to which a dollar value could be readily assigned.

Risk adjustment factor

After rating risks or benefits, both groups of participants were asked to judge the acceptability of the level of risk currently associated with each item. The instructions included the following:

> This is not the ideal risk. Ideally, the risks should be zero. The acceptable level is a level which is 'good enough,' where 'good enough' means you think that the advantages of increased safety are not worth the costs of reducing

risk by restricting or otherwise altering the activity. For example, we can make drugs 'safer' by restricting their potency; cars can be made safer at a cost, by improving their construction or requiring regular safety inspection; we may, or may not, feel restrictions are necessary.

If an activity's present level of risk is acceptable, no special action need be taken to increase its safety. If its riskiness is unacceptably high, *serious action*, such as legislation to restrict its practice, should be taken. On the other hand, there may be some activities or technologies that you believe are currently safer than the acceptable level of risk. For these activities, the risk of death could be higher than it is now before society would have to take serious action.

On their answer sheets, participants were provided with three columns labelled: (a) 'Could be riskier: it would be acceptable if it were – times riskier'; (b) 'It is presently acceptable'; and (c) 'Too risky: to be acceptable, it would have to be – times safer'. These risk adjustment factors were used to establish levels of acceptable risk.

Rating scales

As their final task, participants were asked to rate each activity or technology on nine seven-point scales, each of which represented a dimension which has been hypothesized to influence perceptions of actual or acceptable risk (e.g. Lowrance, 1976). These scales, in the order and wording in which they were described, were:

1 Voluntariness of risk: Do people get into these risky situations voluntarily? If for a single item some of the risks are voluntarily undertaken and some are not, mark an appropriate spot towards the centre of the scale. (The scale was labelled: 1 = voluntary; 7 = involuntary.)
2 Immediacy of effect: To what extent is the risk of death immediate – or is death likely to occur at some later time? (1 = immediate; 7 = delayed.)
3 Knowledge about risk: To what extent are the risks known precisely by the persons who are exposed to those risks? (1 = known precisely; 7 = not known.)
4 Knowledge about risk: To what extent are the risks known to science? (1 = known precisely; 7 = not known.)
5 Control over risk: If you are exposed to the risk of each activity or technology, to what extent can you, by personal skill or diligence, avoid death while engaging in the activity? (1 = uncontrollable; 7 = controllable.)
6 Newness: Are these risks new, novel ones or old, familiar ones? (1 = new; 7 = old.)
7 Chronic–catastrophic: Is this a risk that kills people one at a time (chronic risk) or a risk that kills large numbers of people at once (catastrophic risk)? (1 = chronic; 7 = catastrophic.)
8 Common–dread: Is this a risk that people have learned to live with and can think about reasonably calmly, or is it one that people have great dread for – on the level of a gut reaction? (1 = common; 7 = dread.)
9 Severity of consequences: When the risk from the activity is realized in the form of a mishap or illness, how likely is it that the consequence will be fatal? (1 = certain

not to be fatal; 7 = certain to be fatal.) Green (1974) has referred to this as the 'sporting chance' factor.

Participants rated all 30 activities and technologies on each scale before proceeding to the next.

Participants

Members of the Eugene, Oregon, League of Women Voters and their spouses were asked to participate in the study in return for a contribution to the organization's treasury. In all, 76 individuals (52 women and 24 men) returned completed, anonymous questionnaires. Spouses received the same set of questionnaires and were instructed not to discuss the tasks until they were completed. They indicated having spent an average of two hours on the three tasks. Although League members and spouses are by no means representative of all American adults, they do constitute an extremely thoughtful, articulate and influential group of private citizens. If there are systematic relationships between people's judgements of risk and benefit, they should be found in these participants' responses. While the particular relationships found here might differ from those found with other populations, the opinions of League members may be quite similar to those of many of the private citizens most heavily engaged in the public policymaking process.

Results

Perceived risk and benefit

Because arithmetic means tend to be unduly influenced by occasional extreme values, geometric means were used to describe the data. They are calculated by taking the log of each score, finding the arithmetic mean of those logs and then finding the antilog of the arithmetic mean. Columns 1 and 2 of Table 6.1 present the geometric means of all risk and benefit judgements for each item.

Many of the substantive results in this table appear to be accurate reflections of the attitudes of a generally liberal, environmentally minded group, the League of Women Voters. Especially interesting are the low benefit attributed to food colouring, spray cans and handguns, and the great difference between the evaluations of non-nuclear and nuclear electric power. Although these specific judgements are quite revealing, the main purpose of this study was not to poll the attitudes of any particular group of citizens, but to examine the relationships between perceived benefit and risk.

Figure 6.2 presents these judgements in a perceived risk–benefit space analogous to Starr's revealed risk–benefit space (Figure 6.1). In general, perceived risk *declined* slightly with overall benefit, motor vehicles being the only item which rates high on both scales. The overall best-fit line had a negative slope $(\bar{y} = -0.19x + 107.6; r = -0.20; p>0.25)$. The axes in Starr's Figure 6.1 are logarithmic. Replotting our data in Figure 6.2 using log geometric means left the relationship unchanged $(y = -0.18x + 2.18; r = -0.23)$.

Table 6.1 *Mean judgements of risk and benefit from 30 activities and technologies*

Activity or technology	Perceived benefit	Perceived risk	Risk adjustment factor[a]		Acceptable level of risk[b]	
	(Geometric mean)		Risk subjects	Benefit subjects	Risk subjects	Benefit subjects
			(Geometric mean)			
1. Alcoholic beverages	41	161	4.7	4.2	34	38
2. Bicycles	82	65	1.6	1.4	41	46
3. Commercial aviation	130	52	1.2	1.4	43	37
4. Contraceptives	113	50	2.1	1.9	24	26
5. Electric power[c]	274	52	1.2	0.9	43	58
6. Fire fighting	178	92	1.2	1.0	77	92
7. Food colouring	16	31	2.7	3.4	11	9
8. Food preservatives	44	36	2.6	2.8	14	13
9. General (private) aviation	53	114	2.3	1.8	50	63
10. Handguns	14	220	17.1	17.5	13	13
11. High school and college football	35	37	1.8	1.6	21	23
12. Home appliances	133	25	1.1	1.0	23	25
13. Hunting	30	82	2.9	2.1	28	39
14. Large construction (dams, bridges, etc.)	142	91	2.0	1.4	46	65
15. Motorcycles	29	176	5.1	5.5	35	32
16. Motor vehicles	187	247	7.3	4.9	34	50
17. Mountain climbing	28	68	1.1	0.9	62	76
18. Nuclear power	52	250	32.2	25.9	8	10
19. Pesticides	87	105	10.5	8.5	10	12
20. Power mowers	30	29	1.7	1.3	17	22
21. Police work	178	111	2.3	1.3	48	85
22. Prescription antibiotics	209	30	1.4	1.2	21	25
23. Railroads	185	37	1.4	1.1	26	34
24. Skiing	38	45	1.1	1.0	41	45
25. Smoking	20	189	15.2	15.3	12	12
26. Spray cans	17	73	8.6	6.9	8	11
27. Surgery	164	104	2.2	1.6	47	65
28. Swimming	68	52	1.2	0.9	43	58
29. Vaccinations	194	17	1.0	0.7	17	24
30. X-rays	156	45	2.1	1.3	21	35
All responses	69	69	2.7	2.2		
Coefficient of concordance	0.77	0.50	0.50	0.50		

[a] Values greater than one mean that the item should be safer; values less than one mean that the item could be riskier.

[b] Acceptable levels of risk were calculated by dividing column 2 by columns 3 and 4 respectively.

[c] Non-nuclear.

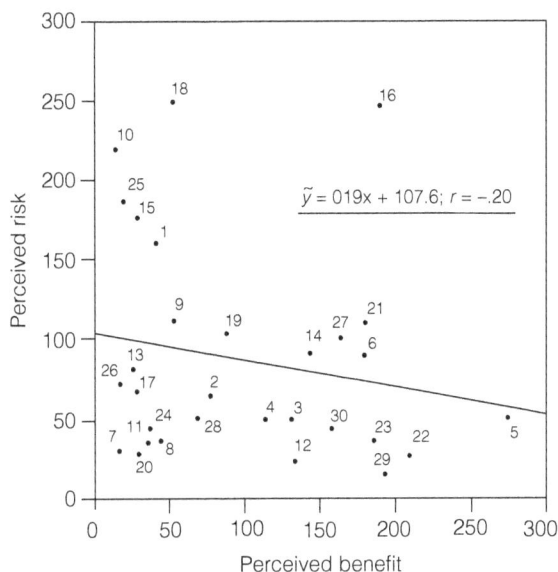

Figure 6.2 *Relationship between perceived risk and perceived benefit*

Examination of columns 1 and 2 in Table 6.1 provides insight into the nature of the perceived risk–benefit relationship. Society presently tolerates a number of activities that our participants rated as having very low benefit and very high risk (e.g. alcoholic beverages, handguns, motorcycles, smoking) as well as a number of activities perceived to have great benefit and relatively low risk (e.g. prescription antibiotics, railroads, vaccinations).

Could these differences between our results and Starr's be artefacts of technical differences between our research procedures? In particular, are they due to our use of additional technologies and different units of measurement? We will consider these factors in turn. We can, however, make no statement about the degree to which our results depend on the participant population studied.

Different items

Figure 6.3 compares the perceived (lower figure) and revealed (upper figure) risk–benefit spaces for the 8 of our 30 items used also by Starr (1969). The computed space is Otway and Cohen's (1975) recalculation of Starr's original data. Although the scale differences make it difficult to compare the two figures directly, it is clear that both the nature of the relationship and the relative costs and benefits of the various items were quite different. For this subset, as for the full set of items, risk decreased somewhat with benefit in the perceived space.

Different units

Allowing people to consider all benefits accruing from an activity, not just those readily expressed in dollars, may have been responsible for some of the difference between our

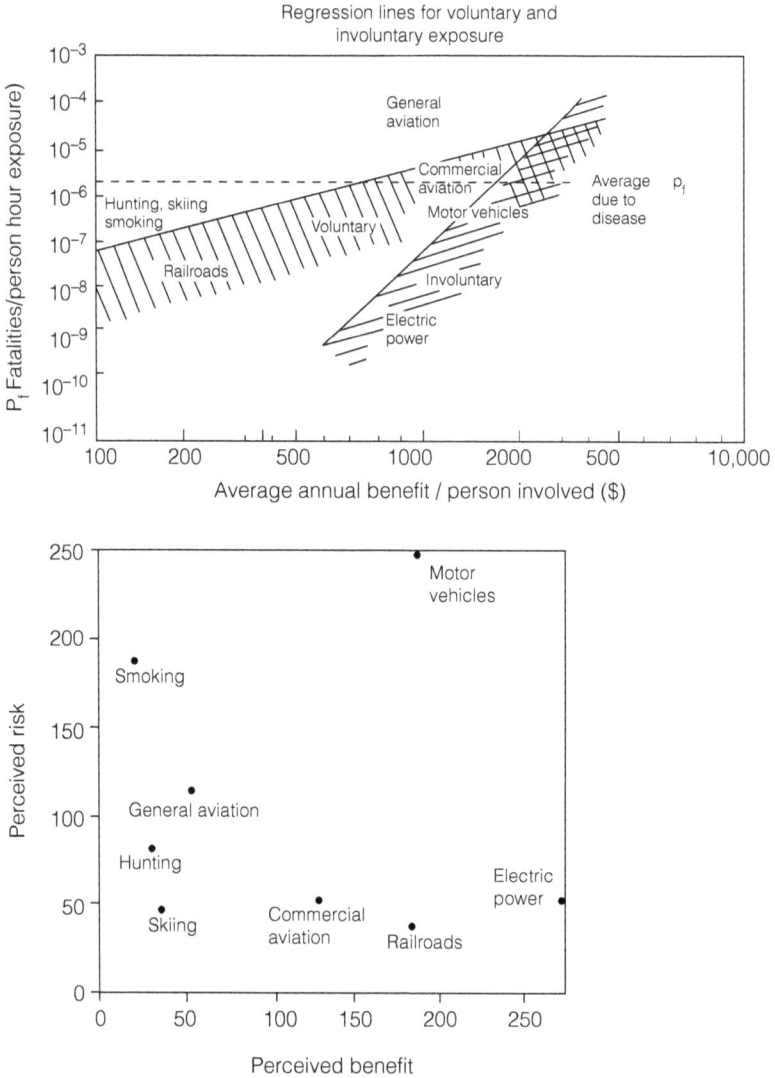

Figure 6.3 *Relationship between perceived risk and perceived benefit for the items studied by Starr (1969) and Otway and Cohen (1975) (above) and the present subjects (below)*

results and Starr's. For example, railroads and electric power appear to be relatively more beneficial in the perceived space, perhaps reflecting the not-readily quantifiable environmental benefits of the former and the 'great flexibility in patterns of living' (Starr, 1972, p29) conferred by the latter. Here, we believe that there are advantages to using the comprehensive measure of benefit.

Another difference between our units of measurement and Starr's was that we considered total risk and benefit to society, not just consequences per person exposed.

25 of the 30 activities and technologies used in this study have risks and/or benefits for all or almost all members of society. For these, use of risk and benefit per participant (Starr's measure) would produce a figure whose pattern is identical to that in Figure 6.2 ($\bar{y}$ = −0.20x + 109.7; r = −0.21 without those items, compared to $\bar{y}$ = −0.19x + 107.6; r = −0.20 with them).

Finally, we have argued that the unit 'risk per year' exposure used here is equal or superior to the unit 'risk per hour' exposure used by Starr. Whether this change of unit was responsible for differences in our results is a topic for future research. Starr reported that the change made little difference in his computations, although that need not also be the case with subjective estimates.

Risk adjustment factor

Columns 3 and 4 of Table 6.1 present the geometric means of our participants' judgements of the acceptability of the risk levels associated with the various items. As indicated by the preponderance of items for which the mean adjustment factor is greater than one, people thought that most items should be made safer; this occurred despite instructions emphasizing that such a rating indicated the need for serious societal action. Of the 2280 acceptability judgements, roughly half indicated that the item in question was too risky; 40 per cent indicated that its current risk level was appropriate and 10 per cent indicated that it could be riskier still. There were, however, relatively few items which people believed should be made *much* safer, namely alcoholic beverages, handguns, motorcycles, motor vehicles, nuclear power, pesticides, smoking and spray cans.

Perceived risk was correlated 0.75 and 0.66 with risk adjustment factor ratings for the risk and benefit groups, respectively. Thus, both groups felt that the higher the risk, the more it should be reduced.

Participants in our study made these risk adjustment ratings after ordering and rating the 30 items for either perceived benefits or perceived risks. Comparing columns 3 and 4 shows that for 24 of the 30 items, the current risk level was judged more acceptable (less in need of change) by those people who had previously considered benefits than by those who had previously dwelt on risks. Thus, the way in which activities and technologies are considered may affect the acceptability of their risk levels.

A 'level of acceptable risk' was determined for each item by dividing its perceived risk (column 2 of Table 6.1) by the geometric mean adjustment factor (column 3 or 4 of Table 6.1). This was done separately for people who had previously judged risk first and those who had judged benefit first. The results are shown in columns 5 and 6 of Table 6.1. For example, for alcoholic beverages, the level of acceptable risk was 161/4.7 = 34.2 for perceived risk participants and 161/4.2 = 38.3 for perceived benefit participants.

Figure 6.4 compares each item's acceptable risk level with its perceived benefit. It shows what societal risk–benefit trade-offs would be if current risk levels were adjusted to acceptable levels. In this figure, the level of acceptable risk increased with the level of perceived benefit, although the relationship was not strong. According to this inferred relationship, participants in our study believed that more risk should be tolerated with more beneficial activities.

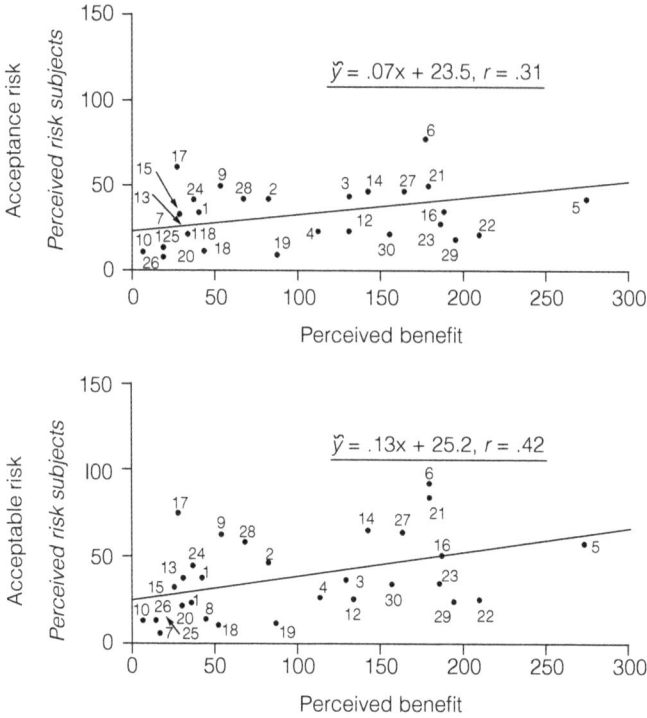

Figure 6.4 *Relationship between perceived benefit and acceptable risk*

Inter-participant agreement

In order to assess how well participants agreed with one another in their judgements, Kendall's coefficient of concordance was computed for each task. This index reflects the average rank-order correlation between the judgements of all pairs of participants (Siegel, 1956). The values shown at the bottom of Table 6.1 are moderate to high (all being significantly different from zero at $p < 0.001$) and indicate that people substantially agreed in their rankings, particularly when they evaluated benefits (column 1).

Rating scales

Table 6.2 presents the arithmetic mean ratings of the nine risk characteristics for the 30 items. Since people in the perceived risk and perceived benefit groups produced very similar judgements (difference in means less than 1.00 in almost every case), their responses were pooled. There was also considerable agreement among people within each of the two groups, as reflected by the moderately high coefficients of concordance.

Perceived risk and benefit

Correlations between the nine risk characteristics and perceived risk and benefit are shown in Table 6.3. None of the risk characteristics correlated significantly with perceived benefit (column 1). Perceived risk was found to correlate with dread and severity but not with any of the other characteristics.

Starr (1969) hypothesized that the trade-off between risk and benefit is mediated by degree of voluntariness. If so, we would expect a tendency for voluntary activities to lie above the common regression line shown in Figure 6.2 and involuntary activities to lie below it. This was not the case. In Figure 6.5, the 30 items are dichotomized into the 15 most and 15 least voluntary. Regression lines for the voluntary and involuntary subsets were virtually identical.

If voluntariness is conceptualized as a continuous rather than a dichotomous variable, then according to Starr's hypothesis an item lying high above the common regression line should be very voluntary (have a rating near 1); an item lying far below that line should be very involuntary (have a rating near 7). Let us define a deviation score as the signed vertical distance between each point in the risk–benefit space and the regression line; positive deviation scores belong to points above the line. These deviation scores reflect the variance in the risk scores that cannot be accounted for by the benefit scores. The correlation between these deviation scores and the voluntariness ratings indicates the proportion of this unexplained variance which can be accounted for by the voluntariness measure. Starr's hypothesis suggests that this correlation would be negative (high positive deviations going with low voluntariness ratings). As can be seen from column 3 of Table 6.3, this was not the case *(r = 0.13)*.

However, two other risk characteristics, commonness and severity, did correlate with the deviations from the regression line. If we drew a figure for each of these scales like Figure 6.5, we would find two roughly parallel regression lines, one lying above the other. With the scale common/dread, we would find that items whose consequences are more dread tend to have higher perceived risk, at all levels of benefit, than items with more common consequences. Similarly, the line for the more severe (certain to be fatal) risks would lie above the line for less severe risks.

Acceptable risk

The fact that *perceived* risk was unrelated to voluntariness does not necessarily contradict Starr's claim that the voluntary nature of an activity influences its *acceptable* risk level. Table 6.4 presents the correlations between each risk characteristic and various aspects of acceptability. The significant correlations in the first column indicate that activities with the most dread and certainly fatal consequences were deemed most in need of risk reduction. The significant correlations in the second column show that if risks were adjusted to an acceptable level, then higher risk levels would be tolerated for old, voluntary activities with well known and immediate consequences. The correlations in the third column show the extent to which each qualitative risk characteristic accounts for variance in acceptable risk unexplained by perceived benefit. These correlations were significant for each of the first six characteristics. Thus, for any given level of benefit, greater risk was tolerated if that risk was voluntary, immediate, known precisely, controllable and familiar.

The relationship between voluntariness and acceptable risk level is further illustrated in Figure 6.6 which shows the separate regression lines for the 15 most and least voluntary activities and technologies. Figure 6.6 clearly shows a double

Table 6.2 *Mean ratings for nine characteristics of risk*

	Voluntariness 1 = voluntary	Immediacy 1 = immediate	Known to exposed 1 = precisely	Known to science 1 = precisely
1. Alcoholic beverages	2.10	5.34	3.77	1.98
2. Bicycles	1.90	2.82	3.27	2.80
3. Commercial aviation	2.80	1.85	3.24	2.12
4. Contraceptives	2.74	5.69	4.66	3.88
5. Electric power (non-nuclear)	4.40	2.82	3.98	2.68
6. Fire fighting	2.40	2.33	1.98	2.25
7. Food colouring	5.86	6.26	6.40	4.77
8. Food preservatives	5.65	6.18	6.39	4.76
9. General aviation	2.20	1.66	2.96	2.60
10. Handguns	3.42	1.65	2.64	2.41
11. H. S. and college football	1.90	3.52	3.66	3.11
12. Home appliances	3.61	2.97	4.47	2.90
13. Hunting	2.01	1.66	2.62	2.64
14. Large construction	3.07	2.23	2.77	2.51
15. Motorcycles	1.87	1.76	2.69	2.17
16. Motor vehicles	4.04	2.33	3.14	2.31
17. Mountain climbing	1.15	1.78	1.83	2.49
18. Nuclear power	6.51	5.08	5.85	4.83
19. Pesticides	5.77	5.57	5.50	4.41
20. Power mowers	2.23	2.99	3.31	2.60
21. Police work	2.44	2.14	2.05	2.25
22. Prescription antibiotics	4.44	4.33	5.40	3.91
23. Railroads	3.42	2.91	3.66	2.68
24. Skiing	1.28	2.45	2.47	2.51
25. Smoking	1.85	6.11	2.86	2.15
26. Spray cans	3.80	6.06	5.43	4.16
27. Surgery	4.28	2.71	3.84	2.86
28. Swimming	1.64	1.76	2.87	2.68
29. Vaccinations	3.82	3.71	4.84	2.82
30. X-rays	4.38	6.15	5.05	3.28
$\bar{X}$	3.24	3.49	3.78	2.98
σ	1.47	1.70	1.33	0.87
Coefficient of concordance — Benefit Ss	0.59	0.59	0.53	0.30
Risk Ss	0.62	0.66	0.61	0.35

standard in risk tolerance for voluntary and involuntary activities, like that found by Starr in Figure 6.1. Note, however, that the *y*-axis in Figure 6.6 is 'acceptable risk level' and not 'current risk level'. The participants in our study believed that a double standard would be appropriate if risk levels were made acceptable. This was also

Controllability 1 = can't be controlled	Newness 1 =new	Chronic–catastrophic 1 = chronic	Common–dread 1 = common	Severity of consequences 1 = certain not to be fatal
5.57	6.61	1.79	1.92	4.40
4.99	5.19	1.30	1.74	3.77
2.18	4.24	6.09	3.39	5.72
3.11	2.25	1.49	3.14	4.08
4.25	5.09	2.66	1.72	4.52
4.03	6.01	2.84	2.62	4.42
2.70	2.66	2.82	3.24	3.59
2.70	2.73	2.82	3.32	3.66
3.99	4.08	3.40	3.15	5.63
4.05	5.69	2.10	4.40	5.67
4.15	4.78	1.40	1.95	3.15
4.85	4.39	1.38	1.43	3.08
4.45	6.14	1.59	2.79	4.91
3.91	5.04	3.04	2.61	4.77
4.08	4.31	1.59	3.02	5.19
4.19	4.73	3.28	3.04	4.57
4.98	5.63	1.32	2.57	4.80
1.36	1.35	6.43	6.42	5.98
2.14	2.22	4.75	5.21	4.87
5.13	3.70	1.16	1.75	2.75
3.76	5.50	2.07	3.05	4.35
2.77	2.87	2.35	2.19	3.82
3.22	5.49	4.49	1.75	3.60
4.73	4.69	1.06	1.92	3.15
4.43	5.04	1.68	2.89	5.01
3.60	1.89	3.82	3.62	4.27
2.39	4.95	1.14	4.04	4.68
5.17	6.50	1.16	1.89	4.78
2.53	4.50	1.88	2.03	3.62
2.37	4.02	1.99	2.58	4.20
3.73	4.41	2.50	2.85	4.37
I.10	1.41	1.43	1.12	0.85
0.40	0.59	0.58	0.45	0.45
0.42	0.65	0.57	0.47	0.50

reflected in the large negative correlation between voluntariness scores and deviations from the perceived benefit-acceptable risk regression line noted above. Figures like Figure 6.6 would show a similar double standard for each of the first six risk characteristics in Table 6.4.

Table 6.3 *Correlations between rating scales and perceived risk and benefit*

Scale	Perceived benefit	Perceived risk	Deviations from perceived benefit–perceived risk regression line[a]
Voluntariness (1 = voluntary)	0.24	0.08	0.13
Immediacy (1 = immediate)	−0.15	−0.07	−0.11
Known to exposed (1 = known precisely)	0.04	−0.20	−0.22
Known to science (1 = known precisely)	−0.16	−0.17	−0.21
Controllability (1 = uncontrollable)	−0.29	−0.04	−0.06
Newness (1 = new)	0.14	0.05	0.08
Chronic (1 = chronic)	0.12	0.30	0.29
Common/dread (1 = common)	−0.26	0.64*	0.54*
Severity of consequences (1 = certain not to be fatal)	−0.10	0.67*	0.66*

[a] as shown in Figure 6.2.
* $p < 0.001$.

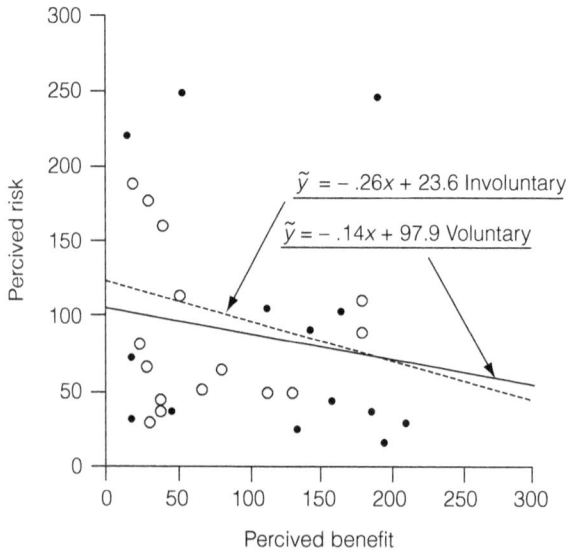

Figure 6.5 *Relationship between perceived risk and perceived benefit for voluntary (circled) and involuntary hazards*

Table 6.4 *Correlation between rating scales and measures of acceptable risk (perceived risk and perceived benefit groups combined)*

Scale	Risk adjustment factor	Level of acceptable risk[a]	Deviations from perceived benefit–level of acceptable risk regression line[b]
Voluntariness (1 = voluntary)	0.38*	−0.47†	−0.64‡
Immediacy (1 = immediate)	0.28	−0.64‡	−0.64‡
Known to exposed (1 = known precisely)	0.21	−0.68‡	−0.75‡
Known to science (1 = known precisely)	0.29	−0.57‡	−0.58‡
Controllability (1 = uncontrollable)	−0.30	0.40*	0.48†
Newness (1 = new)	−0.34	0.60‡	0.60‡
Chronic (1 = chronic)	0.45*	0.22	−0.25
Common/dread (1 = common)	0.75‡	−0.29	−0.24
Severity of consequences (1 = certain not to be fatal)	0.54‡	0.17	0.22

* $p < 0.05$.   † $p < 0.01$.   ‡ $p < 0.001$.
[a] Perceived risk divided by risk adjustment factor.
[b] As shown in Figure 6.3.

Factor analysis of risk characteristics

Ratings of the various task characteristics tended to be highly intercorrelated, as shown in Table 6.5. For example, risks faced voluntarily tended to be known to the exposed individual ($r = 0.83$); new risks tended to be judged less controllable ($r = 0.64$), etc. The intercorrelations were sufficiently high to suggest that they might be explained by a few basic dimensions of risk underlying the nine characteristics. In order to identify such underlying dimensions, we conducted principal components factor analyses (Rummel, 1970) for risk participants and for benefits participants, separately. The unrotated factor loadings for the two groups were so similiar (the mean absolute difference between loadings was 0.05) that they were averaged (Table 6.6). A varimax rotation was applied to these factors, but it produced no improvement in interpretability and will not be discussed.

Two orthogonal factors appeared sufficient to account for the intercorrelations shown in Table 6.5. The factor loadings shown in Table 6.6 indicate the degree to which each risk characteristic correlated with each of the two underlying factors. The first factor correlated highly with all characteristics except severity of consequences. The

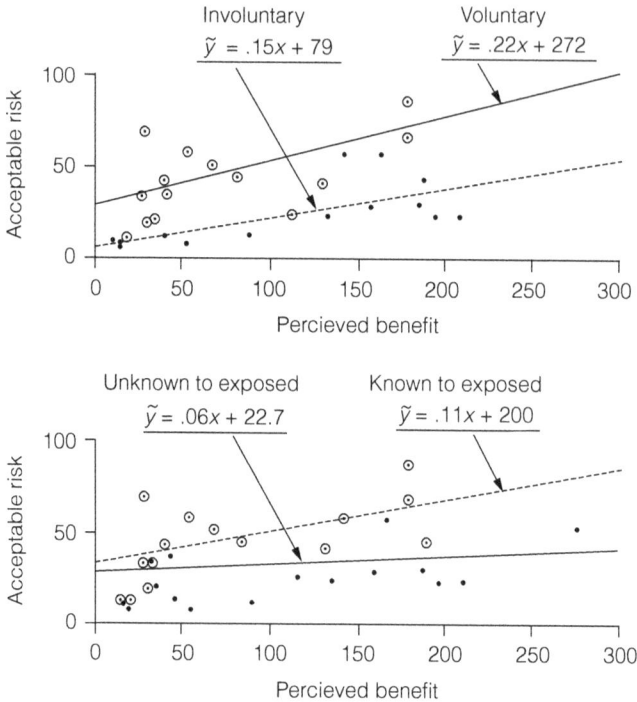

Figure 6.6 *Relationship between perceived benefit and acceptable risk for voluntary (circled)–involuntary and known (circled)–unknown items*

second factor was associated with severity of consequences and, to a lesser extent, with common/dread and chronic/catastrophic. The communality index in Table 6.6 reflects the extent to which the two factors accounted for each of the ratings. The communalities were high, indicating that this two-factor solution did a good job of representing the ratings for the nine scales.

Just as each of the 30 items had a (mean) score on each of the nine risk characteristics, we can obtain a score for each item on each factor. These factor scores enable us to plot the 30 items in the space defined by the two factors. As might be expected from the similarity of the factor solutions for risk and for benefit participants, these plots were very similar for the two groups. The mean absolute difference between factor scores was 0.10 for Factor 1 and 0.18 for Factor 2. The correlations between factor scores for the two groups were 0.99 for Factor 1 and 0.98 for Factor 2. Given the extraordinary similarity of the plots for these two independent groups, their factor scores were averaged. Figure 6.7 plots these scores for the 30 items.

This plot helps clarify the nature of the two factors. The upper extreme of Factor 1 was associated with new, involuntary, highly technological items, which have delayed consequences for masses of people. Items low on the first factor were familiar, voluntary activities with immediate consequences at the individual level. High scores (right-hand

Table 6.5 *Rating scale intercorrelations*[a]

Scale		Vol.	Immed.	Known to Exposed	Known to Science	Control	New	Chronic	Common	Severity
Voluntariness (1 = voluntary)			0.54*	0.83*	0.75*	-0.76*	-0.65*	0.55*	0.55*	0.06
Immediacy (1 = immediate)				0.78*	0.68*	-0.42	-0.63*	0.16	0.25	-0.22
Known to exposed (1 = known precisely)					0.87*	-0.63*	-0.78*	0.35	0.31	-0.22
Known to science (1 = known precisely)						-0.60*	-0.83*	0.35	0.46	-0.14
Controllability (1 = uncontrollable)							0.64*	-0.63*	-0.64*	-0.24
Newness (1 = new)								-0.46	-0.53*	0.05
Chronic (1 = chronic)									0.60*	0.46
Common (1 = common)										0.63*
Severity of consequences (1 = certain not to be fatal)										

[a] These correlations were computed separately for the risk and benefits group and then averaged (using Fisher's Z transformation).

* $p < 0.001$.

Table 6.6 *Factor loadings across nine risk characteristics (risk and benefit subjects averaged)*

Scale	Vol.	Immed.	Exposed	Science	Known to Control	Known to New	Chronic	Common	Severity	λ	Percentage of variance accounted for
Factor 1	0.89	0.70	0.88	0.88	−0.83	−0.87	0.62	0.67	0.11	5.30	58.9
Factor 2	0.03	−0.45	−0.39	−0.28	−0.24	0.14	0.55	0.60	0.91	1.90	21.1
Communality	0.79	0.69	0.93	0.86	0.75	0.78	0.69	0.81	0.84		

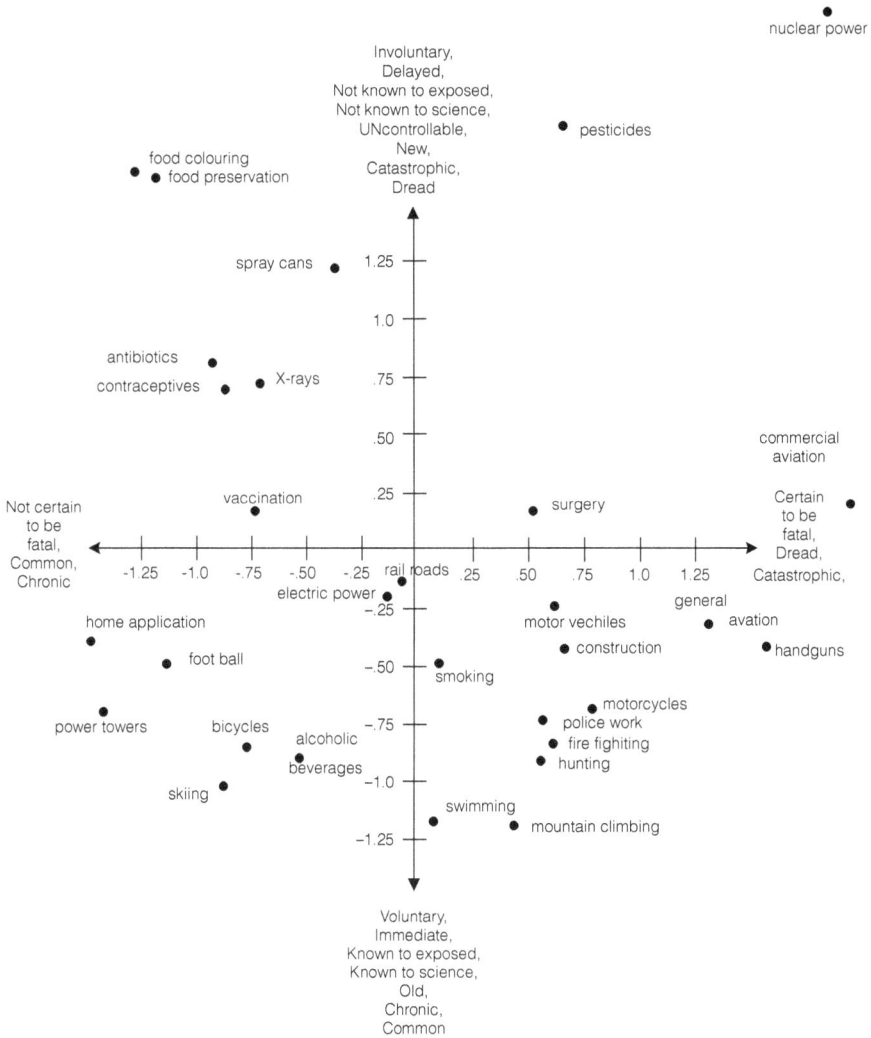

Figure 6.7 *Location of risk items within the two-factor space*

side) on Factor 2 were associated with events whose consequences are certain to be fatal (often for large numbers of people) should something go wrong. It seems appropriate to label Factors 1 and 2 as 'Technological Risk' and 'Severity', respectively.

One of the more remarkable features of this factor space was the unique position (isolation) of nuclear power. Clearly, the participants in our study viewed the risks from nuclear power as qualitatively different from those of the other activities. Figures 6.8a and 6.8b highlight these differences by comparing the risk ratings for nuclear power and two ostensibly similar technologies, X-rays and non-nuclear electric power. Although

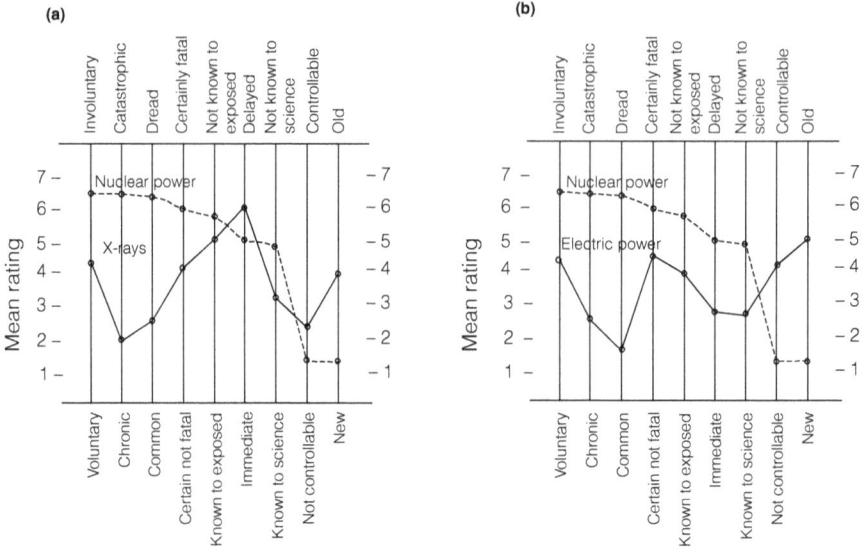

Figure 6.8 *Risk ratings for nuclear power, X-rays and electric power*

X-rays and nuclear power both rely on radioactivity, nuclear power was perceived as markedly more catastrophic and dreaded. For those who believe that nuclear power is just another kind of energy, the discrepancies shown in Figure 6.8b should be very surprising. How widely these perceptions are shared by people other than members of the League of Women Voters and their spouses is a matter for future research.

Multivariate determination of acceptable risk levels

In Figure 6.1, Starr's goal was to show a way to predict level of acceptable risk as a function of benefit and voluntariness. Rowe (1977) has done a similar analysis using qualitative aspects of risk other than voluntariness. A generalization of these approaches would be a formula specifying acceptable risk level as a function of benefit and all relevant qualitative aspects of risk. We have done this using the two risk dimensions derived by the factor analysis of the nine qualitative risk scales. A multiple regression equation predicting acceptable risk level as a function of perceived benefit, Factor 1 and Factor 2 yielded a multiple R of 0.76 ($F = 12.2$; df $= 3, 26$; $p < 0.0001$). This means that we can do a good job of predicting the acceptable risk levels shown in Table 6.1 from judgements of benefits and several risk characteristics. How such a formula may be used to guide future policymaking is also a topic for future research.

A similar analysis was performed on judgements of perceived (current) risk. The multiple R for predicting perceived risk from perceived benefit and the two factor scores was 0.67 ($F = 6.96$; df $= 3, 26$; $p < 0.005$). However, perceived risk judgements could be predicted just as well using the single qualitative variable 'severity of consequences' and ignoring perceived benefit and the other qualitative scales.

Discussion

Methodologically, the main result of this study was that the task we posed to the participants was tractable. That is, it was possible to ask people for complex judgements about difficult societal problems and receive orderly, interpretable responses. Substantively, the most important findings were:

- For many activities and technologies, current risk levels were viewed as unacceptably high. These differences between perceived and acceptable risk indicated that the participants in our study were not satisfied with the way that market and other regulatory mechanisms have balanced risks and benefits. Given this perspective, such people may also be unwilling to accept revealed preferences of the type uncovered by Starr as a guide for future action. In particular, the high correlations between perceived levels of existing risk and needed risk adjustment indicated that our participants wanted the risks from different activities to be considerably more equal than they are now. As shown in Table 6.1, they wanted the most risky item on our list of 30 to be only 10 times as risky as the safest.
- There appeared to be little systematic relationship between the perceived existing risks and benefits of the 30 activities and technologies considered here. Nor are risks entered into voluntarily perceived as greater than involuntary risks at fixed levels of benefit. Such relationships appeared to emerge in Starr's revealed risk–benefit space.
- However, there was a consistent, although not overwhelming, relationship between perceived benefit and acceptable level of risk. Despite their desire for more equal risks from different activities, our respondents believed that society should accept somewhat higher levels of risk with more beneficial activities. They also felt that society should tolerate higher risk levels for voluntary, than for involuntary activities. Thus, they believed that Starr's hypothesized relationships should be obtained in a society in which risk levels are adequately regulated. In addition, other characteristics of risk besides voluntariness, namely perceived control, familiarity, knowledge and immediacy, also induced double standards for acceptable risk. Thus, these expressed preferences indicate that determining acceptable risk may require consideration of other characteristics besides benefits.
- The nine characteristics hypothesized by various authors to influence judgements of perceived and acceptable risk were highly intercorrelated. They could be effectively reduced to two dimensions. One dimension apparently discriminated between high- and low-technology activities, with the high end being characterized by new, involuntary, poorly known activities, often with delayed consequences. The second dimension primarily reflected the certainty of death given that adversity occurs. Consideration of these two factors in addition to perceived benefit made acceptable risk judgements highly predictable. Conceivably, policymakers might use such relationships to predict public acceptance of the risk levels associated with proposed technologies.

Given the contrasts between our study and Starr's, the question arises, 'Who is right?' We believe that neither approach is, in itself, definitive. The particular relationships that

Starr uncovered were based upon numerous ad hoc assumptions and applied to only a small set of possible technologies. Our own study used but one of the psychophysical measurement procedures possible, applied to a rather special participant population.[2] We are, at present, engaged in additional studies employing different types of respondents and different judgement methods. Answering the question 'How safe is safe enough?' is going to require a multi-method, multidisciplinary approach, in which the present work and Starr's are but two components.

Balancing the results of these various approaches also depends upon one's conceptualization of the policymaking process. A definitive revealed-preference study would be an adequate guide to action only if one believed that rational decision-making is best performed by experts formalizing past policies as prescriptions for future action. A definitive expressed-preference study would be an adequate guide only if one believed that people's present opinions should be society's final arbiter and that people act on their expressed preferences. The obvious reservation that many people would have about the former approach is that it is highly conservative, enshrining current economic and social relationships; an obvious problem with the latter approach is that it allows people to change planning guidelines at will, possibly resulting in social chaos.

For most people, presumably, both present opinions and past behaviour are relevant to social policy. The believer in expressed preferences cannot ignore existing economic arrangements. On the other hand, the public will resist even the best-laid plans if they feel that policymakers have not adequately considered their desires. Assume that future research finds that a representative sample of properly informed citizens, queried by means of appropriate methods, evaluates the seriousness of hazards not only by their statistical and 'economic' risks, but also according to qualitative features like voluntariness and controllability. The legitimacy of these desires will have to be explored and debated. For example, implementing a double standard for voluntary risks may prove, upon analysis, to be acceptable while the desire to make dreaded technologies especially safe may be found to have unreasonable consequences. Even if the public's desires are ignored, either with or without analysis, there is no guarantee that they will go away. Pressure on politicians and regulators may force laws based on more 'rational' economic considerations to be implemented in accordance with these 'irrational' desires. Indeed, the current functioning of our regulatory system might be better understood as a partial reflection of such pressures.

Although we have de-emphasized the substance of our respondents' judgements about specific technologies in order to concentrate on more general relationships between those judgements, such opinions from members of the League of Women Voters are quite likely to appear in regulatory hearings and elsewhere. If League members believe that nuclear power has low benefit relative to its level of risk, it is as much a political fact of life as the League members' failure to see any systematic trade-off between existing risks and benefits.[2]

The present study raised several questions worthy of further investigation. One intriguing finding was that people viewed current risk levels as more acceptable after they had ordered current benefits in depth (Table 6.1, columns 3 and 4). Does this imply that the way technologies are presented, say, in regulatory hearings, can affect the way in which they are evaluated? More research is needed into how to present the public with the information needed to give new technologies a fair hearing.

A second question is triggered by the observed inverse relationship between perceived risks and benefits. Could this have occurred because participants in the benefit group were unable to estimate gross benefits rather than net benefits? If people in the benefit group did take risk into consideration, high-risk activities would have been rated as relatively lower in benefit and low-risk activities would have been viewed as relatively higher in benefit, much like the observed pattern. Future work should consider the advantages of having people judge multiple aspects of benefit (e.g. economic aspects, physical and mental health, convenience, etc.) separately. These could then be weighted and amalgamated into an overall, multi-attribute measure. This approach may reduce or eliminate possible contamination from the risk side.

Finally, what is the relationship between these attitudes about risk and people's responses to measures designed to ameliorate risks? If people believe that motor vehicles should be five times safer, does this mean that they would accept any immediate, Draconian step designed to attain that goal? Does it mean that a fivefold reduction in risk is a long-term goal for society and that meaningful (but not necessarily drastic) steps should be taken until that goal is reached, or does it mean that the adjustment ratios expressed here only measure relative concerns about the risk levels of various activities? A more behaviourally relevant scale of acceptability should be developed, with clearer implications for regulatory actions.

Notes

1   Preliminary results indicate that the risk–benefit relationships obtained with the League of Women Voters subjects replicated almost exactly when a group of university students made the same sorts of judgements. A second study asked students to judge acceptable risks directly, instead of using an adjustment factor. The direct ratings correlated about 0.77 with ratings produced by another group using the indirect adjustment method of the present study. These results indicate an encouraging degree of cross-method consistency.

2   In November of 1976, half a year after distribution of our questionnaire, Oregon voters decided the fate of a nuclear safeguards ballot measure that if passed would have curtailed, and perhaps stopped, the development of nuclear power in Oregon. In response to a survey preserving their anonymity, 95 per cent of the participants in our study indicated voting in favour of the safeguards measure (i.e. against nuclear power) compared with 42 per cent supporting it statewide. Thus, the voting behaviour of our League subjects matches the anti-nuclear sentiments they expressed in their risk and benefit judgements.

References

Acton, J. P. (1973). 'Evaluating public programs to save lives: The case of heart attacks', *Rand Corporation Report R–950-RC*, January.

Golant, S. and Burton, I. (1969). 'Avoidance response to the risk environment', Natural Hazards Research Working Paper No. 6, Dept. of Geography, University of Toronto.

Green, C. H. (1974). 'Measures for safety'. Unpublished manuscript. Center for Advanced Study, University of Illinois, Urbana.

Fischhoff, B. (1977). 'Cost-benefit analysis and the art of motorcycle maintenance', *Policy Sciences*, 8, 177–202.

Kates, R. W. (1975). 'Risk assessment of environmental hazard', *SCOPE Report 8*, International Council of Scientific Unions, Paris, France.

Lichtenstein, S., Slovic, P., Fischhoff, B., Combs, B. and Layman, M. (1978). 'Tudged frequency of low-probability lethal events', *Journal of Experimental Psychology: Human Learning and Memory*, 4, 551–578

Linnerooth, J. (1975). 'The evaluation of life saving: A survey', *Research Report 75–21*, International Institute for Applied Systems Analysis, Laxenburg, Austria, July.

Liska, A. E. (Ed.), (1975). *The Consistency Controversy.* New York: Wiley.

Lowrance, W. W. (1976). *Of Acceptable Risk.* Los Altos, Calif.: Wm. Kaufman, Inc.

Maynard, W. S., Nealey, S. M., Hebert, J. A. and Lindell, M. K. (1976). 'Public values associated with nuclear waste disposal', *Report BNWL-1997 (UC-70)*, Battelle Memorial Institute, Human Affairs Research Center, Seattle, Washington, June.

Otway, H. (1975). 'Risk assessment and societal choices', *Research Memorandum 75–2*, International Institute for Applied Systems Analysis, Laxenburg, Austria, February.

Otway, H. J. and Cohen, J. J. (1975). 'Revealed preferences: Comments on the Starr benefit-risk relationships', *Research Memorandum 75–5*, International Institute for Applied Systems Analysis, Laxenburg, Austria, March.

Otway, H. J., Maderthaner, R. and Guttman, G. (1975). 'Avoidance response to the risk environment: A cross cultural comparison'. *Research Report 75–14.* International Institute for Applied Systems Analysis, Laxenburg, Austria, May.

Otway, H. J. and Pahner, P. D. (1976). 'Risk assessment', *Futures*, 8, 122–134.

Rappaport, E. (1974). 'Economic analysis of life-and-death decision making'. Appendix 2 in *Report No. Eng 7478*, School of Engineering and Applied Science, UCLA, Nov.

Rowe, W. D. (1977). *An Anatomy of Risk.* New York: Wiley.

Rummel, R. J. (1970). *Applied Factor Analysis.* Evanston: Northwestern Univ. Press.

Siegel, S. (1956). *Nonparametric Statistics for the Behavioral Sciences.* New York: McGraw-Hill.

Slovic, P., Fischhoff, B. and Lichtenstein, S. (1977). 'Behavioral decision theory', *Annual Review of Psychology*, 28, 1–39.

Starr, C. (1969). 'Social benefit versus technological risk', *Science*, 165, 1232–1238.

Starr, C. (1972). 'Benefit-cost studies in sociotechnical systems'. In Committee on Public Engineering Policy, *Perspective on Benefit-Risk Decision Making.* Washington, DC: National Academy of Engineering.

Starr, C., Rudman, R. and Whipple, C. (1976). 'Philosophical basis for risk analysis', *Annual Review of Energy*, 1, 629–662.

Torrance, G. (1970). 'Generalized cost-effectiveness model for the evaluation of health programs', *McMaster University Faculty of Business Research Series, No. 101.*

Wyler, A. R., Masuda, M. and Holmes, T. H. (1968). 'Seriousness of illness rating scale', *Journal of Psychosomatic Research*, 11, 363–374.

7

Risk as Feelings

George F. Loewenstein, Elke U. Weber, Christopher K. Hsee and Ned Welch

> The worst disease here is not radiation sickness. The truth is that the fear of Chernobyl has done more damage than Chernobyl itself. (Specter, 1996)

Decision-making under risk and uncertainty has been one of the most active and interdisciplinary research topics in judgement and decision-making (J/DM). Stimulated in part by the existence of a strong normative benchmark, expected utility (EU) theory, both psychologists and economists have made important theoretical and empirical contributions. These include tests of EU and its assumptions, identification of a wide range of deviations from EU predictions, and the development of alternative descriptive models such as prospect theory and other rank- and sign-dependent EU-type models (for recent summaries, see Harless and Camerer, 1994; Luce and von Winterfeldt, 1994; Starmer, 2000). EU-type theories also have wide currency in social and industrial-organizational psychology; take for example Ajzen and Fishbein's (1980) theory of reasoned action and the health belief model (Becker, 1974). The convergence in the theoretical perspectives of psychologists and economists in this area has been greater than for any other topic of mutual interest to the two disciplines.

Part of this convergence can be traced to a common implicit, and thus largely unquestioned, theoretical orientation. With some important exceptions (e.g. Janis and Mann, 1977; Mann, 1992; Slovic et al, 2002), both psychologists and economists who study risky choice adhere to what could be characterized as a consequentialist perspective. We use the term *consequentialist* in its conventional sense to mean that people make decisions on the basis of an assessment of the consequences of possible choice alternatives.

As illustrated in Figure 7.1, EU-type theories posit that risky choice can be predicted by assuming that people assess the severity and likelihood of the possible outcomes of choice alternatives, albeit subjectively and possibly with bias or error, and integrate this information through some type of expectation-based calculus to arrive at a decision. Feelings triggered by the decision situation and imminent risky choice are seen as epiphenomenal – that is, not integral to the decision-making process. In this sense J/DM theorists assume (either implicitly or explicitly) that risky decision-making is essentially a cognitive activity. Many choice theorists are deliberately agnostic about the psychological processes underlying the patterns of choice that their models predict. However, modellers who are explicit about process (e.g. Payne et al, 1993; Lopes, 1995)

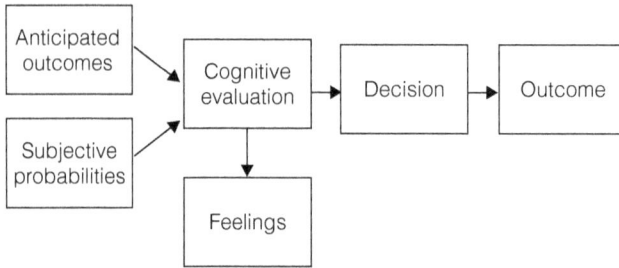

Figure 7.1 *Consequentialist perspective*

typically articulate algebraic accounts of underlying processes that are cognitive in character. Overt or covert cognitive information evaluation and integration are assumed to underlie the full gamut of risk-related decisions, from health and safety decisions such as dieting, seatbelt use and smoking to choices about recreational and workplace activities.

In this chapter, we propose a distinction between anticipatory emotions and anticipated emotions. *Anticipatory emotions* are immediate visceral reactions (e.g. fear, anxiety, dread) to risks and uncertainties. *Anticipated emotions* are typically not experienced in the immediate present but are expected to be experienced in the future. To the extent that J/DM research has addressed emotions, the emotions that have been taken into account are anticipated emotions. Several J/DM theories of risky choice provide a prominent role for such emotions, which include the disappointment or regret that might arise from counterfactual comparisons (Bell, 1982, 1985; Loomes and Sugden, 1982, 1986; Mellers et al, 1997, 1999). As illustrated in Figure 7.2, decision-makers are assumed to anticipate how they will feel about obtaining different outcomes as the result of various counterfactual comparisons. These anticipated emotions are a component of the expected consequences of the decision; they are emotions that are expected to occur when outcomes are experienced, rather than emotions that are experienced at the time of decision. The decision-making process in these theories is still modelled as the implicitly cognitive task of predicting the nature and strength of future emotions in response to possible decision outcomes and weighting them according to their likelihood of occurring.

Likewise, in Isen's work examining the impact of affect on decision-making (e.g. Isen and Patrick, 1983; Isen and Geva, 1987; Nygren et al, 1996), the assumed role of affect is anticipated rather than anticipatory. Isen and her colleagues have investigated the role of positive affect on risky decision-making, presenting research participants with simple decision tasks after inducing positive affect by, for example, giving them a small bag of candy. Although happy decision-makers are generally more optimistic about their probability of winning a given lottery (Isen and Patrick, 1983), they are much less willing to gamble than controls. Isen and colleagues (e.g. Isen et al, 1988) explain this effect in terms of what they call a *mood maintenance hypothesis* – that people in a good mood are reluctant to gamble because losing might undermine their good mood. This is inherently consequentialist reasoning.

Anticipated outcomes (including anticipated emotions) → Cognitive evaluation → Decision → Outcome (including emotions)

Subjective probabilities → Cognitive evaluation

Cognitive evaluation → Feelings

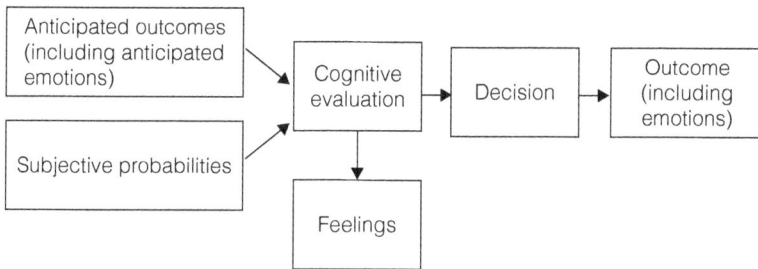

Figure 7.2 *Consequentialist perspective with anticipated emotions*

Whereas decision researchers have focused mainly on anticipated emotions, researchers in fields outside of decision-making, such as neuroscience and social psychology, have focused instead on the role of anticipatory emotions in decision- making. In contrast to the historical view of emotions (and other 'passions') as destructive influences on decision-making, much of the new work highlights the role played by emotions as informational inputs into decision-making and the negative consequences that result when such inputs are blocked.[1] For example, Damasio's somatic marker hypothesis posits that normal decision-making is guided by somatic reactions to deliberations about alternatives that provide information about their relative desirability. In support of this perspective, Damasio and colleagues (Damasio, 1994; Bechara et al, 1997) show that certain neurological abnormalities that block such somatic reactions but produce minimal cognitive deficits lead to significant impairments of risky decision-making. Other research by Wilson and colleagues (e.g. Wilson and Schooler, 1991; Wilson et al, 1993) shows that the quality of decision-making suffers when affective inputs are suppressed by having decision-makers think systematically about the pros and cons of a decision.

Research by Zajonc (1980, 1984a, 1984b), Bargh (1984), and LeDoux (1996) likewise shows that affective reactions to stimuli are often more rapid and basic than cognitive evaluations. Such immediate affective responses, the researchers have argued, provide organisms with a fast but crude assessment of the behavioural options they face, which makes it possible to take rapid action. An even more recent interpretation of the evidence, that is consistent with an early argument by Simon (1967), holds that these rapid emotional reactions serve as a mechanism to interrupt and redirect cognitive processing toward potentially high-priority concerns, such as imminent sources of danger (Armony et al, 1995, 1997; de Becker, 1997). Armony et al (1997) commented that:

> a threatening stimulus occurring outside of the focus of attention may fail to be processed by cortical systems (as its representation is filtered out by a topdown attentional influence). In contrast, the direct pathway is not subject to this type of filtering, and therefore will transmit the information about the threatening stimulus to the amygdala, regardless of whether or not that stimulus occurs in the focus of attention. (p33)

A similar argument, with respect to anxiety as opposed to fear, has been advanced by Luu et al (1998), who argued that 'appropriate levels of anxiety reflect the highest level of normal motivational control of working memory, through which the operations of memory in planning and behavioural sequencing are continually linked with adaptive significance' (p578).

Clore and Schwarz's affect-as-information hypothesis (Schwarz and Clore, 1983; Clore et al, 1994) draws on very different types of evidence to reach a similar conclusion. As presented in Clore (1992), the affect-as-information hypothesis is a model of how feelings influence (social) judgements. Judgements of others, for example, are affected by the positive and negative feelings of liking and disliking. The critical difference between the affect-as-information and other social judgement models that address the role of affect is that, according to the affect-as-information perspective, affect has a direct effect (as a sample of experience of the object of judgement) rather than being mediated by affect-congruent memories or concepts. The affect-as-information hypothesis correctly predicts that feelings during the judgement or decision process affect people's judgements or choices in those cases where the feelings are (correctly or through misattributions) experienced as reactions to the imminent judgement or decision. If feelings are attributed to a source that is normatively irrelevant to the decision at hand, their impact is reduced or eliminated (Schwarz and Clore, 1983; but see Winkielman et al, 1997).

Most directly relevant to our focus on decision-making under risk, and also consistent with the positive view of emotions, Slovic and collaborators (e.g. Slovic et al, 1991a, b; Finucane et al, 2000; Slovic et al, 2002) have proposed an 'affect heuristic' that highlights the importance of affect for risk perceptions and risk-related behaviour. Over the past 20 years, Slovic, Fischhoff, and Lichtenstein have explored the emotional bases of risk judgements using a range of innovative methods. Adopting a psychometric paradigm (e.g. Fischhoff et al, 1981), these researchers found that people's perceptions of the risks of hazardous technologies or activities are influenced by risk dimensions that have little to do with consequentialist aspects (i.e. possible outcomes and their probabilities).[2] Peters and Slovic (1996) have subsequently found that the 'psychological' dimensions of risk can be distilled into two primary factors: *dread*, defined by the extent of perceived lack of control, feelings of dread, and perceived catastrophic potential, and *risk of the unknown*, the extent to which the hazard is judged to be unobservable, unknown, new, or delayed in producing harmful impacts. The first of these dimensions clearly suggests an affective rather than cognitive evaluation of hazards.

Although neither the affect-as-information hypothesis nor the affect heuristic rule out the possibility that affective reactions to decisions can diverge from cognitive evaluations, neither perspective draws attention to such divergences or their consequences for behaviour. In contrast, other strands of literature in psychology most closely associated with the clinical literature suggest that emotions often conflict with cognitive evaluations and can in some situations produce pathologies of decision-making and behaviour. Research on anxiety, for example, shows that emotional reactions to a risky situation often diverge from cognitive evaluations of risk severity (Ness and Klaas, 1994). When such departures occur, moreover, the emotional reactions often exert a dominating influence on behaviour and frequently produce behaviour that does not appear to be adaptive. Fear causes us to slam on the brakes instead of steering into the skid, immobilizes us when we have greatest need for strength, causes sexual dysfunction, insomnia, ulcers, and gives us dry mouth and jitters at the very moment when there is the greatest premium on clarity and eloquence. Most people, therefore, have at least occasionally experienced their own emotions as a destructive influence that they wish they could turn off. As Rolls (1999) wrote:

> the puzzle is not only that the emotion is so intense, but also that even with our rational, reasoning capacities, humans still find themselves in these situations, and may find it difficult to produce reasonable and effective behaviour for resolving the situation. (p282)

Rolls argues that such divergences between emotional reactions and cognitive evaluations arise because:

> in humans, the reward and punishment systems may operate implicitly in comparable ways to those in other animals. But in addition to this, humans have the explicit system [closely related to consciousness] which enables us consciously to look and predict many steps ahead. (p282)

The divergence of emotional responses from cognitive evaluations of risks, as well as the potency of emotional responses in influencing behaviour, are evident in the large numbers of individuals who suffer from often-debilitating fear- and anxiety-related disorders who, in the words of one anxiety researcher, are typically 'well aware that there is little or nothing to fear in situations they find so difficult' (Barlow, 1988, p13). Even people who are not suffering from full-blown phobias commonly experience powerful fears about outcomes that they recognize as highly unlikely (such as aeroplane crashes) or not objectively terrible (such as public speaking); in contrast, many experience little fear about hazards that are both more likely and probably more severe (such as car accidents). The divergence between emotional reactions to, and cognitive evaluations of, risk is a common source of the feeling of intrapersonal conflict (see, e.g., Schelling, 1984). As Schelling documented, people often use sophisticated tactics to override their emotional responses to situations – to 'conquer their fears'.

In other related developments, psychologists from different sub-disciplines (clinical, social and cognitive) have been drawing similar distinctions between two qualitatively different modes of information processing (e.g. Epstein et al, 1992; Sloman, 1996; Chaiken and Trope, 1999; Windschitl and Weber, 1999). Sloman, for example, distinguished between rule-based and associative processing. Rule-based processing is a relatively controlled form of processing that operates according to formal rules of logic and evidence and is mediated by conscious appraisal of information. A response driven by *rule-based processing* follows from the execution of one or more rules that are assumed to be relevant to the task (e.g. *modus ponens* or the conjunction rule). *Associative processing* is a more spontaneous form of processing that operates by principles of similarity and temporal contiguity. In associative processing, the situational context influences responses directly, just as associatively based priming influences the recognition of a target word. Pathways and patterns of activation follow principles of similarity and temporal contiguity; the stronger the association between two concepts (which depends on similarity, repeated joint exposure, etc.), the more activation passes from one to another. Because associative processing is not mediated by conscious appraisal it is difficult to suppress its influence on judgements and decisions.

In support of his two-process dichotomy, Sloman (1996) provided examples from reasoning, categorization, and judgement research in which people find two simultaneously contradictory responses – one presumably mediated by associative processing and the other by rule-based processing – to be compelling for a given problem. For example, although people know that a whale does not fit the classification of 'fish', statements like 'technically a whale is a mammal' suggest that people are influenced by the similarity between whales and fish. Windschitl and Weber (1999) showed that associative processing of contextual information affected judgements of subjective likelihood even in situations where numeric estimates of likelihood were provided by credible experts.

Focusing narrowly on the topic of decision-making under risk, we attempt to integrate these two strands of literature, one showing that emotions inform decision-making and the other showing that emotional responses to risky decision situations – that is, anticipatory emotions – often diverge from cognitive evaluations. As demonstrated by the many studies that support the somatic marker, affect-as-information, and affect heuristic theories, emotional reactions and cognitive evaluations typically work in concert to guide reasoning and decision-making. However, anticipatory emotional reactions sometimes diverge from cognitive evaluations and, when they do, the emotional reactions often exert a dominating influence on behaviour. We attempt to explain when and why such emotional reactions diverge from cognitive evaluations of risk and to explain how these responses interact to determine behaviour. The theoretical framework we propose, which we label the *risk-as-feelings hypothesis*, provides a parsimonious account of a number of risk-related phenomena that are not explained by existing consequentialist models of risky decision-making.

The risk-as-feelings hypothesis, illustrated in Figure 7.3, postulates that responses to risky situations (including decision-making) result in part from direct (i.e. not cortically mediated) emotional influences, including feelings such as worry, fear, dread or anxiety. People are assumed to evaluate risky alternatives at a cognitive level, as in traditional models, based largely on the probability and desirability of associated consequences. Such cognitive evaluations have affective consequences, and feeling states also exert a reciprocal influence on cognitive evaluations. At the same time, however, feeling states are postulated to respond to factors, such as the immediacy of a risk, that do not enter into cognitive evaluations of the risk and also respond to probabilities and outcome values in a fashion that is different from the way in which these variables enter into cognitive evaluations. Because their determinants are different, emotional reactions to risks can diverge from cognitive evaluations of the same risks. As illustrated in Figure 7.3, behaviour is then determined by the interplay between these two, often conflicting, responses to a situation. Note that the term *decision* in Figures 7.1 and 7.2 is deliberately replaced with *behaviour* in Figure 7.3. This substitution reflects the observation that many types of emotion-driven risk-related behaviours, ranging from panic reactions (e.g. slamming on the brake when one skids on ice) to the agoraphobic individual's inability to leave the house, do not seem to reflect decisions in the sense that the term is usually used.

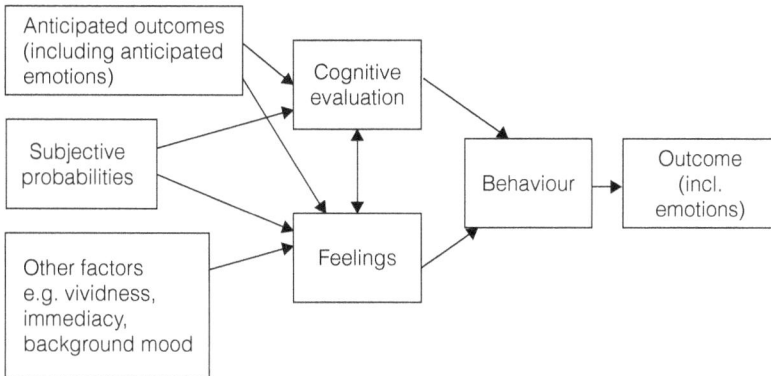

Figure 7.3 *Risk-as-feelings perspective*

The risk-as-feelings hypothesis is similar to the somatic marker hypothesis, the affect-as-information perspective and the affect heuristic in drawing attention to the important role played by affect in decision-making, but the risk-as-feelings hypothesis has a somewhat different focus. Although these approaches do not rule out the possibility that emotional reactions could diverge from cognitive reactions, they focus mainly on the complementary role of the two systems. They assume that affect typically plays an informational role in decision-making – that it provides inputs into decision-making that help people to evaluate alternative courses of action, albeit not always in a normative fashion. In contrast to these other theories, the risk-as-feelings hypothesis posits that, in addition, emotions often produce behavioural responses that depart from what individuals view as the best course of action. Our intent in this chapter is to begin to make sense of when and why such divergences occur.

In highlighting the role played by emotions in risk-related decision-making, the research we review is representative of an emergent interest in the role played by emotions in decision-making more generally. For example, Kahneman and co-authors (Kahneman and Ritov, 1994; Kahneman et al, 1998, 1999) observed that when jurors make decisions or when the public makes contingent valuations of public goods, their judgements are often erratic and cannot be understood from an economic preference perspective. However, these responses can be interpreted as a manifestation of the decision-maker's gut feelings toward the target at the time of decision-making. Luce et al, (1997, 1999) studied another type of decision-moment feeling – trade-off difficulty emotions. They found that trade-off difficulty in decision-making can evoke negative emotions that bear no relationship to the valence of the consequences but that in turn lead decision-makers to alter their coping strategies or avoid the decision altogether. Loewenstein (1996, 1999) has studied the role of emotions and other 'visceral factors' such as hunger, sexual arousal and pain in decision-making (see also Loewenstein and Lerner, 2008).

The next section lays out the risk-as-feelings hypothesis in detail and presents evidence supporting each of its specific assumptions. The second section discusses the determinants of risk-related feelings to explain why such feelings often diverge from cognitive evaluations of risk severity and reviews a wide range of phenomena that are consistent with the risk-as-feelings perspective but are difficult to explain in terms of standard cognitive-consequentialist approaches. The third section concludes with a discussion of further predictions of the risk-as-feelings hypothesis and implications for public policy.

Risk-as-Feelings Hypothesis

If risk-related feelings and cognitive evaluations had identical determinants as well as consequences for behaviour, the risk-as-feelings hypothesis would be little more than an alternative description of the psychological processes underlying decision-making, and anticipatory feelings would not be required as an intervening construct. However, people's emotional reactions to risks depend on a variety of factors that influence cognitive evaluations of risk only weakly or not at all. These include the vividness with which consequences can be imagined, personal exposure to or experience with outcomes, and past history of conditioning. Cognitive assessments of risk, on the other hand, tend to depend on more objective features of the risky situation, such as probabilities of outcomes and assessments of outcome severity. Even when feelings about risk are influenced by these objective features, the functional form of such dependence is different. For example, it has been demonstrated that feelings about risk are largely insensitive to changes in probability, whereas cognitive evaluations do take probability into account. As a result, feelings about risk and cognitive risk perceptions often diverge, sometimes strikingly.

Evidence from different areas of psychology provides support for different aspects of the risk-as-feelings hypothesis, as illustrated in Figure 7.3. Some elements are not controversial. For example, few would question that cognitive evaluations give rise to affective responses, although there is debate about the relationship between specific cognitions and specific emotions (e.g. Roseman, 1984; Scherer, 1984; Smith and Ellsworth, 1985; Ellsworth and Smith, 1988; Ortony et al 1988).

There is also little disagreement that important influences operate in the reverse direction, from emotion to cognition. From a neurophysiological perspective, the finding that emotions exert a powerful influence on judgements is not surprising. As LeDoux (1996) noted, 'emotions can flood consciousness ... because the wiring of the brain at this point in our evolutionary history is such that connections from the emotional systems to the cognitive systems are stronger than connections from the cognitive systems to the emotional systems' (p19). Numerous studies have found that people in good moods make optimistic judgements and choices and that people in bad moods make pessimistic judgements and choices (Isen et al, 1978; Bower, 1981, 1991; Johnson and Tversky, 1983; Schwarz and Clore, 1983; Kavanagh and Bower, 1985; Mayer et al, 1992; Wright and Bower, 1992; Mayer and Hanson, 1995). For example, Johnson and Tversky found that people who read sad newspaper articles subsequently gave higher risk estimates for a variety of potential causes of death (e.g. floods, disease) than people who read happy newspaper articles. More recent research has gone beyond the valence approach to examine the different effect of different specific emotions of the same valence on judgements and choices. Most relevant to the framework proposed here, many studies have found effects of fear and anxiety on various types of judgements that tend to favour cautious, risk-averse decision-making (Lerner and Keltner, 1999, 2000). Eysenck (1992), for example, proposed that highly anxious individuals attend preferentially to threat-related stimuli and interpret ambiguous stimuli and situations as threatening, and a number of studies have supported these predictions (e.g. Eysenck et al, 1987; Vasey et al, 1996; Derakshan and Eysenck, 1997). Raghunathan and Pham (1999) found that induced anxiety increased individuals' preference for low-risk, low-reward options, whereas induced sadness had the opposite effect. Lerner and Keltner (2000) found that fearful individuals make relatively pessimistic risk assessments and relatively risk-averse choices.

The two more controversial aspects of the theoretical framework summarized in Figure 7.3 are:

1   that feelings can also arise without cognitive mediation (probabilities, outcomes, and other factors can directly give rise to feelings); and
2   that the impact of cognitive evaluations on behaviour is mediated, at least in part, by affective responses (cognitive evaluation gives rise to feelings that in turn affect behaviour).

We focus on these two points in the remainder of this section.

Feelings need not be cognitively mediated

There is considerable support for the notion that the pathway from risky stimulus to emotional reaction can be direct, that is, not mediated by any cognitive evaluation of the situation except for the most basic perceptual processing. Evidence for the affect-as-information hypothesis (Schwarz and Clore, 1983; Clore et al, 1994) in social cognition supports the direct effect of feelings on judgements and decisions over indirect (cognitively mediated) effect interpretations that assume that feelings selectively prime semantic concepts (i.e. Bower, 1981, 1992). Clore (1992) provided a summary of two decades of research that shows direct effects of emotions on judgement. The idea that feelings need not be cognitively mediated is also supported by the research of Zajonc (1980, 1984a, 1984b), who first argued for greater speed and automaticity of affective over cognitive reactions and showed that people can have an affective reaction to a stimulus before they know what it is they are reacting to. For example, sudden, unexpected noises can cause fear well before we determine the source of the noise. Zajonc also showed that memory for affective reactions can be dissociated from memory for details of a situation, with the former often being better. An example is that we often remember whether we liked or disliked a particular person, book or movie without being able to remember any details other than our affective reaction (Bargh, 1984).

Recent research by LeDoux and his colleagues (summarized in LeDoux, 1996) provides the anatomical neurological underpinnings for such direct effects. LeDoux and colleagues have shown that there are direct neural projections from the sensory thalamus (which performs crude signal processing) to the amygdala (which is widely believed to play a critical role in the processing of affective stimuli) that are not mediated by cortical processing. More recently, Servan-Schreiber and Perlstein (1998), in research with humans, have shown that intravenous injections of procaine, which produce powerful emotional responses, also produce amygdal activation. People who receive such injections report experiencing panic sensations and other powerful feelings that are disturbing precisely because they have no obvious cognitive antecedents. Other research has found that when the amygdala and other fear sites are stimulated electrically, people verbally report powerful feelings of foreboding (Panksepp, 1985, 1998). These evoked fears are often described in metaphoric terms; for example, 'Somebody is now chasing me', 'just like entering into a long, dark tunnel', or 'surf coming from all directions', as if the cortex attempts to make sense of these disembodied forebodings (Panksepp, 1998, p214). Whatever the reason for these crude, rapid, emotional responses, all of this research suggests that powerful emotional responses can occur with minimal, or possibly no, mediation by higher-level cognitive processes.

Feelings as determinants of behaviour

Diverse evidence also supports the proposition that affect mediates, at least in part, the relationship between an individual's cognitive evaluation of risk and his or her behavioural response to it. The idea that emotions exert a direct and powerful influence on behaviour receives ample support in the psychological literature on emotions. Zajonc (1998) in his chapter on emotions in the *Handbook of Social Psychology* argued that the defining characteristic of emotions is that they are designed to help people make approach-avoidance distinctions (whereas cognitions help people make true-false distinctions). Frijda (1986) has been a major proponent of the idea that a change in action readiness is the central core of an emotion and has shown that qualitatively distinct emotional states can be distinguished, not only on the basis of the cognitive appraisals that give rise to them, but also in terms of the state of action readiness that they create (Frijda et al, 1989).

A number of authors have postulated that emotions play a critical role in rational, risk-averse, forward-looking, decision-making. Liddell (cited in Barlow, 1988) referred to anxiety as the 'shadow of intelligence'. 'The capacity to experience anxiety and the capacity to plan', Barlow noted, are 'two sides of the same coin' (p12). Cottle and Klineberg (1974) argued that people only care about the delayed or uncertain consequences of their decisions to the degree that contemplating such consequences evokes immediate affect. In support of this view, they cited the effects of frontal lobotomies which, they believe, create a deficiency in areas of the brain that somehow underlie the capacity for images of absent events to generate experiences of pleasure or discomfort (p15). The neurosurgeons who performed these operations wrote of their frontal lobotomy patients that 'the capacity for imagination is still present, and certainly not sufficiently reduced to render the patients helpless, and affective responses are often quite lively, [but there is] a separation of one from the other' (Freeman and Watts, 1942, p303). Consistent with the notion that such emotions are critical for forward-looking decision-making, these surgeons noted that such patients were highly impulsive and risk-taking and generally seemed 'confined to what is here and now'.

More recent work by Damasio lends further support to this perspective. Damasio and colleagues (Damasio, 1994; Bechara et al, 1997) argued that decision-makers encode the consequences of alternative courses of action affectively and that such 'somatic markers' are an essential input into decision-making. Like Cottle and Klineberg (1974), Damasio argued that the prefrontal cortex plays a critical role in translating cognitive inputs from the cortex into terms that the emotional brain can understand. The prefrontal lobe is one terminus for dopaminergic neural pathways that are widely viewed as playing a critical role in volitional behaviour.

Damasio and collaborators conducted a study in which patients suffering damage to the prefrontal cortex and non-brain-damaged individuals played a game in which the objective was to win as much money as possible (Bechara et al, 1997). Players earned hypothetical money by turning over cards on which were written either monetary gains or losses. On any given turn, individuals could draw from any of four decks, two of which included high payments ($100) and two of which contained lower payments ($50). The high-paying deck, however, also included occasional very large losses, to the point where these decks had a net negative expected value. Bechara et al (1997) found that both non-patients and those with prefrontal damage began by sampling from all four decks, and both groups avoided high-paying decks immediately after penalty cards were encountered. Compared to non-patients, those with prefrontal damage returned to the high-paying decks more quickly after suffering a loss. As a result of this tendency, they often went 'bankrupt' despite a (reportedly) strong desire to win and a thorough understanding of the game. One possible interpretation of the patients' behaviour is that even though they 'knew' the high-paying deck was risky, their inability to experience fear when contemplating a draw from one of those decks made risky draws more palatable. Consistent with this interpretation, subsequent research using the same task found in a sample of non-patients that those who were higher in reactivity to negative events (as measured by two standard scales) were more prone to sample from the lower paying but safer decks of cards (Peters and Slovic, in press).

It should be noted that the lack of emotional responses does not necessarily lead to poor decisions. It is the specific design of Damasio's (1994; Bechara et al, 1997) experiment that makes his patients with frontal damage go bankrupt. One could easily design an experiment where the expected value of the high-risk deck (that contains some large losses) is actually higher than that of the low-risk deck. In this case, prefrontal damaged patients would do better in the long run than non-patients, because the fear in the latter group would hinder them from choosing from the risky but higher expected-value deck. Indeed, there may be a real-world analogue of such an experiment; because of fear and myopic loss aversion, most employees have historically foregone substantial financial gains by investing their retirement in safe bond or money market funds rather than in equities, even though the long-term return of equities is often many times higher (Benartzi and Thaler, 1995; Gneezy and Potters, 1997; Thaler et al, 1997).

The anomalous behaviour of patients with frontal damage might be consistent with a consequentialist view of decision-making if their emotional reaction to losing was simply less intense than that of non-patients. In this case, their strategy could be seen as a reasonable adaptation to different subjective feedback. However, they did not appear to be operating under different incentives. They were highly engaged in the task and wanted to win. After encountering a penalty card, they avoided the high-risk deck for a few turns (but returned to the high-risk decks more quickly than the non-patients). Where the patients with frontal damage differed from non-patients was in the arousal they experienced immediately before cards were turned over. In later phases of the game, when individuals had had experience drawing from all four decks, most of them drew an occasional card from one of the high-risk decks. Contemplating this selection evoked a galvanic skin conductance response in non-patients in the moments before making their choice, but no such reaction in patients with frontal damage. Damasio concluded from this research that anticipatory emotions – somatic markers – play a critical role in decision-making by encoding in a tangible fashion a summary of the likely consequences of a particular action. Lacking such somatic markers, his frontal-lesioned patients did not take account of the future consequences of their choices and, as a result, made bad decisions. They also had difficulty *making* decisions, even trivial ones. Anticipatory emotional reactions thus seem to facilitate the process of risky decision-making and to be a crucial input for good decisions.

Damasio's research (Damasio, 1994) derived further support from observations of another abnormal population: criminal psychopathic individuals. Like frontal patients, criminal psychopathic individuals are characterized by insensitivity to the future consequences of their behaviour (to themselves as well as other people). Although the neurological bases of this disorder are still not well understood, there also appears to be a connection to a specific emotional deficit. During the 1940s, researchers speculated that the inability of psychopathic individuals to take account of future consequences of their actions, or the impact of their actions on others, could be due to a defect in their propensity to experience fear (Cleckley, 1941). In support of this hypothesis, Lykken (1957) showed that, compared to controls, sociopathic individuals have less intense physiological reactions to a conditioning stimulus that had been previously paired with a painful electric shock. Hare (1965, 1966) showed that sociopathic individuals have less intense physiological reactions to the prospect of an impending painful shock. Patrick (1994) demonstrated that sociopathic individuals display fewer physiological symptoms of negative affect when exposed to aversive stimuli than controls (see also Williamson et al, 1991; Fowles and Missel, 1994).[3]

In summary, consistent with the notion that anticipatory emotions play a critical role in risk aversion and far-sighted decision-making, several populations who do not feel or fear the future in the same way that others do make decisions that display a profound disregard for future consequences. We acknowledge, however, that none of these studies conclusively demonstrates a causal link, because the observed correlations between affective deficiencies and decision myopia may result from some type of collateral damage to neural systems. However, evidence from a quite different stream of research points to a similar conclusion.

Eisenberg et al (1995) asked people who differed in trait anxiety and depression to make a series of choices between pairs of more and less risky options. For some of the choices, the riskier option was the default (it did not involve taking action), whereas the less risky option did involve taking action. For other choice pairs, the riskier option involved taking an action. The researchers found that trait anxiety was strongly and positively correlated with risk aversion, whereas depression was related to a preference for options that did not involve taking an action. In a second study reported in the same article, participants were asked to make these types of decisions not only for themselves, but also for a hypothetical other person. They found that trait anxiety did not correlate with risk aversion for decisions made on behalf of another person.

In a study that produced similar results to those of Eisenberg et al (1995), Hsee and Weber (1997) examined whether individuals could accurately predict the risk preference of others who were described either in generic (the average student on campus) or specific (another student sitting across the room) terms. Research participants were asked to choose between riskless monetary gains and risky monetary gains and also to predict the choices of others who were described in a generic or specific fashion. Participants were generally risk averse in their own choices, and their predictions of risk preference for another specific student (whom they did not know but could observe across the room) were close to their own risk preferences. However, their predictions for the average student on campus were closer to risk neutrality. Hsee and Weber hypothesized that people's personal risk preference is driven at least in part by emotional reactions to risky options, or, as Lopes (1987) put it, that risk preference reflects a compromise between greed and fear. To the extent that risk aversion is the dominant response to risky decisions, negative feelings (i.e. fear, dread or anxiety) toward risk tend to dominate positive feelings. When people predict the risk preference of another individual, they can base their prediction on their own feelings and reactions to the risky choice situation (i.e. predict by projection), which would be expected to occur when the 'other' is a concrete individual. When the prediction is for an abstract 'other', people find it more difficult to project and may ignore the impact of positive or negative emotional reactions on the decision, arriving at a prediction much closer to risk neutrality.

In a new study that we conducted for this chapter, we obtained further support for the idea that the self–other discrepancies in risk preferences are produced by self–other discrepancies in feelings toward risky options. We asked 115 college students to imagine the following scenario: they were riding in a taxi and found out that the driver was drunk. There were no other taxis around or other means of transportation. They could either (a) remain in the taxi (a relatively risky option) or (b) get out of the taxi and walk to their destination five miles away (a lower-risk option). Participants were asked how worried they would feel if they remained in the taxi cab and to predict how the average student at their university would feel if he or she remained in the cab. Participants were also asked whether they would get out of the cab and to predict the decision of the average student at their university. The results were consistent with the risk-as-feelings hypothesis. With respect to feelings, respondents rated themselves (on a scale from 0 = not worried at all to 5 = extremely worried) as significantly more worried than the average student (Ms = 3.71 and 3.16, t = 4.09, $p < .001$). In decisions, respondents also rated themselves (on a scale from 0 = not likely at all to 5 = extremely likely) as significantly more likely to get out of the cab than the average student (Ms = 2.93 and 2.39, t = 3.45, $p < .001$). Moreover, the self–other difference in decision was highly correlated across respondents with the self–other difference in feelings (r = .58, $p < .001$).

Additional support for the idea that affect plays an important role in behavioural intentions comes from a series of studies conducted by Slovic and his collaborators. In a typical study, participants free-associate about a concept of interest to the experimenters–for example, different states and cities (Slovic et al, 1991b), a nuclear waste repository (Slovic et al, 1991a), or health-related behaviours (Benthin et al, 1995) – and then provide affective ratings of these associations. These affective ratings are shown to correlate strongly with attitudes and self-predicted behaviour, such as desire to vacation or retire in particular states and cities, willingness to accept a nuclear waste repository in one's state, and the propensity to engage in health-related behaviours. Slovic and co-authors have also shown that, whereas risks and benefits tend to be positively associated in the real world (because high-risk activities are only tolerated to the extent that they provide benefits), they are negatively associated in people's minds (Alhakami and Slovic, 1994; Finucane et al, 2000). This negative relationship, they find, stems from people's reliance on general affective evaluations in making risk and benefit judgements. Through a kind of halo effect, activities that have a negative affective valence are seen as both high in risk and low in benefit.

Summary

In this section, we have sought to establish the central role that feelings play in determining people's choices and other responses under conditions of risk and uncertainty. The risk-as-feelings hypothesis suggests that feelings play a much more prominent role in risky decision-making than they are given credit for by the cognitive–consequentialist tradition of J/DM research. Behavioural evidence suggests that, to the extent that emotional reactions to, and cognitive evaluations of, risky choice options are dissociated, risk preference is often determined by the former. Emotional reactions guide responses not only at their first occurrence, but also through conditioning and memory at later points in time, serving as somatic markers. Patient populations who lack these markers not only have difficulty making risky decisions, but they also choose in ways that turn their personal and professional lives to shambles. Thus, feelings may be more than just an important input into decision-making under uncertainty; they may be necessary and, to a large degree, mediate the connection between cognitive evaluations of risk and risk-related behaviour.

Determinants of Feelings

As we noted in the introduction, the risk-as-feelings hypothesis is only interesting if the addition of feelings as a predictor variable makes risky choice more predictable, both within and across different decision domains and contexts. This can only be the case if emotional reactions have determinants that differ from those that drive cognitive evaluations. In this section we show that divergences between emotional and cognitive reactions occur for two reasons. First, emotions respond to the two central input variables of cognitive consequentialist accounts of risk-related perception and behaviour – probabilities and outcomes – in a fashion that is different from cognitive evaluations of riskiness. Second, emotions are influenced by situational variables that play only a minor role in cognitive evaluations. These factors include the time-course of the decision (i.e. the time between the decision and the realization of the outcome of the decision), non-consequentialist aspects of the decision outcomes (e.g. their vividness or the associations they evoke), and evolutionary preparedness for certain emotional reactions.

In addition to reviewing each of these discrepancies between emotional reactions to, and cognitive evaluations of, risk, we discuss phenomena observed in the laboratory and in natural settings that can be explained by such discrepancies but which are difficult to explain in conventional consequentialist terms. When viewed through the lens of consequentialist models such as the expected utility model, people's risk-taking behaviour often appears to be highly variable and inconsistent across domains and situations (MacCrimmon and Wehrung, 1986; Schoemaker, 1990; Isaac and James, 2000). Barsky et al (1997), for example, classified respondents to the Health and Retirement Survey (a large-scale panel study of older Americans) into four categories of risk tolerance on the basis of three questions that measured their degree of risk aversion for hypothetical decisions involving a change of job. They found that the resultant measure of risk tolerance correlated only very weakly with other risk-related behaviours such as drinking, smoking and investment decisions. Weber et al (2002) similarly found only weak correlations between self-reports of risk-taking in decisions involving either financial, health, social, ethical or recreational risks. To the extent that the risk-as-feelings hypothesis identifies situational factors that can influence risk-taking that would not be predicted by consequentialist models, it can help explain the content- and context-specific nature of risk-taking.

Effects of vividness

One of the most important determinants of emotional reactions to future outcomes is the vividness with which those outcomes are described or represented mentally (Damasio, 1994). To the extent that anticipatory emotions are generated in response to mental imagery about the experience of decision outcomes, factors that influence the occurrence or vividness of mental images are likely to be important determinants of anticipatory emotions.[4]

One such factor is individual differences in mental imagery. Several studies find a correlation between people's self-reported ability to form mental images and visceral responses that are plausibly related to anticipatory emotion. For example, compared with non-vivid imagers, vivid imagers salivate significantly more while thinking about their favourite food (White, 1978), become more sexually aroused in structured fantasy exercises (Smith and Over, 1987), and have greater ability to voluntarily increase their heart rate using visual imagery (Carroll et al, 1979). Consistent with the idea that imagery influences affective response, Miller et al (1987) reported that enhancing individuals' ability to form vivid images through training increases their visceral response to personalized scripts designed to elicit particular affective reactions, such as anger and fear.

Vividness, and hence the strength of anticipatory emotions, depends not only on individual differences in mental imagery ability, but also on situational factors, such as how an outcome is described. Nisbett and Ross (1980) illustrated this effect by contrasting two descriptions of the same event. In the first description, one learns that 'Jack sustained fatal injuries in an auto accident'. This description of death evoked weaker emotional reactions than the second description that 'Jack was killed by a semi trailer that rolled over on his car and crushed his skull' (p47).

The effect of vividness on emotional responses to risk may help explain some common patterns of insurance purchase behaviour that are anomalous within the consequentialist framework. Consequentialist models of risky choice (e.g. EU theory) predict that insurance purchases depend exclusively on the magnitude of the loss, its probability, the cost of insurance, and the consumer's wealth and risk tolerance, all variables that are immune to differences in the description of potential losses. Consideration of anticipatory emotions, on the other hand, suggests that the description of the outcomes may matter. Images of losses that evoke vivid negative mental imagery should lead to greater willingness to purchase insurance. Evidence supporting this prediction comes from Johnson et al (1993), who found that people were willing to pay more for airline travel insurance covering death from 'terrorist acts' (a highly imaginable event) than death from 'all possible causes' (which, of course, implicitly subsumes terrorist acts in addition to a range of other causes but does not spontaneously bring fear-provoking mental images to mind). At the opposite extreme, people tend to be underinsured against hazards that evoke relatively pallid mental images. Flood insurance is notoriously difficult to sell, even when premiums are heavily subsidized (*Insurance Advocate*, 1994; Kunreuther, 1976). Consequentialist explanations for this phenomenon would focus on systematic failures to predict the true devastation of a flood or on actuarially optimistic estimates of a flood's likelihood. Slovic et al (1980), on the other hand, speculated that people's willingness to insure against small-probability losses may be related to how much these potential losses cause worry or concern. A number of studies have shown that knowing someone who has been in a flood or earthquake, or having been in one oneself, greatly increases the likelihood of purchasing insurance (Browne and Hoyt, 2000). Although these findings could be explained in consequentialist terms as resulting from an increase in individuals' expectations of experiencing a flood or earthquake in the future, the effect remains significant even after controlling for subjective expectations (Kunreuther et al, 1978).

The importance of personal experience has also been noted in other areas. Weinstein (1989) presented evidence showing that the effect of the personal experience of adverse consequences on subsequent precautionary or self-protective behaviour goes beyond what one would expect if its main effect is to simply provide 'additional information that is inserted into a decision equation' (p47). Weinstein documented how personal experience can modify people's emotional reactions to risky situations in complex, situation- and domain-specific ways – for example, increasing feelings of worry, resulting in an increase in self-protective behaviour in some domains, but also decreasing feelings of controllability in other situations, with the opposite effect on precautionary responses. In a similar vein, Hendickx et al (1989) found that warnings are more effective when they are linked to people and anecdotes (and hence emotionally involving) than when they are based on statistics, suggesting that anxiety induction through the use of vividness manipulations can produce desirable changes in risk behaviours.

Anxiety induction is not, however, a panacea when it comes to promoting self-protective behaviour. Besides the fact that evoking anxiety saddles people with the hedonic burden of the anxiety itself, it can also induce defensive reactions that undermine efforts at risk mitigation. Thus, for example, Janis and Feshbach (1953) found that high levels of fear induced by a message about dental hygiene led to defensive avoidance, that is, subsequent warding off of exposures to the content of the message. Leventhal and Watts (1966) exposed visitors to a state fair to motion pictures dealing with smoking and lung cancer that were designed to elicit high, medium or low levels of fear. Consistent with defensive avoidance, the researchers found that higher levels of fear led to less willingness to get an X-ray but did produce a decrease in smoking relative to the other two groups. Thus, high levels of fear led to both information avoidance and some degree of risk mitigation. More recently, Lieberman and Chaiken (1992) found that defensive processing was heightened when the fear-inducing content of a message was personally relevant, as generally is the case with breast cancer. Indeed, there have been suggestions in the literature on breast self-exams that women's anticipatory anxiety about cancer prevents them from examining themselves (Bernay et al, 1982; O'Malley and Fletcher, 1987; Murray and McMillan, 1993).

Insensitivity to probability variations

In the EU model, the value of a prospect is equal to the sum of the utilities of outcomes that could be experienced, weighted by their likelihood of occurrence. Probabilities and outcomes thus have symmetrical effects on evaluations. This is not the case for emotional reactions. Changes in probability within some broad mid-range of values have little effect on anticipatory emotions perhaps because, as just discussed, emotions arise in large part as a reaction to mental images of a decision's outcomes (Damasio, 1994). Because such images are discrete and are not much affected by probabilities, the emotions that arise from them are likewise insensitive to variations in probability. One's mental image of what it would be like to win the state lottery, for example, is likely to be about the same, whether there is a 1 in 10,000,000 chance of winning or a 1 in 10,000 chance of winning. The mental image of winning $10,000,000 or $10,000, on the other hand, is likely to be very different. This is not to say that fear responses are completely unaffected by probabilities, but they are largely unaffected by orders-of-magnitude differences at the extreme (e.g. between a 1 in 100,000,000 chance of winning the lottery and a 1 in 100,000 chance).

Psychophysical studies of anxiety illustrate the relatively small role probability plays in anticipatory emotion. In these experiments, research participants experienced a series of countdown periods of stated length at the end of which they received, with some stated probability, a painful electric shock of varying intensity. Anxiety is operationalized by changes in participants' heart rate and skin conductance during the countdown period. The general finding from this research is that people's physiological responses to the impending shock are correlated with their expectations about the intensity of the shock – that is, bigger shocks elicited greater arousal (Deane, 1969). The probability of receiving the shock, however, does not affect arousal (Snortum and Wilding, 1971; Monat et al,1972; Bankhart and Elliott, 1974; Elliott, 1975) except for trials in which the probability is stated to be zero. Evidently, the mere thought of receiving a shock is enough to arouse individuals, but the precise likelihood of being shocked has little impact on level of arousal. These results suggest that feelings of fear or worry in the face of decisions under risk or uncertainty have an all-or-none characteristic; they may be sensitive to the possibility rather than the probability of negative consequences.

In a study designed to investigate cross-cultural differences in risky decision-making, Weber and Hsee (1998) asked participants to provide maximum buying prices for risky investment options that differed in the probabilities with which gains or losses of different magnitude would be realized. Although not reported in Weber and Hsee, participants were also asked to rate, for each investment option, the degree of worry or concern they would experience between the time they invested in the option and the time they would find out which outcome actually occurred. Whereas maximum buying prices were sensitive to both probability and outcome levels, $F(1, 6634) = 4.64$ and 5.12, respectively, $ps < .05$, reported feelings of worry were far less sensitive to probability levels, $F(1, 6634) = 1.69, p > .10$. A similar dissociation between intellectual judgements of risk and emotional reactions expressed by judgements of worry has been reported by Sjöberg (1998) in a study of subjective risk perceptions.

The observation that some changes in probability affect risky decisions more than others has been confirmed by many studies of decision-making (for a review, see Camerer, 1989) and has been incorporated into the predictions of many non-EU models as non-linearities in the probability weighting function (e.g. Kahneman and Tversky, 1979). One of the most robust observations in the domain of decision-making under uncertainty is the overweighting of small probabilities, particularly those associated with extreme outcomes (see Prelec, 1998). Many of the famous EU anomalies, such as the Allais paradox and the common ratio effect (see Kahneman and Tversky, 1979, for a description of both), can be explained parsimoniously in such terms (Camerer, 1995, p637). A 1 per cent change in the probability of an aversive event seems trivial when there is already a 49 per cent chance, but is likely to cause great concern, and concomitant effort to avert it, if it changes the chances from none at all to 1 per cent, that is, away from the certainty of not being exposed. Viscusi and Magat (1987), for example, found that people were willing to pay considerably more to reduce the risk of inhalation poisoning or skin poisoning from an insect spray from 5 in 10,000 to 0 than from 15 in 10,000 to 5 in 10,000.

Although these non-linearities in probability weights have been extensively documented and have a well-known label (the *certainty effect;* Kahneman and Tversky, 1979), relatively little work has been done to explain them. Incorporating emotional reactions into the prediction equation helps to explain these phenomena. As the probability of an aversive event passes the zero threshold, a consequence that was previously of no concern now becomes a source of worry. Subsequent increments in probability, however, have little additional emotional impact and, presumably for this reason, have little impact on choice.

In a recent paper, Rottenstreich and Hsee (1999) found not only that people were insensitive to probability variations, but also that such insensitivity depended on the emotional impact of the associated outcomes. This result lends support to the risk-as-feeling hypothesis, according to which people should be more insensitive to probability variations for emotional and vivid outcomes than for pallid outcomes. In one study, Rottenstreich and Hsee asked participants to indicate the largest amount of money they would be willing to pay to avoid an undesirable outcome that occurred with different levels of probability. The undesirable outcome was either a loss of $20 (a relatively pallid outcome) or a brief but painful electric shock (a more emotional-visceral outcome). The results were dramatic. When the outcome was pallid (losing $20), the participants were quite sensitive to probability variations: the dollar value placed on the uncertain outcome changed from $1 (for $p = .01$) to $18 (for $p = .99$). However, when the outcome evoked emotion (receiving an electric shock), participants were extremely insensitive to probability variations: the dollar value changed only from $7 (for p = .01) to $10 (for p = .99). In other words, when probability increased by a factor of 99 (from 1 to 99 per cent), the value of the uncertain prospect increased by less than a factor of 1.5 (from $7 to $10). Rottenstreich and Hsee (1999) replicated these results using positive outcomes as well. For example, when the outcome was a $500 discount on their tuition (a relatively pallid outcome), students were quite sensitive to probability variations. However, when the outcome was a $500 coupon they could use for their dream trip to Paris and Rome (a more emotion-laden outcome), students were less sensitive to probability variations.

Although most consequentialist decision theories consider probability weighting as independent of the nature of the outcome, the findings of Rottenstreich and Hsee (1999) suggest that the impact of probability depends strongly on the nature of the outcome. The probability weighting function is flatter (i.e. more overweighting of small probabilities) for vivid outcomes that evoke emotions than for pallid outcomes. It seems that the overweighting of small probabilities is a result of feelings of fear and hope – fear in the case of a negative outcome and hope in the case of a positive outcome.

The relationship between probabilities and emotions can help to explain one of the major paradoxes in decision-making under uncertainty: the prevalence of simultaneous gambling and purchasing of insurance. According to EU, risk aversion (which motivates insurance purchase) is caused by diminishing marginal utility of wealth (or increasing marginal disutility of poverty). If this is the case, then people who, through purchases of insurance, reveal themselves to be risk averse should not purchase actuarially unfair lottery tickets. Friedman and Savage (1948) argued that the observed pattern of behaviour suggests that utility functions take a complicated S-shaped form. Markowitz (1952) critiqued Friedman and Savage's explanation by demonstrating that it produced many unrealistic behavioural predictions, and advanced an alternative formulation that assumed (a) that people care about losses and gains relative to some reference point (usually the status quo) rather than about absolute levels of wealth and (b) that they evaluate losses and gains with a value function that is generally risk averse for gains and risk-seeking for losses. Kahneman and Tversky (1979) further developed Markowitz's model by adding a non-linear probability weighting function that overweighted small probabilities of both losses and gains. Prospect theory and similar models explain gambling on the basis of an overweighting of small probabilities of a gain (which is, however, countered by the general tendency toward risk aversion for gains) and insurance purchases on the basis of an overweighting of small probabilities of a loss (which is mitigated by the tendency towards risk-seeking for losses).

Although the overweighting of small probabilities may be partly responsible for lottery playing and insurance purchases, the overweighting of small probabilities may, itself, stem from the disproportionate fear and pleasurable anticipation evoked by such prospects, as discussed earlier. Consistent with this prediction, Hogarth and Kunreuther (1995) found that, when people make decisions regarding investment in protective measures such as warranties, they do not think about probabilities of malfunctions unless these figures are given to them. Rather, they use arguments such as peace of mind or sleeping well at night to defend their positions. Only when probabilities are explicitly provided do people include them as part of their reasoning. Marketers of insurance in fact rarely provide probabilities; instead, they tend to emphasize qualitative or emotional considerations. Likewise, lottery marketers highlight the pleasure of anticipation associated with lottery purchases with slogans such as 'buy a dream'. Middle class and lower middle class families who are struggling to make ends meet can savour the possibility that their money problems may come to an instant end when the weekly number is drawn.

The affective response to risks may also help to address another anomaly in the literature on risk-taking. For many risky decisions, the moment of uncertainty resolution is different from the time when consequences are actually realized. In some cases, moreover, individuals have some degree of control over when uncertainty is resolved. People can choose whether and when to be tested for diseases such as Huntington's chorea, HIV, or genetic markers associated with increased vulnerability to various types of cancer. Students can decide when to pick up grades, and parents can decide whether and when to learn the sex of a foetus. In some cases, early resolution can only be obtained at a cost. For example, in plea bargaining, early resolution can be achieved at the cost of accepting the prosecutor's offer. In all types of negotiations, the party who can wait longer typically does better; succumbing to the desire for early resolution in the form of a settlement, therefore, usually comes at the expense of a less favourable settlement.

Consequential models of risk-taking predict that early resolution will be preferred if other decisions have to be made that depend on the value of the obtained outcome (Markowitz, 1959; Mossin, 1969; Spence and Zeckhauser, 1972). For example, knowing the value of one's year-end bonus should help one to make more rational spending decisions during the intervening year. Studies that have tested this prediction have generally found, consistent with consequentialist models, that people do typically prefer early resolution of uncertainty. However, there are important exceptions to this general preference for early resolution. Specifically, people often prefer to delay resolution of uncertainty for gambles with small probabilities of gains or large probabilities of losses (Ahlbrecht and Weber, 1996). Elster and Loewenstein (1992, p228) argued that, in these cases, delayed resolution is desirable because it provides utility from anticipation. Small probabilities of large gains provide substantial utility from 'savouring' the gamble (Loewenstein, 1987) even when there is actually little likelihood of winning. Large probabilities of losses also provide utility from savouring because they are cognitively reframed as a (virtually) certain loss plus a small probability of a gain. Delaying resolution is desirable in these cases because it prolongs the period of hopeful anticipation. Consistent with this interpretation, Lovallo and Kahneman (2000) found an extremely strong positive correlation between people's evaluations of the attractiveness of a set of gambles and their willingness to delay those gambles. Recent theories that deal with delayed resolution preference have introduced considerations of utility derived from anticipation – hope, fear and dread (Pope, 1985; Chew and Ho, 1994; Caplin and Leahy, 1997).

Time interval between decision and realization of outcome

One of the most important determinants of fear that is likely to be relatively uncorrelated with cognitive assessments of risk is the time between the decision and the realization of its outcomes. As the prospect of an uncertain aversive event approaches in time, fear tends to increase, even when cognitive assessments of the probability or likely severity of the event remain constant (Loewenstein, 1987; Paterson and Neufeld, 1987; Roth et al, 1996). Breznitz (1971) informed individuals that they would receive a strong electric shock in either 3, 6 or 12 minutes. The average heart rate was lower for the distant warning group than for either of the other two groups, which did not differ from one another. Monat (1976) threatened individuals with an electric shock that they were told would occur after 1, 3 or 12 minutes. Heart rate, galvanic skin response, and self-reported anxiety were all inversely related to the duration of the waiting period. Such a temporal pattern of fear is highly adaptive; organisms that experienced similar levels of fear toward distant and immediate risks would be unlikely to survive long in a hostile environment. Indeed, one of the characteristics of certain types of stress disorders is the tendency to ruminate over risks that are remote in time (e.g. Nolen-Hoeksema, 1990; Sapolsky, 1994) or to continue to experience fear toward no longer threatening events that happened in the past (e.g. Barlow, 1988).

The increase in fear just before the 'moment of truth' has a range of diverse consequences. Several studies have found that people lower their expectations just prior to receiving important self-relevant information (e.g. Nisan, 1972; Shepperd et al, 1996; Sanna, 1999). Welch (1999) showed that the increase in fear before the moment of outcome resolution has behavioural consequences. In one study, students were offered a payment of $1 in exchange for telling a joke in front of a class the following week. When the appointed time arrived, both students who had agreed to tell the joke and those who had declined to do so were given the opportunity to change their minds. As predicted by the risk-as-feelings hypothesis, with the added assumption that fear increases as the moment of taking a risky action draws near, there was substantial 'chickening out'. 67 per cent of those who initially volunteered to tell a joke (6 out of 9) decided not to when the time came, but none of those who had initially declined the offer (0 out of 49) changed their mind and decided to tell a joke at the last minute ($p < .01$).

Other studies have provided more direct evidence that pessimistic shifts and chickening out are caused by emotional changes. Savitsky et al (1998) found that pessimistic shifts are associated with an increase in arousal. In a different study, Welch (1999) incorporated an explicit test of the hypothesis that chickening out was caused by affective reactions. The design of the study was identical to the study just described except that half of the students watched a fear-inducing film clip (two minutes from Kubrick's *The Shining*) before making their initial choice about whether to tell the joke in front of the class. Table 7.1 presents the results for the two groups. As can be seen, risk-taking was sensitive to both the temporal proximity of the risk and the immediate mood state induced by the film, with less risk-taking occurring when fear was aroused by the immediacy of the risky action or the scary film clip. The tendency to chicken out at the last minute undoubtedly overlaps in many situations with the tendency, demonstrated in research by Liberman and Trope (1998), for people to place greater weight on practical considerations (e.g. do I really have the time to attend the conference?) relative to more vague dimensions of desirability (the topic matter to be discussed at the conference) as moment of taking an action draws near. Both effects produce changes in behaviour with the passage of time; the increase in fear leads people

Table 7.1 *Effect of fear manipulation on fear, choice at Time 1, and choice at Time 2*

Response	No fear induction (n = 30)	Fear induction (n = 32)	Significance of difference
Self-reported fear about telling the joke[a]	6.1	7.3	p < .04
Agree to tell a joke at Time 1 (%)	33	6	p < .03
Agree to tell a joke at Time 2 (%)	13	0	ns

Note. Time 1 = 1 week before joke would be told; Time 2 = just before joke would be told.
[a]Measured on a 0–10-point scale.

to change their minds about taking risks, whereas the effect discussed by Liberman and Trope leads people to change their minds about actions that are desirable in a gestalt sense but have practical drawbacks.

Public panics

It is well established that decision-makers' emotional states can affect their cognitive evaluations of a risk (e.g. Johnson and Tversky, 1983). These cognitive evaluations, in turn, can affect the individual's emotional states. Because these effects exert reciprocal, self-reinforcing influences, there is a potential for self-reinforcing feedback effects. Fear increases arousal and arousal increases the intensity of new fear responses (Lang, 1995). Feedback processes of this type have the potential to create unstable situations in which relatively mild fears rapidly build into a panic reaction. One prominent theory of panic attacks (at the level of the individual) is precisely based on such a feedback process – namely, the idea that fearful thoughts (induced by a focus on internal bodily sensations) produce further bodily sensations, which intensify fears, which increase physiological reactions, and so on (Beck and Emery, 1985; Clark, 1986).

Attacks of panic can be seen at a societal level (Bartholomew, 1997). Such social panics are characterized by an explosion of public concern about a problem – typically unconnected with any sudden change in the underlying risk – followed by an also-sudden collapse of concern (Weinstein, 1989, p37). Well-publicized panics include outbreaks of Koru in Asia (an epidemic of fear in which people believe that their genitals are shrinking; Gwee, 1968; Chakraborty et al, 1983), unsubstantiated rumuors of mad 'slashers' and 'gassers' on the loose (Jacobs, 1965), and, recently in the United States, hysterical reactions to herpes and disappearing children (Loewenstein and Mather, 1990).

Panics are typically set off by highly vivid cases, or clusters of cases, that receive concentrated media attention (Weinstein, 1989, p46). As with individual-level panics, public panics seem to be fuelled, in part, by an interplay between anxiety, fear and subjective probabilities. Evidence supporting such a dynamic interplay of risk perceptions and anxiety comes from field studies. According to Simon Wessely, who has conducted several case studies of mass panics (see, e.g. Wessely, 1987; Wessely and Wardle, 1990; David and Wessely, 1995), almost all cases fit a common pattern. Someone observes a fear-inducing event or is exposed to a vivid frightening rumour, begins to experience anxiety, displays symptoms such as hyperventilating or collapsing that others see, and those others begin to get anxious themselves. As Wessely (cited in Gladwell, 1999) described it, 'before you know it everyone in the room is hyperventilating and collapsing' (p24). Feelings clearly play a prominent role in this process.

Evolutionary preparedness

Although cognitive evaluations of the likelihood and magnitude of outcomes are relatively domain independent, the work of Garcia and other researchers in the 1970s (see Seligman, 1971) suggests that the ability of events to evoke fear and other emotional reactions is restricted by biological or evolutionary preparedness. Humans and other animals seem to be preprogrammed to experience certain types of fears. For example, cage-reared rats who have never been exposed to a cat show signs of fear if exposed to the smell of cat fur (Panksepp, 1998). In some cases such preparedness seems to vary over the life course. For example, stranger fear has been observed in humans in a wide range of cultures, usually develops between 4 and 9 months of age, peaks around 12.5 months, and does not require aversive experience with strangers to develop (Menzies, 1995).

Beyond such preprogrammed fears, primates and humans seem to be biologically prepared to become fear-conditioned to certain objects (e.g. snakes, spiders, water and enclosed spaces) but not to others (but see McNally, 1987). Öhman (1986), for example, found superior conditioning using fear-relevant slides of snakes and spiders as conditional stimuli as compared to fear-irrelevant conditioned stimuli such as slides of flowers and mushrooms or geometric figures. More recent studies have followed up on Lazarus's research on subliminal influences (e.g. Lazarus and McCleary, 1951) by demonstrating that subliminal presentations of fear-relevant, but not of fear-irrelevant, conditioned stimuli are sufficient to elicit conditioned responses. Öhman and Soares (1993) argued that subliminal evocation of fear may help explain the irrationality of fears and phobias 'because their origin rests in cognitive structures that are not under the control of conscious intentions' (p129; see also Öhman and Soares, 1994).

In many instances of phobias, the inability to uncover any traumatic conditioning history has led to a search for alternative mechanisms. One mechanism, which has received substantial documentation in animal research, has been labelled *vicarious conditioning*. Mineka and colleagues (e.g. Cook and Mineka, 1990; Mineka and Cook, 1993) have demonstrated strong and persistent vicarious conditioning of snake fear in rhesus monkeys. In a prototypical experiment, cage-raised monkeys do not initially show a fear-reaction to snakes but developed one almost instantly after witnessing a fear response from a wild-reared monkey. Subsequent research indicated that vicarious conditioning also exhibits the phenomenon of preparedness. Cage-reared monkeys developed a fear reaction after viewing a tape in which another monkey appeared to react fearfully to a snake, but they did not develop such a reaction when, in a similar tape, the same monkey reacted fearfully to a flower stimulus.

Besides showing very rapid acquisition, certain types of fears also exhibit resistance to extinction. Even when fear conditioning is extinguished through repeated presentation of a conditioned stimulus (e.g. a tone) in the absence of the aversive unconditioned stimulus (e.g. a shock), the fear conditioning of the original association is not lost but remains latent. Such latency has been demonstrated in studies of spontaneous recovery of fear conditioning (Pavlov, 1927) and in studies in which reinstatement of conditioning has been shown to follow presentation of the unconditioned stimulus (Bouton and Swartzentruber, 1991; Bouton, 1994) or as a result of severing connections between the amygdala and the cortex (LeDoux, 1996). The latter finding suggests that the cortex plays an important role in the extinction of fear conditioning and is consistent with the idea that cortical and subcortical processing of fear may often be at odds with one another. The fear is, in a sense, still there, but either the subjective experience of fear or the behavioural response to it is cortically suppressed.

The critical implication of the research on evolutionary preparedness is that people are likely to react with little fear to certain types of objectively dangerous stimuli that evolution has not prepared them for, such as guns, hamburgers, automobiles, smoking and unsafe sex, even when they recognize the threat at a cognitive level. Types of stimuli that people are evolutionarily prepared to fear, such as caged spiders, snakes or heights (when adequate safety measures are in place), evoke a visceral response even when, at a cognitive level, they are recognized to be harmless.

It is tempting to draw a connection between such discrepancies in cognitive evaluations and fear reactions and the often-lamented discrepancy between scientists' and the lay public's concern for risks. Just as an animal might be very slow to develop fear toward an unfamiliar poison-emitting flower, there may also be a lag between cognitive and emotional reactions toward risks for which we are not prepared to have emotional reactions. On the one hand, even when environmental policymakers have become convinced that the existing information about the probability and negative consequences of risks such as global warming or radon warrant precautionary action, such sacrifices may require a level of public fear that does not exist. On the other hand, public alarm over risks that experts view as inconsequential, such as Alar or cyanide in Chilean grapes, can force the hand of reluctant policymakers (Slovic et al, 1994; Gregory et al, 1995, 1996).

Summary

The research reviewed in this section can be summarized as follows. First, fear as the emotional response experienced in risky situations reacts to probabilities and outcomes in a manner that is very different from that postulated by EU theory and its generalizations. Second, fear depends on a variety of factors that are not part of such models. Fear typically peaks just before a threat is experienced and is highly dependent on mental imagery (and thus subject to vividness effects). Fear responses also seem to be conditioned, in part, by our evolutionary make-up; we may be prepared to learn very rapidly about some types of risks but much more slowly about others. Fear responses are evoked, often by crude or subliminal cues. Fear conditioning may be permanent, or at least far longer lasting than other kinds of learning. To the extent that these differences exist between the calculus of objective risk and the determinants of fear, and to the extent that fear does, in fact, play an important role in risk-related behaviours, behaviour in the face of risk is unlikely to be well described by traditional consequentialist models.

Conclusions

Although decision-making under risk has been a central topic of decision theory, the decision-theoretic approach to decision-making under risk has largely ignored the role played by emotions. Whereas some theorists have considered the effects of emotions experienced after the decision (i.e. emotions elicited by good or bad outcomes), very little attention has been given to the impact of emotions experienced *during* the decision-making process. In contrast, such anticipatory emotions play a prominent role in clinical and social psychological theory and research and have received recent attention from neuroscientists.

People react to the prospect of risk at two levels: they evaluate the risk cognitively, and they react to it emotionally. Although the two reactions are interrelated, with cognitive appraisals giving rise to emotions and emotions influencing appraisals, the two types of reactions have different determinants. Cognitive evaluations of risk are sensitive to the variables identified by decision theory, namely probabilities and outcome valences. Although emotions do respond to cognitive evaluations, they can also arise with minimal cognitive processing (Zajonc, 1980), and people can experience fear reactions without even knowing what they are afraid of. In contrast to cognitive evaluations, emotional reactions are sensitive to the vividness of associated imagery, proximity in time, and a variety of other variables that play a minimal role in cognitive evaluations. Moreover, although emotional reactions are also sensitive to probability and outcome valence, the functional relationships are quite different from those for cognitive evaluations. As a result of these differences, people often experience a discrepancy between the fear they experience in connection with a particular risk and their cognitive evaluation of the threat posed by that risk.

Implications for research

One important implication of the risk-as-feelings hypothesis is that those doing risk-related research should make it a routine practice to collect information on emotional reactions to risks, in addition to such traditional measures as probabilities and outcome values. Ideally, such measures would include physiological measures as well as self-reports. Two areas in which these measures could provide useful information are gender and age-related changes in risk-taking.

When it comes to gender, large numbers of studies have found that male individuals tend to be more risk averse than female individuals (see Byrnes et al, 1999, for a recent meta-analysis). These differences are particularly pronounced when it comes to physical, or life-threatening, risks (Hersch, 1997), but have also been observed in other domains such as investment decisions (Bajtelsmit et al, 1997). Very little of this research has paid explicit attention to the role of risk-related emotions. There is, however, some intriguing evidence suggesting that gender differences in risk-taking may be linked to parallel differences in emotional responsiveness. Several studies have found that female individuals report more and better imagery than male individuals (see Harshman and Paivio, 1987, for a review of several studies) and that they experience emotions more intensely than male individuals, on average. When men and women are asked to recall their saddest memory, positron emission tomography scans indicate that brain activity increases significantly more in the female brain than in the male brain (George, 1999). Of greatest relevance to the risk-as-feelings hypothesis, women report experiencing nervousness and fear more intensely than men do (Stapley and Haviland, 1989; Brody et al, 1990; Fujita et al, 1991; Brody, 1993). Further studies are needed to determine whether observed male–female differences in risk-taking may be mediated by differences in emotional reactions to risks. If true, it would be interesting to examine whether women are more risk-seeking in situations to which they respond less emotionally than men.

There is also a possibility that emotional changes associated with *aging* may help to explain observed age-based differences in risk-taking, and specifically adolescents' high risk-taking propensities. One popular explanation for adolescent risk-taking is the so-called invulnerability hypothesis according to which adolescent risk-taking stems from feelings of invulnerability (see, e.g., Burger and Burns, 1988; Whitley and Hern, 1991). From a decision-making perspective, the invulnerability hypothesis implies that adolescents either do not consider some potentially harmful consequences of risky behaviour or underestimate the likelihood of these consequences happening to them. Despite its popularity, however, there is surprisingly little evidence that supports the invulnerability hypothesis and some evidence that conflicts with it. Beyth-Marom et al (1993) and Quadre et al (1993), for example, compared adolescents and adults on their cognitive evaluations of the consequences of engaging or not engaging in various risky behaviours. Contrary to the invulnerability hypothesis, these studies found relatively few differences in the subjective probabilities of negative outcomes. The possibility that age-based differences in risk-taking are affectively mediated (and possibly the result of differences in the vividness of mental simulations of behaviour), therefore, merits further exploration.

A second pressing need in basic research is to examine the effects of *intense* emotions on risk-taking and behaviour. Most of the current research on the effects of emotions examines relatively mild emotions that are induced using techniques such as guided imagery. It is exactly at such low levels of intensity that emotions are most likely to play the largely advisory role emphasized by many of the current theories reviewed in the introduction. The clinical literature on fear and anxiety may have been the area in which cognition–emotion conflicts are most prevalent in part because the emotions examined in clinical settings and with clinical populations are much more intense than those elicited in the laboratory with non-clinical populations. Eliciting powerful emotions in normal populations is certainly problematic; perhaps the best opportunities for such research occur in naturalistic settings in which emotions reliably run high (e.g. just before parachuting, or in the courtroom).

Policy implications

Individuals' emotional reactions to risks not only often differ from their cognitive evaluations of those risks; they also often diverge from the evaluations of experts. Public perception of the risks of silicone implants in causing auto-immune diseases, for example, led Dow Corning to stop production of implants in 1992 and file for bankruptcy in 1995, despite two major medical reports that revealed no evidence of silicone-related illnesses and a clean bill of health from the American College of Rheumatology (Cowley, 1995). Controversies about the licensing of technologies such as genetic engineering or the siting of facilities such as landfills, incinerator plants, or halfway houses for the mentally handicapped tend to be fuelled primarily by emotional reactions to the risks, rather than by scientific evaluations of objective risk levels. Although the controversy about location of the high-level nuclear waste repository generates powerful emotions, large numbers of people seem amazingly unconcerned about the fact that high-level nuclear waste is currently being stored at nuclear reactors that are in close proximity to major population centres. Referring to the current controversy about the Department of Energy's nuclear waste disposal plans for Yucca Mountain (Nevada), Slovic et al (1991a) described officials from the Department of Energy, the nuclear industry and their technical experts as 'profoundly puzzled, frustrated, and disturbed by public opposition that many of them consider to be based on irrationality and ignorance' (p1603). Whereas business or government experts have clear quantitative definitions of such risks on the basis of objective data or models, members of the general public often seem to evaluate the same options in very different ways. Much of the early work by Slovic et al (1986) on psychological risk dimensions was funded by the Nuclear Regulatory Commission (NRC) to explain how public perception of the riskiness of nuclear technology could differ so drastically from the estimates provided by NRC engineers. In the intervening years, these differences in perception have shown no sign of diminishing. Future research should continue to investigate whether these differences in perception are the result of differences in the degree to which risks are processed cognitively versus affectively by different segments of the population.

The divergence between the emotional reactions of the public to risks and professionals' appraisals of risks creates a significant dilemma for policymakers. On the one hand, many policymakers would like to be responsive to public attitudes and opinions. On the other hand, there is a strong rationale for basing public policy on the best scientific assessments of risk severity. Sunstein (2000) justified cost–benefit analysis precisely on the basis that it provides an impartial assessment of programmes that are resistant to the influence of public fears. He noted that governments allocate the limited resources for risk mitigation in an inefficient fashion in part because they are responsive to lay judgements about the magnitude of risks. Sunstein then cited results from diverse lines of research showing that a government that could insulate itself from such misinformed judgements could save tens of thousands of lives and tens of billions of dollars annually. Consistent with the risk-as-feelings hypothesis, Sunstein attributed the public's misinformed judgements in part to emotional influences:

> Risk-related objections can be a product not so much of thinking as of intense emotions, often produced by extremely vivid images of what might go wrong ... The role of cost–benefit analysis is straightforward here. Just as the Senate was designed to have a 'cooling effect' on the passions of the House of Representatives, so cost–benefit analysis might ensure that policy is driven not by hysteria or alarm, but by a full appreciation of the effects of relevant risks and their control. (p16)

Sunstein argued further that cost–benefit analysis could not only act as a check on unwarranted fears (e.g. Alar), but could also serve to introduce regulation of risks that are objectively threatening but that do not elicit visceral reactions in the populace (e.g. lead in gasoline and radon in homes).

Simply disregarding the public's fears and basing policy on the experts, however, is difficult in a democracy and ignores the real costs that fears impose on people, as is well documented in the literatures on stress and anxiety. The best policy, then, would be one that involves mitigating real risks and irrational fears. Although clinical treatment of anxiety disorders 'represents one of the great success stories of applied psychological science' (Bouton et al, 2001, p4), there is very little research on fear-reduction strategies that might be effective at a societal level.

In this chapter we have proposed a model of risky choice that highlights the role of anticipatory emotions – immediate visceral reactions (e.g. fear, anxiety, dread) to risks and uncertainties that arise at the time of decision-making. The model is fundamentally different from the consequentialist approach that characterizes most existing risky-choice theories. Consequentialist models, to the extent that they include emotions at all, tend to incorporate anticipated emotions – emotions that are expected to result from the consequences of the decision. By taking account of the role of anticipatory emotions that are experienced at the moment of decision-making, our model explains a variety of phenomena that have puzzled decision theorists who have attempted to explain them at a purely cognitive level.

Although the focus of this chapter has been on choices under risk, the basic theme can be applied to any type of decision, whether it involves risks or not. Like theories of risky choice, most theories of riskless choice, including multi-attribute utility theories, also take a consequentialist perspective, assuming that decisions are made to maximize the utility of future consequences. Even theories that do take emotions into consideration typically view emotions as a consequence of one's decision. In contrast, our model, and the substantial body of research on which it is based, suggest that gut feelings experienced at the moment of making a decision, which are often quite independent of the consequences of the decision, can play a critical role in the choice one eventually makes.

Notes

1   The same pattern can be seen in the popular press and literature. Witness a recent *Newsweek* article titled 'Don't Ignore Your Fear' (1997) a *Spiegel* (1997) article titled 'Die Macht der Gefuehle' (The power of feelings), or the recent popular bestseller *The Gift of Fear: Survival Signals that Protect Us from Violence* (de Becker, 1997).

2   Holtgrave and Weber (1993) demonstrated that Slovic et al's risk dimensions have explanatory power even after controlling for the effect of probabilities and outcomes. They attempted to explain subjective assessments of a wide variety of financial and health and safety risks on the basis of both probabilities and utilities – as captured by a simplified version of Luce and Weber's (1986) conjoint expected-risk model – and Slovic et al's (1986) psychometric risk dimensions. The best fits were obtained by a hybrid model that added Slovic et al's three *dread* risk dimensions to the conjoint expected-risk model. These results

suggest that even evaluations of the risk of financial investments have emotional components that are not completely described by the objective components of cognitive information-integration models.

3   More recent research casts some doubt on these earlier results. One study compared psychopathic and non-psychopathic incarcerated men and found no difference in trait anxiety or fear between the two groups (Schmitt and Newman, 1999). Another study compared psychopathic and non-psychopathic incarcerees' performance on Damasio's card sort task (Schmitt et al, 1999). Although psychopathic incarcerated men did not perform differently from non-psychopathic incarcerated men, individuals high in trait anxiety became more risk averse relative to those low in trait anxiety as they gained experience with the cards.

4   In a study that illustrates the importance of mental imagery, Shiv and Huber (2000; see also Shiv and Fedorikhin, 1999) asked individuals to choose between a series of two-choice alternatives. In all cases, one was inferior on a pallid dimension (e.g. a higher price), and the other was inferior on a fear-inducing dimension (e.g. no power protection on a computer). In a 2 × 2 factorial design, some individuals were asked to think about their feelings about each of the products and others were not, and some individuals were instructed to *not* use imagery when they made their choice and others were not. The main finding was that encouraging individuals to think about their feelings about the products increased the weight placed on the fear-inducing dimension, but only when they were not instructed to not use imagery (i.e. when they were, presumably, using it). Asking individuals to not imagine using the product inhibited the impact of feelings on choice.

References

Ahlbrecht, M., and Weber, M. (1996). The resolution of uncertainty: An experimental study. *Journal of Institutional and Theoretical Economics, 152*, 593–677.

Ajzen, I., and Fishbein, M. (1980). *Understanding attitudes and predicting behavior.* Englewood Cliffs, NJ: Prentice Hall.

Alhakami, A. S., and Slovic, P. (1994). A psychological study of the inverse relationship between perceived risk and perceived benefits. *Risk Analysis, 14*, 1085–1096.

Armony, J. L., Servan-Schreiber, D., Cohen, J. D., and LeDoux, J. E. (1995). An anatomically-constrained neural network model of fear conditioning. *Behavioral Neuroscience, 109*, 246–256.

Armony, J. L., Servan-Schreiber, D., Cohen, J. D., and LeDoux, J. E. (1997). Computational modeling of emotion: Explorations through the anatomy and physiology of fear conditioning. *Trends in Cognitive Sciences, 1*, 28–34.

Bajtelsmit, V. L., Bernasek, A., and Jianakoplos, N. A. (1997). Gender differences in pension investment allocation decisions. *Journal of Risk and Insurance, 16*, 135–147.

Bankhart, C. P., and Elliott, R. (1974). Heart rate and skin conductance in anticipation of shocks with varying probability of occurrence. *Psycho-physiology, 11*, 160–174.

Bargh, J. A. (1984). Automatic and conscious processing of social information. In R. S. Wyer and T. K. Srull (Eds.), *Handbook of social cognition* (Vol. 3, pp. 1–43). Hillsdale, NJ: Erlbaum.

Barlow, D. H. (1988). *Anxiety and its disorders: The nature and treatment of anxiety and panic.* New York: Guilford Press.

Barsky, B., Juster, F. T., Kimball, M. S., and Shapiro, M. D. (1997). Preference parameters and behavioral heterogeneity: An experimental approach in the health and retirement study. *Quarterly Journal of Economics, 112*, 537–579.

Bartholomew, R. (1997, May/June). Collective delusions: A skeptic's guide. *Skeptical Inquirer*, pp. 29–33.

Bechara, A., Damasio, H., Tranel, D., and Damasio, A. R. (1997). Deciding advantageously before knowing the advantageous strategy. *Science, 275*, 1293–1295.

Beck, A. T., and Emery, T. (1985). *Anxiety disorders and phobias*. New York: Basic Books.

Becker, M. H. (1974). The health belief model and personal health behavior. *Health Education Monographs, 2*, 324–508.

Bell, D. E. (1982). Regret in decision making under uncertainty. *Operations Research, 30*, 961–981.

Bell, D. E. (1985). Disappointment in decision making under uncertainty. *Operations Research, 33*, 1–27.

Benthin, A., Slovic, P., Moran, P., Severson, H., Mertz, C. K., and Gerrard, M. (1995). Adolescent health-threatening and health-enhancing behaviors: A study of word association and imagery. *Journal of Adolescent Health, 17*, 143–152.

Benartzi, S., and Thaler, R. H. (1995). Myopic loss aversion and the equity premium puzzle. *The Quarterly Journal of Economics, 110*, 73–92.

Bernay, T., Porrath, S., Golding-Mather, J. M., and Murray, J. (1982). The impact of breast cancer screening on feminine identity: Implications for patient education. *Breast, 8*, 2–5.

Beyth-Marom, R., Austin, L., Fischhoff, B., Palmgren, C., and Quadrel, M. (1993). Perceived consequences of risky behavior: Adolescents and adults. *Developmental Psychology, 29*, 549–563.

Bouton, M. E. (1994). Conditioning, remembering, and forgetting. *Journal of Experimental Psychology, 20*, 219–231.

Bouton, M. E., and Swartzentruber, D. (1991). Sources of relapse after extinction in Pavlovian and instrumental learning. *Clinical Psychology Review, 11*, 123–140.

Bouton, M. E., Mineka, S., and Barlow, D. H. (2001). A modern learning theory perspective on the etiology of panic disorder. *Psychological Review, 108*, 4–32.

Bower, G. H. (1981). Mood and memory. *American Psychologist, 36*, 129–148.

Bower, G. H. (1991). Mood congruity of social judgment. In J. Forgas (Ed.), *Emotion and social judgment* (pp. 31–54). Oxford, England: Pergamon Press.

Bower, G. (1992). How might emotions affect learning. In S.-A. Christianson (Ed.), *The handbook of emotion and memory: Research and theory* (pp. 3–31). Hillsdale, NJ: Erlbaum.

Breznitz, S. (1971). A study of worrying. *British Journal of Social and Clinical Psychology, 10*, 271–279.

Brody, L. R. (1993). On understanding gender differences in the expression of emotion. In S. L. Ablon, D. Brown, E. J. Khantzian, and J. E. Mack (Eds.), *Human feelings: Explorations in affect development and meaning* (pp. 87–121). Hillsdale, NJ: Analytic Press.

Brody, L. R., Hay, D., and Vandewater, E. (1990). Gender, gender role identity and children's reported feelings toward the same and opposite sex. *Sex Roles, 21*, 363–387.

Browne, M. J., and Hoyt, R. E. (2000). The demand for flood insurance: Empirical evidence. *Journal of Risk and Uncertainty, 20*, 271–289.

Burger, J. M., and Burns, L. (1988). The illusion of unique invulnerability and the use of effective contraception. *Personality and Social Psychology Bulletin, 14*, 264–270.

Byrnes, J. P., Miller, D. C., and Schafer, W. D. (1999). Gender differences in risk taking: A meta-analysis. *Psychological Bulletin, 125*, 367–383.

Camerer, C. (1989). An experimental test of several generalized utility theories. *Journal of Risk and Uncertainty, 2*, 61–104.

Camerer, C. (1995). Individual decision making. In J. H. Kagel and A. E. Roth (Eds.), *Handbook of experimental economics* (pp. 587–683). Princeton, NJ: Princeton University Press.

Caplin, A., and Leahy, J. (1997). *Psychological expected theory and anticipatory feelings.* Unpublished manuscript, New York University, Department of Economics.

Carroll, D., Baker, J., and Preston, M. (1979). Individual differences in visual imagery and the voluntary control of heart rate. *British Journal of Psychology, 70*, 39–49.

Chaiken, S., and Trope, Y. (Eds.) (1999). *Dual process theories in social psychology.* New York: Guilford Press.

Chakraborty, A., Das, S., and Mukherji, A. (1983). Koro epidemic in India. *Transcultural Psychiatric Research Review, 20*, 150–151.

Chew, S. H., and Ho, J. L. (1994). Hope: An empirical study of attitude toward the timing of uncertainty resolution. *Journal of Risk and Uncertainty, 8*, 267–288.

Clark, D. M. (1986). A cognitive approach to panic. *Behavior Research and Therapy, 24*, 461–470.

Cleckley, H. (1941). *The mask of sanity.* St. Louis, MO: C. V. Mosby.

Clore, G. L. (1992). Cognitive phenomenology: Feelings and the construction of judgment. In L. L. Martin and A. Tesser (Eds.), *The construction of social judgments* (pp. 133–163). Hillsdale, NJ: Erlbaum.

Clore, G. L., Schwarz, N., and Conway, M. (1994). Affective causes and consequences of social information processing. In R. S. Wyer and T. K. Srull (Eds.), *Handbook of social cognition* (Vol. 1, pp. 323–417). Hillsdale, NJ: Erlbaum.

Cook, M., and Mineka, S. (1990). Selective associations in the observational conditioning of fear in Rhesus monkeys. *Journal of Experimental Psychology: Animal Behavior Processes, 16*, 372–389.

Cottle, T. J., and Klineberg, S. L. (1974). *The present of things future.* New York: Free Press.

Cowley, G. (1995, November 13). Silicone: Juries vs. science. *Newsweek*, p. 75.

Damasio, A. R. (1994). *Descartes' error: Emotion, reason, and the human brain.* New York: Putnam.

David, A. S., and Wessely, S. C. (1995). The legend of Camelford: Medical consequences of a water pollution accident. *Journal of Psychosomatic Research, 39*, 1–9.

Deane, G. (1969). Cardiac activity during experimentally induced anxiety. *Psychophysiology, 6*, 17–30.

de Becker, G. (1997). *The gift of fear: Survival signals that protect us from violence.* Boston: Little, Brown, and Company.

Derakshan, N., and Eysenck, M. W. (1997). Interpretive biases for one's own behavior and physiology in high-trait-anxious individuals and repressors. *Journal of Personality and Social Psychology, 73*, 816–825.

Eisenberg, A. E., Baron, J., and Seligman, M. E. P. (1995). *Individual differences in risk aversion and anxiety* (Working Paper). University of Pennsylvania, Department of Psychology.

Elliott, R. (1975). Heart rate in anticipation of shocks which have different probabilities of occurrences. *Psychological Reports, 36*, 923–931.

Ellsworth, P. C., and Smith, C. A. (1988). From appraisal to emotion: Differences among unpleasant feelings. *Motivation and Emotion, 12*, 271–302.

Elster, J., and Loewenstein, G. (1992). Utility from memory and anticipation. In G. Loewenstein and J. Elster (Eds.), *Choice over time* (pp. 213–234). New York: Russell Sage.

Epstein, S., Lipson, A., Holstein, C., and Huh, E. (1992). Irrational reactions to negative outcomes: Evidence for two conceptual systems. *Journal of Personality and Social Psychology, 62*, 328–339.

Eysenck, M. W. (1992). *Anxiety: The cognitive perspective.* Hove, England: Erlbaum.

Eysenck, M. W., MacLeod, C., and Matthews, A. (1987). Cognitive functioning and anxiety. *Psychological Research, 49*, 189–195.

Finucane, M., Alhakami, A., Slovic, P., and Johnson, S. M. (2000). The affect heuristic in judgments of risks and benefits. *Journal of Behavioral Decision Making, 13*, 1–17.

Fischhoff, B., Lichtenstein, S., Slovic, P., Derby, S. L., and Keeney, R. L. (1981). *Acceptable risk.* Cambridge, England: Cambridge University Press.

Fowles, D. C., and Missel, K. A. (1994). Electrodermal hyporeactivity, motivation, and psychopathy: Theoretical issues. In D. C. Fowles, P. Sutker, and S. Goodman (Eds.), *Progress in experimental personality and psychopathy research 1994: Special focus on psychopathy and antisocial behavior: A developmental perspective* (pp. 263–283). New York: Springer.

Freeman, W., and Watts, J. W. (1942). *Psychosurgery; intelligence, emotion and social behavior following prefrontal lobotomy for mental disorders.* Springfield, IL: Charles C. Thomas.

Friedman, M., and Savage, L. (1948). The utility analysis of choices involving risk. *Journal of Political Economy, 56*, 279–304.

Frijda, N. H. (1986). *The emotions.* Cambridge, England: Cambridge University Press.

Frijda, N. H., Kuipers, P., and ter Schure, E. (1989). Relations among emotion, appraisal, and emotional action readiness. *Journal of Personality and Social Psychology, 57*, 212–228.

Fujita, F., Diener, E., and Sandvik, E. (1991). Gender differences in negative affect and well-being: The case for emotional intensity. *Journal of Personality and Social Psychology, 61*, 427–434.

George, M. R. (1999, Spring/Summer). National Institute of Mental Health, research described in do male and female brains respond differently to severe emotional stress?: In a flurry of new research, scientists are finding tantalizing clues. *Newsweek* (Special Edition: What Every Woman Needs to Know), pp. 68–71.

Gladwell, M. (1999, July 12). Is the Belgian Coca-Cola hysteria the real thing? *New Yorker*, pp. 24–25.

Gneezy, U., and Potters, J. (1997). An experiment on risk taking and evaluation periods. *Quarterly Journal of Economics, 112*, 631–645.

Gregory, R., Flynn, J., and Slovic, P. (1995). Technological stigma. *American Scientist, 83*, 220–223.

Gregory, R., Slovic, P., and Flynn, J. (1996). Risk perceptions, stigma, and health policy. *Health and Place, 2*, 213–220.

Gwee, A. L. (1968). Koro: Its origin and nature as a disease entity. *Singapore Medical Journal, 9*, 3.

Hare, R. D. (1965). Psychopathy, fear arousal and anticipated pain. *Psychological Reports, 16*, 499–502.

Hare, R. D. (1966). Temporal gradient of fear arousal in psychopaths. *Journal of Abnormal and Social Psychology, 70*, 442–445.

Harless, D. W., and Camerer, C. F. (1994). The predictive utility of generalized expected utility theories. *Econometrica, 62*, 1251–1289.

Harshman, R. A., and Paivio, A. (1987). Paradoxical sex differences in self-reported imagery. *Canadian Journal of Psychology, 41*, 303–316.

Hendickx, L., Vlek, C., and Oppewal, H. (1989). Relative importance of scenario and information and frequency information in the judgment of risk. *Acta Psychologica, 72*, 41–63.

Hersch, J. (1997). Smoking, seat belts, and other risky consumer decisions: Differences by gender and race. *Managerial and Decision Economics, 11*, 241–256.

Hogarth, R., and Kunreuther, H. (1995). Decision making under ignorance: Arguing with yourself. *Journal of Risk and Uncertainty, 10*, 1015–1036.

Holtgrave, D., and Weber, E. U. (1993). Dimensions of risk perception for financial and health-and-safety risks. *Risk Analysis, 13*, 553–558.

Hsee, C. K., and Weber, E. U. (1997). A fundamental prediction error: Self–other discrepancies in risk preference. *Journal of Experimental Psychology: General, 126*, 45–53.

Insurance Advocate (1994). Flood disasters noted by those in jeopardy but they still don't buy flood insurance. *Insurance Advocate, 105*, 17.

Isaac, R. M., and James, D. (2000). Just who are you calling risk averse? *Journal of Risk and Uncertainty, 20,* 177–187.

Isen, A. M., and Geva, N. (1987). The influence of positive affect on acceptable level of risk: The person with a large canoe has a large worry. *Organizational Behavior and Human Decision Processes, 39,* 145–154.

Isen, A. M., and Patrick, R. (1983). The effect of positive feelings on risk-taking: When the chips are down. *Organizational Behavior and Human Performance, 31,* 194–202.

Isen, A. M., Shalker, T. E., Clark, M., and Karp, L. (1978). Affect, accessibility of material in memory, and behavior: A cognitive loop? *Journal of Personality and Social Psychology, 36,* 1–12.

Isen, A. M., Nygren, T. E., and Ashby, F. G. (1988). Influence of positive affect on the subjective utility of gains and losses: It is just not worth the risk. *Journal of Personality and Social Psychology, 55,* 710–717.

Jacobs, N. (1965). The phantom slasher of Taipei: Mass hysteria in a non-Western society. *Social Problems, 12,* 318–328.

Janis, I. L., and Feshbach, S. (1953). Effects of fear-arousing communications. *Journal of Abnormal and Social Psychology, 48,* 78–92.

Janis, I. L., and Mann, L. (1977). *Decision making: A psychological analysis of conflict, choice, and commitment.* New York: Free Press.

Johnson, E. J., and Tversky, A. (1983). Affect, generalization, and the perception of risk. *Journal of Personality and Social Psychology, 45,* 20–31.

Johnson, E. J., Hershey, J., Meszaros, J., and Kunreuther, H. (1993). Framing, probability distortions, and insurance decisions. *Journal of Risk and Uncertainty, 7,* 35–51.

Kahneman, D., and Ritov, I. (1994). Determinants of stated willingness to pay for public goods: A study in the headline method. *Journal of Risk and Uncertainty, 9,* 5–38.

Kahneman, D., and Tversky, A. (1979). Prospect theory: An analysis of decision under risk. *Econometrica, 47,* 263–291.

Kahneman, D., Schkade, D. A., and Sunstein, C. R. (1998). Shared outrage and erratic awards: The psychology of punitive damages. *Journal of Risk and Uncertainty, 16,* 49–86.

Kahneman, D., Ritov, I., and Schkade, D. (1999). Economic preferences or attitude expressions? An analysis of dollar responses to public issues. *Journal of Risk and Uncertainty, 19,* 203–237.

Kavanagh, D. J., and Bower, G. H. (1985). Mood and self-efficacy: Impact of joy and sadness on perceived capabilities. *Cognitive Therapy and Research, 9,* 507–525.

Kunreuther, H. (1976). Limited knowledge and insurance protection. *Public Policy, 24,* 227–261.

Kunreuther, H., Ginsburg, R., Miller, L., Sagi, P., Slovic, P., Borkan, B., and Katz, N. (1978). *Disaster insurance protection: Public policy lessons.* New York: Wiley.

Lang, P. J. (1995). The emotion probe: Studies of motivation and attention. *American Psychologist, 50,* 372–385.

Lazarus, R., and McCleary, R. (1951). Autonomic discrimination without awareness: A study of subception. *Psychological Review, 58,* 113–122.

LeDoux, J. (1996). *The emotional brain.* New York: Simon and Schuster.

Lerner, J. S., and Keltner, D. (2000). Beyond valence: Toward a model of emotion-specific influences on judgment and choice. *Cognition and Emotion, 14,* 473–494.

Lerner, J. S., and Keltner, D. (2001). *Fear, anger, and risk. Journal of Personality and Social Psychology 81,* 146–159.

Leventhal, H., and Watts, J. (1966). Sources of resistance to fear arousing communications on smoking and lung cancer. *Journal of Personality, 34,* 155–175.

Liberman, N., and Trope, Y. (1998). The role of feasibility and desirability considerations in near and distant future decisions: A test of temporal construal theory. *Journal of Personality and Social Psychology, 75,* 5–18.

Lieberman, A., and Chaiken, S. (1992). Defensive processing of personally relevant health messages. *Personality and Social Psychology Bulletin, 18*, 669–679.

Loewenstein, G. (1987). Anticipation and the valuation of delayed consumption. *Economic Journal, 97*, 666–684.

Loewenstein, G. (1996). Out of control: Visceral influences on behavior. *Organizational Behavior and Human Decision Processes, 65*, 272–292.

Loewenstein, G. (1999). A visceral account of addiction. In J. Elster and O. J. Skog (Eds.), *Getting hooked: Rationality and addiction* (pp. 235–264). Cambridge, England: Cambridge University Press.

Loewenstein, G., and Lerner, J. (2002). The role of emotion in decision making. In R. J. Davidson, H. H. Goldsmith, and K. R. Scherer (Eds.), *The handbook of affective science*. Oxford, England: Oxford University Press.

Loewenstein, G., and Mather, J. (1990). Dynamic processes in risk perception. *Journal of Risk and Uncertainty, 3*, 155–170.

Loomes, G., and Sugden, R. (1982). Regret theory: An alternative theory of rational choice under uncertainty. *Economic Journal, 92*, 805–824.

Loomes, G., and Sugden, R. (1986). Disappointment and dynamic consistency in choice under uncertainty. *Review of Economic Studies, 53*, 271–282.

Lopes, L. L. (1987). Between hope and fear: The psychology of risk. In L. Berkowitz (Ed.), *Advances in experimental social psychology* (Vol. 20, pp. 255–295). San Diego, CA: Academic Press.

Lopes, L. L. (1995). Algebra and process in modeling risky choice. In J. R. Busemeyer, R. Hastie, and D. L. Medin (Eds.), *Decision making from a cognitive perspective. The psychology of learning and motivation* (Vol. 32, pp. 177–220). New York: Academic Press.

Lovallo, D., and Kahneman, D. (2000). Living with uncertainty: Attractiveness and resolution timing. *Journal of Behavioral Decision Making, 13*, 179–190.

Luce, M. F., Bettman, J. R., and Payne, J. W. (1997). Choice processing in emotionally difficult decisions. *Journal of Experimental Psychology: Learning, Memory, and Cognition, 23*, 384–405.

Luce, M. F., Bettman, J. R., and Payne, J. W. (1999). Emotional tradeoff difficulty and choice. *Journal of Marketing Research, 36*, 143–159.

Luce, R. D., and von Winterfeldt, D. (1994). What common ground exists for descriptive, prescriptive, and normative utility theories? *Management Science, 40*, 263–279.

Luce, R. D., and Weber, E. U. (1986). An axiomatic theory of conjoint, expected risk. *Journal of Mathematical Psychology, 30*, 188–205.

Luu, P., Tucker, D. M., and Derryberry, D. (1998). Anxiety and the motivational basis of working memory. *Cognitive Therapy and Research, 22*, 577–594.

Lykken, D. T. (1957). A study of anxiety in the sociopathic personality. *Journal of Abnormal and Social Psychology, 55*, 6–10.

MacCrimmon, K. R., and Wehrung, D. A. (1986). *Taking risks: The management of uncertainty.* New York: The Free Press.

Mann, L. (1992). Stress, affect, and risk taking. In Y. J. Frank (Ed.), *Risk-taking behavior* (Wiley Series in Human Performance and Cognition, pp. 202–230). Chichester, England: John Wiley and Sons.

Markowitz, H. (1952). The utility of wealth. *Journal of Political Economy, 60*, 151–158.

Markowitz, H. M. (1959). *Portfolio selection.* New York: Wiley.

Mayer, J. D., and Hanson, E. (1995). Mood-congruent judgment over time. *Personality and Social Psychology Bulletin, 21*, 237–244.

Mayer, J. D., Gaschke, Y. N., Braverman, D. L., and Evans, T. W. (1992). Mood-congruent judgment is a general effect. *Journal of Personality and Social Psychology, 63*, 119–132.

McNally, R. J. (1987). Preparedness and phobias: A review. *Psychological Bulletin, 101*, 283–303.

Mellers, B. A., Schwartz, A., Ho, K., and Ritov, I. (1997). Decision affect theory: Emotional reactions to the outcomes of risky options. *Psychological Science, 8*, 423–429.

Mellers, B., Schwartz, A., and Ritov, I. (1999). Emotion-based choice. *Journal of Experimental Psychology: General, 128*, 332–345.

Menzies, R. G. (1995). The uneven distribution of fears and phobias: A nonassociative account. *Behavioral and Brain Sciences, 18*, 305–306.

Miller, G. A., Levin, D., Kozak, M., Cook, E., McLean, A., and Lang, P. (1987). Individual differences in imagery and the psychophysiology of emotion. *Cognition and Emotion, 1*, 367–390.

Mineka, S., and Cook, M. (1993). Mechanisms involved in the observational conditioning of fear. *Journal of Experimental Psychology: General, 122*, 23–38.

Monat, A. (1976). Temporal uncertainty, anticipation time, and cognitive coping under threat. *Journal of Human Stress, 2*, 32–43.

Monat, A., Averill, J. R., and Lazarus, R. S. (1972). Anticipatory stress and coping reactions under various conditions of uncertainty. *Journal of Personality and Social Psychology, 24*, 237–253.

Mossin, J. (1969). A note on uncertainty and preferences in a temporal context. *American Economic Review, 59*, 172–173.

Murray, M., and McMillan, C. (1993). Social and behavioral predictors of women's cancer screening practices in Northern Ireland. *Journal of Public Health Medicine, 15*, 147–153.

Ness, R. M., and Klaas, R. (1994). Risk perception by patients with anxiety disorders. *Journal of Nervous and Mental Disease, 182*, 466–470.

Newsweek (1997, July 21). Don't ignore your fear. p. 78.

Nisan, M. (1972). Dimension of time in relation to choice behavior and achievement orientation. *Journal of Personality and Social Psychology, 21*, 175–182.

Nisbett, R., and Ross, L. (1980). *Human inference: Strategies and shortcomings of social judgment.* Englewood Cliffs, NJ: Prentice Hall.

Nolen-Hoeksema, S. (1990). *Sex differences in depression.* Stanford, CA: Stanford University Press.

Nygren, T. E., Isen, A. M., Taylor, P. J., and Dulin, J. (1996). The influence of positive affect on the decision rule in risk situations: Focus on outcome (and especially avoidance of loss) rather than probability. *Organizational Behavior and Human Decision Processes, 66*, 59–72.

Öhman, A. (1986). Face the beast and fear the face: Animal and social fears as prototypes for evoluationary analyses of emotion. *Psychophysiology, 23*, 123–145.

Öhman, A., and Soares, J. J. F. (1993). On the automatic nature of phobic fear: Conditioned electrodermal responses to masked fear-relevant stimuli. *Journal of Abnormal Psychology, 102*, 121–132.

Öhman, A., and Soares, J. J. F. (1994). Unconscious anxiety: Phobic responses to masked stimuli. *Journal of Abnormal Psychology, 103*, 231–240.

O'Malley, M. S., and Fletcher, S. W. (1987). Screening for breast cancer with breast self-examination: A critical review. *Journal of the American Medical Association, 257*, 2196–2203.

Ortony, A., Clore, G. L., and Collins, A. (1988). *The cognitive structure of emotions.* Cambridge, England: Cambridge University Press.

Panksepp, J. (1985). Mood changes. In P. I. Vinken, G. W. Buyn, and H. L. Klawans (Eds.), *Handbook of clinical neurology. Revised series: Vol. 1. Clinical neuropsychology* (pp. 271–855). Amsterdam: Elsevier Science.

Panksepp, J. (1998). *Affective neuroscience.* New York: Oxford University Press.

Paterson, R. J., and Neufeld, R. W. J. (1987). Clear danger: Situational determinants of the appraisal of threat. *Psychological Bulletin, 101*, 404–416.

Patrick, C. J. (1994). Emotion and psychopathy: Startling new insights. *Psychophysiology, 31*, 415–428.

Pavlov, I. P. (1927). *Conditioned reflexes.* London: Oxford University Press.

Payne, J. W., Bettman, J. R., and Johnson, E. (1993). *The adaptive decisionmaker.* Cambridge, England: Cambridge University Press.

Peters, E., and Slovic, P. (1996). The role of affect and worldviews as orienting dispositions in the perception and acceptance of nuclear power. *Journal of Applied Social Psychology, 26,* 1427–1453.

Peters, E., and Slovic, P. (2000). The springs of action: Affective and analytical information processing in choice. *Personality and Social Psychology Bulletin, 26,* 1465–1475

Pope, R. (1985). Timing contradictions in von Neumann and Morgenstern's axioms and in Savage's 'sure thing' proof. *Theory and Decision, 18,* 229–261.

Prelec, D. (1998). The probability weighting function. *Econometric, 66,* 497–529.

Quadrel, M. J., Fischhoff, B., and Davis, W. (1993). Adolescent (in)vulnerability. *American Psychologist, 48,* 102–116.

Raghunathan, R., and Pham, M. T. (1999). All negative moods are not equal: Motivational influences of anxiety and sadness on decision making. *Organizational Behavior and Human Decision Processes, 79,* 56–77.

Rolls, E. T. (1999). *The brain and emotion.* New York: Oxford University Press.

Roseman, I. (1984). Cognitive determinants of emotions: A structural theory. In P. Shaver (Ed.), *Review of personality and social psychology* (Vol. 5, pp. 11–36). Beverly Hills, CA: Sage.

Roth, W. T., Breivik, G., Jorgensen, P. E., and Hofmann, S. (1996). Activation in novice and expert parachutists while jumping. *Psychophysiology, 33,* 63–72.

Rottenstreich, Y., and Hsee, C. K. (1999). *Money, kisses and electric shocks: On the affective psychology of probability weighting.* Working paper, The University of Chicago.

Sanna, L. J. (1999). Mental simulations, affect, and subjective confidence: Timing is everything. *Psychological Science, 10,* 339–345.

Sapolsky, R. M. (1994). *Why zebras don't get ulcers: A guide to stress, stress-related diseases, and coping.* New York: Freeman.

Savitsky, K., Medvec, V. H., Charlton, A. E., and Gilovich, T. (1998). What, me worry?: Arousal, misattribution, and the effect of temporal distance on confidence. *Personality and Social Psychology Bulletin, 24,* 529–536.

Schelling, T. (1984). Self-command in practice, in policy, and in a theory of rational choice. *American Economic Review, 74,* 1–11.

Scherer, K. R. (1984). On the nature and function of emotions: A component process approach. In K. R. Scherer and P. Ekman (Eds.), *Approaches to emotion* (pp. 293–317). Hillsdale, NJ: Erlbaum.

Schmitt, W. A., and Newman, J. P. (1999). Are all psychopathic individuals low-anxious? *Journal of Abnormal Psychology, 108,* 353–358.

Schmitt, W. A., Brinkley, C. A., and Newman, J. P. (1999). Testing Damasio's somatic marker hypothesis with psychopathic individuals: Risk takers or risk averse? *Journal of Abnormal Psychology, 108,* 538–543.

Schoemaker, P. J. H. (1990). Are risk-preferences related across payoff domains and response modes? *Management Science, 36,* 1451–1463.

Schwarz, N., and Clore, G. L. (1983). Mood, misattribution, and judgments of well-being: Information and directive functions of affective states. *Journal of Personality and Social Psychology, 45,* 513–523.

Seligman, M. E. P. (1971). Phobias and preparedness. *Behavior Therapy, 2,* 307–320.

Servan-Schreiber, D., and Perlstein, W. M. (1998). Selective limbic activation and its relevance to emotional disorders. *Cognition and Emotion, 12,* 331–352.

Shepperd, J. A., Ouellette, J. A., and Fernandez, J. K. (1996). Abandoning unrealistic optimism: Performance estimates and the temporal proximity of self-relevant feedback. *Journal of Personality and Social Psychology, 70,* 844–855.

Shiv, B., and Fedorikhin, A. (1999). Heart and mind in conflict: The interplay of affect and cognition in consumer decision making. *Journal of Consumer Research, 26,* 278–292.

Shiv, B., and Huber, J. (2000). The impact of anticipating satisfaction on choice. *Journal of Consumer Research, 27,* 202–216.

Simon, H. A. (1967). Motivational and emotional controls of cognition. *Psychological Review, 57,* 386–420.

Sjöberg, L. (1998). Worry and risk perception. *Risk Analysis, 18,* 85–93.

Sloman, S. A. (1996). The empirical case for two systems of reasoning. *Psychological Bulletin, 119,* 3–22.

Slovic, P., Fischhoff, B., and Lichtenstein, S. (1980). Facts and fears: Understanding perceived risk. In R. Schwing and W. Albers Jr. (Eds.), *Societal risk assessment: How safe is safe enough?* (pp. 181–216). San Francisco: Jossey-Bass.

Slovic, P., Fischhoff, B., and Lichtenstein, S. (1986). The psychometric study of risk perception. In V. T. Covello, J. Menkes, and J. Mumpower (Eds.), *Risk evaluation and management* (pp. 3–24). New York: Plenum Press.

Slovic, P., Flynn, J. H., and Layman, M. (1991a). Perceived risk, trust, and the politics of nuclear waste. *Science, 254,* 1603–1607.

Slovic, P., Layman, M., Kraus, N., Flynn, J., Chalmers, J., and Gesell, G. (1991b). Perceived risk, stigma, and potential economic impacts of a high-level nuclear waste repository in Nevada. *Risk Analysis, 11,* 683–696.

Slovic, P., Flynn, J., and Gregory, R. (1994). Stigma happens: Social problems in the siting of nuclear waste facilities. *Risk Analysis, 14,* 773.

Slovic, P., Finucane, M., Peters, E., and MacGregor, D. (2002). The affect heuristic. In T. Gilovich, D. Griffin, and D. Kahneman (Eds.), *Intuitive judgment: Heuristics and biases.* Cambridge, England: Cambridge University Press.

Smith, C. A., and Ellsworth, P. C. (1985). Patterns of cognitive appraisal and emotional response related to taking an exam. *Journal of Personality and Social Psychology, 52,* 475–488.

Smith, D., and Over, R. (1987). Male sexual arousal as a function of the content and the vividness of erotic fantasy. *Psychophysiology, 24,* 334–339.

Snortum, J. R., and Wilding, F. W. (1971). Temporal estimation of heart rate as a function of repression-sensitization score and probability of shock. *Journal of Consulting and Clinical Psychology, 37,* 417–422.

Specter, M. (1996, March 31). 10 years later, through fear, Chernobyl still kills in Belarus. *New York Times,* p. 1.

Spence, M., and Zeckhauser, R. (1972). The effect of timing of consumption decisions and the resolution of lotteries on the choice of lotteries. *Econometrica, 40,* 401–403.

Spiegel. (1997, September 29). Die Macht der Gefuehle [The power of feelings]. *Spiegel, 39,* 244–265.

Stapley, J. C., and Haviland, J. M. (1989). Beyond depression: Gender differences in normal adolescents' emotional experiences. *Sex Roles, 20,* 295–308.

Starmer, C. (2000). Developments in non-expected utility theory: The hunt for a descriptive theory of choice under risk. *Journal of Economic Literature, 38*(2), 332–383.

Sunstein, C. (2000). Cognition and cost-benefit analysis. *Journal of Legal Studies, 29,* 1059

Thaler, R., Tversky, A., Kahneman, D., and Schwartz, A. (1997). The effect of myopia and loss aversion on risk taking: An experimental test. *Quarterly Journal of Economics, 112,* 647–661.

Vasey, M. W., El-Hag, N., and Daleiden, E. L. (1996). Anxiety and the processing of emotionally threatening stimuli: Distinctive patterns of selective attention among high- and low-test-anxious children. *Child Development, 67,* 1173–1185.

Viscusi, K., and Magat, W. (1987). *Learning about risk.* Cambridge, MA: Harvard University Press.

Weber, E. U., and Hsee, C. K. (1998). Cross-cultural differences in risk perception but cross-cultural similarities in attitudes towards risk. *Management Science, 44*, 1205–1217.

Weber, E. U., Blais, A.-R., and Betz, N. (2002). A domain-specific risk-attitude scale: Measuring risk perceptions and risk behaviors *Journal of Behavioral Decision Making*, 15, 263–290.

Weinstein, N. D. (1989). Effects of personal experience on self-protective behavior. *Psychological Bulletin, 105*, 31–50.

Welch, E. (1999). *The heat of the moment*. Doctoral dissertation, Department of Social and Decision Sciences, Carnegie Mellon University.

Wessely, S. (1987). Mass hysteria: Two syndromes? *Psychological Medicine, 17*, 109–120.

Wessely, S., and Wardle, C. J. (1990). Mass sociogenic illness by proxy: Parentally reported epidemic in an elementary school. *British Journal of Psychiatry, 157*, 421–424.

White, K. D. (1978). Salivation: The significance of imagery in its voluntary control. *Psychophysiology, 15*, 196–203.

Whitley, B., and Hern, A. (1991). Perceptions of vulnerability to pregnancy and the use of effective contraception. *Personality and Social Psychology Bulletin, 17*, 104–110.

Williamson, S., Harpur, T. J., and Hare, R. D. (1991). Abnormal processing of affective words by psychopaths. *Psychophysiology, 28*, 260–273.

Wilson, T. D., and Schooler, J. W. (1991). Thinking too much: Introspection can reduce the quality of preferences and decisions. *Journal of Personality and Social Psychology, 60*, 181–192.

Wilson, T. D., Lisle, D. J., Schooler, J. W., Hodges, S. D., Klaaren, K. J., and LaFleur, S. J. (1993). Introspecting about reasons can reduce post-choice satisfaction. *Personality and Social Psychology Bulletin, 19*, 331–339.

Windschitl, P. D., and Weber, E. U. (1999). The interpretation of likely depends on context, but 70% is 70%, right? The influence of associative processes on perceived certainty. *Journal of Experimental Psychology: Learning, Memory, and Cognition, 25*, 1514–1533.

Winkielman, P., Zajonc, R. B., and Schwarz, N. (1997). Subliminal affective priming resists attributional interventions. *Cognition and Emotion, 11*, 433–465.

Wright, W. F., and Bower, G. H. (1992). Mood effects on subjective probability assessment. *Organizational Behavior and Human Decision Processes, 52*, 276–291.

Zajonc, R. B. (1980). Feeling and thinking: Preferences need no inference. *American Psychologist, 35*, 151–175.

Zajonc, R. B. (1984a). The interaction of affect and cognition. In K. R. Scherer and P. Ekman (Eds.), *Approaches to emotion* (pp. 239–246). Hillsdale, NJ: Erlbaum.

Zajonc, R. B. (1984b). On primacy of affect. In K. R. Scherer and P. Ekman (Eds.), *Approaches to emotion* (pp. 259–270). Hillsdale, NJ: Erlbaum.

Zajonc, R. (1998). Emotions. In D. Gilbert, S. Fiske, and G. Lindzey (Eds.), *Handbook of social psychology* (Vol. 1, pp. 591–632). New York: Oxford University Press.

Part III

Communication About Risk

8

Accounting for the Social Context of Risk Communication

Branden B. Johnson

The emerging field of risk communication has emphasized the meaningful conveyance of technical information from risk experts to laypeople. This chapter argues that the social context of risk communication is just as important, and sometimes more important, than the technical issues with which the field has largely been concerned. Messages are ultimately conveyed from person to person; what and how risk messages are received will be affected by our relations with the communicator, other humans and the material artefacts concerned. Although the importance of social context has been 'recognized', this recognition has been relatively superficial.

A first approximation of 'social context' is compared here to the current emphasis in risk communication. The examples used in this chapter deal with hazardous waste, hazardous facility siting and natural disasters, but the arguments made apply as well to other hazards (e.g. radon, occupational safety and health). The focus is on how lay receivers of risk messages are affected by social context, but the influence of social context on the construction of risk messages is also important.[1] Tasks for risk communicators which combine the technical and social context approaches are suggested, and some barriers to the use of risk communication based on social context are briefly noted.

Defining Social Context

A multidimensional concept

The social context approach assumes that relationships with other people affect the degree to which individuals attend to, understand and use technical information about risks. The field is too young to yield a comprehensive definition of social context, but important factors include social networks, economic resources, political rights and responsibilities, histories and ideologies. It is important to note that these factors vary in importance in different risk communication situations. For example, the context for siting a hazardous waste facility will be different than that for enhancing occupational safety: workers' apparently voluntary risk assumption in an economic context reduces their ability to act on risk information relative to that of site residents, who wield more political power.[2] And the statutory differences between low-level nuclear waste and chemical waste management vary the constraints on public and governmental willingness and ability to come to agreement on waste facility siting.[3] It is thus critical for success to 'know your risk communication problem ... [and] objectives ... [and] listen to your audience and know their concerns'.[4]

Social networks

The extent, complexity and membership of social networks can affect the speed and accuracy with which messages about hazards are transmitted. Such networks also affect message credibility and the definition of the receiver's concerns (e.g. preservation of family or responsibility to the community).

At Love Canal those most concerned about the risks were well connected in the neighbourhood, particularly the young parents, and became increasingly unwilling to trust official information; the unconcerned were relatively isolated from their neighbours.[5] In another community, people who identified pollution of the local lake (a Superfund site) as a major community problem were more likely to have intense social interactions and attachment to the community than those who cited unemployment, a much more prominent local problem.[6] Contrary findings[7] that attachment to place results in low concern about hazardous waste may be due to offsetting concerns (see below) about economic impacts of waste management.

Ties to place also appear to increase actions (e.g. evacuation) to reduce vulnerability to natural hazards.[8] Credible sources of evacuation warnings increase with community involvement and social connections,[9] and discussion of a hurricane threat with neighbours is critical to whether evacuation is actually undertaken.[10] (Where hazard experience is frequent, as in Hawaiian volcanic eruptions, social networks apparently become unimportant in evacuation decisions.)[11]

Economic resources

Risk communications may seem to elicit irrational responses if the economic benefits and costs pertinent to message recipients are ignored by or unknown to communicators. Whether a community has a diversified economic base will influence the salience and interpretation of risk messages. Where management of abandoned hazardous waste appears to threaten local economic viability, health risks will tend to be denied.[12] Nuclear power plants or waste facilities which promise to reduce local economic distress may evoke lower risk concerns. However, protecting existing economies (as with abandoned hazardous waste) appears to be more important to local perceptions of facility risks than the chance of enhancing the future economy. The economic vulnerability of a population alters what risk message is received by its members, which is why such vulnerability has been criticized as an unethical criterion for hazardous facility siting.[13]

In the face of natural hazards people may live in clearly dangerous places or refuse to evacuate when warned of imminent disaster. This apparently non-rational behaviour has been linked to a lack of the capital and organizational resources that would allow people to avoid or reduce their exposure to hazards.[14] Conversely, the availability of resources can help people reduce their vulnerability to natural disasters,[15] though the expectation of post-disaster assistance (e.g. from government) can reduce hazard preparations despite risk communications.[16]

Distribution of political rights and responsibilities

There must be a perceived match between such rights and responsibilities, and the benefits, costs, and risks of a proposed action, if technical risk communication is to be taken at face value. Power – i.e. who makes the decisions about what risks are carried and by whom?[17] – is the social relationship at issue here. Power has been identified as a vital issue in siting radioactive and chemical waste facilities,[18] with residents demanding monitoring, design and closure powers as the price of facility acceptance. Rayner and Cantor[19] use a case study in acceptance of new nuclear technologies to argue that the salient issues are not technical ones like hazard magnitude or probability, but principles for achieving consent to a technology, distributing liabilities and investing trust in institutions.

Risk communication which ignores these points is likely to fail, unless power is not seen by message recipients as salient to the hazard at issue. Natural hazards usually fall into the latter category. But power can be pertinent where proposed controls to avoid future disaster (e.g. restrictions on floodplain land use) are deemed obstacles to local political and economic opportunities. The perception after a disaster that damages are due to acts or omissions of humans (instead of being due to an act of God) will also make political rights and responsibilities pertinent to natural hazard communications.

History

Perceptions of communicator legitimacy and trustworthiness are affected by the history of the relations between risk communicator and message recipient. The process of risk communication itself becomes part of the continuing experience of communicator and recipient. For example, the experience of states with the Department of Energy over siting high-level radioactive waste facilities has exacerbated rather than resolved conflicts.[20] 'Good' reputations may be less influential in eliciting trust than 'bad' reputations are in losing it: there is some evidence[21] on low-level nuclear waste disposal that past performance, no matter how good, is no guarantee of acceptance where the hazard is highly dreaded. Mistaken history can be as significant for risk communication as the real thing. For example, officials have been known to delay hurricane warnings, and thus hamper evacuation, for fear of a non-existent 'cry-wolf' syndrome from previous mistaken warnings.[22]

What makes things more difficult for the risk communicator is that the history of its relations with other groups may be communicated to the message recipient, to the detriment of the communicator's plans. For example, citizen groups increasingly link those who have already fought local siting of hazardous waste facilities to people in towns which are candidates for such sites. In combination with media tales about unsuccessful waste management, these links make the risk communications of facility proposers less believable. Comparisons of the communicating institution to other institutions dealing with the problem may also be made by message recipients. For example, federal and state agencies were unable to provide risk estimates or clean-up resources for a case of groundwater contamination. Combined with trust in local government, this failure resulted in low concern about the contamination despite official risk communications.[23]

Ideologies

The ideologies of communicator and recipient affect their identification of risks and benefits, acceptance of a risk communicator and of proposals for resolving disputes. These ideologies are often concerned with the issue of power discussed earlier, but they can also be concerned with 'the state of society' more generally. (Although ideology may seem to be a belief system that transcends particular social contexts, it has been argued that it arises from and is maintained by face-to-face communications with others.)[24]

Rayner and Cantor argue[25] that 'the critical question facing societal risk managers is not "How safe is safe enough? [i.e. technical risks]," but "How fair is safe enough?"' They suggest that different institutional settings will generate different ideologies. For example, entrepreneurial types will prefer market mechanisms to determine who bears losses (e.g. from new nuclear technologies), assume consent is implied in the allocation of one's money and express confidence in successful individuals. Egalitarian environmentalists, however, will prefer a strict-fault system of liability and assume consent to risk is contained only in explicit statements made through trusted participatory institutions (e.g. town meetings). Because both sides' risk communications are structured by their ideologies about liability, consent and trust, to a large extent they end up talking past each other.

The State of the Art and Its Limits

A technical emphasis

The social context factors discussed above have been recognized to some extent by people in risk communication. For example, Covello et al. – sophisticated communicators – recently reviewed the literature.[26] Among their suggestions were the tackling of 'lack of trust and credibility', 'resource, legal, and institutional constraints on analysis, authority, and actions', and 'limited [expert and official] understanding of the ... concerns ... of individual citizens and public groups' – all valid issues of social context.

However, this review's coverage (and, by extension, that of the field in general) of the social context of risk communication is less than it might be. Relatively little of the review addresses social context issues: some 72 per cent (41 of 57) of its recommendations are concerned with avoiding mistakes in conveying technical information to lay audiences. Examples of these recommendations are:

> use simple, graphic, and concrete material, avoiding technical language wherever possible ... identify, acknowledge, and explain uncertainties in risk

estimates ... when people ask personal questions – such as, 'Can I drink the water?' – respond in a personal way without minimizing the risks and uncertainties ... recognize the power of subtle changes in the way information is presented and use such knowledge responsibly ... [27]

This technical approach to risk communication is undoubtedly important. Messages must address the problems citizens have in processing scientific information. They must simultaneously acknowledge scientific uncertainties, through such means as presenting data in different numerical or pictorial ways.[28] The technical emphasis is also important because 'these recommendations may seem obvious, but are nonetheless continually and consistently violated in practice'.[29] For example, Missouri residents screened for dioxin contamination were sent registered letters informing them that they had abnormal blood and/or urine results. Apparently no explanation of the results – including what 'abnormal' meant in the circumstances – was enclosed. A state official agreed that:

> it is highly technical [information]... But we expect they will find technical support [from family doctors, to explain the results and] to continue with their own health care... I wouldn't be alarmed by the letters... But then, I'm not one of those people.[30]

In a world which can produce such risk 'communications', a simple emphasis on how to transfer technical information to laypeople should not be lightly dismissed (though the official's response also indicates several problems in the social context of that communication).

The technical emphasis in the risk communication literature is partly due as well to the relative inaccessibility of research on social context. In some cases, presentations of research are so harshly critical of hazard managers that it is not surprising that institutional communicators dismiss these findings. In other cases, these points appear in literature which is about 'risk selection' or 'hazard perception' or 'environmental politics', rather than explicitly about risk communication. And even when such findings are available, they usually emphasize what happens when the social context of risk communication is *ignored*. This is true of the review by Covello et al., for example; and it is the norm, not the exception. Recognition that the social context of risk communication has an impact is far more advanced than understanding of how positive results can be achieved by taking it into account.

However, the technical emphasis in even state-of-the-art risk communication may also be due to less noble factors than need or lack of alternatives. Risk communicators tend to be either technical risk experts, or employed as their representatives. A technical emphasis is desirable to them because it emphasizes their expertise compared to the lack of it among those to whom they are communicating. Expertise acts as a technical sieve for consensus on facts, but it also labels certain paths to knowledge (and certain path-takers) as better than others.[31] Thus the technical emphasis in current risk communication is *both* justifiable technically *and* suspect for its implications for the relative power of groups in hazard management.

Missing perspectives

Face-to-face communication between two people includes the words spoken, tone of voice, facial expression and body language. Its content, on all these levels, is constrained by such factors as whether others are present and who they are; the past relationship of the speakers; and whether the agreed-upon text of the talk is that of conversation, interview, debate, interrogation, joking or gossip. Talk is thus a multi-layered, multi-channelled activity carrying many meanings at once.

Risk communication is an equally rich activity. However, the technical focus noted above is the equivalent of the 'words spoken' in a conversation. In some communications – whether general conversation or risk-related – this is sufficient. But in most cases a major, sometimes even dominant, role is played by the non-spoken and subtextual aspects of communication. These aspects of risk messages are carried by their 'social context'.

Risk communication restricted to conveying technical information will ultimately fail to communicate, because it misses most of what is going on; messages about risks may be sent but will not be received. Furthermore, the current approach threatens to ignore the fact that risk communication is a *two*-way process. One-way, impoverished risk communication will ultimately become mere ritual, without power to improve management of hazardous activities. This holds true whether it is deployed with good intentions or as a cynical plan to manipulate policy. Emphasis on purely technical communication will prevent its practitioners from perceiving several important aspects of their enterprise.

Unintended messages can be important

The scientific content of messages (e.g. official risk assessments) is important, but is only a small portion of the overall message that is sent. All of the communicator's actions are potential messages, and explicit risk communications may have negligible effects if the rest of 'the message' contradicts them or makes them irrelevant. For example, reassurance that water from a municipal facility is safe to drink followed by the facility's closing – even if the shutdown is unrelated to chemical contamination – is unlikely to be a credible risk communication.[32] In drought situations, water conservation programmes lose credibility if the same utilities which promote voluntary conservation then raise rates to offset the consequent falling revenues.[33]

This overall message is also evaluated in the context of others' (agencies, firms, activists) actions, which send similar messages relevant to potentially risky activities. Take the example of opposition to the restart of the undamaged reactor at Three Mile Island. Distrust of the Nuclear Regulatory Commission's neutrality and competence was not the only reason for local rejection of NRC risk messages. Local activists were also affected by such actions as cheating by utility operators and the governor's opposition to restart.[34] New Jersey's early easing of restrictions on water use during the 1980–1981 drought threatened the credibility of water conservation programmes in neighbouring New York City.[35] Technical risk communication ignores such influences on message reception.

Risks are not all that is at issue

'Risk' is by no means the only matter of interest in communications between organizations and groups, though the risk communication literature often fails to make that explicit. Decisions of government agencies and firms take into account many other factors as well (e.g. benefits, alternative projects and policies, institutional goals, prescriptions for society). Everyone 'knows' this implicitly, but failure to explicitly include these factors in the message threatens its dismissal as irrelevant or self-serving (i.e. disguising political or economic interests as technical matters). The risk focus may also mean loss of an opportunity to directly address (and perhaps resolve) potential conflict on these other issues. For example, local opposition to a hazardous waste facility may be partly due to concerns about noise and property values; an exclusive focus on safety concerns will overlook these other issues.

This does not mean that bringing policy benefits into the picture will encourage benefit–risk trade-offs and acceptance of the communicator's proposal. It may do so in some cases, but the larger point is that what is at stake is what institutions and society should do, and messages ignoring this are unlikely to convey conviction. Statutory constraints and professional biases may make it difficult to raise these other issues, underlining the importance of the social context of risk *communicators*, but should not be arguments against making the attempt.

A theory of risk communication should integrate the technical and social context approaches. The ideal theory would be a middle-range one, concrete enough to provide guidance for practitioners but general enough to explain varying message responses across issues and audiences. Our knowledge of how factors in social context interact – much less their relation to technical communication – is too meagre to allow for formulation of that theory now. Detailed suggestions about the application of social context to risk communication are also premature. However, some practical options can be suggested.

Communication Tasks Within the Social Context Perspective

The risk communicator can start to deal with the message recipient's social context by undertaking the following tasks:

- the *change in recipients' behaviour*[36] which is desired as an outcome of the risk communication must be clearly defined;
- the information which the recipient wants, as well as needs, should be identified; and
- the most appropriate communicator for the situation should be selected, if there is any room for manoeuvre on this point.

Even without definitive information about the effects of social context on reception of risk messages, undertaking these tasks can improve the performance of institutional risk communicators.

Defining Outcomes

Without a definition of desired behavioural outcomes which will shape message content, risk communication is likely to be misdirected or otherwise unsuccessful. This may seem obvious, but as the Missouri example discussed earlier indicates, all too often communicators assume that the conclusions to be drawn from their messages are self-evident. In the 'Show Me' state, as elsewhere, 'showing' one's data is not enough. The presentation of the data should vary according to whether the purpose of risk communication is information and education, personal and disaster risk reduction, or joint problem solving.

Information and education

The first category of risk communication listed in the literature review by Covello et al. is 'informing and educating people about risks, risk assessment and risk management in general'. Although this particular discussion is benign, the lack of specificity of this category makes it suspect. There is often a hidden agenda to such efforts – e.g. encouraging public acquiescence in institutional decision-making. Reassuring messages are certainly far more common than concern-raising ones.

However, simple scientific and risk 'literacy' is important for meaningful participation of laypeople in hazard management, and certain steps can be taken to promote useful education. This kind of communication needs to match transmitted concepts to the pre-existing concepts and skills of the message recipients.[37] For example, if people are concerned about groundwater contamination this might be a base for educating them about harmful effects of unsafe disposal of household chemicals.[38] Use of social networks to facilitate transmission *and* joint learning of the material can be useful where the risk issue is important to local residents. Involvement of recipients in a hands-on application of the information – e.g. in lay risk assessments of possible hazardous waste sites[39] – can also enhance learning.[40]

Officials and experts may also learn things of value, in addition to their policy preferences, from citizen risk communicators. Citizens can gather data otherwise unavailable to officials because of professional ignorance or the expense of collecting it. For example, using lay volunteers to collect site-specific rainfall and streamflow data to add to National Weather Service data has been proposed to identify specific flood locations in New York State.[41] Citizen risk assessment may identify hazardous waste problems previously unknown to officials.[42] Ad hoc efforts of this sort are already occurring in communities around the country, and in one case[43] lay risk assessment allegedly led to a US Environmental Protection Agency (EPA) suspension of forestry uses of certain pesticides. Although this trend chagrins experts who dispute the validity of lay assessments, cooperative efforts could avoid invalid results and extend agency resources. The possibility of 'data mediation' has also been raised in some quarters.[44]

Personal and disaster risk reduction

Both of these types of risk communication are intent upon affecting individual- and family-level behaviour in large populations. The goal is to facilitate coping behaviours by removing constraints on them (e.g. cost, ability and relevance), in part by providing information about these factors and seeking to shift the salience of such behaviours.

For example, addressing relevant concerns (e.g. protection of family and conservation of economic resources) may be helped by exploiting cultural images of disaster, like chemical gas clouds,[45] or fear of hurricane-spawned tornadoes that is greater than fear of the hurricanes themselves.[46] Although 'high-threat or fear campaigns' should be avoided,[47] accurate, low-emotion presentation of aspects of the hazard pertinent to citizens may be useful. This is particularly true for hazards such as hurricanes, where previous experience with the hazard appears to reduce a person's propensity to evacuate.[48]

Joint problem solving

The arena of joint problem solving and conflict resolution is the part of risk communication most obviously affected by social context, because issues of power and process become paramount here. The conflict over siting nuclear and hazardous waste facilities may require redistribution of political rights and responsibilities.[49] This possibility raises technical and political questions about where responsibility for such facilities should be located, but it is also likely to arouse opposition from current hazard managers. Cultural (or value) analysis may be helpful in identifying specific decision processes, compensation, incentives and independent technical capabilities that will overcome distrust of hazard managers.[50]

O'Hare[51] suggests that the 'impact statement' approach to agency provision of information is misguided for controversial actions. Since the magnitude of policy or project impacts is among the items at dispute, government should restrict itself to providing general information (e.g. the kinds of impacts expected). Many alternatives should be discussed as early and for as long as possible, with at least some aspects of the policy or project adjustable for a wide range of values. For example, proposing a single waste facility design for a single location at the very beginning of public involvement is to court disaster. Any party should have the resources needed to participate, and be able to propose new alternatives at any time.

O'Hare also suggests that the regulatory agency act as a conduit for information passed between parties. Anyone could ask that a given datum be passed to anyone else. The source of this information would be clearly identified in case the recipient wished to take that into account in evaluating the datum's validity. Deadlines would have to be set for this exchange and debate of information, and for the refinement of policy alternatives. But by fostering mutual development and consideration of information about risk-carrying activities, the chances of joint problem solving may be enhanced.

Identifying desired information

The second task recommended to risk communicators is based on the notion that laypeople hold different conceptions of pertinent information than do hazard managers.[52] Yet risk communicators often assume that they know what information is needed by the message recipient. Because 'the amount of information in a single message … is … unique to a single user', with this assumption an agency could only hope to meet all information demands by supplying all data it had; this would overwhelm the analytic capacities of recipients.[53] Identifying information desired by interested parties is thus more than just a ploy to placate them. It is necessary to avoid wasted resources in both risk communication and general hazard management. The assumption that experts know lay information needs is likely to be wrong in many cases.[54] It may also violate norms about the respective rights and responsibilities of institutions and citizens. After all, if citizens cannot be responsible for defining the information they want, what meaningful role can they possibly play in decision-making?

The importance of attending to citizens' information needs – defined by their social contexts – is highlighted by Sharlin's study[55] of the EPA's failed risk communication programme about ethylene dibromide. In line with professional norms, that programme focused on aggregate risks, while citizens were interested in their personal risks. The public relief that followed EPA's ban of EDB emphasizes the earlier point that risk communication encompasses far more than the explicit process institutions label 'risk communication'.

Providing recipients with the technical and economic resources to produce their *own* information can help risk communicators ensure that all pertinent information is available to all parties, and that the decision-making process is acceptable.[56] Officials and experts will be concerned about the quality of information provided by other sources, particularly its putative lack of 'objectivity'. But we will not know whether non-official data can be useful until these institutions rethink their own interests so as to support its provision.

Identifying the appropriate communicator

The credibility of communicators will affect reception of risk messages. Appropriate selection of communicators can help to assure the most trustworthy person, group or institution for the target audience(s) is responsible. But there are limits to the range of available and acceptable communicators. For example, the Department of Energy's general loss of credibility in siting radioactive waste repositories may be offset by its near-monopoly of pertinent technical knowledge (in conjunction with the equally suspect Nuclear Regulatory Commission and nuclear industry). Politically credible state and local governments may lack technical credibility.[57] To these problems must also be added social context constraints set by statute, and organizational or professional refusal to relinquish control.

Trust is perhaps the best-known social context factor in the hazard management field. Yet at the moment it is easier to say that trust is important than to define its components and how it grows, though it is probably multidimensional (arguments that it is solely a political or technical issue are probably naive). Furthermore, the presence of distrust has uncertain effects on risk communication, due to the heavy burden of enquiry, complexity and uncertainty it imposes on the distrusting people.[58] Trust may exist not because one has no reservations, but because the issue is too small or the need for expert action too immediate to behave otherwise.[59] In short, clearly defining what is meant by 'credibility' for communicator selection will require more experience.

The ability of the hazard manager/risk communicator to provide political and economic resources to resolve communication problems is also important, since such resources are needed for appropriate distribution of rights and responsibilities. For example, agencies are unlikely to keep alternatives open (as discussed earlier) for siting of hazardous waste facilities in those states where government enters the process only after private firms have selected sites. In such cases the firm has control – usually by government default – of resources that the agency needs to do this particular risk communication job (e.g. through site negotiation).

Obstacles to accounting for social context

Although integration of the social context approach with the technical approach should dramatically improve risk communication, there are some caveats. Given the obvious problems with a purely technical approach to such hazards as nuclear power and chemical waste, it can be tempting for advocates of social context to argue its primacy in all situations for all hazards. Unfortunately, a 'theory' which purports to explain everything – particularly with the multidimensional definition of social context proposed here – is no theory at all. Specification of the conditions under which the theory does and does not operate is critical. Some constraints on the influence of social networks, economic resources and political rights have been noted here, for example, but considerable empirical work will be needed to confirm and extend these speculations.

There are also several practical limits to implementation of a social context approach to risk communication. First, efforts to take into account the social context of message recipients may require more resources than agencies, firms and professional associations are able or willing to give, even though without them the resources that are spent may be wasted. Second, information credibility may require an ongoing relationship between the parties. With such a relationship any given piece of information is harder to reject, because past data from that source have been accepted and future data may be acceptable.[60] This suggests that 'shotgun' risk communications to the general public should be de-emphasized relative to targeting of organized groups (e.g. environmentalist or neighbourhood groups). However, both officials and these groups may see long-term cooperation as too costly.

Third, it must be re-emphasized that the social context approach is alien to most government and corporate officials. It requires skills they lack and discounts those they have. In some situations it may also call upon them to yield professional and organizational power to ordinary citizens and other institutions. Resistance to such sacrifices can be expected, particularly since the success of social context approaches cannot be guaranteed in their current underdeveloped state.

Ultimately, these obstacles are likely to be overcome, because the current misunderstandings can serve only short-term interests of both the experts and the public,[61] and technical risk communication has been unable to resolve this stalemate. Conscientious hazard managers will make sacrifices and take creative gambles in order to improve unsatisfactory hazard management. They can be helped by social scientists who are willing to make proposals that take into account the constraints on managers' ability to implement the social context approach whole-heartedly. Although this may mean less than satisfactory compromises in the short term, managers who experience success will be willing to try more creative experiments.

Conclusions

Short suggests that antagonists in hazard management may be forced to cooperate 'in the search for solutions to mutually threatening conditions'.[62] Risk communication is a means for finding such solutions. But an exclusive emphasis on the conveying of technical risk information will founder on the implicit assumptions that only one kind of information from a single (expert) source needs to (and will) be conveyed. Risk communication is more than just communication about risks; in the end it encompasses the issue of how hazards are defined and controlled.

The social context approach seeks to rectify this problem by emphasizing the role of social networks, economic resources, political rights and responsibilities, history and ideologies in the reception of risk messages. This approach is no panacea; the slowly growing recognition that technical approaches are insufficient is offset by our limited understanding of the specific impacts of social context and the difficulty of getting hazard managers to implement the social context tasks suggested here. But our need to explore new approaches will eventually overcome these obstacles.

It is important to recognize that no single approach will do. Attention to the conveyance of technical information must go hand-in-hand with attention to the role of contextual factors in affecting its reception, and in raising issues not addressed by the technical information. To assume that social context is all, and there is no objective knowledge that should be communicated, is as blind as assuming that only technical data are salient. Although the desire for generalization is understandable, rules for proper risk communication will tend to be situation-specific. Political issues are much more important than technical information in conflicts over hazardous facilities and hazardous wastes, but that does not mean that technical information is useless. In other situations power becomes less important, and technical data and other social context factors more so.

In short, despite its intellectual and practical challenges (and perhaps because of them), the middle way which respects the roles of both technical and contextual information in risk communication seems the most fruitful. It implies a partnership between citizen and expert in hazard management, which seems particularly appropriate in a society which lauds both science and democracy.

Notes

1   See, for example, Branden B. Johnson and Vincent T. Covello, eds., *The Social and Cultural Construction of Risk: Essays on Risk Selection and Perception* (Dordrecht, Holland: Reidel, 1987), and Branden B. Johnson, 'The Social Construction of Science and Hazard Assessment' (Paper presented at the Annual Meeting of the Society for Social Studies of Science, Pittsburgh, PA, 23–25 October 1986).

2   Branden B. Johnson, 'Risk Education and Hazard Management in the Workplace: The Role of Workers' and Executives' Social Relations' (Paper presented at the Annual Meeting of the Society for Risk Analysis, Boston, MA, 9–12 November 1986).

3   Branden B. Johnson, 'Public Concerns and the Public Role in Siting Nuclear and Chemical Waste Facilities', *Environmental Management* 11 (1987): 571–586.

4   Vincent Covello, Detlof von Winterfeldt, and Paul Slovic, *Risk Communication: An Assessment of the Literature on Communicating Information About Health, Safety and Environmental Risks*, draft preliminary report to the Environmental Protection Agency (Institute of Safety and Systems Management, University of Southern California, Los Angeles, CA, 11 January 1986), p. 35.

5   Martha R. Fowlkes and Patricia Y. Miller, 'Community and Risks at Love Canal', in Johnson and Covello, *Construction of Risk*, 55–78.

6   Branden B. Johnson and Bradley H. Baltensperger, 'An Empirical Test of Alternative Hazard Perception Models' (Paper presented at the Annual Meeting of the Association of American Geographers, Minneapolis, MN, 4–7 May 1986).

7   John D. Powell, 'Assault on a Precious Commodity: The Local Struggle to Protect Groundwater', *Policy Studies Journal* 14 (1985): 62–69; Janet Fitchen, Jenifer Heath and

June Fessenden-Raden, 'Risk Perception in Community Context: A Case Study', in Johnson and Covello, *Construction of Risk*, 31–54.

8 See, for example, K. Jill Kiecolt and Joanne M. Nigg, 'Mobility and Perceptions of a Hazardous Environment', *Environment and Behavior* 14 (1982): 131–154.

9 Ronald W. Perry, *The Social Psychology of Civil Defense* (Lexington, MA: Lexington Books, 1982).

10 Harry E. Moore, Fred L. Bates, M. V. Layman, and V. J. Parenton, *Before the Wind: A Study of Hurricane Carla*, NAS/NRC Disaster Study Number 19 (Washington, DC: National Academy of Sciences, 1963).

11 John H. Sorenson and Phil J. Gersmehl, 'Volcano Hazard Warning System: Persistence and Transferability', *Environmental Management* 4 (1980): 125–136.

12 See, for example, David Morell and Christopher Magorian, *Siting Hazardous Waste Facilities: Local Opposition and the Myth of Preemption* (Cambridge, MA: Ballinger, 1982), 35–42; Fitchen et al., 'Risk Perception', op cit, note 7.

13 Johnson, 'Public Concerns', op cit, note 3.

14 See, for example, Paul Susman, Phil O'Keefe, and Ben Wisner, 'Global Disasters, A Radical Interpretation', in Kenneth Hewitt, ed., *Interpretations of Calamity* (Boston: Allen and Unwin, 1983), 263–283.

15 Ian Burton, Robert W. Kates, and Gilbert F. White, The *Environment as Hazard* (New York, NY: Oxford University Press, 1978).

16 Sallie A. Marston, 'The Political Economy of the Earthquake Hazard in California' (Paper presented at Annual Meeting of the Association of American Geographers, San Antonio, TX, 26 April 1982).

17 Roger E. Kasperson, 'Six Propositions on Public Participation and Their Relevance for Risk Communication', *Risk Analysis* 6 (1986): 275–281; see also Peter M. Sandman, *Explaining Environmental Risk: Some Notes on Environmental Risk Communication* (Washington, DC: US Environmental Protection Agency, November 1986).

18 Richard J. Bord, 'Public Cooperation as a Social Problem: The Case of Risky Wastes' (Paper presented at Annual Meeting of the American Association for the Advancement of Science, Chicago, IL, 14–18 February 1987); E. Brent Sigmon, 'Achieving a Negotiated Compensation Agreement in Siting: The MRS Case', *Journal of Policy Analysis and Management* 6 (1987): 170–179; Johnson, 'Public Concerns', op cit, note 3.

19 Steve Rayner and Robin Cantor, 'How Fair Is Safe Enough? The Cultural Approach to Societal Technology Choice', *Risk Analysis* 7 (1987): 3–9.

20 See, for example, Gary L. Downey, 'Federalism and Nuclear Waste Disposal: The Struggle Over Shared Decision Making', *Journal of Policy Analysis and Management* 5 (1985): 73–99; Sigmon, 'Achieving', op cit, note 18.

21 Richard J. Bord, Philip J. Ponzurick, and Warren F. Witzig, 'Community Response to Low-Level Radioactive Waste: A Case Study of an Attempt to Establish a Waste Reduction and Incineration Facility', *IEEE Transactions on Nuclear Science* 32 (1985): 4466–4471.

22 R. P. Savage, J. Baker, J. H. Golden, A. Kareem, and B. R. Manning, *Hurricane Alicia: Galveston and Houston, TX, August 17–18, 1983* (Washington, DC: National Academy of Sciences, 1984).

23 Fitchen et al., 'Risk Perception', op cit, note 7.

24 See, for example, Mary Douglas and Aaron Wildavsky, *Risk and Culture* (Berkeley, CA: University of California Press, 1982); James F. Short, Jr., 'The Social Fabric at Risk: Toward the Social Transformation of Risk Analysis', *American Sociological Review* 49 (1984): 711–725.

25 Rayner and Cantor, 'How Fair', 3, op cit, note 19.

26 Covello et al., *Risk Communication*, op cit, note 4.

27   Ibid., 16–18.
28   See, for example, Baruch Fischhoff and Don MacGregor, 'Judged Lethality: How Much People Seem to Know Depends Upon How They Are Asked', *Risk Analysis* 3 (1983): 229–236; Harald Ibrekk and M. Granger Morgan, 'Graphical Communication of Uncertain Quantities to Non-Technical People' (Department of Engineering and Public Policy, Carnegie-Mellon University, Pittsburgh, PA, October 1986, manuscript).
29   Covello et al., *Risk Communication*, 7, op cit, note 4.
30   'Dioxin Screening Tests Alarm Missouri Residents', *New York Times*, 21 April 1983, Y-8.
31   Johnson, 'Social Construction of Science', op cit, note 1.
32   Philip Shabecoff, 'Uncertainties of a Chemical-Filled World Come Home to a Denver Suburb', *New York Times*, 19 April 1987, Y-19.
33   Karen De Witt, 'As Consumers Save Water, Rates Go Up', *New York Times*, 29 October 1979, A-9.
34   Edward J. Walsh, 'Challenging Official Risk Assessments via Protest Mobilization: The TMI Case', in Johnson and Covello, *Construction of Risk*, 85–101.
35   Clyde Haberman, 'City Not Ready To Start Easing Curbs on Water', *New York Times*, 21 May 1981, B-4.
36   Behaviour change should be emphasized in defining communication outcomes, because it is often a precursor (rather than consequence) of attitudinal change; see, for example, Irwin Deutscher, *What We Say/What We Do: Sentiments and Acts* (Glenview, IL: Scott, Foresman, 1973). Behaviour can also be easier to change and observe than attitudes, and it provides a more concrete basis for possible negotiation about appropriate hazard management.
37   Joseph D. Novak, *A Theory of Education* (Ithaca, NY: Cornell University Press, 1977); Joseph D. Novak and D. Bob Gowin, *Learning How to Learn* (New York, NY: Cambridge University Press, 1984).
38   Bonney F. Hughes, *Knowledge, Beliefs and Actions of Elmira Water Customers Related to Groundwater, Contamination of Groundwater, and Toxicology*, MS thesis, Cornell University, January 1986.
39   Branden B. Johnson, 'Citizen Risk Assessment,' research proposal submitted to the National Science Foundation (Michigan Technological University, Houghton, MI, 1987).
40   See, for example, Robert Glaser, 'Educating and Thinking: The Role of Knowledge,' *American Psychologist* 39 (1984): 93–104.
41   Flood Loss Reduction Associates, *Prototype Local Flood Warning Plan* (Albany, NY: Department of Environmental Conservation, 1984).
42   Johnson, 'Citizen Risk Assessment', op cit note 39.
43   Carol Van Strum, *A Bitter Fog: Herbicides and Human Rights* (San Francisco, CA: Sierra Club Books, 1983), 163–165.
44   See, for example, Donald B. Straus, 'Mediating Environmental, Energy and Economic Trade-Offs: A Case Study of the Search for Improved Tools for Facilitating the Process' (Paper presented at Annual Meeting of the American Association for the Advancement of Science, Denver, CO, 20–25 February 1977).
45   Lee Wilkins, *Media Coverage of Quick Onset Hazards: Toward a Definition of Memorable News; The Bhopal Example*, Final Report to the National Science Foundation (School of Journalism and Mass Communication, University of Colorado, Boulder, CO, December 1986).
46   Carlton Ruch and Larry Christensen, *Hurricane Message Enhancement* (Texas A&M University, College Station, TX, 1981).
47   Covello et al., *Risk Communication*, 22, op cit, note 4.
48   See, for example, Louisiana Department of Public Safety, *Southeast Louisiana Hurricane Study, Evacuation Behavioral Survey*, Final Report (Office of Emergency Preparedness, Baton Rouge, LA, 1984).

49   See, for example, Robert C. Mitchell and Richard T. Carson, 'Protest, Property Rights, and Hazardous Waste', *Resources*, 85 (1986): 6–9; Johnson, 'Public Concerns', op cit, note 3.

50   See, for example, Rayner and Cantor, 'How Fair', op cit, note 19; Ward Edwards and Detlof von Winterfeldt, 'Public Values in Risk Debates', *Risk Analysis* 7 (1987): 141–158.

51   Michael O'Hare, 'Information Management and Public Choice', in John P. Crecine, ed., *Research in Public Policy Analysis and Management*, Volume 1 (Greenwich, CT: JAI Press, 1981), 236.

52   Paul Slovic, Baruch Fischhoff, and Sarah Lichtenstein, 'Facts and Fears: Understanding Perceived Risk', in Richard C. Schwing and Walter A. Albers, Jr., eds., *Societal Risk Assessment: How Safe Is Safe Enough?* (New York, NY: Plenum, 1980), 181–213.

53   O'Hare, 'Information Management,' 236, 240 and 245, op cit, note 51.

54   See, for example, Ian MacIver, *Urban Water Supply Alternatives: Perception and Choice in the Grand Basin, Ontario*, Research Paper No. 126 (Department of Geography, University of Chicago, Chicago, IL, 1970); Kerry Thomas, Elisabeth Swaton, Martin Fishbein, and Harry J. Otway, 'Nuclear Energy: The Accuracy of Policy Makers' Perceptions of Public Beliefs', *Behavioral Sciences* 25 (1980): 332–344.

55   Harold I. Sharlin, 'Macro-Risks, Micro-Risks, and the Media: The EDB Case', in Johnson and Covello, *Construction of Risk*, 183–197.

56   In addition to the earlier discussion on information and education, see O'Hare, 'Information Management', op cit, note 51; and Kasperson, 'Six Propositions', op cit, note 17.

57   Johnson, 'Public Concerns', op cit, note 3.

58   Burkart Holzner and Evelyn Fisher, 'Knowledge in Use: Considerations in the Sociology of Knowledge Application', *Knowledge: Creation, Diffusion, Utilization* 1 (1979): 223.

59   Sandman, *Explaining Environmental Risk*, 19–20, op cit, note 17.

60   O'Hare, 'Information Management', 243–244, op cit, note 51.

61   Sandman, *Explaining Environmental Risk*, 22, op cit, note 24.

62   Short, 'Social Fabric at Risk', 718, author's italics, op cit, note 24.

9

Risk Communication and Management in the 21st Century

Ragnar E. Löfstedt

It is fair to say that European regulation can be divided into an old model of regulatory decision-making, that I label consensual, and a new model of regulatory decision-making that I label participatory-transparent.[1] The old model of regulatory decision-making, put in place as early as 1842 in the United Kingdom following the passage of the Factory Laws, had the following features (e.g. see Lundqvist, 1980; Ashby and Anderson, 1981; Kelman, 1981; Brickman et al, 1985; Vogel, 1986):

- It was based on consensual styles of regulation in which policymakers and industry met behind closed doors and made regulatory decisions.
- It was elitist in nature, with regulatory decisions made in consultation with a number of elite groups including heads of industry, senior regulators, and representatives from trade unions. These groups were seen to represent society at large.

This model of regulatory decision-making was also inherently flexible. Regulators made a point of working out possible problems with the regulatees, be it at national and/or local level. For example in the annual report of the British Alkali and Clean Air Inspectorate in 1973 it states that '[t]he Chief Inspector, with the help of his deputies, lay down the broad national policies and, provided they keep within their broad lines, inspectors in the field have plenty of flexibility to take into account local circumstances and make suitable decisions' (Vogel, 1986, p82).

The old consensual model of regulatory decision-making was widespread throughout Europe, ranging from Sweden, to Germany, France and the UK, and it was by in large praised by academics, industry and regulators. As the journal *Chemical and Industry* in its regular reviews of the then UK Alkali Inspectorate argued in 1949, '[t]he alkali inspectors are a remarkable body of men. Any inspectors who are not looked upon by the inspected as having only nuisance value must be remarkable, and that is most certainly the case with the alkali inspectors. They have to administer an Act and a number of Orders which could easily become an intolerable nuisance to industry were they not intelligently and helpfully administered' (Ashby and Anderson, 1981, p103).

Similarly, a number of academic studies produced in the early 1980s praised the old model. In one thorough review comparing and contrasting chemical controls in three

European nations as well as the United States, the authors argue that '[w]hile US agencies are hampered by inexperience and by frequent changes in the upper echelons, European bureaucracies, particularly those with technical expertise, remain better insulated against the winds of electoral politics. Regulatory agencies are staffed by professional civil servants who are not subject to removal with every change in government. At the same time they are steeped in the history and tradition of bureaucratic decision making ...' (Brickman et al, 1985, p305).

The general public accepted these arrangements. As late as 1979, for example, only 4 per cent of British respondents in a survey on public perceptions toward regulators felt that a close collaboration between industry and the regulator was improper (Hayward and Berki, 1979). In addition, at this time there was widespread public trust throughout Europe toward policymakers and regulators. The public seldom became involved in the policymaking process nor were they expected to do so. Environmental groups who were not part of the establishment, such as Greenpeace and Friends of the Earth, tried to get their voices heard but in more cases than not they were not listened to by the powers that be. The top-down form of risk communication, in which regulators/government communicated in a one-way fashion to the public, was the modus operandi.

Declining Levels of Public Trust

Since these academic studies of the 1980s, the risk communication and management climate in Europe has changed tremendously. The primary reason for this change has to do with the erosion of the general public's trust toward industry and regulators. There have been a number of explanations of why the public's trust toward these bodies has decreased so dramatically, including the rise of 24-hour television and the Internet leading to the public not having to take policymakers' comments for granted, to the centralization of government, and the amplification of risk by the media (Giddens, 1990; Nye et al, 1997).

That said, the single most important factor to the decline in public trust has to do with the sheer number and size of regulatory scandals that have plagued Europe over the last 15 years or so (Löfstedt and Vogel, 2001). Among the more significant scandals include the Belgian dioxin crisis of the summer of 1999, the tainted blood scandal in France, and the UK and European BSE (mad cow disease) crisis in the 1990s. These scandals should not be underestimated. The Belgian dioxin crisis which involved dioxin entering the Belgian food supply via contaminated animal fat used in animal feed supplied to Belgian, French and Dutch farms, for example, had significant repercussions. Because the Belgian government did not promptly go public with the knowledge of the crisis, it was accused of a self-serving cover-up leading to the resignations of two cabinet ministers and the ousting of the ruling party in a national election (Lok and Powell, 2000).

The BSE crisis, in which UK government ministers continued to reassure the public that BSE was not transmissible to humans even after it had begun to cross species barriers, also had significant repercussions. John Major, the prime minister at the time of the BSE crisis, viewed it as the worst crisis since the 1956 Suez debacle, while the

Table 9.1 *The decline in public trust*

	Early 1980s (%)	Mid-1990s (%)
Finland	65	33
Germany	51	29
Spain	48	37

then European Commissioner for Agriculture Franz Fischler viewed BSE as the biggest crisis the European Union had ever had (Ratzan, 1999).

In terms of decline in public trust, in a 15-year period from the early 1980s to the mid-1990s, according to the World Values Survey, the public's confidence in parliament has fallen significantly in many European countries (Newton and Norris, 2000) (see Table 9.1).

In the countries where I have conducted most of my research, namely the UK and Sweden, the public's trust toward policymakers has fallen. In the UK, polls indicate that the public's trust decreased from 39 to 22 per cent in the period 1974–1996 (House of Lords, 2000), while trust in Swedish policymakers has declined from 65 per cent in 1968 to 30 per cent in 1999 (Holmberg and Weibull, 1999).

The issue of falling trust levels is important. First, past research indicates that it is much easier to destroy trust than to build it (Slovic, 1993). It is therefore highly unlikely that regulators in the UK, for example, will be able to rebuild public trust levels to the same height as they were prior to the BSE scandal, although one should note that the falling trust levels have tapered off. Second, research that Paul Slovic, myself and others have done over recent years shows that public trust is one of the most important explanatory variables of the public's perceptions of risk (Löfstedt, 1996). That is, if the public trusts regulators they will perceive risks to be less than when they do not trust regulators. In fact, there is a correlation between low public-perceived risk and a high level of public trust and vice versa. In sum, as the public becomes increasingly distrustful, the public is increasingly risk averse.

This is one of the primary reasons why there is such a high level of public concern in the UK with regard to a wide range of scares ranging from food safety issues (Is it safe to eat farmed Scottish salmon or not?) to public health (Should my child get the MMR jab?[2]). Hence, in countries such as the UK, where public distrust is rampant, it is not surprising that risks and various alarms dominate the news.

The New Model of Regulatory Decision-Making

As the levels of public trust toward regulators and policymakers have declined, researchers such as Giandomenico Majone have concluded that the consensual model of regulatory decision-making in Europe is now dead (Majone and Everson, 2001). The number and size of the scandals throughout Europe made this model unacceptable in the eyes of the public. In the ashes of the consensual model, a new model of regulatory decision-making has taken shape.

This model, developed in an ad hoc and very much muddling-through fashion, and which is arguably more advanced in some nations (such as the UK) than others (such as Sweden), has the following characteristics (Royal Commission on Environmental Pollution, 1998; European Commission, 2001; UK Strategy Unit, 2002; Löfstedt, 2004):

- It aims to be more inclusive than exclusive, encouraging greater public and stakeholder participation in the policymaking process, either via citizen panels or citizen juries or by having stakeholders participate in policymaking round tables.
- It calls for regulatory strategies to be completely open and transparent (e.g. putting draft recommendations on the Internet) and for regulators to be accountable for any policy that they propose.
- Regulators are asked to take more account of environmental and social values and to use the precautionary principle and other risk-averse measures more frequently.
- It aims for a distinct separation of risk assessment (science) from risk management (policymaking).
- Science has received a different role. The media increasingly questions scientific findings, and many stakeholders and the public take the view that scientists are just another stakeholder.

The marked change of events is well summarized by the Health and Safety Executive in its study, *Reducing Risks, Protecting People* (1999) when it states: 'The need for public explanation of the basis for decisions about the regulation of risks now arises in wide areas of public policy-making. In former times, the issue hardly ever featured, at least outside the circle of technical specialists' (piii). Similarly, the conversion to the new model of regulatory decision-making is well argued by the UK Strategy Unit's 2002 report on risk when it states that '[d]epartments and agencies should make earning and maintaining public trust a priority in order to help them advise the public about risks they may face. There should be more openness and transparency, wider engagement of stakeholders and the public, wider availability of choice and more use of 'arm's-length' bodies such as the Food Standards Agency to provide advice on risk decisions' (p3).

The Teething Problems

Not everyone is happy with the new model of regulatory decision-making. Many scientists and regulators would welcome a return of the consensual style of regulatory decision-making. It is clear, however, that Western Europe will be unable to revert to it due to the nature and depth of the regulatory scandals that have taken place. That said, the new model of regulation, at least as implemented in Europe, is not problem-free. There are a series of teething problems that have resulted from this European experimentation. These teething problems have to date not been dealt with adequately in either a theoretical or practical fashion. So, what are some of the issues? I will now discuss the characteristics of the new approach of regulatory decision-making.

Greater public and stakeholder participation

Regulators operating in this model of decision-making are encouraged to seek greater public and stakeholder participation. Although this is indeed a worthwhile goal it needs to be made clear that achieving this objective is not problem-free. Participants tend to be self-selecting. Most people, believe it or not, do not want to participate in policymaking. They prefer to go home after work, put their feet up, have a glass of wine with their loved ones and discuss the day, rather than participate in a citizen panel.

There are many examples of this. A few years ago I was involved in evaluating a citizen panel project in the North Blackforest in Baden Wurttemberg (Germany) (Löfstedt, 1999). Using random sample techniques, the research group there invited some 5440 citizens to participate in the panels. Of those asked, 198 actually accepted and 191 participated, giving a response rate of 3.5 per cent. Those that did participate had, on the whole, two things in common: they were left of centre politically and they had time to spare – in effect, not representing the majority of the Christian Democratic Union-leaning Baden Wurttemberg population. Although these panels came up with a sensible outcome in the end, to almost everyone's disbelief, the issue is still one of self-selection. How can we encourage the silent majority to participate even when they do not want to? This is an issue that needs to be addressed, otherwise the UK government's public participation efforts, be they with regard to the siting of a nuclear waste depository or determining whether the country should grow genetically modified (GM) crops, will be a waste of time and money.

One way to address the conundrum of the self-selection process is to focus more on face-to-face ethnographic interviews rather than engage in mass public dialogue campaigns, as this would better uncover how the public actually perceives the risk in question. These types of studies, based on cognitive mapping, or mental models process, developed by Baruch Fischhoff and others, coordinate the knowledge of diverse experts as well as securing public understanding of the analytical results leading to better (proactive) risk communication strategies (Morgan et al, 2002).

Past research indicates that involving the public and stakeholders in the policymaking process does lead to greater public trust. There are two primary explanations for this. First, as Thomas Schelling (1960) noted, when the public and the stakeholders have been brought into the policymaking process early on they feel ownership of the outcome of the exercise. Second, if policymakers have taken note of the public's and stakeholders' concerns, these same groups feel listened to and are more likely to accept a decision (Renn et al, 1995). However, upon further reflection, this is not as clear-cut as it seems. In many cases, for example, involving stakeholders can actually increase distrust in the policymaking process rather than the other way around.

Some years ago I evaluated a risk communication exercise for the Swedish National Chemical Inspectorate with regard to banning the use of antifouling paints by pleasure boat owners (Löfstedt, 2001). Part of the inspectorate's risk communication exercise focused on engaging a number of stakeholders, such as the Swedish Yacht Club Association, to ensure stakeholder buy-in. The exercise misfired as the stakeholders argued forcefully that the boat owners would oppose and disobey any ban. These stakeholders mentioned, for example, that they were sure that their members would consider sailing to Estonia and buying even nastier chemicals than what were available in Sweden, or buying antifouling paints via the web from other European countries. The associations also questioned the science that the ban was based on and told the Chemical Inspectorate that they felt unfairly picked on. In sum, the various Swedish boating federations were trying to inject distrust into the inspectorate's decision for a ban to kill it off. They were ultimately unsuccessful, however, as the results of my study and subsequent analyses indicated that the Swedish boat owners wanted to protect the environment as much as possible and that they would be happy to comply. In this case the stakeholders wanted to promote their agenda at the price of destroying the boat owners' trust in the policymaking process of the Swedish Chemical Inspectorate.[3]

Regulatory strategies should be open and transparent

Policymakers throughout Europe and elsewhere argue that the policymaking process should be as transparent as possible (European Commission, 2001; UK Strategy Unit, 2002). This includes placing policy deliberations on the Internet, making actual correspondence between policymakers, the public and lobbyists publicly available, and encouraging scientists to participate to a greater degree in the public eye. It is difficult to disagree with this. Many of the past regulatory scandals in Europe came to fruition primarily because the regulatory policymaking process was non-transparent, with decisions made behind closed doors and where the principal actors did not take into account a wide array of social and environmental values. Indeed, the issue of wider transparency in policymaking is crucial in the eyes of many policymakers to rebuild public trust (European Commission, 2001).

A transparent process, however, is not problem-free. A series of issues arises. First, it encourages the public, both directly and indirectly, to make their own decisions about what food they should eat, what car they should buy, and what policymakers they should believe in, based either directly on information available via the web or through the lens of the media rather than from the regulators themselves. This means that the public increasingly has to make risk management decisions based on a number of criteria, many of which are unscientific – for example, a stakeholder's ability to speak or an individual's charisma or looks.

It is because of this type of environment that the public in the UK, for example, has become so concerned about the MMR vaccine. Also, is it in the regulators' best interest to see risks amplified when they should in fact be attenuated? In the farmed Scottish salmon scare, for example, this was caused by a number of US scientists trying to act as policymakers. That is, using their study which showed higher levels of PCBs in farmed salmon from Scotland than from wild salmon caught off the coast of Alaska, and then applying US Environmental Protection Agency (EPA) food consumption guidelines, set for anglers catching recreational fish rather than US Food and Drug Administration (FDA), UK Food Standards Agency (FSA), or World Health Organisation (WHO) guidelines, they concluded that the farmed salmon was unsafe to eat. This study, in the name of transparency, was quickly circulated throughout Europe and the US, leading to widespread concern that one should not eat farmed salmon, despite the significant health benefits of doing so. Is it in this case reasonable to expect the public, let alone the media, to compare regulatory guidelines from different agencies in different countries as a basis to decide whether farmed salmon is safe to eat?

Greater transparency also leads to the development of so-called policy vacuums (Powell and Leiss, 1997). The proposing and making of regulations are in many cases about issues management. In the days of consensual-style regulation, regulatory decisions were not announced before a consensus had been reached, in effect stifling any possible debate regarding whether the regulation was needed in the first place. Today, in a transparent environment, the conflicts and deliberations are for everyone to see, and more importantly, for everyone who wants to, to try to influence. This causes information vacuums, as those in power, the regulators, are not always quick enough to respond concretely to a regulatory uncertainty, thus leaving it vulnerable to attack by more trusted bodies. For a body to exert its influence in this new environment it needs to have three things going for it; namely, public trust, a well-toned communication machine, and speed on the ground (for a great discussion, see Leiss, 2001).

In the UK, it is increasingly the non-governmental organizations (NGOs) who have earned as well as mastered these skills at the cost of regulators and industry. In many cases this is not a problem, as the interests of the NGOs are not dissimilar to those of the government, but in some cases it can be. There are many examples of UK regulators indirectly losing control of the regulatory agenda because of this policy vacuum, ranging from the recent ghost ship fiasco, to the GMO debate, and the siting of a nuclear waste depository. If the regulators want to regain the public's trust in an era of increased policy transparency, they will have to address these three key factors.

Increased transparency in the policymaking process also leads to the growth of scientific pluralism (Jasanoff, 1990). As scientists start airing their grievances in public rather than behind closed doors as in the past, the likelihood of one group of scientists being pitted against another in the media increases exponentially. One example of this was at the height of the Swedish acrylamide scare in April 2002, at which time findings from rodent studies put forward by toxicologists showing that acrylamide was a possible human carcinogen were publicly questioned by epidemiologists, leading to a rise of public distrust toward scientists (Löfstedt, 2003).

The use of the precautionary principle and the growth of risk aversion

In the new model of regulatory decision-making, driven by public distrust, regulators are becoming increasingly risk averse. Concerned about a new possible scandal lurking around the corner, they take the view that it is better to be safe than sorry. In the risk-averse world, one regulatory philosophy that has become increasingly fashionable is that of the precautionary principle.

What the precautionary principle actually means, however, is difficult to pinpoint, as studies indicate up to 19 formulations (Sandin, 1999), although suffice it to say that the most common usage of it is that one needs to take action when an activity raises threats to the environment or human health. Many member state countries, most notably Germany and Sweden, have used the precautionary principle with some degree of success for 30 years (Löfstedt et al, 2002), and a recent study by the European Environment Agency espoused the virtues of it (EEA, 2001). Even the European Commission has become involved regarding the meaning of the precautionary principle, and in the year 2000 published a communication to clarify its meaning, concluding that the principle should be placed within an existing framework of risk management (European Commission, 2000).

There is now a concern within elements of the European Commission and elsewhere that it may be misused, so rather than being an added tool to a risk assessors tool box it becomes a law unto itself. Questionable rulings over the past few years include the European Commission's decision to ban the importation of groundnuts from Africa, citing the precautionary principle (although scientific studies indicate that eating these ground nuts increases the rate of liver cancer by 1 death in 100 million people) (see Chapter 14). If the use of the precautionary principle is to remain a credible regulatory tool, then it needs to be used within the parameters set out by the European Commission's communication, as its misuse will lead to public and stakeholder distrust of European regulators and worse policymaking overall.

Separation of risk assessment from risk management

In Europe, the delineation of risk assessment and management was for many years unclear, because the focus was more on determining the criteria of the risk management process while still taking into account that it can be influenced by social values (Fairman et al, 1998; Royal Commission on Environmental Pollution, 1998; Fairman, 1999). Over the past three years there has been a fundamental shift in this thinking. In 1998 the RCEP argued that scientists should not be seen to be making policy, and hence risk assessment should be separated from risk management.

The European Commission has also argued that this is necessary in order to restore public trust in the policymaking process (e.g. Byrne 2000). Initial European research does support Byrne's claims. For example, a 2002 poll conducted on 3000 consumers in the UK for the FSA, the agency in charge of risk assessment, indicated that 60 per cent of the consumers now claim to be very or somewhat confident in the agency's role in protecting health with regard to food safety. This is a 10 per cent increase in consumer confidence levels since 2000 (FSA, 2003). Similarly, results from the US, and in this case the US Environmental Protection Agency in the early 1980s, does indicate that a separation of risk assessment from risk management did increase public trust in the regulatory body.

The issue, however, is whether this is always a good thing. In 1996, the US National Research Council published a report entitled *Understanding Risk*, which argued that the two areas should be combined, taking the view that all types of actors should be involved in the risk characterization process and that there should be continuous feedback throughout the whole risk management cycle. Other policymakers take the view that a separation is not practically possible, as the scientists in charge of the risk assessment should at least offer their advice to the policymakers in charge of the risk management process.

The role of science

In the new model of regulatory decision-making, scientists do not play the prominent role that they once did. Rather, scientific results today are increasingly questioned by the media, stakeholders, the public and other scientists claiming contrary evidence (O'Brien, 2000). There are several reasons for this demotion, one of which having to do with past scandals. With regard to BSE, for example, scientists were wrong to categorically state in the late 1980s that there was no link between BSE and vCJD (the human variant). In addition, studies indicate that public information is important and should not be quickly discounted by scientists. One study that strongly supports this case had to with government scientific experts pitted against Cumbrian sheep farmers, who had seen their sheep contaminated by radiation after the Chernobyl accident. The research showed that the procedures for the affected sheep, provided by scientists at the Ministry of Agriculture, Food and Fisheries (MAFF) and other government bodies, did not consider the sheep farmers' local knowledge. As the MAFF scientists turned out to be wrong and the sheep farmers right, it led to the scientists losing their credibility in the eyes of the sheep farmers (see Wynne, 1992, 1996).

However, the question remains how often does this occur? Should scientists have only equal weight with local knowledge or stakeholder intuitions? Is the sheep case more of an exception to the rule? These questions are difficult to answer, but one clearly needs to take into account the consequences of downplaying scientific results in the setting of regulations. For example, by not focusing enough on the scientific dimension, the media has amplified the controversy around the MMR jab as a national health risk, with more than 50 per cent of the public now confused as to whether there is a link between the jab and child autism (although this may now be shifting following Wakefield's study being recently discredited) and concerns around whether British industries should be involved in boat disposal. In sum, ignoring science can be perilous.

Conclusions

The new model of regulatory decision-making, as outlined in this chapter, is here to stay. The levels of public distrust toward authorities are simply too high to consider anything else. Yet there are many issues that still need to be analysed and resolved. If policymakers are encouraging greater public participation in the policymaking process, how can we reduce self-selection bias? How can we ensure that the stakeholders participating in the policymaking process really want to build trust? How can we ensure that transparency in policymaking does not lead to unnecessary amplification of risks and public confusion? What is needed to halt the misuse of the precautionary principle? These and related issues key to the formation of the new regulatory model need further attention and analyses in order to ensure the development of a better regulatory framework for Europe, taking into account the needs for improving public health and the environment.

Acknowledgements

The research and development of this chapter has been supported by a contract from the Canadian Privy Council Office, as well as grants from Pfizer Global Research and Development and the Swedish Research Foundation via the Centre for Public Sector Research, University of Goteborg. I am grateful to the following individuals who have commented on an earlier version of this chapter: Åsa Boholm, Frederic Bouder, E. Donald Elliot, Robyn Fairman, Baruch

Fischhoff, George Gray, Ortwin Renn and Fred Thompson. Earlier versions of this chapter were presented at a seminar to the Law School at George Mason University on 15 March 2004 and as an inaugural lecture for my chair in risk management at King's College, London, on 23 March 2004.

Notes

1   The idea of dividing regulation into old and new models comes from an excellent article by William Leiss (2000) who applies it to Canada's risk management experience.
2   The MMR jab refers to the measles, mumps and rubella vaccine. There has been a heated debate in the UK as to whether infants should be given this vaccine, as one UK scientific study suggested a link between the MMR vaccine and autism. Although this study (initially published in *Lancet* in 1998) was based on a small sample size and has yet to be replicated in either the UK or anywhere else in the world, it led to massive media and public outcry. In fact, today some 50 per cent of the UK general public believe that there may be a link between autism and the MMR vaccine, even though a vast majority of medical experts dispute such a link. Public concern about the MMR vaccine has led to take-up levels of the vaccine falling in the UK from approximately 90 per cent in 1998 to just over 80 per cent in 2002.
3   It should, however, be made clear that on the whole and in many cases the policy preferences of interest group members are more likely to reflect those of the general public than those of the leaders of these special interest groups. One of the main reasons for this is that the leaders of the special interest groups must justify themselves and therefore take a more radical position than that of their members (Downs, 1957; Zald and McCarthy, 1987; Ellis and Thompson, 1997).

References

Ashby, E., and M. Anderson. 1981. *The Politics of Clean Air.* Oxford, UK: Oxford University Press.

Breyer, S. 1993. *Closing the Vicious Circle.* Cambridge, MA: Harvard University Press.

Brickman, R., S. Jasanoff, and T. Ilgen. 1985. *Controlling Chemicals: The Politics of Regulation in Europe and the United States.* Ithaca, NY: Cornell University Press.

Byrne, D. 2000. 'Food Safety: Continuous Transatlantic Dialogue Is Essential'. *European Affairs* 1: 80–5.

Downs, A. 1957. *An Economic Theory of Democracy.* London: Harper Collins.

EEA (European Environment Agency). 2001. *Late Lessons from Early Warnings: The Precautionary Principle 1896–2000.* Copenhagen: EEA.

Ellis, R. J., and F. Thompson. 1997. 'Culture and Environment in the Pacific Northwest'. *American Political Science Review* 91: 885–97.

European Commission. 2000. *Communication from the Commission on the Precautionary Principle.* COM 2000 1 Final: Brussels: European Commission.

———. 2001. *European Governance: A White Paper.* COM 2001 428 Final. Brussels: European Commission.

Fairman, R. 1999. 'A Commentary on the Evolution of Environmental Health Risk Management: A US Perspective'. *Journal of Risk Research* 2: 101–13.

Fairman, R., C. D. Mead, and W. P. Williams. 1998. *Environmental Risk Assessment: Approaches, Experiences, and Information Sources.* Copenhagen: EEA.

FSA (Food Standards Agency). 2003. *Consumer Attitudes Survey 2002.* London: FSA.

Giddens, A. 1990. *The Consequences of Modernity.* Cambridge, UK: Polity Press.

Hayward, J., and R. Berki. 1979. *State and Society in Contemporary Europe.* Oxford, UK: Robertson.

Health and Safety Executive. 1999. *Reducing Risks. Protecting People.* Consultation Document. London: Health and Safety Executive.

Holmberg, S., and L. Weibull, eds. 1999. *Ljusnande Framtid.* Gothenburg, Sweden: SOM Institute, University of Gothenburg.

House of Lords. 2000. *Select Committee on Science and Technology: Science and Society.* London: Stationery Office.

Jasanoff, S. 1990. *The Fifth Branch: Science Advisors as Policy Makers.* Cambridge, MA: Harvard University Press.

Kelman, S. 1981. *Regulating America, Regulating Sweden: A Comparative Study of Occupational Safety and Health Policy.* Cambridge, MA: MIT Press.

Leiss, W. 2000. 'Between Expertise and Bureaucracy: Risk Management Trapped at the Science-Policy Interface'. pp. 49–74 in G. B. Doern and T. Reed, eds., *Risk Business: Canada's Changing Science-based Policy and Regulatory Regime.* Toronto: University of Toronto Press.

———. 2001. *In the Chamber of Risks.* Montreal: McGill-Queen's University Press.

Löfstedt, R. E. 1996. 'Risk Communication: The Barseback Nuclear Plant Case'. *Energy Policy* 24: 689–96.

———. 1999. 'The Role of Trust in the North Blackforest: An Evaluation of a Citizen Panel Project'. *Risk: Health. Safety and Environment* 10: 10–30.

———. 2001. 'Risk and Regulation: Boat Owners' Perceptions of Recent Antifouling Legislation'. *Risk Management: An International Journal* 3: 33–46.

———. 2003. 'Science Communication and the Swedish Acrylamide "Alarm"', *Journal of Health Communication* 8: 407–30.

———. 2004. 'The Swing of the Regulatory Pendulum in Europe: From Precautionary Principle to (Regulatory) Impact Analysis'. *Journal of Risk and Uncertainty* 28: 237–60.

Löfstedt, R. E., B. Fischhoff, and I. Fischhoff. 2002. 'Precautionary Principles: General Definitions and Specific Applications to Genetically Manipulated Organisms (GMOs)'. *Journal of Policy Analysis and Management* 21: 381–407.

Löfstedt, R. E., and D. Vogel. 2001. 'The Changing Character of Regulation: A Comparison of Europe and the United States'. *Risk Analysis* 21: 399–406.

Lok, C, and D. Powell. 2000. 'The Belgian Dioxin Crisis of the Summer of 1999: A Case Study in Crisis Communication and Management'. Guelph, Ontario: Department of Food Science, University of Guelph.

Lundqvist, L. J. 1980. *The Hare and the Tortoise: Clean Air Policies in the United States and Sweden.* Ann Arbor: University of Michigan Press.

Majone, G., and M. Everson. 2001. 'Institutional Reform: Independent Agencies, Oversight, Coordination and Procedural Control'. pp. 129–68 in O. DeSchutter, N. Lebessis, and J. Paterson, eds., *Governance in the European Union.* Luxembourg: Office for the Official Publications of the European Communities.

Morgan, M. G., B. Fischhoff, A. Bostrom, and C. J. Atman. 2002. *Risk Communication: A Mental Models Approach.* New York: Cambridge University Press.

National Research Council. 1996. *Understanding Risk.* Washington, DC: National Academy Press.

Newton, K., and P. Norris. 2000. 'Confidence in Public Institutions: Fear, Culture, or Performance?' pp. 52–73 in S. Pharr and R. Putnam, eds., *Disaffected Democracies: What's Troubling the Trilateral Countries?* Princeton, NJ: Princeton University Press.

Nye, J. S. Jr., P. D. Zelikow, and D. C. King, eds. 1997. *Why People Don't Trust Government.* Cambridge, MA: Harvard University Press.

O'Brien, M. 2000. *Making Better Environmental Decisions: An Alternative to Risk Assessment.* Cambridge, MA: MIT Press.

Powell, M., and W. Leiss. 1997. *Mad Cows and Mother's Milk.* Montreal: McGill-Queen's University Press.

Ratzan, S., ed. 1999. *The Mad Cow Crisis: Health and the Public Good.* London: University College London Press.

Renn, O., T. Webler, and P. Wiedemann, eds. 1995. *Fairness and Competence in Citizen Participation.* Dordrecht, Netherlands: Kluwer.

Royal Commission on Environmental Pollution. 1998. *Setting Environmental Standards.* London: Stationery Office.

Sandin, P. 1999. 'Dimensions of the Precautionary Principle'. *Human and Ecological Risk Assessment* 6: 445–58.

Schelling, T. 1960. *The Strategy of Conflict.* Cambridge, MA: Harvard University Press.

Slovic, P. 1993. 'Perceived Risk, Trust and Democracy'. *Risk Analysis* 13: 675–82.

UK Strategy Unit. 2002. *Risk: Improving Government's Capability to Handle Risk and Uncertainty.* Summary Report. London: Strategy Unit, Cabinet Office.

Vogel, D. 1986. *National Styles of Regulation: Environmental Policy in Great Britain and the United States.* Ithaca, NY: Cornell University Press.

Wynne, B. 1992. 'Sheep Farming After Chernobyl: A Case Study in Communicating Scientific Information'. In B.V. Lewenstein, ed., *When Science Meets the Public.* Washington, DC: American Association for the Advancement of Science.

_____. 1996. 'May the Sheep Safely Graze? A Reflexive View of the Expert-Lay Knowledge Divide'. pp. 44–83 in S. Lash, B. Szerszynski, and B. Wynne, eds., *Risk, Environment and Modernity: Towards a New Ecology.* London: Sage.

Zald, M. N., and J. D. McCarthy. 1987. *Social Movements in an Organisational Society: Collected Essays.* New Brunswick, NJ: Transaction Publishers.

Part IV

Trust and Post-Trust

10

Exploring the Dimensionality of Trust in Risk Regulation

Wouter Poortinga and Nick F. Pidgeon

Introduction

Trust has become a popular research subject in the social sciences during the last two decades. Trust is considered to lubricate social interactions on various levels so that these function smoothly and harmoniously (e.g. Tyler and Degoey, 1996), it is thought to reduce social uncertainty and complexity (Luhmann, 1979; Barber, 1983; Earle and Cvetkovich, 1995), and is seen to be an important element of social capital and as a prerequisite for a healthy and flexible economy and democracy (e.g. Putnam, 1993; Fukuyama, 1995; Dekker, 1999; Kasperson et al, 1999; Cook, 2000).

Also, in the field of risk research there is now general agreement that trust in risk management institutions may be an important factor in perception and acceptance of risks. This issue was first raised by Wynne (1980), who argued that with technological risks some of the differences between 'expert' and 'lay' perspectives could be traced to differing evaluations of the trustworthiness of risk managing institutions. The relationship between trust and risk perception has since gained widespread attention (e.g. Renn and Levine, 1991; Pidgeon et al, 1992; Slovic, 1993). Furthermore, trust is seen as one prerequisite for effective risk communication (e.g. Kasperson et al, 1992), while distrust may be associated with stigmatization of technologies, such as nuclear power (Flynn et al, 2001) as well as social amplification effects following major failures of risk regulation (see Freudenburg, 2003; Kasperson et al, 2003).

The dimensionality of trust

Although it is now widely recognized that trust in institutions plays an important role in risk perceptions and responses to risk communication, there have been many debates regarding what constitute and what contribute to trust. In other words, what factors make people trust or distrust risk regulatory or other institutions. In very general terms, Rousseau et al (1998) argue that trust, as conceptualized across a number of disciplines, can be defined as: 'a psychological state comprising the intention to accept vulnerability based upon the behaviour of positive expectations of the intentions of or behaviour of another' (p395). However, this definition does not, in itself, explain why people might be willing to accept vulnerability. Classical work on interpersonal trust suggests that it is mainly a two-dimensional concept based on competence and care (or 'trustworthiness'). Half a century ago, Hovland et al (1953) identified these two aspects in their seminal social psychological research programme on communication and persuasion. In a series of experiments, in which they varied specific characteristic of the communicator, they found that someone accepts information more easily when the communicator is seen as an expert (i.e. is a good source for valid assertions) and when the communicator is seen as being trustworthy, in the sense that the source is seen as willing to communicate the assertions he or she considers most valid (i.e. has no motives to promote a particular view or has lack of intent to persuade). However, more recent discussions suggest that there may be various 'levels' of social trust (e.g. Renn and Levine, 1991; Kasperson et al, 1992; Greenberg and Williams, 1999) such as 'interpersonal' versus 'institutional/social', or 'local' versus 'global'. Accordingly, more nuanced theoretical and practical understandings of the notion of trust have begun to emerge, recognizing that it may often be considered to be complex and multidimensional, as illustrated in the following quote:

> 'We trust you' may mean that we believe you can give us right answers and reliable information. It may mean that we believe that you are honest, and will tell us all that you know. Or it may mean that we trust your judgement, and rely on you for decisions which are wise, impartial, ethical and in the public interest. We may trust you in one of these ways, without trusting you in the others. In this case, if a pollster asks us whether we trust you, what are we to say? (House of Lords, 2000, paragraph 2.29)

Within risk research, a wide range of theoretical (e.g. Renn and Levine, 1991; Kasperson et al, 1992; Johnson, 1999) and empirical studies (e.g. Frewer et al, 1996; Peters et al, 1997; Metlay, 1999) have been conducted to identify the core elements of trust. That is, they have examined what kind of evaluative judgements contribute to the creation or destruction of trust in risk regulatory or other institutions. For example, in their review of the literature on trust, Renn and Levine (1991) identify five core components or attributes, namely:

1. *perceived competence*, which represents the degree of technical expertise of the source;
2. *objectivity*, reflecting the absence of bias in information;
3. *fairness*, or the degree to which the source takes into account all relevant points of view;
4. *consistency*, or the predictability of arguments and behaviour based on past experience and previous communication efforts; and
5. *faith*, which reflects the perception of 'good will' of the source.

Similarly, Kasperson et al (1992) identify four key dimensions that play an important role in the development and maintenance of trust:

1. *commitment*, as social trust involves some degree of vulnerability, one wants to make sure that the trustee is fully committed to the mission, goal, or fiduciary obligation;

2. *competence*, since trust can only exist when a person or institution is competent in the thing it is obliged to do, so that someone should not only be committed to his or her fiduciary responsibilities, but should also fulfil it competently;
3. *caring*, a perception that an institution acts in a way that shows concern for the people who put their trust in it; and finally
4. *predictability*, in that people tend to trust people or organizations that are consistent. Predictability of arguments and behaviour means that people know what to expect from a particular person or organization.

These and other scholars (e.g. Mishra, 1996) have distinguished a wide range of seemingly different aspects of trust. All of these aspects have some face validity, i.e. they all seem to reflect important components of trust under some circumstances. However, it is not always completely clear whether the public distinguishes between the different theoretical features of trust. For example, the categories *objectivity* and *fairness* of Renn and Levine (1991) may not be completely independent. A source that takes into account all relevant points of view may be perceived as more objective. Likewise, some people may not discriminate between the aspects of trust that Kasperson et al (1992) call *commitment* and *caring*. Perceptions of whether an institution acts in a caring way may influence perceptions of whether that institution fulfils its fiduciary obligations.

Recently, Metlay (1999) has criticized researchers for making discussions about trust unnecessarily difficult. He argues that some researchers have the tendency to distinguish additional shades of meaning in the concept of trust, although it is not at all clear whether these are indeed (empirically) discernible aspects of trust. Metlay's study of judgements of trust in the US Department of Energy (DoE) suggests that trust is not complex and multifaceted, but a rather simple concept based on two distinctively different components: (1) a tightly interconnected set of *affective* beliefs about institutional behaviour, which Metlay calls 'trustworthiness'; and (2) perceptions of how *competent* the institution is. There is other empirical evidence to support this claim that, rather than being based on a large number of components, trust is mainly a two-dimensional concept based on competence and care (or 'trustworthiness'). As mentioned earlier, Hovland et al (1953) identified these two aspects in their early work on trust. Also Jungermann et al (1996) found, in a study about communicating the risks of hazardous chemical facilities, that trust in information sources could be described by a two-factor solution, rather similar to that reported by Metlay, representing *honesty* and *competence*.

Evidence for trust as a two-dimensional construct has been mainly found using factor-analytical statistical techniques. A criticism of this approach is that respondents are typically asked to use scales that are predetermined by the researcher, rather than characteristics that are selected by the respondents themselves. As a consequence, the resulting factor structure may not correctly represent the public's dimensions of trust. Frewer et al (1996) have tried to avoid this criticism by personalizing their questionnaires on trust in relation to food-related hazards. In a series of studies, they constructed a personalized questionnaire by first asking respondents to indicate their own reasons for trusting or distrusting a number of possible sources of food risk information. In this way, respondents could rate each of the information sources on the dimensions they themselves thought were important. Frewer et al (1996) found a two-factor structure that could best describe the reasons for trusting or distrusting various information sources, later validated with a more representative population sample. The first component comprised the characteristics: truthful, good track record, trustworthy, favour, accurate, factual, public welfare, responsible, knowledgeable, and (negatively) the characteristics: distorted, proven wrong in the past, and biased. The second factor consisted of the characteristics: accountable, self-protection, and a vested interest versus sensationalism component. While Frewer et al (1996) did not themselves label the two components, their first factor seems once again to reflect a *general trust* evaluation of an information source, interestingly encompassing *both* competence and care components. The second factor is more difficult to interpret, but seems to encompass a *vested interest* or *accountability* factor. Using a selection of the characteristics of Frewer et al (1996), French et al (2002) identified similar dimensions of trust. A principal-components analysis (PCA) showed that the evaluation of a (hypothetical) food risk communication could be described by two dimensions, which related to the perceived credibility of the information provided and the reputations of these organizations. Like Frewer et al (1996), the first component was a general trust dimension that encompassed competence as well as care. Although the second factor also included the aspect of 'accountability', it was more closely related to what Barber (1983) calls fiduciary responsibility, as it also covered 'responsibility', and 'proven wrong in the past'.

In conclusion, there would seem to be two slightly differing empirical models of the dimensionality of trust. The first model, arising from the work of Metlay (1999), consists of the dimensions of a *general trustworthiness* factor alongside one of *competence*. The second model, from the work of Frewer et al (1996), overlaps partially with that of Metlay in that it also points to a *general trustworthiness* dimension (including both competence and care) together with a separate *vested interest* dimension. A primary objective of the present article then is to test which of these two models best describes trust in government risk regulation on a range of issues.

Salient value similarity

Earle and Cvetkovich (1995) have argued that for most people it is far too demanding to base trust on evidence of competence and fiduciary responsibilities. According to Earle and Cvetkovich (1995), social trust is particularly critical where complex socio-technical systems generate risks that are remote from everyday experience. However, most people will not have the resources or interest to make a detailed assessment of whether or not it is worthwhile to trust a particular institution. Earle and Cvetkovich (1995) argue that it is more likely that under complex circumstances trust is based on agreement and sympathy rather than on carefully reasoned arguments or direct knowledge (see also Langford, 2002). In other words, people base their trust judgements on whether they feel that the other person or organization shares the same values, i.e. is seen as having the same understanding of a specific situation. Although conventional trust concepts (such as competence) are often used in *discourses* on trust, Earle and Cvetkovich (1995) reason that this is without regard to whether these really are the critical factors underlying people's trust judgements. Rather, people may use these concepts to provide an explanation for their general agreement, sympathy or trust in an institution because espoused value similarity may not be regarded as a socially acceptable response. This salient value similarity (SVS) approach of Earle and Cvetkovich (1995) has been applied successfully in a number of studies (e.g. Chapter 11; Earle and Cvetkovich, 1995, 1997, 1999; Siegrist et al, 2001). However, it has not been examined whether the SVS approach has indeed an 'additional' value in explaining trust in the regulation of risk. In his own study, Metlay (1999) reports an indirect test of the value-similarity thesis, for which he found little evidence. In the current study we provide a more direct test of this possibility.

Aims of the Study

This study reports data from one part of a major quantitative survey conducted in Great Britain during 2002, which had a main focus of making a detailed *comparative analysis* of five risk cases on various risk-relevant topics. This study examined people's perceptions of the British government and its policy with regard to several risk cases, namely, climate change, radiation from mobile phones, radioactive waste, genetically modified food (GM food) and human genetic testing on a wide range of trust-related aspects. These cases were chosen because they are all prominent societal risk issues, and have complementary as well as contrasting facets of risk, benefits and uncertainty. They all involve scientific knowledge, public trust in science, and risk regulation, allowing for tests of governmental competence in this area. In addition they are all themes that are covered by various surveys of public opinion, but where a richer set of contextually referenced and comparative data is lacking.

The current study had a number of discrete objectives:

1. To investigate possible differential levels of trust in government regulation across the different risk contexts. This will be done in relation to several attributes that are generally seen to constitute trust (see Measures section). Our expectation is that, given the rather different nature and histories of the five risk issues chosen, significant cross-issue differences in patterns of trust ratings will emerge.
2. To empirically investigate the relationship between a range of concepts that might be thought of as comprising distinctive 'dimensions' of trust. In particular, whether people's perception of government's risk policies can be described by a limited number of underlying dimensions. The design provides a test of the two empirical models, noted above, of Metlay (1999) and Frewer et al (1996). That is, whether the evaluation of government's risk policies on the five risk cases could best be described by the dimensions of *general trustworthiness* and *competence* (Metlay, 1999), or by the dimensions of *general trust* and *vested interests* (Frewer et al, 1996).
3. To enhance Metlay's original set of survey items in order to permit a more direct examination of whether the SVS approach of Earle and Cvetkovich (1995) has an additional value in predicting trust in risk regulation over and above the more conventional conceptualizations noted above.

The Survey

Procedure and respondents

Data for this study were collected in the summer of 2002 (see Poortinga and Pidgeon, 2003). The quantitative survey was administered in Britain (England, Scotland and Wales) by the market research company MORI. Fully trained and supervised market research interviewers carried out face-to-face interviews with people in their own homes, which lasted on average about 30 minutes. The survey was run in 126 sample points. Interviewers approached selected addresses within these sample points until they reached the quotas for gender, age and work status. The quotas were reflective of the actual profile in each of the sampling points. The total sample of 1547 people aged 15 years and older comprised of five *separate* quota samples of about 300 respondents, each covering one of the five risk cases (see Table 10.1). So, respondents were presented with a set of *standardized* questions on only one of the five risk issues listed above.

Measures

Evaluation of government

Respondents were asked to evaluate the British government on how they thought it handles the five risk cases. People were presented with various standardized statements on the government and its policy on one of the five risk cases, depending on the version of the questionnaire. The statements were selected from a review of previous work on trust (e.g. Renn and Levine, 1991; Frewer et al, 1996; Peters et al, 1997; Johnson, 1999; Metlay, 1999). Eleven items were designed to measure the trust-related aspects of *competence, credibility, reliability, integrity* (vested interests), *care, fairness* and *openness* (see Table 10.1). The scores could vary from 1: 'totally disagree' to 5: 'totally agree'.

Value similarity

Two items were included that were aimed at measuring the extent to which the government was seen as having the same values with regard to the five risk cases. These items were adapted from earlier work of Earle and Cvetkovich (1995) and Siegrist et al (2000; reprinted as Chapter 11 in this volume). People were asked to indicate to what extent they agreed with the statements 'The government has the same opinion as me about [issue X]', and 'The government has the same ideas as me about [issue X]', where again the issue was the relevant risk case for the questionnaire version. Answers could be given on a five-point scale from 1: 'totally disagree' to 5: 'totally agree'.

Trust in risk regulation

Trust in risk regulation was measured using two items. People were asked whether they agreed with the statement 'I feel that current rules and regulations are sufficient to control [issue X]' as well as the statement 'I feel confident that the British government adequately regulates [issue X]', where issue X (one of the five risk cases) again depended on the version of the questionnaire that the respondent received. Responses to the two items were given on a scale ranging from 1: 'totally disagree' to 5: 'totally agree'.

Results

Comparing the five risk cases

Multivariate analyses of variance (MANOVAs) were conducted to examine whether people differed in their mean responses across the five cases with respect to the 11 items evaluating the government, whether government was seen as having the same values with regard to the five risk cases, and whether there were overall differences in trust in risk regulation. Where the MANOVAs were statistically significant (i.e. with respect to differences between the five risk cases) Tukey's multiple pairwise procedure for post hoc comparisons was used to establish which of the specific risk case means differed from the others.

It appeared that the government and its policies were evaluated differently across the five risk cases (F(44, 4714) = 1.78, p < 0.001). However, what is immediately striking about Table 10.1 is how few real differences there are in people's evaluation of government with respect to the different risk cases. The mean scores, while they differ *between* different questions, only rarely differ *within* any specific question. This high level of across-issue agreement is surprising, given that each risk issue was evaluated by a different (albeit carefully matched) sample of respondents, and that each of the cases was chosen because of its particular contrasting facets and histories. For example, human genetic testing is a relatively 'new' issue and might also be expected to hold higher perceived benefits than would GM food. Indeed, a range of other psychometric items included in the survey, but not reported here (see Poortinga and Pidgeon, 2003), did confirm that people held different beliefs about the risks, benefits and other aspects of the individual five risk issues themselves.

Overall, the mean results showed a moderate lack of endorsement of government across the items. Mean responses were below the scale mid-point for most of the 'positive' items such as competence (except the item regarding availability of skilled people), care and fairness, whereas the mean responses were above the scale mid-point for 'negative' items such as influence by industry, changes policies, and distorts facts. Interestingly, the item with the lowest average agreement was the one designed to measure the concept of *openness*. In Britain the need for greater openness in government risk handling was a key recommendation of the official enquiry into the BSE 'mad cow' disease crisis (Phillips et al, 2000).

The right-hand column of Table 10.1 shows the questionnaire items where the MANOVA reached statistical significance, and different subscripts in the table indicate where specific means differed from each other (Tukey's test p < 0.05). Note though that the statistical effect sizes for all of these differences are small (of the order of 0.2 or 0.3).

There were consistent significant differences in the two perceived value similarity items across the five risk cases (F(8, 2582) = 3.24, p < 0.001). More people agreed with the statement that the government has the same opinion about radiation from mobile telephones than about GM food, and more people agreed that the government has the same ideas about mobile phones than about climate change and GM food. However, the average responses to both items were once more below the middle of the scale, meaning that people did not see the government as having the same values as themselves with regard to any of the five risk cases. A reliability analysis showed that

Table 10.1 *Evaluation of government*

Risk statement	Climate change	Mobile phones	Radioactive waste	GM food	Genetic testing	p-value
Competence						
The government is doing a good job with regard to...	2.42_a (0.97)	2.52_{ab} (0.88)	2.66_b (0.84)	2.45_{ab} (1.00)	2.68_b (0.99)	<0.01
The government is competent enough to deal with ...	2.60 (1.08)	2.61 (1.06)	2.59 (1.03)	2.51 (1.16)	2.71 (1.17)	n.s.
The government has the necessary skilled people to carry out its job with regard to ...	2.99 (1.09)	2.93 (1.01)	3.08 (1.02)	2.85 (1.07)	3.09 (1.15)	n.s.
Credibility						
The government distorts facts in its favour regarding ...	3.71 (0.93)	3.49 (0.95)	3.68 (0.94)	3.71 (0.90)	3.50 (1.12)	<0.01
Reliability						
The government changes policies regarding ... without good reasons	3.53 (0.89)	3.41 (0.83)	3.41 (0.88)	3.60 (0.94)	3.45 (0.99)	n.s
Integrity (vested interests)						
The government is too influenced by industry regarding ...	3.73 (0.86)	3.57 (0.83)	3.58 (0.87)	3.65 (0.91)	3.54 (0.94)	n.s.
Care						
The government is acting in the public interest with regard to ...	2.68 (1.01)	2.82 (0.94)	2.72 (0.95)	2.62 (1.13)	2.79 (1.11)	n.s.
The government listens to concerns about ... raised by the public	2.59 (0.99)	2.68 (0.97)	2.67 (0.96)	2.53 (1.05)	2.70 (1.12)	n.s.
The government listens to what ordinary people think about ...	2.30 (0.97)	2.41 (0.96)	2.35 (0.98)	2.27 (1.05)	2.38 (1.05)	n.s.

Fairness						
I feel that the way the government makes decisions about … is fair	2.53 (0.91)	2.61 (0.83)	2.63 (0.87)	2.45 (1.01)	2.55 (1.02)	n.s.
Openness						
The government provides all relevant information about … to the public	2.15 (0.92)	2.19 (0.91)	2.07 (0.88)	2.08 (0.95)	2.05 (1.04)	n.s.
Value similarity						
The government has the same opinion as me about …	2.46_{ab} (0.97)	2.63_{b} (0.90)	2.44_{ab} (0.87)	2.29_{a} (1.06)	2.47_{ab} (1.00)	<0.01
The government has the same ideas about … as me	2.33_{a} (0.93)	2.57_{b} (0.92)	2.45_{ab} (0.89)	2.29_{a} (0.98)	2.43_{ab} (0.97)	<0.01
Trust in risk regulation						
I feel that current rules and regulations in the UK are sufficient to control …	2.62_{a} (1.08)	2.86_{ab} (0.93)	2.67_{a} (0.99)	2.65_{a} (1.10)	2.92_{b} (1.10)	<0.001
I feel confident that the British government adequately regulates …	2.59 (1.11)	2.67 (0.97)	2.74 (1.00)	2.61 (1.05)	2.75 (1.20)	n.s.
Sample size (N)	321	319	306	296	305	

Note: The scale ranged from 1: 'strongly disagree' to 5: 'strongly agree'; standard deviations are given in parentheses. Means with different subscripts are significantly different from each other.

one *value-similarity* scale could be constructed from the two items (Cronbach's α between 0.77 and 0.85 for the five cases).

Also, differences in trust in risk regulation were found across the five risk cases ($F(8, 2724) = 3.54$, $p < 0.001$). Table 10.1 shows that overall trust in risk regulation was not high for any of the five risk issues. The mean responses to the two items designed to measure this were below the scale mid-point for all cases. Small differences were found in one of these items. It appeared that more people felt that current rules and regulations in the United Kingdom are sufficient to control genetic testing than to control radioactive waste, climate change, and GM food. The reliability of both items was sufficient in each of the five risk cases (Cronbach's α between 0.65 and 0.81), so a *trust in risk regulation* variable was constructed combining the two.

The dimensionality of trust

To examine whether the 11 statements evaluating government could be described by a number of underlying dimensions, *separate* PCAs with varimax rotation were conducted for each of the five risk cases. As the results were similar for all risk cases, one single PCA was conducted across all risk cases. This also allows comparisons between the five risk cases on the resulting factors.

Table 10.2 shows that the PCAs in each of the five risk cases produced very similar factor solutions. The initial 11 items were described by two main components, which accounted for between 58.0 per cent and 68.2 per cent of the original variance. In each of the five risk cases the first component, which accounted for about 40 per cent of the variance, comprised the items designed to measure competence, care, fairness and openness. This can be interpreted as a *general trust* component. That is, it represents a general evaluation of government policy on the five risk issues. The second component, which accounted for about 20 per cent of the variance of the original items, was concerned with credibility, reliability and integrity (vested interest). The items 'the government distorts facts in its favour regarding ...', 'the government changes policies regarding ... without good reasons,' and 'the government is too influenced by industry regarding ...' loaded high on this second component in all five risk cases. The latter component found here reflects a sceptical view on how risk policies are brought about, and was labelled as such (*scepticism*). Once more, this high level of stability in the factor solution is surprising, given that each risk issue was evaluated by different respondents.

The explanatory power of value similarity

In order to examine whether the SVS approach has an additional value in explaining trust, two sets of multiple regression analyses were conducted for the five risk cases separately. The first regression model (Model 1) included the factors resulting from the overall factor analysis on the evaluation of government. In the second regression model (Model 2), the combined value similarity scale was added to this initial set of predictors. The differences in explained variance between the two regression models were used as an indicator for the importance of value similarity to trust in risk regulation across the five risk cases. Another indication that value similarity is an important determinant of trust in risk regulation is if its addition to the regression models leads to decreased

Table 10.2 *Factor loadings after varimax rotation*

	Climate change		Mobile phones		Radioactive waste		GM food		Genetic testing		Overall	
	1	2	1	2	1	2	1	2	1	2	1	2
The government is doing a good job	**0.80**	-0.11	**0.75**	-0.27	**0.73**	-0.18	**0.77**	-0.39	**0.79**	-0.30	**0.77**	-0.25
The government is competent enough	**0.72**	-0.26	**0.71**	-0.27	**0.76**	-0.16	**0.74**	-0.42	**0.81**	-0.29	**0.76**	-0.27
The government has the necessary skilled people	**0.57**	-0.20	**0.47**	-0.35	**0.70**	0.13	**0.66**	-0.31	**0.71**	-0.07	**0.65**	-0.12
The government distorts facts in its favour	-0.23	**0.80**	-0.23	**0.86**	-0.22	**0.73**	-0.28	**0.82**	-0.19	**0.83**	-0.23	**0.82**
The government changes policies without good reasons	-0.23	**0.81**	-0.21	**0.88**	-0.09	**0.86**	-0.22	**0.86**	-0.27	**0.83**	-0.22	**0.84**
The government is too influenced by industry	-0.11	**0.73**	-0.36	**0.60**	-0.24	**0.76**	-0.35	**0.73**	-0.19	**0.74**	-0.24	**0.73**
The government is acting in the public interest	**0.73**	-0.18	**0.65**	-0.30	**0.70**	-0.28	**0.73**	-0.30	**0.75**	-0.25	**0.72**	-0.26
The government listens to concerns raised by the public	**0.72**	-0.06	**0.72**	-0.21	**0.71**	-0.24	**0.77**	-0.15	**0.79**	-0.09	**0.75**	-0.13
The government listens to what ordinary people think	**0.68**	-0.16	**0.75**	-0.25	**0.70**	-0.28	**0.82**	-0.26	**0.76**	-0.26	**0.75**	-0.24
I feel that the way the government makes decisions is fair	**0.79**	-0.29	**0.75**	-0.20	**0.75**	-0.29	**0.77**	-0.37	**0.79**	-0.28	**0.77**	-0.28
The government provides all relevant information to the public	**0.71**	-0.23	**0.76**	-0.20	**0.56**	-0.26	**0.76**	-0.19	**0.70**	-0.30	**0.69**	-0.25
Eigenvalue	4.25	2.13	4.14	2.42	4.08	2.29	4.77	2.73	4.83	2.40	4.45	2.33
Explained variance	38.6	19.4	37.6	22.0	37.1	20.8	43.4	24.8	43.9	21.9	40.5	21.2
Average agreement	2.53	3.66	2.60	3.49	2.61	3.55	2.48	3.64	2.65	3.51	2.58	3.57
Cronbach's α	0.87	0.74	0.88	0.78	0.87	0.75	0.92	0.82	0.92	0.78	0.90	0.77

Note: The scale ranged from 1: 'totally disagree' to 5: 'totally agree'. Factor loadings higher than 0.40 are in bold. Factor interpretations: (1) general trust; (2) scepticism.

Table 10.3 *Standardized regression coefficients*

	Climate change	Mobile phones	Radioactive waste	GM food	Genetic testing
Model 1					
General trust	0.42*	0.38*	0.57*	0.59*	0.59*
Scepticism	−0.16**	−0.24*	−0.33*	−0.24*	−0.39*
R²	19.0	22.1	38.4	44.2	47.6
Adj. R²	18.4	21.4	37.9	43.6	47.1
Model 2					
General trust	0.43*	0.24**	0.47*	0.46*	0.43*
Scepticism	−0.18**	−0.18**	−0.31*	−0.17**	−0.33*
Value similarity	−0.01	0.22***	0.12	0.20***	0.26*
R²	19.4	24.0	39.5	45.3	53.6
Adj. R²	18.4	22.9	38.8	44.5	53.0

Note: *$p < 0.001$; **$p < 0.01$; ***$p < 0.05$; dependent variable is trust in risk regulation.

regression coefficients for the other independent variables. In either case, value similarity would be a significant predictor for trust in risk regulation.

Table 10.3 shows the results of the analyses for each of the two models. When trust in the regulation of the five risk cases were regressed onto the two components resulting from the overall factor analysis (Model 1) both the general trust and scepticism components were highly significant in all five risk cases (top half of Table 10.3). The explained variance of trust in risk regulation varied between about 20 and 50 per cent. The two predictors best explained trust in the regulation of genetic testing, GM food and radioactive waste, but were less successful in the explanation of trust in the regulation of climate change and the regulation of radiation from mobile phones. In Model 2 (bottom half of Table 10.3), where the combined value similarity scale was added to the initial set of predictors, the explained variance of trust in risk regulation only marginally increased for most risk cases. Only genetic testing saw a reasonable increase in explained variance of about 6 per cent. In Model 2, general trust remained the strongest predictor for trust in risk regulation across the five cases. If less strong than general trust, scepticism was also a significant predictor of trust in the regulation of all five cases. Value similarity appeared to be the weakest predictor of trust in risk regulation, being a strong (additional) predictor of trust in the regulation of genetic testing, and a less strong but still significant predictor in the context of mobile phones and GM food. The addition of value similarity to the five regression models did not greatly affect the regression coefficients of general trust and scepticism, although it did somewhat decrease the regression coefficients of general trust and scepticism in the contexts of radiation from mobile phones, GM food and genetic testing.

Discussion

This study has dealt with how people perceive government and its policies toward risk regulation in different risk contexts. The first aim was to compare evaluations across the five rather different risk cases, i.e. climate change, radiation from mobile phones, radioactive waste, GM food and genetic testing. Here, evaluation of government on the various trust-related items was surprisingly similar for each of the five risk cases, with only very few specific differences. Although there were some significant differences in perceived value similarity between the risk cases, they were once more small. The average responses of most items were somewhat below the mid-point value for all of the five cases. Likewise, there were only minor differences in overall trust in risk regulation, with people having the highest trust in the regulation of genetic testing and the lowest trust in the regulation of climate change, radioactive waste and GM food. Again, the average response was below the middle of the scale for all risk cases, indicating that, in general, there is a tendency toward distrust in government.

The second aim of this study was to explore the dimensionality of trust. Our initial expectation had been that trust in government with regard to the five risk cases would be in accordance with the findings of Metlay (1999). That is, the evaluation of government could best be described by a component that represents technical competence, and one that represents a general trustworthiness dimension, encompassing care for the public interest (among other things). Although a clearly interpretable two-factor solution was found for each of the five risk cases, the results were in the event closer to those obtained by Frewer et al (1996). The first component in the current results, reproduced across five different issues and samples of respondents, was concerned with a wide range of trust-relevant aspects, such as competence, care, fairness and openness. As such, this factor can be interpreted as a *general trust* dimension, albeit one that conflates the competence and care dimensions found by Metlay. The second factor obtained here resembled the vested interest factor of Frewer et al (1996). However, in the present study the second factor also included the aspects of credibility and reliability. This factor seems to reflect a sceptical view regarding how risk policies are brought about and enacted, and was therefore labelled here as a *scepticism* dimension. Again, the results were surprisingly similar across the five risk cases, as the same two-factor solution was found in each of the different samples.

It is an interesting question as to what has caused the differences in results between this study and the findings of Metlay (1999). In both studies the same statistical technique of PCA with varimax rotation was used to examine whether the original items reduced to a smaller number of dimensions. Moreover, there were close similarities between the items used in our and Metlay's studies to measure the different aspects of trust. Even one of the five risk cases in the current study (radioactive waste) was similar to the one investigated by Metlay.

There are at least two plausible explanations for the differences in results. The first explanation might reside in cross-cultural differences. It may be that there are key differences between British and American samples in relation to beliefs about trust. If true, this would also account for the similarities of the current findings to the models of Frewer et al (1996) and French et al (2002). A second, more plausible and theoretically interesting explanation locates the differences in the survey populations and in the evaluated institution(s). Whereas in the current study the survey was administered to representative samples of the British public, Metlay (1999) used a selective sample of people interested in the management of radioactive waste, and who had participated in a long-running exercise involving at least one hour per week over the course of one year.

Moreover, Metlay looked at trust in a specific government department: i.e. the DoE. As a result of these two factors Metlay's respondents may have had more specific and stable attitudes about the management of radioactive waste (and in particular the competence of DoE in its handling of this issue). By contrast, the current study asked people to evaluate government in general. The minor differences in mean scores and factor structure between the five risk cases suggest that people evaluated government policy as a whole, rather than specific governmental policy or decisions with respect to each of the five risk cases. So, rather than the evaluation of a specific institution, people may have assessed the wider political and administrative system of *risk governance*. As noted at the start of this chapter, it is often argued that there may be various 'levels' of social trust. It may well be that the level evoked in any particular study will vary as a function of familiarity with the institution being judged. In particular, the more specific the evaluated subject, the more likely it is that someone will have more differentiated views. This could also help to explain why some recent studies, which take a more locally grounded approach to issues of public understanding of risk and trust, elicit much more complex referents for these concepts, and their relationship with such things as economic dependence, place, identity and stigma (e.g. Irwin et al, 1996; Greenberg and Williams, 1999; Williams et al, 1999; Bush et al, 2002; Bickerstaff and Walker, 2003; Horlick-Jones et al, 2003). Clearly, there are further fruitful research avenues – both quantitative and qualitative – to be conducted on the relationship between issues of institutional trust and locally grounded risk perceptions. It also is worth noting here that the operation of affect is seen as an increasingly important part of the way in which lay perceptions of risk issues are constructed (Alakhami and Slovic, 1994; Finucane et al, 2000; Langford, 2002; Slovic, 2004). In this sense our current results are rather more in line with Metlay's findings than might first seem the case, in that people's judgements can be described with relation to a dominant, predominantly affective, dimension of trustworthiness, with competence loading alongside a range of more clearly affective variables. Note that the second factor identified here, that of scepticism, intuitively has affective properties too. The current results therefore suggest that there is much further interesting research to be done concerning the way institutions (rather than just risks) are affectively perceived, how this relates to an institution's historical record of competence, whether this varies with different levels of familiarity or 'closeness' to the institution, and how this then feeds through into evaluations of (different levels of) trust.

The third aim of this study was to examine whether the value-similarity approach of Earle and Cvetkovich (1995) has an additional value in explaining trust in risk regulation, compared to more conventional aspects of trust. The current results suggest that value similarity may not contribute universally to people's conceptualizations of risk regulation. Having said that, while value similarity is the least important factor in explaining trust in risk regulation, it still was a significant predictor in the contexts of radiation from mobile phones, GM food and genetic testing. These three issues are just the risk cases that are either highly polarized (GM food) or that are (relatively) new issues that have not fully developed yet (radiation from mobile phones and genetic testing). That is, it is still unclear whether radiation from mobile phones has adverse health effects, and people may not yet have a clear idea what to think about genetic testing, as the consequences of this technology are not yet fully understood. This seems to suggest that in some contexts, especially in those with low familiarity, value similarity is indeed of special importance – a finding that is in line with the SVS approach of Earle and Cvetkovich (1995). Although in the present study it was examined whether value similarity has an *additional* value to more conventional aspects of trust, it could also be argued that the variables used here to measure general trust and scepticism (such as the item 'the government is acting in the public interest') also have value implications. Siegrist et al (2000; reprinted as Chapter 11 in this volume) argue that the SVS approach should not be seen as a substitute for other models of trust. That is, SVS does not exclude the conventional aspects of trust if those are considered salient for the pertaining risk case. From that perspective, the current study seems to suggest that for some cases (especially genetic testing) other value aspects than the ones measured by the factors general trust and scepticism are important as well. This line of reasoning, however, raises questions about the nature and measurement of value similarity as a separate concept or heuristic to come to trust judgements, as well as about the precise relationship between value similarity and other trust-relevant aspects. Future theoretical and empirical research should address whether value similarity is indeed a (empirical and psychological) discernable aspect of trust and how this interacts with other evaluations of (risk regulatory) institutions.[1]

Reflecting upon the overall pattern of results, Trettin and Musham (2000) have recently questioned the importance of enhancing trust in institutions. That is, the public does not necessarily expect or see trust as an achievable goal in their relation with institutions. Recent evidence from more qualitative work suggests that the public does not necessarily consider 'trust' to be the most appropriate word to describe their relationship with risk management institutions (Wynne et al, 1993). Two decades ago Barber (1983) had already observed that:

> The public is less passively deferential in its relations with experts and others in authority and is more likely to take an active part in monitoring the fulfillment of professionals' claims to absolute trustworthiness. (Barber, 1983, p134)

According to Barber (1983) (see also O'Neill, 2002), the importance of full trust tends to be exaggerated. The public has become more competent and knowledgeable enough to have 'effective' distrust. Distrust in this sense is not destructive, but can be seen as an essential component of political accountability in a participatory democracy.

Pidgeon et al (2003) posit that what is frequently called trust or distrust exists along a continuum, ranging from uncritical emotional acceptance to (downright) rejection. Somewhere between these extremes a healthy type of distrust can be found that Pidgeon et al call *critical trust*. Critical trust can be conceptualized as a practical form of reliance on a person or institution combined with some healthy scepticism. The current study provides quantitative evidence for the existence of this conceptualization of trust, which, until now, has mainly been identified in qualitative work (see, e.g. Irwin et al, 1996; Walls et al, 2003; Poortinga et al, 2004). The two trust components that were found in this study show that different degrees of general trust could coexist with different degrees of scepticism. Based on these two independent components, a typology of trust is proposed that ranges from full trust to a deep type of distrust (see Figure 10.1). The situation in which someone has high general trust in and is not sceptical about a certain institution can be said to be one of trust. That is, one is likely to accept decisions and communications from this particular organization. This would compare to what Walls et al (2003) call 'uncritical emotional acceptance'. However, a high degree of general trust can also coexist with a relatively high level of scepticism. This situation could best be described as critical trust. One may be willing to rely on information, but one is still somewhat sceptical, and thus may still (constructively) question the correctness of the received information. The situation in which general trust is low, combined with low scepticism, is labelled as distrust. Although distrust would not be a preferred situation, it could be contrasted to a more deep type of distrust: cynicism, a situation in which one not only has no trust in a specific institution, but one is also sceptical about its intentions. In the latter situation one is likely to simply reject everything that comes from a particular organization. As noted above, the current aggregate results display both moderate general distrust, alongside moderate scepticism (although individual respondents might be expected to hold distinct positions in the space shown in Figure 10.1).

The proposed typology of trust raises some interesting questions both for risk policy and the direction of future trust research. In policy terms decision-makers may well be confusing 'critical trust' with outright 'distrust' or rejection. Of course, these are not the same thing. Nor do they necessarily demand similar policy responses. For example, instead of focusing on how to increase trust in risk management organizations, it could be more fruitful to give attention to the interaction between institutional structures, agency behaviour, and qualitative properties of perceptions of trust. That is, what kind of relationship between people and risk management institutions is achievable and desirable? For a functioning society it could well be more suitable to have critical but involved citizens in many situations.

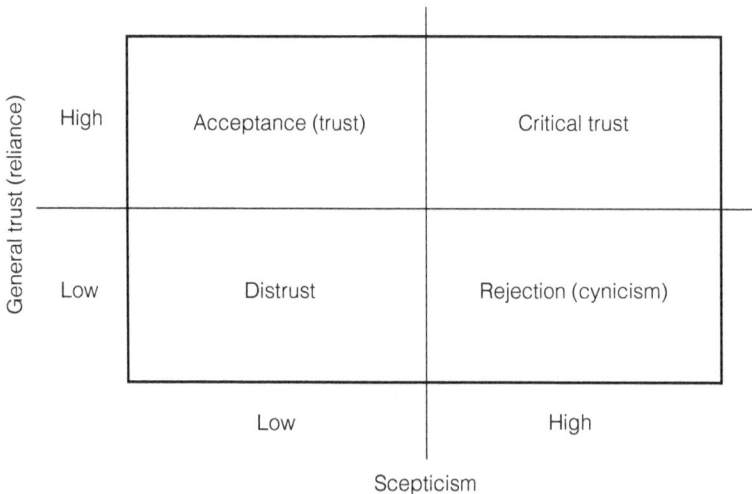

Figure 10.1 *A typology of trust in government*

Acknowledgements

Work reported in this chapter was partly supported by the Program on Understanding Risk, funded by a grant of the Leverhulme Trust (RSK990021), and was partly supported by a grant from the ESRC Science in Society Program (L144250037). The authors would also like to thank the Leverhulme team, Ian Langford and others who have helped us in various ways. Special thanks goes to Daniel Metlay for a number of helpful discussions and his comments on an earlier version of this chapter.

Note

1 Subsidiary analysis using structural equation modelling suggests that the relationship between value similarity, the 'conventional' aspects of trust, and trust in risk regulation may be more complex than our current discussion allows. The results of that analysis will be reported in a subsequent article.

References

Alakhami, A. S., and Slovic, P. (1994). A psychological study of the inverse relationship between perceived risks and perceived benefit. *Risk Analysis, 14,* 1085–1096.

Barber, B. (1983). *The Logic and Limits of Trust,* New Brunswick: Rutgers University Press.

Bickerstaff, K., and Walker, G. (2003). The place(s) of matter: Matter out of place – Public understandings of air pollution. *Progress in Human Geography, 27,* 45–67.

Bush, J., Moffatt, S., and Dunn, C. E. (2002). Contextualisation of local and global environmental issues in north-east England: Implications for debates on globalisation and the 'risk society'. *Local Environment, 7,* 119–133.

Cook, K. S. (2000). *Trust in Society.* New York: Russell Sage.

Dekker, P. (1999). Niveaus van vertrouwen in landen van de Europese Unie [Levels of trust in countries of the European Union]. In A. E. Bonner et al (Eds.), *Recente Ontwikkelingen in Het Marktonderzoek Jaarboek 1999.* Haarlem: De Vriescheborg.

Earle, T. C., and Cvetkovich, G. T. (1995). *Social Trust. Towards a Cosmopolitan Society.* London: Praeger.

Earle, T. C., and Cvetkovich, G. T. (1997). Culture, cosmopolitanism, and risk management. *Risk Analysis, 17(1),* 55–65.

Earle, T. C., and Cvetkovich, G. T. (1999). Social trust and culture in risk management. In G. T. Cvetkovich and R. E. Löfstedt (Eds.), *Social Trust and the Management of Risk.* London: Earthscan.

Finucane. M. L., Alhakami, A. S., Slovic, P., and Johnson, S. M. (2000). The affect heuristic in the judgment of risks and benefits. *Journal of Behavioral Decision Making, 13,* 1–17.

Flynn, J., Slovic, P., and Kunreuther, H. (2001). *Risk Media and Stigma: Understanding Public Challenges to New Technologies.* London: Earthscan.

French, S., Maule, J., Mythen, G., and Wales, C. (2002). *Trust and Risk Communication (Technical Report).* Leeds/Manchester: Manchester Business School/Leeds University Business School.

Freudenburg, W. R. (2003). Institutional failure and the organizational amplification of risks. In N. F. Pidgeon, R. K. Kasperson, and P. Slovic (Eds.), *The Social Amplification of Risk.* Cambridge: Cambridge University Press.

Frewer, L. J., Howard, C., Hedderley, D., and Shepherd, R. (1996). What determines trust in information about food-related risks? Underlying psychological constructs. *Risk Analysis, 26(4),* 473–485.

Fukuyama, F. (1995). *Trust: The Social Virtues and the Creation of Prosperity.* New York: Free Press.

Greenberg, M. R., and Williams, B. (1999). Geographical dimensions and correlates of trust. *Risk Analysis, 19(2),* 159–169.

Horlick-Jones, T., Sime, J., and Pidgeon, N. F. (2003). The social dynamics of environmental risk perception. In N. F. Pidgeon, R. K. Kasperson, and P. Slovic (Eds.), *The Social Amplification of Risk.* Cambridge: Cambridge University Press.

House of Lords. (2000). *Science and Society, 3rd Report.* London: HSMO. (Available at www.parliament.the-stationery-office.co.uk/pa/ldl99900/ldselect/ldsctech/ 38/3801.htm.)

Hovland, C. I., Janis, I. L., and Kelley H. H. (1953). *Communication and Persuasion. Psychological Issues of Opinion Change.* New Haven: Yale University Press.

Irwin, A., Dale, A., and Smith, D. (1996). Science and hell's kitchen: The local understanding of hazard issues. In A. Irwin, and B. Wynne (Eds.), *Misunderstanding Science? The Public Reconstruction of Science and Technology.* Cambridge: Cambridge University Press.

Johnson, B. B. (1999). Exploring dimensionality in the origins of hazard related trust. *Journal of Risk Research, 2(4),* 325–354.

Jungermann, H., Pfister, H. R., and Fischer, K. (1996). Credibility, information preferences, and information interests. *Risk Analysis, 16(2),* 251–261.

Kasperson, R. E., Golding, D., and Tuler, S. (1992). Social distrust as a factor in siting hazardous facilities and communicating risk. *Journal of Social Issues, 48(4),* 161–187.

Kasperson, R. E., Golding, D., and Kasperson, J. X. (1999). Risk, trust and democratic theory. In G. Cvetkovich and R. E. Löfstedt (Eds.), *Social Trust and the Management of Risk.* London: Earthscan.

Kasperson, R. E., Kasperson, J. X., Pidgeon, N. F., and Slovic, P. (2003). The social amplification of risk: Assessing fifteen years of research and theory. In N. F. Pidgeon, R. K. Kasperson, and P. Slovic (Eds.), *The Social Amplification of Risk.* Cambridge: Cambridge University Press.

Langford, I. H. (2002). An existential approach to risk perception. *Risk Analysis, 22(1),* 101–120.

Luhmann, N. (1979). *Trust and Power.* New York: Wiley.

Metlay, D. (1999). Institutional trust and confidence: A journey into a conceptual quagmire. In G. T. Cvetkovich and R. E. Löfstedt (Eds.), *Social Trust and the Management of Risk.* London: Earthscan.

Mishra, A. (1996). Organizational responses to crisis: The centrality of trust. In R. M. Kramer and T. R. Tyler (Eds.), *Trust in Organizations: Frontiers of Theory and Research.* London: Sage.

O'Neill, O. (2002). *A Question of Trust.* Cambridge: Cambridge University Press.

Peters, R. G., Covello, V. T., and McCallum, D. B. (1997). The determinants of trust and credibility in environmental risk communication: An empirical study. *Risk Analysis, 17(1),* 43–54.

Phillips, L., Bridgeman, J., and Ferguson-Smith, M. (2000). *The Report of the Inquiry into BSE and Variant CJD in the UK.* London: The Stationery Office. (Available at www.bseinquiry.gov.uk.)

Pidgeon, N. F., Hood, C, Jones, D., Turner, B., and Gibson, R. (1992). Risk perception. In *Risk Analysis, Perception and Management: Report of a Royal Society Study Group* (Ch. 5, pp. 89–134). London: The Royal Society.

Pidgeon, N. F., Walls, J., Weyman, A., and Horlick-Jones, T. (2003). *Perceptions of and Trust in the Health and Safety Executive as a Risk Regulator.* Research Report 2003/100, Norwich: HSE Books.

Poortinga, W., and Pidgeon, N. F. (2003). *Public Perceptions of Risk, Science and Governance. Main Findings of a British Survey on Five Risk Cases (Technical Report).* Norwich: Centre for Environmental Risk.

Poortinga, W., Bickerstaff, K., Langford, I. H., Niewöhner, J., and Pidgeon, N. F. (2004). The British 2001 foot and mouth crisis: A comparative study of public risk perceptions, trust and beliefs about government policy in two communities. *Journal of Risk Research, 7(1)*, 73–90

Putnam, R. D. (1993). *Making Democracy Work. Civic Traditions in Modern Italy.* Princeton: Princeton University Press.

Renn, O., and Levine, D. (1991). Credibility and trust in risk communication. In R. E. Kasperson and P. J. M. Stallen (Eds.), *Communicating Risks to the Public.* The Hague: Kluwer.

Rousseau, D. M., Sitkin, S. B., Burt, R. S., and Camerer, C. (1998). Not so different after all: A cross-discipline view of trust. *Academy of Management Review, 23(3)*, 393–404.

Siegrist, M., Cvetkovich, G. T., and Gutscher, H. (2001). Shared values, social trust, and the perception of geographic cancer clusters. *Risk Analysis, 21(6)*, 1047–1053.

Slovic, P. (2004). Perceived risk, trust and democracy. *Risk Analysis, 13(6)*, 675–682.

Slovic, P. (in press). Risk as analysis and risk as feelings: Some thoughts about affect, reason, risk, and rationality. *Risk Analysis, 24*, 311–322.

Trettin, L., and Musham, C. (2000). Is trust a realistic goal of environmental risk communication? *Environment and Behavior, 32(3)*, 410–426.

Tyler, T. R., and Degoey, P. (1996). Trust in organizational authorities. In R. M. Kramer and T. R. Tyler (Eds.), *Trust in Organizations. Frontiers of Theory and Research.* London: Sage.

Walls, J., Pidgeon, N. F., Weyman, A., and Horlick-Jones, T. (2003). *Critical Trust: Understanding Lay Perceptions of Health and Safety Risk Regulation. Journal of Risk Research (Report).* Norwich: Centre for Environmental Risk.

Williams, B. L., Brown, S., and Greenberg, M. (1999). Determinants of trust perceptions among residents surrounding the Savannah River nuclear weapons site. *Environment and Behavior, 31*, 354–371.

Wynne, B. (1980). Technology, risk and participation: On the social treatment of uncertainty. In J. Conrad (Ed.), *Society, Technology and Risk Assessment.* New York: Academic Press.

Wynne, B., Waterton, C., and Grove-White, R. (1993). *Public Perceptions and the Nuclear Industry in West Cumbria.* Lancaster: Centre for the Study of Environmental Change.

11

Salient Value Similarity, Social Trust and Risk/Benefit Perception

Michael Siegrist, George Cvetkovich
and Claudia Roth

Introduction

Risk managers have become keenly aware that in democratic countries perceptions of a technology's risks and benefits are important components of the entire political decision process, from initial decisions to develop a technology or product, to the acceptance of management approaches to risk mitigation. The present study investigates two important issues concerning the public's acceptance of technology related to risk and benefit perception. The first issue is the functional relationship between risk perceptions and benefit perceptions. It could be assumed that the two are inversely and causally related (Frewer et al, 1998). This implies that the acceptability of a perceived high-risk technology could be increased by identifying and emphasizing its benefits (and hence reducing the perceived risk).

In contrast to this assumption is the possibility that risk perceptions and benefit perceptions are both affected by a third evaluation concerning the technology. This second issue, the possibility of a third variable influencing both risk and benefit perceptions, is explored by examining the possibility that both risk perceptions and benefit perceptions are affected by judgements of trust of those in charge of managing the technology.

Risk and benefit perception

Negative correlations among judgements of risk and judgements of benefit have been found for a number of different technologies (Gregory and Mendelsohn, 1993; Alhakami and Slovic, 1994; Frewer et al, 1998). Several explanations for the observed associations have been offered. Alhakami and Slovic (1994) speculate that people may assess hazards in terms of general attitudes (favourable or unfavourable). If people prefer consistency among their beliefs this results in devaluation of risks and the elevation of benefits for technologies perceived as favourable. For technologies perceived as unfavourable the mechanism would work the other way, resulting in higher perceived risks and lower perceived benefits associated with the technology. However, Alhakami and Slovic (1994) emphasized that their study was not specifically designed to test this or other possible explanations for the negative correlation between perceived risks and perceived benefits. Gregory and Mendelsohn (1993) concluded that people incorporate some benefits in their risk assessments. In other words, risk ratings are 'net' measures.

Frewer et al (1998) assumed that favourableness of a technology is affected by perceptions of risks and benefits that are functionally related to each other. They also argued that it may be possible to change perceived risks by changing perceptions of benefits. There are reasons to hesitate in accepting that emphasizing the benefits associated with a technology results in a decreased risk perception. The observed correlations between benefits and risks perceived do not mean that there is a causal relationship between the two variables. Rather than being causally linked it may be that both risk and benefit perceptions are influenced by a third, unmeasured variable. One likely third-variable candidate is social trust. It has been found that the significant negative relationship between perceptions of risks and benefits of gene technology vanished or diminished when the level of social trust was held constant (Siegrist, 1999, 2000). The present study investigates the possibility that negative correlations between benefits and risk are observed when social trust is not accounted for.

Social trust and risk/benefit perception

Social science research has identified a number of characteristics of perceivers correlated to differences in judgements about the riskiness of technologies. These have included lay public/expert differences (Fischhoff et al, 1982) and cultural values and other worldview differences (Douglas and Wildavsky, 1982; Buss and Craik, 1983; Buss et al, 1986; Dake, 1991; Peters and Slovic, 1996; Earle and Cvetkovich, 1997; Brenot et al, 1998; Marris et al, 1998) as well as ethnic and gender differences (Brody, 1984; Flynn et al, 1994; Greenberg and Schneider, 1995; Davidson and Freudenburg, 1996).

Social science research has also identified a number of characteristics of hazards correlated to differences in judgements about the riskiness of technologies. These have included level of knowledge, uncertainty, voluntariness, newness, catastrophic potential, and control over risk (Slovic, 1987). Social science's efforts to understand risk perceptions have expanded from the above listed variables to social trust (Renn and Levine, 1991; Slovic, 1993; Cvetkovich and Löfstedt, 1999).

Social trust[1] is the willingness to rely on those who have the responsibility for making decisions and taking actions related to the management of technology, the environment, medicine, or other realms of public health and safety. We believe that it is generally true that being able to determine who to trust is most important in those situations where the individual lacks the interest, time, abilities, knowledge or other resources to personally make decisions and take actions. Science and technology are areas where many individuals seem to lack such resources.

The importance of social trust to risk/benefit perceptions

It has been shown that confidence in laws controlling gene technology and social trust in companies as well as in the scientists doing genetic modification research is important for perceiving the technology as acceptable and safe (Siegrist, 1999, 2000). People who trusted these institutions and professions perceived less risks and more benefits associated with biotechnology than people who did not. Similar results have been found for other technologies. Social trust had an important influence on the risk perception of a nuclear waste repository (Flynn et al, 1992), on the risks associated with hazardous waste disposals (Bord and O'Connor, 1992; Groothuis and Miller, 1997), on the perceived risk of a chemical plant (Jungermann et al, 1996), and on the acceptance of food irradiation (Bord and O'Connor, 1990).

Sjöberg (1998) questioned the importance of social trust as an explanation of perceived risk. He argued that Swedish data showed a much weaker relationship between social trust and perceived risk of nuclear waste. He concluded that the importance of social trust might be limited. One aim of the present study was to investigate the influence of social trust on perceived risk and perceived benefits for different technologies or products using a non-US sample.

Why social trust is important to risk/benefit perceptions

People do not possess an elaborate knowledge about science and technology (Gregory and Miller, 1998). Based on empirical data, Miller (1998) concluded that three out of four people in the United States and Europe lack the necessary scientific literacy to understand information utilizing basic scientific constructs such as molecules or radiation. Due to lack of knowledge and interest most people do not directly assess benefits and risks associated with different technologies. When there is insufficient knowledge or technical background for making first-hand risk assessments, social trust is needed to reduce the complexity facing people (Luhmann, 1989; Earle and Cvetkovich, 1995).

Public reactions and attitudes toward new technologies are guided by the social trust and confidence people have in companies and government agencies. Results of a study investigating perception of 25 hazards support that trust becomes important when individual resources to make decisions and take actions are limited (Siegrist and Cvetkovich, 1999). Strong correlations between social trust and judged risks and benefits were observed for hazards about which people did not possess much knowledge. As expected, no significant correlations between social trust and perceived risks and benefits were found for hazards about which people were knowledgeable.

Social trust: How does it work?

The present study uses the salient value similarity (SVS) model, developed by Earle and Cvetkovich (1995). There are two key components of the model: salient values and value similarity.

Salient values

Salient values consist of the individual's sense of what the important goals (ends) and/or processes (means) are that should be followed in a particular situation. Salient values are an aspect of the individual's understanding of the meaning of a specific situation. The inferred meaning of a situation could include an understanding of what problem is being faced, what options are available, and how effective each might be. The modifier 'salient' was chosen to emphasize that the individual concludes that specific values are important in one situation given its meaning, but that other values may be important in another situation with a different meaning. For example, a person might conclude that equal sharing is an important value in relationships with family members but that entrepreneurial and competitiveness values are important in business relationships. The construct of salient values contrasts to the more common social science practice of categorizing an individual as believing in one or a single set of dominant values that are applied across most situations (distinguishing people, for example, as either egalitarians or individualists).

Salient values are further characterized as being:

- Generalizations that might apply in more than one situation. The saliency of values varies with the meaning of the situation. Situations with similar inferred meanings will make similar values salient.
- Potentially changeable in saliency. As inferred meaning changes so will the saliency of values. Meaning could change, for example, as the individual learns more about a particular hazard. Personal experiences, discussions with family and friends, and media reports could all change the inferred meaning of a technology and affect the saliency of values (Renn et al, 1992; Kasperson and Kasperson, 1996).
- Most often rapid, implicit, unarticulated and automatically elicited, rather than slow, explicit, articulated and arrived at on the basis of controlled, systematic logical thought (Cvetkovich, 1999).

Value similarity

Judgements of value similarity involve:

- A conclusion about the values that are salient for the person whose trustworthiness is being judged. This attribution is made on the basis of that person's verbal statements, actions and/or identity (e.g. federal regulator, nuclear plant operator). Understandings that the person has of how the human mind works are also used (Cvetkovich, 1999).
- A comparison of the similarity of the salient values of the perceiver and the person being judged.

Several studies have shown that judged SVS is strongly related to attributions of social trust (Earle and Cvetkovich, 1995, 1997, 1999; Cvetkovich and Löfstedt, 1999). The meaning of the situation determines which values are salient. It is possible to trust the government in one domain where there is SVS and to distrust it in another domain where there is salient value dissimilarity. It is hardly surprising, therefore, that general trust in politicians was found not significantly related to risks perceived (Sjöberg, 1999). A general, non-domain-specific measure of trust in politicians fails to identify SVS.

Rationale of the present study

Based on the reviewed literature and the SVS model, a causal model was developed (Figure 11.1). We postulated that salient values have an influence on social trust in institutions and persons related to the technology. One has social trust in people who share similar salient values.

Past studies have shown that social trust has an influence on risks and benefits perceived (Siegrist, 1999, 2000). Therefore, the model depicted in Figure 11.1 entails

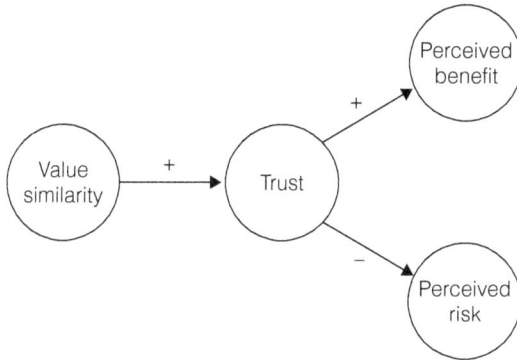

Figure 11.1 *Hypothesized model for perception of different technologies*

causal paths from social trust to perceived risk and perceived benefit. It was expected that when social trust is controlled, the relationship between perceived risk and perceived benefit diminishes. The proposed model may explain perception of different technologies and products.

Method

Participants

A questionnaire, cover letter and prepaid return envelope were sent to 600 randomly selected students at the University of Zürich. The response rate was approximately 44 per cent (N = 261). Forty-nine per cent were males, and 51 per cent were females. The participants' mean age was 27.5 (SD = 6.7) within a range of 19–61 years. Deletion of cases with missing data on variables, which were used for testing the causal models, yielded final sample sizes of 250 for nuclear power, 247 for pesticides, and 247 for artificial sweetener.[2]

Questionnaire

It was hypothesized that the model shown in Figure 11.1 can be used to explain perception of the risks and benefits of different technologies and products. In the present study perception of risk and benefits for pesticide, nuclear power and artificial sweetener were investigated. For all three analyses the same set of variables was used for measuring the salient values. The latent variables 'perceived risk', 'perceived benefit' and 'social trust' in the institutions responsible for or those regulating the technologies were measured using different indicator variables for the three technologies. In the questionnaire, questions regarding pesticides, nuclear power and artificial sweetener were mixed.

Value similarity was assessed using a measurement scale similar to the one used by Earle and Cvetkovich (1995, 1997, 1999). Participants were asked to compare

Table 11.1 *Test statistics for hypothesized models*

Model	χ^2	df	CFI[a]	$\Delta\chi^2$	Δdf
Pesticides					
Model 1	165.44	116	0.97		
Model 2[b]	161.91	115	0.98	3.53	1
Nuclear power					
Model 1	261.16	116	0.93		
Model 2[b]	244.47	115	0.94	16.69*	1
Artificial sweetener					
Model 1	174.97	87	0.94		
Model 2[b]	169.10	86	0.95	5.87*	1

[a] Comparative fit index.
[b] Correlation among error terms of perceived benefit and perceived risk.
* $p < .05$.

themselves with a typical manager of a multinational company (e.g. same goals–different goals). Five semantic differentials were used to measure participants' values. The items are shown in Table 11.1. Seven response categories ranging from 3 to –3 were given.

The variables that were used to measure the latent variables perceived risk, perceived benefit, and social trust associated with pesticides are shown in Table 11.2. Questions related to nuclear power are shown in Table 11.3, and questions related to artificial sweetener are presented in Table 11.4. Six response categories were used that ranged from 'strongly agree' (1) to 'strongly disagree' (6).

Data analysis

The structural equation modelling approach was chosen to test the proposed model. Parameters were estimated using the program EQS, Multivariate Software, Inc. (Bentler, 1993). The univariate distributions of the variables did not indicate strong departures from normal distributions. Analysis was based on covariance matrices, and the maximum likelihood (ML) method was employed. Assessment of model fit was based on the comparative fit index (CFI; Hu and Bentler, 1995), the residual values, and the meaningfulness of the model. The CFI is a fit index and ranges from 0 to 1. A greater value indicates a better fit of the model to the data. It is rather difficult to set a cut-off criterion. However, the CFI should exceed 0.90 (Hu and Bentler, 1995).

A basic assumption of the ML estimation procedure is that the measured variables are continuous and have a normal distribution. Simulation studies have shown that underestimation of parameter becomes severe when there are only a few categories for each variable (e.g. two or three), and that the magnitude of skewness increases (West et al, 1995). In the present study, for all indicator variables six or seven response categories were used. Skewness (ranging from –1.06 to 1.03) and kurtosis (ranging from –1.13 to 0.91) did not indicate strong departures from normality. Nevertheless, based on raw data, the Satorra-Bentler scaled χ^2, the robust CFI, and robust standard errors were computed. Monte Carlo simulations indicated that these test statistics are more reliable than test statistics based on ML when data are not multivariate normal (Chou

Table 11.2 *Factor loading estimates for indicator variables of the pesticide model*

Construct/indicator	Factor loading
Values	
Different persons work in management. One often reads about or hears about managers of multinational companies without knowing them. Nevertheless, one has an image of these managers. Indicate in the following pairs of opposite words how similar or dissimilar you are compared to a manager of a multinational company:	
Same values – different values	0.855
Same goals – different goals	0.713
Acts as I would – acts different than I would	0.833
Thinks like me – thinks unlike me	0.826
Same opinions – different opinions	0.837
Social trust	
The chemical industry is interested in producing pesticides that are environmentally friendly	0.638
Swiss authorities take care that pesticides are used in proportion	0.545
On the whole, pesticides are responsibly dealt with	0.699
Scientists working in the chemical industry do not bother about the consequences of their work	−0.614
Perceived risk	
Pesticides advance nature's ruinous exploitation	0.607
Fruits produced without pesticides are healthier	0.565
Pesticides are a big danger to mankind	0.851
Risks associated with pesticides are still underrated	0.837
Perceived benefit	
Without the use of pesticides even more human beings would suffer from hunger	0.773
Despite some problems, benefits associated with pesticides must not be underrated	0.669
A thorough consideration indicated that a general ban on pesticides would be irresponsible	0.792
Food would be more expensive without pesticides	0.388

and Bentler, 1995). The scaled test statistics were somewhat lower than the ML test statistics, and the robust CFIs were slightly higher than the CFIs based on ML. Because results were virtually identical only the ML results are reported.

First the model depicted in Figure 11.1 was tested. Then a second model that incorporated a covariance term for the disturbance terms of perceived benefit and perceived risk was tested. Because the two models are nested, it is possible to determine whether the χ^2 of the second model is significantly smaller than the value of the first model. The difference of the χ^2 values of the two models can be compared with the theoretical χ^2 distribution with degrees of freedom (df) which are equal to the difference of the df's in the two models.

In the structural modelling approach one can distinguish between free and fixed parameters. Free parameters are estimated using the data, whereas fixed parameters are usually set to zero. The Lagrange multiplier test (LM-test) was used to identify

Table 11.3 *Factor loading estimates for indicator variables of the nuclear power model*

Construct/indicator	Factor loading
Values	
Different persons work in management. One often reads or hears about managers of multinational companies without knowing them. Nevertheless, one has an image of these managers. Indicate in the following pairs of opposite words how similar or dissimilar you are compared to a manager of a multinational company:	
Same values – different values	0.866
Same goals – different goals	0.710
Acts as I would – acts different than I would	0.822
Thinks like me – thinks unlike me	0.823
Same opinions – different opinions	0.828
Social trust	
Scientists working in the field of nuclear power are hardly able to estimate or predict the consequences of their work	–0.545
The responsible authorities accurately control whether legal regulations and restrictions are upheld in nuclear power plants	0.645
Legal regulations regarding the disposal of radioactive waste are sufficient	0.665
Corporations operating nuclear power plants are aware of their responsibility	0.787
Perceived risk	
Risks associated with nuclear power are too high	0.829
Radioactive waste is a big danger for future generations	0.710
I do not worry about dangers associated with nuclear power plants in the industrialized countries	–0.738
Nuclear power is a major technology such as many others; the risks should not be over-dramatized	–0.785
Perceived benefit	
Without nuclear power, industrialized nations would be faced with an energy crisis	0.623
I think that we could renounce nuclear power without any problems	–0.797
Without nuclear power the CO_2 load would be even higher	0.566
Nuclear power is important for our economics	0.727

fixed parameters that should be relaxed to have a better-fitting model. However, parameters should be relaxed only if modifications are theoretically meaningful (Jöreskog, 1993).

Results

For pesticides the hypothesized model yielded a good fit to the data. The CFI was 0.97, and the average of the absolute standardized residuals was 0.04. A second model, in which a correlation term among perceived benefit and perceived risk was included, did not yield a significantly improved fit (Table 11.1). No posteriori model modifications

Table 11.4 *Factor loading estimates for indicator variables of the artificial sweetener model*

Construct/indicator	Factor loading
Values	
Different persons work in management. One often reads or hears about managers of multinational companies without knowing them. Nevertheless, one has an image of these managers. Indicate in the following pairs of opposite words how similar or dissimilar you are compared to a manager of a multinational company:	
Same values – different values	0.861
Same goals – different goals	0.706
Acts as I would – acts different than I would	0.822
Thinks like me – thinks unlike me	0.824
Same opinions – different opinions	0.829
Social trust	
In case of doubt, authorities advocate interests of the food industry and not consumers' interests	−0.630
For the food industry, consumers' health is a matter of secondary importance; just the profit is important	−0.640
Producers of artificial sweetener have done enough research about possible harmful effects	0.678
Artificial sweeteners would not have been licensed if they were harmful	0.637
Perceived risk	
There is not enough knowledge about possible health risks associated with artificial sweeteners	0.557
I believe that artificial sweeteners are rather unhealthy	0.834
Persons who often consume beverages with artificial sweeteners put up with health risks	0.786
Perceived benefit	
Beverages with artificial sweeteners are "positive": sweet and few calories	0.759
Artificial sweeteners are important for cavity prevention	0.537
Without artificial sweeteners even more people would suffer from being overweight	0.372

were necessary. The LM-test indicated that the inclusion of correlations among error terms of indicator variables yielded a slightly better model fit. Because post hoc modifications regarding correlated errors of measurement are problematic without a strong theoretical justification (Hoyle and Panter, 1995), no additional parameters were relaxed. In other words, these parameters remained fixed at zero.

The factor loadings of most variables were rather high (see Table 11.2). For the item 'Food would be more expensive without pesticides', the factor loading was low, but still acceptable. An analysis without this item yielded almost identical results. Therefore, results including all variables are presented here. All causal paths had the predicted sign, and the magnitude was rather high. A substantial part of the variance of the dependent latent variables has been explained.

Standardized estimated regression coefficients are presented in Figure 11.2. In the small circles the coefficients associated with the residual variable are presented. It should

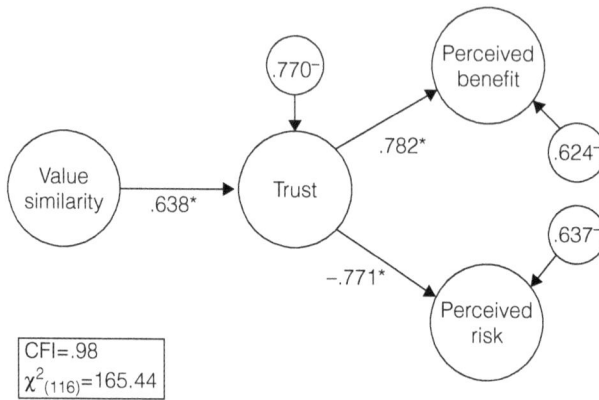

Figure 11.2 *Final model for pesticides. Values represent standardized estimates.**p < *.001*

be emphasized that the standardized solution produced by EQS is different from the solution produced by LISREL, Scientific Software International (Bentler, 1993). In EQS all model variables included in the structural equation system are standardized. In other words, error and disturbance terms are also standardized. The squared disturbance term equals the unexplained variance of the latent variables.

For nuclear power, the fit of the hypothesized model was acceptable (CFI = 0.93). However, the inclusion of a covariance between the disturbance terms of perceived risk and perceived benefit yielded a significantly better-fitting model. Table 11.1 shows that the χ^2 significantly dropped. The final model, which is shown in Figure 11.3, yielded a good fit to the data (CFI = 0.94), and the average of the absolute standardized residuals was 0.04. Results of the measurement models are shown in Table 11.3. All factor loadings were rather high.

The proposed model explained the data for artificial sweetener very well. However, freeing the covariance term among the disturbance term of perceived risk and the disturbance term of perceived benefit significantly improved the fit of the model (see Table 11.1). The final model had a CFI of 0.95, and the average of the absolute standardized residuals was 0.04. The standardized regression coefficients are shown in Figure 11.4. Factor loadings of the indicator variables for the final version are shown in Table 11.4. The loadings were rather high or at least acceptable.

Discussion

The proposed model explained the perception of pesticides, nuclear power and artificial sweetener very well. As expected, SVS determined the level of social trust participants had in institutions responsible for regulating the technology or the product. Social trust had a positive influence on perceived benefits and a negative influence on perceived risks. The

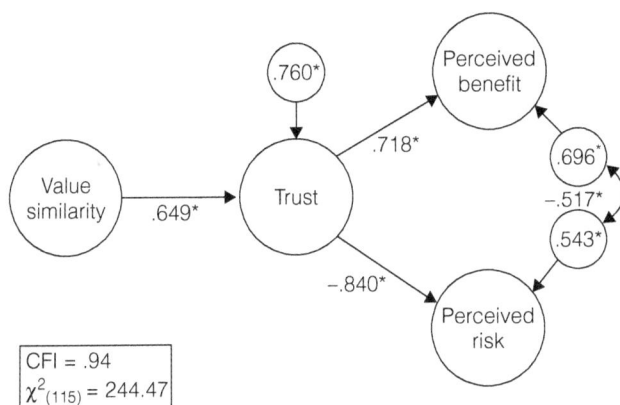

Figure 11.3 *Final model for nuclear power. Values represent standardized estimates. *p < .001*

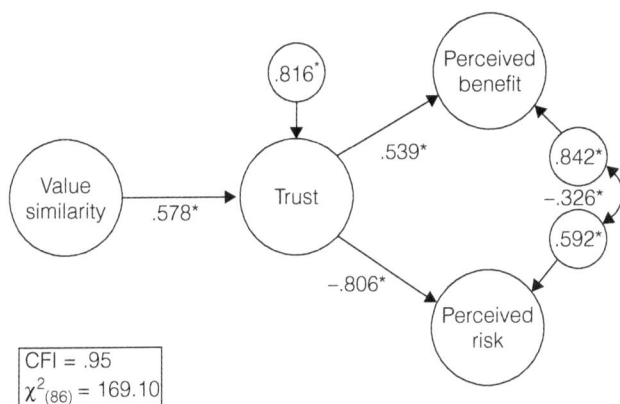

Figure 11.4 *Final model for artificial sweetener. Values represent standardized estimates. *p < .001*

findings for gene technology (Siegrist, 1999, 2000) have been successfully replicated for the three technologies investigated by this study. The psychometric paradigm has shown that perceived dreadfulness and the extent to which a hazard is judged to be unknown determine risks perceived (Slovic, 1987). In the present study, hazards were investigated that were found in previous studies to be perceived as rather unknown. Therefore, present findings may not explain perception of hazards located in other areas of the 'cognitive map'.

Some limitations of the present study should be addressed. Covariances were used to test a causal model. We cannot rule out the possibility that alternative models exist – even with different directions of causality – that also fit the data very well. However, based on theoretical considerations we believe that the proposed causal model is the most meaningful. A further limitation is that perceptions of students only were investigated. Future studies have to address the question as to whether the proposed model explains the perceptions of a general public as well.

Social trust and risk/benefit perceptions

A substantial part of the variance of risks and benefits perceived was explained by social trust. Therefore, results of the present study clearly contradict Sjöberg's (1998) notion that the explanation for power of trust is rather limited. The results suggest that the explanation power of trust depends on how it is operationalized. An unspecified measure of social trust (e.g. general social trust in government in all situations) might well explain much less variance.

People who cannot evaluate the assessed risks and promised benefits of a technology will rely on the assessments of experts. However, experts are not a homogeneous group (Kraus et al, 1992; Sjöberg, 1998). For almost all technologies there are specialists who are in favour of the technology and there are experts who have objections against it. Laypeople will have social trust in experts who appear to hold similar values. People will, therefore, accept as true the risks and benefits identified by experts who share their values.

Relationship of risk and benefit perceptions

In different studies significant correlations among perceived benefit and perceived risk have been found (Gregory and Mendelsohn, 1993; Alhakami and Slovic, 1994; Frewer et al, 1998). The present analyses held the level of social trust constant, resulting in a significantly decreased correlation between benefits and risks perceived. No significant correlation was found for pesticides. For artificial sweetener the correlation was significant, but the association was rather low. A substantial correlation was found for nuclear power; nevertheless, social trust had an important influence on perceived risk. Results of the present study suggest that it may not be possible to change risk perception by emphasizing benefits associated with a technology. At least partially, the findings for the perception of gene technology (Siegrist, 1999, 2000) have been confirmed for other technologies.

The importance of values for the emergence of social trust has significant implications. People's values are not easily changed. However, social trust might be increased if a technology is framed in such a way as to reflect the public's salient values. For applications of gene technology it has been shown that certain food applications can be framed in such a way that they are perceived as similar to medical applications (Siegrist and Bühlmann, 1999). As a result they were assessed as more beneficial and were more accepted than other food applications. In contrast, emphasizing lower production cost of genetically engineered food could result in decreased trust, because the public may believe that only companies will profit.

The SVS model of trust

Results of the present study support the prediction that value similarity evokes social trust (Earle and Cvetkovich, 1995). Trusting someone involves a risk that the person will act unreliably. A strategy reducing this risk is to rely on those individuals who we sense will follow what we consider to be appropriate guidelines and general principles for setting goals and procedures – those with similar salient values.

Many economists and organizational psychologists equate trust with cooperation and, as a result, emphasize the influence of perceived competence on the emergence of trust (Mayer et al, 1995; Sheppard and Sherman, 1998; Wicks, Berman. and Jones, 1999). In the field of risk management the role of competence in establishing trust has been stressed as well (Renn and Levine, 1991; Peters et al, 1997; Petts, 1998; Hunt et al, 1999).

Reviews of our work indicate that some have a misunderstanding that the SVS model is being proposed as a substitute for competency as an explanation of trust. The SVS model leads to the expectation that perceived competency affects trust when competency is a salient value. SVS allows for the operation of multiple influences, including perceived competence, that emerge from the subjectively defined understandings and meanings of the situation by the individual. As such, we argue that SVS is a more basic and general model than one that specifies that trust is exclusively based on competency or another particular value. What is important are the values salient in the mind of the person risking trusting, not the mind of the theorist.

Acknowledgement

This article is based on work supported by the Swiss National Science Foundation under grant #8210–053512.

Notes

1   The adjective 'social' is used to emphasize the class of people being trusted (those with formal responsibilities within organizations) who may not be personally known to the individual making the trust attribution.
2   There were only a few cases with missing values; deletion of cases with missing values seemed justified. Nevertheless, additional analyses using pairwise deletion were conducted. The two approaches yielded virtually identical results.

References

Alhakami, A. S., and Slovic, P. (1994). A psychological study of the inverse relationship between perceived risk and perceived benefit. *Risk Analysis, 14*, 1085–1096.

Bentler, P. M. (1993). *EQS: Structural equations program manual.* Los Angeles: BMDP Statistical Software.

Bord, R. J., and O'Connor, R. E. (1990). Risk communication, knowledge, and attitudes: Explaining reactions to a technology perceived as risky. *Risk Analysis, 10*, 499–506.

Bord, R. J., and O'Connor, R. E. (1992). Determinants of risk perceptions of a hazardous waste site. *Risk Analysis, 12,* 411–416.

Brenot, J., Bonnefous, S., and Marris, C. (1998). Testing the cultural theory of risk in France. *Risk Analysis, 18,* 729–739.

Brody, C. J. (1984). Differences by sex in support for nuclear power. *Social Forces, 63,* 209–228.

Buss, D. M., and Craik, K. H. (1983). Contemporary worldviews: Personal and policy implications. *Journal of Applied Social Psychology, 13,* 259–280.

Buss, D. M., Craik, K. H., and Dake, K. M. (1986). Contemporary worldviews and perception of the technological system. In V. T. Covello, J. Menkes, and J. Mumpower (Eds.), *Risk evaluation and management* (pp. 93–130). New York: Plenum.

Chou, C.-P., and Bentler, P. M. (1995). Estimates and tests in structural equation modeling. In R. H. Hoyle (Ed.), *Structural equation modeling* (pp. 37–55). Thousand Oaks, CA: Sage.

Cvetkovich, G. (1999). The attribution of social trust. In G. Cvetkovich, and R. Löfstedt (Eds.), *Social trust and the management of risk* (pp. 53–61). London: Earthscan.

Cvetkovich, G., and Löfstedt, R. (Eds.). (1999). *Social trust and the management of risk.* London: Earthscan.

Dake, K. (1991). Orienting dispositions in the perception of risk: An analysis of contemporary worldviews and cultural biases. *Journal of Cross-Cultural Psychology, 22,* 61–82.

Davidson, D. J., and Freudenburg, W. R. (1996). Gender and environmental risk concerns: A review and analysis of available research. *Environment and Behavior, 28,* 302–339.

Douglas, M., and Wildavsky, A. (1982). *Risk and culture: An essay on the selection of technological and environmental dangers.* Berkeley: University of California Press.

Earle, T. C., and Cvetkovich, G. T. (1995). *Social trust: Toward a cosmopolitan society.* Westport, CT: Praeger.

Earle, T. C. and Cvetkovich, G. (1997). Culture, cosmopolitanism, and risk management. *Risk Analysis, 17,* 55–65.

Earle, T. C., and Cvetkovich, G. (1999). Social trust and culture in risk management. In G. Cvetkovich and R. E. Löfstedt (Eds.), *Social trust and the management of risk* (pp. 9–21). London: Earthscan.

Fischhoff, B., Slovic, P., and Lichtenstein, S. (1982). Lay foibles and expert fables in judgments about risk. *American Statistician, 36,* 240–255.

Flynn, X., Burns, W., Mertz, C. K., and Slovic, P. (1992). Trust as a determinant of opposition to a high-level radioactive waste repository: Analysis of a structural model. *Risk Analysis, 12,* 417–429.

Flynn, J., Slovic, P., and Mertz, C. K. (1994). Gender, race, and perception of environmental health risks. *Risk Analysis, 14,* 1101–1108.

Frewer, L. J., Howard, C., and Shepherd, R. (1998). Understanding public attitudes to technology. *Journal of Risk Research, 1,* 221–235.

Greenberg, M. R., and Schneider, D. F. (1995). Gender differences in risk perception: Effects differ in stressed vs. nonstressed environments. *Risk Analysis, 15,* 503–511.

Gregory, J., and Miller, S. (1998). *Science in public: Communication, culture, and credibility.* New York: Plenum.

Gregory, R., and Mendelsohn, R. (1993). Perceived risk, dread, and benefits. *Risk Analysis, 13,* 259–264.

Groothuis, P. A., and Miller, G. (1997). The role of social distrust in risk-benefit analysis: A study of the siting of a hazardous waste disposal facility. *Journal of Risk and Uncertainty, 15,* 241–257.

Hoyle, R. H., and Panter, A. (1995). Writing about structural equation models. In R. H. Hoyle (Ed.), *Structural equation modeling* (pp. 158–176). Thousand Oaks, CA: Sage.

Hu, L.-T., and Bentler, P. M. (1995). Evaluating model fit. In R. H. Hoyle (Ed.), *Structural equation modeling* (pp. 76–99). Thousand Oaks, CA: Sage.

Hunt, S., Frewer, L. J., and Shepherd, R. (1999). Public trust in sources of information about radiation risks in the UK. *Journal of Risk Research, 2,* 167–180.

Jöreskog, K. G. (1993). Testing structural equation models. In K. A. Bollen and J. S. Long (Eds.), *Testing structural equation models* (pp. 294–316). Newbury Park, CA: Sage.

Jungermann, H., Pfister, H.-R., and Fischer, K. (1996). Credibility, information preferences, and information interests. *Risk Analysis, 16,* 251–261.

Kasperson, R. E., and Kasperson, J. X. (1996). The social amplification and attenuation of risk. *Annals of the American Academy of Political and Social Sciences, 545,* 95–105.

Kraus, N., Malmfors, T., and Slovic, P. (1992). Intuitive toxicology: Expert and lay judgments of chemical risks. *Risk Analysis, 12,* 215–232.

Luhmann, N. (1989). *Vertrauen: Ein Mechanismus der Reduktion sozialer Komplexität* [Trust: A mechanism for the reduction of social complexity]. Stuttgart, Germany: Enke.

Marris, C., Langford, I. H., and O'Riordan, T. (1998). A quantitative test of the cultural theory of risk perceptions: Comparison with the psychometric paradigm. *Risk Analysis, 18,* 635–647.

Mayer, R. C., Davis, J. H., and Schoorman, F. D. (1995). An integrative model of organizational trust. *Academy of Management Review, 20,* 709–734.

Miller, J. D. (1998). The measurement of civic scientific literacy. *Public Understanding of Science, 7,* 203–223.

Peters, E., and Slovic, P. (1996). The role of affect and worldviews as orienting dispositions in the perception and acceptance of nuclear power. *Journal of Applied Social Psychology, 26,* 1427–1453.

Peters, R. G., Covello, V. T., and McCallum, D. B. (1997). The determinants of trust and credibility in environmental risk communication: An empirical study. *Risk Analysis, 17,* 43–54.

Petts, J. (1998). Trust and waste management information expectation versus observation. *Journal of Risk Research, 1,* 307–320.

Renn, O., Burns, W. J., Kasperson, J. X., Kasperson, R. E., and Slovic, P. (1992). The social amplification of risk: Theoretical foundations and empirical applications. *Journal of Social Issues, 48,* 137–160.

Renn, O., and Levine, D. (1991). Credibility and trust in risk communication. In R. E. Kasperson and P. J. M. Stallen (Eds.), *Communicating risks to the public* (pp. 175–218). Dordrecht, The Netherlands: Kluwer.

Sheppard, B. H., and Sherman, D. M. (1998). The grammars of trust: A model and general implications. *Academy of Management Review, 23,* 422–437.

Siegrist, M. (1999). A causal model explaining the perception and acceptance of gene technology. *Journal of Applied Social Psychology, 29,* 2093–2106.

Siegrist, M. (2000). The influence of trust and perceptions of risks and benefits on the acceptance of gene technology. *Risk Analysis, 20,* 195–203.

Siegrist, M., and Bühlmann, R. (1999). Die Wahrnehmung verschiedener gentechnischer Anwendungen: Ergebnisse einer MDS-Analyse [Perception of different applications of gene technology: Results of an MDS-analysis]. *Zeitschrift für Sozialpsychologie, 30,* 32–39.

Siegrist, M., and Cvetkovich, G. (1999). Perception of hazards: The role of social trust and knowledge. *Risk Analysis, 20,* 713–720.

Sjöberg, L. (1998). Risk perception: Experts and the public. *European Psychologist, 3,* 1–12.

Sjöberg, L. (1999). Perceived competence and motivation in industry and government in risk perception. In G. Cvetkovich and R. E. Löfstedt (Eds.), *Social trust and the management of risk* (pp. 89–99). London: Earthscan.

Slovic, P. (1987). Perception of risk. *Science, 236,* 280–285.

Slovic, P. (1993). Perceived risk, trust, and democracy. *Risk Analysis, 13,* 675–682.

West, S. G., Finch. J. F., and Curran, P. J. (1995). Structural equation models with nonnormal variables. In R. H. Hoyle (Ed.), *Structural equation modeling* (pp. 56–75). Thousand Oaks, CA: Sage.

Wicks, A. C., Berman, S. L., and Jones, T. M. (1999). The structure of optimal trust: Moral and strategic implications. *Academy of Management Review, 24*, 99–116.

Part V

Policy and Regulation

12

Risk-Based Decision Analysis in Support of Precautionary Policies

Michael DeKay, Mitchell J. Small, Paul S. Fischbeck,
R. Scott Farrow, Alison Cullen, Joseph B. Kadane, Lester
B. Lave, M. Granger Morgan and Kazuhisa Takemura

Introduction

Risk-based decision analysis provides a structured framework for making rational decisions when outcomes are uncertain. It does so by considering alternative actions intended to enhance benefits or avoid or mitigate losses, the possible outcomes associated with each of these actions, and the probabilities and relative desirabilities of these outcomes. It can also be used to evaluate options for reducing the uncertainty surrounding the probabilities and magnitudes of possible outcomes through diagnostic tests or additional research.

For many proposed activities, such as the introduction of a new drug, the administration of growth hormones to beef cattle, or the incineration of municipal or industrial waste, a clear set of benefits can be anticipated by those who support the action (though the value, allocation and sustainability of these benefits may be subject to controversy). However, the risks associated with these programmes, should 'things not go as planned', are usually much more uncertain. This is often the case when risks arise from low-probability, high-consequence events and processes within complex systems, such as those involving human health, ecology, and socio-cultural institutions. The complexity and low probability of these effects can make it very difficult to assess and reduce the resulting uncertainty – so much so that some believe that problems of this type strain the capabilities of risk-based decision analysis.

Such concerns are part of the motivation for precautionary approaches that would substitute highly protective decision rules for the calculus and trade-offs of risk-based decision-making. In a classic paper, Page (1978) offered a characterization of the type of risk for which support for precautionary approaches is most likely to arise. Page described the (still) emerging set of technological, health and environmental risks for which:

- there is an *ignorance of mechanism* – so that our knowledge of the physical processes that determine the likelihood and magnitude of the risk is poor;

- there is a *potential for catastrophic loss* – so that the harm to the affected individuals and to society as a whole can be very great if the activity or technology entails such a risk;
- there is a *relatively modest benefit* associated with the activity or technology – especially when compared to the potential harm; and
- there is a *low subjective probability* associated with the feared outcome – otherwise, the activity would not be considered, even by its proponents. However, there is often no consensus about the probability of occurrence, due to the rarity or one-of-a-kind nature of the risk, with little or no actuarial history upon which to base estimates.

Page (1978) argued that traditional regulatory approaches are inadequate for such problems. These approaches have often focused solely or primarily on limiting false positives, assuming that new technologies and products are safe and beneficial until proven otherwise. Furthermore, these policies have often failed to address the implications of differences in the distribution of benefits and costs, especially when those exposed to the greatest risk do not receive a commensurate portion of the benefits. It is typical of these activities to involve an *internal transfer of benefits* – often through the marketplace and among willing participants to the transaction; but an *external transfer of costs* – to groups or individuals often unwilling to accept the risk, or even unaware of its presence. Such risks are often *collective*, borne by many people simultaneously. Some are *latent*, not exhibited until far into the future, and/or *irreversible*, making it difficult or impossible to prevent future damages or recover losses. Page argued that such features dictate concern for false positives that lead to restrictions on beneficial activities that are in fact safe *and* concern for false negatives that permit activities that are likely to lead to harmful outcomes. He advocated a modified expected-value approach that balances these concerns within a socially acceptable institutional framework.

Specifically, Page (1978) suggested three modifications to the expected-value approach. First, he argued that consideration of social risk aversion implies greater restrictions on risky activities. In principle, risk aversion can be handled by considering the utilities or desirabilities of the possible outcomes rather than their monetary values (Raiffa, 1968; Keeney, 1982; Clemen, 1996). But as Page noted, it may be very difficult to determine the appropriate amount of risk aversion to build into the analysis. Second, he argued that decision-makers should consider postponing taking actions that may result in irreversible negative outcomes when there is the prospect for obtaining improved information. This focus on the value of information is entirely consistent with traditional decision analysis (Clemen, 1996; Graham, 2001) and with dynamic approaches that consider multiple decision periods (Arrow and Fisher, 1974; Dixit and Pindyck, 1994; Farrow and Morel, 2001). Third, Page argued that the expected-value approach ignores the distribution of costs and benefits, particularly when the costs and benefits occur at different times. However, the results of a decision analysis or benefit–cost analysis should not tie the hands of the decision-maker. It is entirely reasonable to consider the results of such analyses in conjunction with other objectives, such as distributional equity (Arrow et al, 1996; Farrow and Toman, 1999); to conduct a separate analysis for each of the (currently existing) affected parties (Farrow, 1998); or to consider multiple dimensions of value throughout the analysis, searching for options on the outer surface of a multidimensional outcome space (Merkofer and Keeney, 1987; Cohon and Rothley, 1997; Ashford, 1999). Page concluded that the expected-value approach, modified in these ways, suggests 'a more precautionary management of environmental risk, and a lower level of acceptable risk' (p241), compared to approaches that focus primarily on the prevention of false positives.

Since Page's (1978) article, there has been increased emphasis on estimating and balancing the benefits and costs of health, safety and environmental regulations. However, some critics of the risk-analysis approach have argued that the quest for conclusive scientific evidence regarding the impacts of individual products and practices has impaired regulators' ability to protect the public and the environment, and that there is still too much emphasis on preventing false positives as opposed to false negatives (Barrett and Raffensperger, 1999; Cranor, 1999; Fairbrother and Bennett, 1999; Raffensperger and Tickner, 1999). As a result, precautionary approaches for dealing with such risks have been proposed with increasing frequency, and have been embodied in various forms of the *precautionary principle* (e.g. Raffensperger and Tickner, 1999; Commission of the European Communities, 2000). This principle is designed to ensure that the absence of scientific certainty is not used as a reason for postponing actions that are intended to protect people and the environment when there is a credible threat of serious or irreversible harm. The range of adopted and proposed precautionary principles and their interpretations have been discussed in Raffensperger and Tickner's edited volume, and the American and European experiences have been well-documented by Applegate (2000) and Sand (2000), respectively. Articles in issues of the *Journal of Risk Research* (vol. 4, no. 2, 2001; vol. 5, no. 4, 2002), and an issue of *Human and Ecological Risk Assessment* (vol. 6, no. 3, 2000) provide additional perspectives.

In this chapter, it is illustrated how the traditional decision-analytic method can be used to derive thresholds for taking precautionary action to avoid a risky activity. We do *not* attempt to justify the precautionary principle in decision-analytic terms, but formulate our model in a manner that highlights the basis for precautionary decisions. In addition, it is shown how a decision-analytic exposition of a problem reveals the key components about which parties may disagree and on the basis of which negotiated agreements may be realistically constructed.

Decision Analysis and the Precautionary Principle

Traditional applications of decision analysis have considered the health, safety or environmental risks associated with a focal action and related control or mitigation plans designed to reduce these risks or lessen their effects. If the estimated risks are too great or the costs of mitigation too high, the focal activity should be forgone. Such assessments can consider multiple health, environmental, economic and social impacts that occur over time, perhaps with special attention to highly exposed or sensitive individuals or groups. Possible outcome states are typically characterized by weighting and combining various impacts into a single (albeit, uncertain) value or utility scale and weighting them by their (also uncertain) probabilities to generate an expected value or utility for each decision alternative (Raiffa, 1968; Keeney, 1982; Clemen, 1996). Such approaches are designed to clarify trade-offs among different concerns for individual decision-makers, or for multiple stakeholders who share a common view of a decision. This is not to say that different parties must agree on the appropriate course of action, however. Full, rational consideration may show that a decision that appears to have the appropriate amount of 'prudent precaution' for its proponents appears reckless and non-precautionary to opponents with different beliefs and value systems.

Of course, decision rules other than expected utility maximization may also be considered. These include a *maximin* approach in which the decision-maker chooses the alternative that maximizes the minimum possible outcome (i.e. minimizes his or her possible loss). This decidedly precautionary approach may be appropriate in certain decision contexts, especially when the negative outcome constitutes ruin. But it ignores other aspects of the situation, including the probability of the ruinous outcome. Orr (1992) suggested that Pascal adopted the maximin approach in his famous wager regarding the existence of God, and argued that policies regarding global climate change should be based on similar reasoning. Other authors, notably Hacking (1975), have described Pascal's reasoning in terms of dominance and expected utility, with no mention of the maximin approach. For the class of problems considered here (including problems such as global climate change), a strict maximin approach always leads to avoidance of the focal risk, perhaps at the expense of forgone benefits or increases in other risks.

In his recent commentary on the relationships between decision analysis and the precautionary principle, Graham (2001) pointed out that both approaches are concerned with decision-making in the presence of uncertainly. Further, he suggested that the precautionary principle should be refined to address:

- any benefits that are associated with the risky activity;
- the possibility that protective action will lead to other countervailing risks; and
- the value of targeted research investments designed to reduce uncertainty before taking protective action.

In a similar comparison, Keeney and von Winterfeldt (2001) concluded that neither fully resolving uncertainties before taking action nor acting immediately on the side of caution are appropriate as general principles for environmental decision-making, and that a better policy would be to select the alternative with the best balance of costs, risks and benefits on a case-by-case basis. In the context of global climate change, Hammitt (2000) argued that the precautionary principle adds little to benefit–cost analysis, which can incorporate aversion to uncertainty and can more readily integrate cost considerations and concerns about modest as well as severe harms. Similarly, Montgomery and Smith (2000) suggested that an 'act then learn' approach based on a rich decision analysis that includes the value of information collected over time is consistent with a weak form of the precautionary principle, but that decision analysis provides more specific (and therefore more useful) guidance in choosing among policy options. Indeed, the vagueness of the precautionary principle is sometimes seen as its primary weakness (Bodansky, 1991). Recently, the Commission of the European Communities (2000) has attempted to refine the precautionary principle, stating that it should be considered within a structured risk-analysis approach that incorporates (among other things) information regarding the economic and non-economic benefits and costs of the various policy options and the continued collection of relevant scientific information.

Whereas Page's (1978) article suggested that a modified expected-value approach could be used to make regulations more precautionary than they had been, the above review suggests that many authors view the precautionary principle as biased in the other direction. They see the precautionary principle as placing too much emphasis on false negatives, and again suggest that the pros and cons of the various decision alternatives should be considered in a more balanced manner within the traditional framework. Such a view is far from universal, however. For example, Santillo and Johnston (1999) have argued that the precautionary principle is a 'higher-order paradigm' (p928) that is fundamentally incompatible with risk-based approaches.

We do not attempt to resolve this disagreement in this chapter. Rather, a potentially useful framework is presented for thinking about precautionary decisions from a traditional risk-based decision-analytic perspective.

A Decision-Analytic Model for Precaution

In this section, a simple model is derived for a decision about whether to engage in an activity, given uncertainty regarding the associated outcomes. The model is expressed in terms of the level of precaution desired or demanded by a decision-maker. A model for a single decision-maker is presented first, considering his or her prior assessment of risk, his or her valuation of the benefits and risks, and the accuracy of tests or research results suggesting that the activity is safe or unsafe. The model is then extended to two or more decision-makers, considering differences in their priors, their valuations, and their assessments of the information value and credibility of the supporting science.

A simplified decision problem

Consider a decision about whether to engage in a particular activity (e.g. whether to implement a new product or technology). In the simplest form of this problem, it is assumed that the activity is either safe or unsafe, and that there is no test available for collecting additional information prior to the decision. The decision-maker can decide either to engage in the activity or to avoid the activity. This situation is represented by the first two main branches of the decision tree in Figure 12.1. Although problems of this type are by their nature symmetric, we consider avoidance of the activity to be the action of interest. This perspective is consistent with the precautionary principle in the sense that avoiding the activity constitutes taking precautionary action. The four possible outcomes of the decision are a true positive (avoiding the activity when it is unsafe), a false positive (avoiding the activity when it is safe), a false negative (engaging in the activity when it is unsafe), and a true negative (engaging in the activity when it is safe).

It is also assumed that the decision-maker has some means of assessing the relative desirabilities or utilities of the four possible outcomes. These utilities are denoted $U(TP)$, $U(FP)$, $U(FN)$, and $U(TN)$, respectively. Finally, it is assumed that the decision-maker has some subjective probability P that the activity is unsafe. (See Table 12.1 for complete notation.)

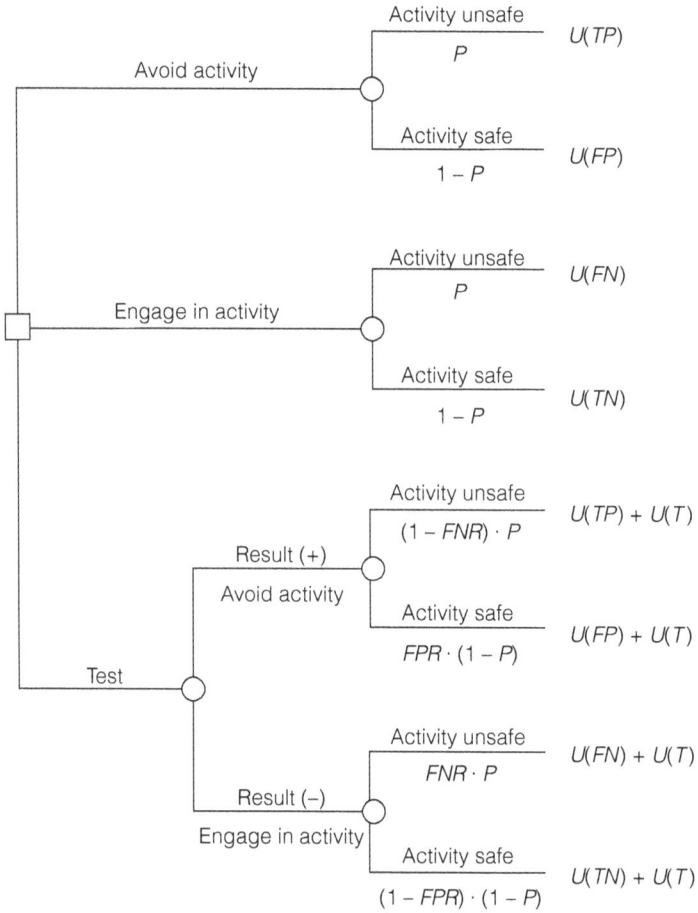

Figure 12.1 *Framework for deciding whether to avoid an activity, engage in the activity, or conduct an additional test (or larger research programme) and follow the result*

Note: See Table 12.1 for notation.

The subjective expected utilities of the two alternatives are determined by weighting the possible outcomes by the appropriate probabilities.

$$SEU(Avoid) = [U(TP) \times P] + [U(FP) \times (1 - P)] \tag{1}$$

$$SEU(Engage) = [U(FN) \times P] + [U(TN) \times (1 - P)] \tag{2}$$

According to decision analysis, the decision-maker should avoid the activity if and only if the subjective expected utility of doing so exceeds that of engaging in the activity.[1]

$$SEU(Avoid) > SEU(Engage) \tag{3}$$

Table 12.1 *Notation*

U(TP)	Utility of a true positive (avoiding the activity when it is unsafe)
U(FP)	Utility of a false positive (avoiding the activity when it is safe)
U(FN)	Utility of a false negative (engaging the activity when it is unsafe)
U(TN)	Utility of a true negative (engaging in the activity when it is safe)
U(T)	Utility of the test itself; usually $U(T) \leq 0$
B	Benefit of avoiding the activity when it is unsafe; $B = U(TP) - U(FN) > 0$
C	Cost of avoiding the activity when it is safe; $C = U(TN) - U(FP) > 0$
FPR	False positive rate of the test (the probability that test indicates that the activity is unsafe given that it is safe)
FNR	False negative rate of the test (the probability that the test indicates that the activity is safe given that it is unsafe)
P	Prior estimate of the probability that the activity is unsafe
P_{EA}	Probability threshold between engaging in the activity and avoiding the activity (when no test is available)
P_{ET}	Probability threshold between engaging in the activity (without testing) and testing (and following the result)
P_{TA}	Probability threshold between testing (and following the result) and avoiding the activity (without testing)

In Figure 12.2, these subjective expected utilities are plotted as functions of P for a generic binary decision, with the end-points of the lines determined by substituting $P = 0$ and $P = 1$ into Equations 1 and 2. As is evident in the figure, the intersection of the lines for *SEU (Avoid)* and *SEU (Engage)* defines a threshold probability P_{EA}. If the probability P that the activity is unsafe is below this threshold, engaging in the activity is the preferred course of action; if P is above this threshold, avoidance is preferred.

Substituting Equations 1 and 2 into Equation 3 and solving for P yields an expression for the threshold in terms of the utilities of the possible outcomes.

$$P_{EA} = \frac{U(TN) - U(FP)}{U(TN) - U(FP) + U(TP) - U(FN)} \quad (4)$$

The utility difference $U(TP) - U(FN)$, which is greater than zero, may be labelled the benefit B of avoiding the activity when it is unsafe. Similarly, the utility difference $U(TN) - U(FP)$, which is also greater than zero, may be labelled the cost C of avoiding the activity when it is safe.[2] In other words, C is an *opportunity cost* equal to the forgone benefits of engaging in a safe activity. Substitution yields a simpler expression.

$$P_{EA} = \frac{C}{C + B} = \frac{1}{1 + (B/C)} \quad (5)$$

Thus, the threshold is a simple function of the benefit and cost of avoiding the activity. Although it may seem odd to consider the benefit and cost of avoiding the activity rather than the benefit and cost of engaging in the activity, this formulation is consistent with current focus on precaution. It is also consistent with analyses of many

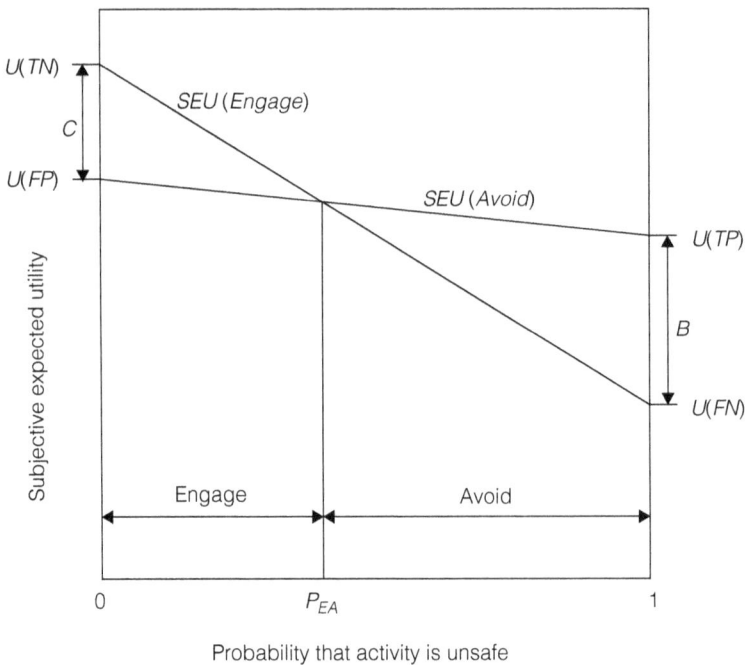

Figure 12.2 *Subjective expected utilities of engaging in an activity and avoiding the activity*

Note: The utilities and the threshold are for a generic decision. For a situation in which a great deal of precaution is warranted, the threshold P_{EA} would be much lower. See Table 12.1 for notation.

other problems in which the decision-maker is concerned with the chance of an undesirable outcome and with the benefit and cost of actions taken to avoid or rectify that outcome. Indeed, this threshold formula and its close cousins, some of which are expressed in terms of odds or likelihood ratios, have been used to evaluate a wide variety of high-consequence decisions. These include taking protective action against inclement weather (Thompson, 1950; Thompson and Brier, 1955; Murphy, 1977; Winkler and Murphy, 1985; Katz and Murphy, 1987), issuing flood and dam-failure warnings (Krzysztofowicz, 1985, 1993; DeKay and McClelland, 1991; DeKay, 1995), implementing environmental clean-up and remediation (Massman and Freeze, 1987; Hobbs et al, 1988; Freeze et al, 1990; Dakins et al, 1994, 1996; Wolfson et al, 1996a, 1996b, 1997), initiating medical treatments (Pauker and Kassirer, 1975; Sox et al, 1988; Merz et al, 1992), establishing legal standards of proof (Kaplan, 1968; Cullison, 1969; Connolly, 1987; DeKay, 1996), and numerous applications of signal detection theory (Green and Swets, 1966; Macmillan and Creelman, 1991; Swets, 1992; Swets et al, 2000).

The threshold in Equation 5 is a measure of precaution – a *standard of proof* that reflects the fact that false positives and false negatives may not be valued equally. It is a simple expression of how sure a decision-maker has to be that an activity is unsafe before he or she avoids that activity. One minus this threshold is an expression of how sure a decision-maker has to be that an activity is safe before he or she engages in that activity.

Proponents of the precautionary principle have argued that the standard of proof for taking protective action should be lower than customary scientific standards (Cranor, 1999; Tickner, 1999). For example, Cranor suggested that one of several less stringent legal definitions (e.g. 'preponderance of the evidence') might be more appropriate. In the present model, Equation 5 yields a very low decision threshold when a false negative is particularly undesirable and the benefit of avoidance is far greater than the cost. For example, a dam failure that is not preceded by an adequate warning may result in many fatalities (DeKay and McClelland, 1991, 1993), and the cost of evacuation may be relatively small compared to the value placed on those lives. DeKay and McClelland (1991) estimated that thresholds for warnings at some dams in the Western US should be 0.01, 0.001 or lower, depending on the topography, the population at risk, and the value of a statistical (i.e. unidentified) life. Thus, a dam-failure warning might be issued if the probability of dam failure were perceived to be greater than 1 in 1000. This threshold may appear surprising low to some, but it reflects a degree of precaution that is appropriate in this situation. In other situations, the thresholds resulting from Equation 5 may be very different because, as Ashford (1999, p203) has noted, 'the cost of being wrong in one instance may be vastly different from the cost of being wrong in another'.

Although it would be ideal to have a detailed analysis of the probability and magnitude of potential harm for each product, technology or activity, the case-by-case approach can be very expensive and time-consuming. It might be reasonable, therefore, to consider categories of cases (e.g. earthen dams above populated canyons, or persistent bioaccumulative chemicals) rather than individual cases, at least at the outset (see Fredholm, 2000). In our view, it is entirely reasonable to base estimates of the probability P that a specific persistent bioaccumulative chemical is unsafe and the benefit B of avoiding that chemical on evidence regarding the harmful health and environmental effects associated with other similar chemicals (i.e. on *base rates*). Thus, the approach here allows for the possibility for taking precautionary action for entire classes of cases if P exceeds the appropriate standard of proof. Of course, if additional evidence is available for a specific case, that information should be used to tailor the decision accordingly. In the next section is discussed the possibility of collecting additional information regarding the probability that a product, technology or activity is unsafe.

Collecting additional information

In some instances, the decision-maker has the option of collecting additional information before deciding whether to engage in the activity. This information may come from a distinct diagnostic procedure (e.g. an assay or a rodent test for carcinogenicity) or from a broader research programme. For simplicity, we refer to the data collection effort as a 'test' and assume that it provides additional information regarding the probability that the activity is unsafe.[3] A positive result indicates that the activity is unsafe, and a negative result indicates that the activity is safe.

The accuracy of the test may be expressed in terms of its false positive rate *FPR* and its false negative rate *FNR*. *FPR* is the probability that the test indicates that the activity is unsafe, given that it is safe, or *P(Test Result + | Activity Safe)*. FNR is the probability that the test indicates that the activity is safe, given that it is unsafe, or *P(Test Result – | Activity Unsafe)*.

Once the test is conducted, the result may be used to update the probability that the activity is unsafe via Bayes' theorem. If the test result is positive, the probability that the activity is unsafe is revised upward.

$$P(Active\ Unsafe\,|\,Test\ Result\ +) = \frac{(1-FNR) \times P}{[(1-FNR) \times P] + [FPR \times (1-P)]} \tag{6}$$

If the test result is negative, the probability that the activity is unsafe is revised downward.

$$P(Active\ Unsafe\,|\,Test\ Result\ -) = \frac{FNR \times P}{[FNR \times P] + [(1-FPR) \times (1-P)]} \tag{7}$$

The decision-maker may then compare the revised probability *P(Activity Unsafe | Test Result)* to the threshold in Equation 5 to determine whether to engage in the activity. As before, he or she should engage in the activity if *P(Activity Unsafe | Test Result)* < P_{EA} and avoid the activity if *P(Activity Unsafe | Test Result)* > P_{EA}.

For the test to be worthwhile, it must be accurate enough to change the decision. For example, if avoiding the activity is originally preferred because *P* > P_{EA}, the test has value only if a negative result can lower the probability estimate enough to make *P(Activity Unsafe | Test Result)* < P_{EA}, so that engaging in the activity is preferred. If the test is not accurate enough to move the probability estimate to the other side of the threshold, there is no point in performing the test. Therefore, it would make sense to consider whether the test is worthwhile at the outset, before the test is conducted.[4]

From this perspective, the decision-maker has three choices, as depicted in Figure 12.1. He or she may engage in the activity without testing, avoid the activity without testing, or conduct the test. If the test is conducted, it is assumed that the decision-maker will engage in the activity if the result is negative (indicating that the activity is safe) and avoid the activity if the result is positive (indicating that the activity is unsafe). When a test is conducted, the utilities for the possible outcomes are the same as before, except for the addition of a term *U(T)* for the utility of the test itself. Because testing usually costs time and money, and may involve some risk as well, *U(T)* is generally non-positive (it may be zero from the perspective of some parties). The subjective expected utility of testing is given by the following expression.

$$SEU(Test) = [U(TP) \times (1-FNR) \times P] + [U(FP) \times FPR \times (1-P)]$$
$$+ [U(FN) \times FNR \times P] + [U(TN) \times (1-FPR) \times (1-P)] + U(T) \tag{8}$$

This subjective expected utility is plotted in Figure 12.3, along with those of the other two alternatives. Generally, the end-points of *SEU (Test)* are located between the end-points of *SEU (Engage)* and *SEU (Avoid)* because the end-points of *SEU (Test)* are weighted averages of those end-points, plus the (non-positive) utility of the test. Again, the alternative with the highest subjective expected utility should be chosen. As is apparent in the figure, there are now two probability thresholds separating the three

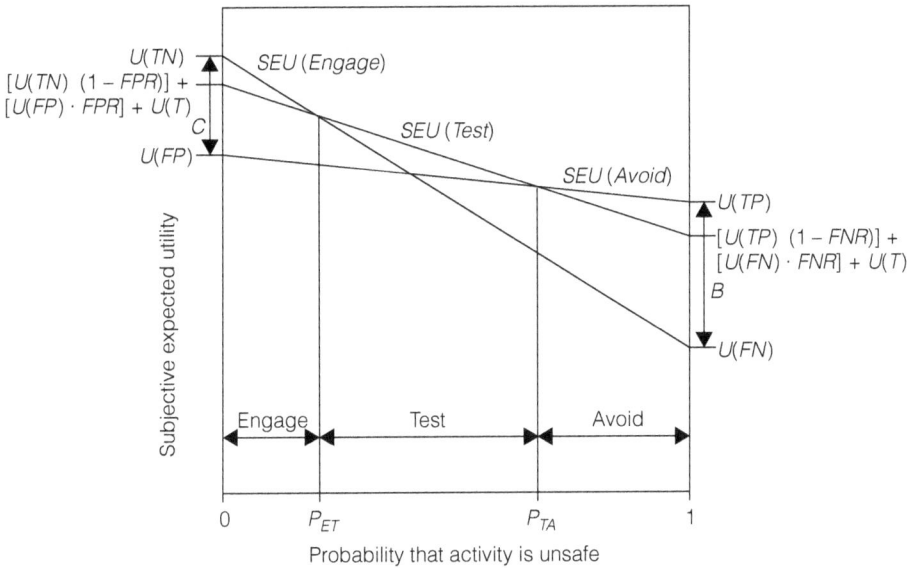

Figure 12.3 *Subjective expected utilities of engaging in an activity, avoiding the activity, and conducting an additional test (or larger research programme) and following the result.*

Note: The utilities and thresholds are for a generic decision. For a situation in which a great deal of precaution is warranted, the thresholds P_{ET} and P_{TA} might be much lower. See Table 12.1 for notation

alternatives. P_{ET} separates engaging in the activity (without testing) from testing (and following the result), and P_{TA} separates testing (and following the result) from avoiding the activity (without testing). The exact values are determined by equating the subjective expected utilities of the two alternatives in question, and solving for P.

$$P_{ET} = \frac{[C \times FPR] - U(T)}{[C \times FPR] + [B \times (1 - FNR)]} \tag{9}$$

$$P_{TA} = \frac{[C \times (1 - FPR)] + U(T)}{[C \times (1 - FPR)] + [B \times FNR]} \tag{10}$$

When the probability P that the activity is unsafe is very low, engaging in the activity without testing is the preferred option. When P is very high, avoiding the activity without testing is the preferred option. When P is somewhere in the middle, it makes more sense to conduct the test and behave in accordance with the result.

Holding the characteristics of the test constant, both thresholds are lower when the benefit of avoidance is large relative to the cost of avoidance (i.e. when $B/C > 1$), as might be the case in situations where precautionary decisions are intuitively appealing. Holding the benefit and cost of avoidance constant, the thresholds are further apart and the range of probabilities for which testing is preferred is wider when the cost and risk of the test are low (i.e. when $U(T)$ is small). Finally, the thresholds are further apart and the range of probabilities for which testing is preferred is wider when the test is more accurate (i.e. when *FPR* and *FNR* are small).

Analogous expressions have been applied in medicine, where such decision problems are common (Pauker and Kassirer, 1980; Sox et al, 1988; DeKay and Asch, 1998).

Ozonoff (1999) has also noted the analogy between errors resulting from medical screening tests and errors in applying the precautionary principle. Although we are not aware of instances in which similar thresholds have been used in other fields, these results should be widely applicable to decisions involving dichotomous testing.

Multiple stakeholders with different values and beliefs

It is a truism that different stakeholders can have very different values, beliefs and preferred decision alternatives (Kunreuther and Linnerooth, 1984; Soderstrom et al, 1984; Jenkins-Smith and Bassett, 1994; Apostolakis and Picket, 1998). In principle, any or all of the probability and utility estimates that are inputs to the decision problem may be different for different parties. In many instances, such differences may reflect the scientific uncertainty that surrounds estimates of the likelihood and severity of possible outcomes. Whether such differences lead to different preferred courses of action depends on their directions and magnitudes. Conversely, if parties prefer different courses of action, it may be useful to assess the parties' probability and utility estimates in order to determine the sources of their disagreement and to highlight possible routes to agreement.

First, the parties may have different beliefs about the probability P that the activity is unsafe. These beliefs may stem from differences in prior experiences, access to information, or trust in the sources of that information (Wynne, 1987; Kadane, 1992; Michael, 1992; Shapin, 1994; Cvetkovich et al, 2002). Differences in P may also result from parties' consideration of different sets of outcomes in the first place.[5]

Second, the parties may have different estimates for the benefit B and cost C of avoiding an activity, and therefore different values for the avoidance threshold P_{EA}. Such differences may result from the fact that the parties value the same outcomes differently, or from the fact that the benefits and costs are not distributed equally among the parties (US Environmental Protection Agency, 1992; Institute of Medicine, 1999; Sexton and Zimmerman, 1999). For example, one party might live near a proposed hazardous waste incinerator, or have a greater need for a genetically engineered pest-resistant crop. Regardless of their source, differences in P_{EA} are interpretable as differences in the levels of precaution desired or required by the parties.

Third, the parties may differ in their beliefs about the accuracy of any test that is performed to determine the safety of the activity. Differences in estimates of *FPR* and *FNR* may also result from differences in prior experiences, access to information, or trust in the sources of that information. Indeed, some parties may ignore the test entirely if they do not believe it is valid (e.g. if a study funded by the tobacco industry concludes that smoking has no adverse health effects).

Fourth, the parties may have different estimates of the utility $U(T)$ of the test itself, because they value the cost and risk associated with the test differently, or because the cost and risk are not distributed evenly among the parties.

Returning to the type of problem considered by Page (1978), it is useful to consider how an opponent and a proponent of a particular activity might differ in their assessments of the above quantities. Although the model has been presented as if the preferred decision alternative follows directly from these inputs (as it should in a consequentialist decision model), there is substantial evidence that people's assessments of 'input' quantities may be biased in the direction of their initially preferred decision alternatives (Montgomery, 1983; DeKay, 1995; Svenson 1996; Russo et al, 1996, 1998, 2000; Boiney et al, 1997). Regardless of the parties' actual decision-making processes, the following differences between a prototypical opponent and a prototypical proponent of a particular activity might be expected.

The probability P that the activity is unsafe is likely to be higher for the opponent than for the proponent. Past efforts by a proponent of an activity to dismiss or hide evidence of harm lowers other parties' trust in the proponent as a source of information. Furthermore, because trust is easy to lose and very difficult to regain (Rothbart and Park, 1986; Slovic, 1993), there may be a considerable time lag between when a proponent shapes up (by conducting business in a more open, honest and respectful manner) and when other parties' perceptions respond to the proponent's new mode of operation.

The benefit B of avoidance is likely to be higher, and the cost C of avoidance lower, for the opponent than for the proponent. Thus, the avoidance threshold P_{EA} is likely to be lower for the opponent than for the proponent, and the opponent may be characterized as more precautionary than the proponent.

The estimate of the false negative rate FNR of the test is likely to be higher for the opponent than for the proponent. This difference may result in part from mistrust of the source of information (Wynne, 1987; Kadane, 1992; Michael, 1992; Shapin, 1994; Cvetkovich et al, 2002), and may also reflect fears of scientific misconduct or hubris (Tversky and Kahneman, 1971; Lichtenstein and Fischhoff, 1977; Stern and Fineberg, 1996; Dumas, 1999; Small and Fischbeck, 1999). Such differences may be especially likely when the proponent conducts or supports the research, unless specific steps are taken to ensure a mutually acceptable design. In the absence of such safeguards, the opponent may believe that those conducting and/or reporting the studies are biased, and that FNR is intentionally underestimated so that a negative result implies more strongly that the activity is safe. Alternatively, the opponent may lack confidence in the quality of the science and believe that the test is less accurate than is claimed. Either of these sources of mistrust raises the opponent's estimate of FNR, relative to the proponent's estimate.

The effect of mistrust on the opponent's estimate of the false positive rate FPR is less clear. On the one hand, the opponent may believe that the scientific study is biased in favour of the activity, and that FPR is intentionally overestimated so that a positive result (which ostensibly indicates that the activity is unsafe) may be dismissed as an error more readily. In this case, the opponent's estimate of FPR would be lower than the proponent's. On the other hand, the opponent may doubt the quality of the science and believe that the accuracy of the test is overstated. In this case, the opponent's estimate of FPR would be higher than the proponent's.[6]

Finally, it is not at all clear whether the opponent or the proponent will place greater emphasis on the cost and risk of testing, because $U(T)$ affects the two thresholds P_{ET} and P_{TA} in opposite directions. The result is likely to depend on whether the default decision is to engage in the activity or to avoid the activity, on implications regarding who has the burden of proof for changing this decision, and on the distribution of the cost and risk of testing.

Although the differences between the opponent and the proponent regarding *FPR* and $U(T)$ are equivocal, differences in their estimates of B, C and *FNR* have relatively straightforward implications for the two thresholds P_{ET} and P_{TA}. For P_{ET}, the opponent's higher estimate of B and lower estimate of C lead to a lower threshold. The opponent's higher estimate of *FNR* raises P_{ET}, but it seems likely that this effect will be smaller than the combined effects of B and C. Thus, the net result for the opponent is a lower threshold and a reduction in the range of probabilities for which engaging in the activity without testing is preferred. For P_{TA}, the opponent's higher estimate of B, lower estimate of C, and higher estimate of *FNR* all lead to a lower threshold. The result is an increase in the range of probabilities for which avoiding the activity without testing is preferred. In summary, both thresholds are likely to be lower for the opponent than for the proponent, reflecting the opponent's more precautionary stance.

An Example Based on International Trade

A simple illustrative case involves an exporter who, with the support of nation N1, requests permission to sell fruit grown there to a second nation N2. Like N1, N2 will engage in this trade only if it is in its best interests to do so. As part of its plan to convince N2 to accept the fruit, N1 proposes a programme of phytosanitation that includes field studies and inspections at points of export (from N1) and import (to N2). For the purposes of this illustration, it is assumed that each nation evaluates its alternatives in a solely financial manner.[7] For the sake of simplicity, we also neglect such considerations as whether N2's refusal in the presence of free-trade agreements might affect N2's exports to N1, whether insurance or bonds might be available should N2 be adversely affected, and whether there is a legal forum in which N2 could sue N1 for damage if importation leads to losses due to insect pests.

If all goes well, and the imported fruit introduces no viable foreign pests to N2, N1 expects increased profits of US$2 million, and N2 expects a net consumer surplus of US$200,000 from decreased fruit prices (including losses to fruit growers in N2). If a foreign pest is introduced to N2, its expected losses from crop and ecological damage are US$500 million (albeit, estimated with great uncertainty). N1 will have an expected loss of US$10 million, as a result of forced produce withdrawals from N2 and loss of business in other nations.

With only this background, how precautionary should N2 be in comparison to N1? If *not* trading is assumed to be the status quo, and the utility of the status quo does not depend on whether trading would have been safe, then we may arbitrarily set $U(TP) = U(FP) = 0$ for both nations.[8] For N1, $U(TN) = $ US$2 million and $U(FN) = -$US$10 million, so the benefit B of *not* trading when trading is unsafe is US$10 million and the cost C of *not* trading when trading is safe is US$2 million. Equation 5 yields a threshold probability P_{EA} of 0.1667 for N1. For N2, $U(TN) = $ US$200,000 and $U(FN) = -$US$500 million, so the benefit B of *not* trading when trading is unsafe is US$500 million and the cost C of *not* trading when trading is safe is US$200,000. The corresponding threshold probability P_{EA} is 0.0004. The appropriate standard of proof for N2 is much more precautionary than that for N1.

Suppose that N1 and N2 agree that the prior probability P of an infestation resulting from fruit trade is 0.01. This value is below N1's decision threshold, but above N2's decision threshold. Accordingly, N1 prefers to trade and N2 prefers not to trade.

Now consider the effectiveness of the phytosanitation programme. Suppose that the programme is funded entirely by N1 at a cost of US$400,000, so $U(T) = -US\$400,000$ for N1 and US$0 for N2. For simplicity, suppose that the fruit trade between N1 and N2 is 'all or none' and that a positive test result leads to the cancellation of the fruit trade for one year. In this model, the false positive rate FPR and the false negative rate FNR represent the system-wide error rates. These aggregate error rates imply that the error rates for specific elements of the phytosanitation programme (e.g. inspections at one border crossing) would be much lower. It would be tedious, but relatively straightforward, to expand the example to allow the different elements of the programme to have different error rates or to allow for finer geographic or temporal limitations on trade. Given this simplification, suppose further that N1 and N2 agree that the false positive rate is very small, $FPR = 0.001$. However, N1 and N2 disagree about the false negative rate. N1 claims that FNR is 0.01, but N2 believes that it is 0.1.

Under these assumptions, the relevant thresholds as seen by N1 are $P_{ET} = 0.0406$ and $P_{TA} = 0.7617$. Both of these thresholds are above N1's prior probability P that the activity is unsafe, so N1 prefers to trade without testing. However, because N2 will not trade without testing (see above), N1 is willing to pay for the testing programme. From N1's perspective, SEU (*Test*) exceeds SEU (*Avoid*) by almost US$1.6 million.

The relevant thresholds as seen by N2 are $P_{ET} = 0.0000004$ and $P_{TA} = 0.0040$. These thresholds are exceedingly low, and N2 still prefers to forgo trade, largely because a negative test result does not provide the assurance necessary to risk a loss of US$500 million. Although a negative result yields a probability P (*Activity Unsafe | Test Result –*) that is an order of magnitude lower than N2's prior probability P (0.0010 instead of 0.01), the revised value is still above N2's original avoidance threshold of 0.0004. In short, N1's offer to fund the testing programme is insufficient to change N2's position.

It is easy to imagine how a situation like the one described here might lead to conflict in international negotiations (e.g. under the General Agreement on Tariffs and Trade, GATT). The resolution of that conflict would depend in large part on which party bears the burden of proof regarding test accuracy, and the feasibility of delaying the decision until higher-quality data arrive. Alternatively, N1 could offer N2 a more equitable distribution of the benefits and risks of trade. These options are discussed further in the following section.

This greatly simplified example assumes a set of well-defined benefits, costs and test characteristics. Although the assumed values are not unreasonable, researchers would have great difficulty in estimating most of these values with any precision, or even in setting the boundaries for the problem (e.g. that a pest infection in N2 will be confined to N2; National Research Council, 2000). Translating expected environmental effects into monetary terms (as one way of comparing these effects with other costs and benefits) is perhaps even more difficult (e.g. Farrow et al, 2000). Doing so involves eliciting, quantifying and summarizing different perceptions and valuations of what is at risk. Still, with these parameters put into focus, our conceptual framework may help to clarify discussions and deliberations, and thereby improve the chances that a mutually acceptable resolution can be identified.

Implications for Conflict Resolution

In applying the proposed model, the proponent of a product, technology or activity that is in fact justified could adopt a number of strategies to promote its interests.

First, the proponent might lower the risks of the activity (if that is possible) or distribute the remaining risks more equitably, perhaps via insurance or other risk-sharing arrangements, thereby reducing differences among parties' estimates of the benefit of avoidance B. In the above fruit-trade example, how low would the benefit of avoidance have to be for the opponent N2 to prefer testing (and following the result) to avoiding trade (without testing)? Setting P_{TA} equal to 0.01 (N1 and N2's original estimate of P) in Equation 10 and solving for B yields a value of about US$198 million for N2. So if all else remained equal, N2's estimate of B would have to drop by at least US$302 million before that nation would prefer testing. If N1's estimate of B were increased by an equivalent amount (to US$312 million) through some sort of risk-sharing arrangement, N1 would also prefer to test, and the parties could undertake testing and trading.

Second, the proponent could distribute the benefits of the activity more equitably, thereby reducing differences among parties' estimates of the cost of avoidance C. In the fruit-trade example, N2's estimate of C would have to be at least US$0.5 million (an increase of at least US$0.3 million) before testing would be preferred to avoidance. If N1's estimate of C were lowered by an equivalent amount, N1 would prefer to trade without testing, but would be willing to pay for the testing programme in order to gain access to N2's markets.

Third, the proponent could attempt to increase other parties' trust in scientific results, perhaps via increased stakeholder participation in the problem formulation and study design,[9] or through independent, third-party studies or reviews, thereby reducing differences among parties' estimates of the false positive rate FPR and the false negative rate FNR. In the fruit-trade example, N2's estimate of FNR would have to be reduced to less than 0.04 before testing would be preferred to avoidance. If N1 also agreed that FNR was about 0.04, N1 would still prefer to trade without testing, but would again be willing to pay for the testing programme.

Of course, the proponent could also adopt some combination of these strategies. For example, N1 could convince N2 to trade by (1) sharing US$150 million of N2's risk, so that N2's estimate of B is reduced to US$350 million; (2) sharing US$100,000 of the benefits of trade, so that N2's estimate of C is increased to US$300,000, and (3) improving or providing more convincing data regarding the phytosanitation programme, so that N2's estimate of FNR is reduced to 0.08.

The direct trade-offs between B, C and FNR in determining N2's preferred action are particularly evident in the odds form of Equation 10.

$$O_{TA} = \frac{P_{TA}}{1 - P_{TA}} = \frac{[C \times (1 - FNR)] + U(T)}{B \times FNR} \tag{11}$$

Because $U(T) = 0$ for N2, proportional changes in B, C and FNR affect this odds threshold to the same degree. In other words, increasing C by some factor increases O_{TA} by the same amount as decreasing B or FNR by that factor. In the fruit-trade example, this factor would need to be a bit higher than 2.5 before N2 would prefer testing to avoidance. Indeed, any combination of changes for which the increase in $C/(B \times FNR)$ is a bit higher than 2.5 times would yield the same result. On the other hand, changing the false positive rate FPR would have almost no effect on O_{TA} or P_{TA}, and no effect on N2's decision.

Although none of these strategies for obtaining agreement among parties is new, our model illustrates their respective roles in a rational, risk-based decision-analytic framework for determining appropriate precautionary levels. The usefulness of the model lies in the fact that it allows the parties to deconstruct the problem into its essential components in a manner that highlights sources of disagreement and possible paths to negotiated agreement.

The Importance of Trust

Recent writings on risk policy have highlighted the importance of trust (e.g., National Research Council, 1989; Kasperson et al, 1992; Slovic, 1993; Stern and Fineberg, 1996; Siegrist and Cvetkovich; 2000). Although the focus here has been on the role of trust in the interpretation of information about probabilities, trust may affect overall judgements of risks and benefits as well. Numerous studies have reported a weak negative relationship between judgements of risk and benefit, reflecting explicit beliefs or perhaps a conscious or unconscious desire to avoid cognitive dissonance (Gregory and Mendelsohn, 1993; Alhakami and Slovic, 1994; Frewer et al, 1998; Finucane et al, 2000). A study by Siegrist and Cvetkovich (2000) suggests that this negative relationship may be due in part to the effects of trust, and that these effects are moderated by respondents' familiarity with the activity or technology. More specifically, greater social trust (i.e. confidence in the competence and honesty of social institutions) is associated with perceptions of lower risks and greater benefits across numerous activities and technologies, and these relationships are stronger for unfamiliar activities and technologies for which people must rely on authorities for the information needed to judge risks and benefits.

As noted earlier, Page (1978) argued that precautionary approaches are especially appropriate for activities or technologies for which we lack the mechanistic understanding or actuarial history needed to support risk estimates. When both scientific and lay estimates of risk are uncertain, there is likely to be a stronger link between trust and perceived risks and benefits. In such situations, the cumulative effects of the lack of trust on the various components of our model are likely to yield decision criteria that are more precautionary.

Implications for Future Research

The implementation of this framework would benefit greatly from an enhanced ability to characterize stakeholder perceptions in sufficiently precise terms to allow for model specification. This improvement is likely to require intensive, directed interviews to ensure that participants fully understand the issues and clearly articulate their positions. Such interviews could take advantage of advances in constructive value elicitation (Fischhoff, 1991, 2000; Gregory et al, 1993; Payne et al, 1999; Satterfield et al, 2000), risk communication (National Research Council, 1989; Fischhoff, 1998; Fischhoff et al, 1998; Riley et al, 2001; Morgan et al, 2002), and statistical elicitation and modelling (Kadane et al, 1980; Wolpert, 1989; Chaloner, 1996; Kadane and Wolfson, 1998; Garthwaite and Al-Awadhi, 2001). In a particularly interesting approach to statistical elicitation for Bayesian models (Kadane, 1980; Winkler, 1980; Wolfson, 1995), participants are asked for their prior beliefs concerning a quantity (e.g. its probability distribution), and what their posterior beliefs would be given specific, new information. The latter is referred to as a predictive distribution and, combined with the prior, allows for derivation of the likelihood function that is being used by the participant to process and interpret the implications of the new data.[10] Such an approach could be especially useful in eliciting from stakeholders the inferences that they might draw from scientific studies conducted by different parties or with different designs. Comparing the results of these elicitations to those from project proponents and their scientific experts could provide direct insight into the effects of beliefs about competency and trust on the other components of the model.

Limitations

The analysis presented in this chapter is limited to a very small number of alternatives and possible outcomes. It can be extended to any number of alternatives and outcomes by using ordinary tools of decision analysis, although the results will not be so conveniently reduced to simple avoidance thresholds. Even so, the limited set of risk options and metrics considered in many analyses have led to scepticism or outright rejection of risk assessment by some stakeholders and scholars (Stern and Fineberg, 1996; Andrews, 1997; Montague, 1998; O'Brien, 2000), and such objections may be difficult to overcome if the practice of risk-based decision analysis is not improved. Risk–benefit and risk–risk decisions regarding natural resource utilization, product introduction, international trade, waste management and environmental clean-up involve multiple stakeholders who influence decisions through a complex set of legal and deliberative processes. Their values and perspectives often differ greatly. Furthermore, risk estimates may lack the *pedigree* of sound, consensual science needed to ensure broad acceptance (Funtowicz and Ravetz, 1992). A broader framing of risk and decision analysis is clearly needed if the approach is to have greater credibility (Jasanoff, 1993; Irwin, 1995; Keller and Sarin, 1995; Stern and Fineberg, 1996; Apostolakis and Pickett, 1998; Miller et al, 1999; Sexton, 1999).

In some circumstances, it may be difficult to apply the proposed model because the parties do not agree about the set of possible alternatives or outcomes. A strong version of this position is advocated by those who favour alternatives analysis over risk analysis, arguing that our efforts would be better spent on characterizing and broadening the option set (O'Brien, 2000). Without knowing what is possible, it is argued, what the benefits and risks are for any option cannot be known. Although we agree that a better understanding of the options leads to a better decision analysis, it is relatively straightforward to include all of the outcomes and alternatives that seem plausible to any party. Some parties may assign probabilities of zero to some outcomes, and some parties may believe that some alternatives are not viable, but the proposed model provides a very clear framework for highlighting such disagreements. We are much less optimistic about the application of the model when the risk problem is so ill-defined and the science so new and uncertain, that the relevant outcomes, probabilities and utilities cannot be specified in a sensible manner by any of the stakeholders (Stern and Fineberg, 1996).

Finally, there is the possibility that others will question the appropriateness of an expected-utility framework for such problems. For example, Allais (1953/1979), Ellsberg (1961), and Lopes (1981) have questioned the normative status of subjective expected-utility theory, and Mellers et al (1998) have reviewed alternative frameworks. Research in the prospect-theory tradition (Kahneman and Tversky, 1979; Tversky and Kahneman, 1992) has shown that people tend to either overweight or ignore outcomes with very small probabilities; and the literature on risk perception (e.g. Chapter 6; Slovic, 1986; Morgan et al, 2001) has shown that riskiness judgements for activities or technologies with the potential for catastrophe are not well captured by the expectation of the loss. Although decision theorists may be able to provide counter-arguments to address normative concerns, and incorporate other 'anomalies' via subjective probabilities and non-linear utility functions (or by pointing out the distinction between normative and descriptive models), there is no guarantee that such answers will satisfy those who have raised these objections.

Conclusions

In any important policy context, making a sensible decision about whether to engage in or avoid a risky activity requires considered judgements about the relative desirabilities (utilities) and likelihoods (probabilities) of the plausible outcomes of the decision. Focusing solely on a single feared outcome, believing only that it would be terrible or that there is some non-zero chance that it will occur, is not a sufficient basis for taking precautionary action.

In this chapter, an attempt has been made to demonstrate the compatibility of a risk-based decision-analytic approach with some of the concerns that motivate precautionary approaches for technological and environmental decision-making. In particular, the proposed decision-analytic model highlights differences between parties' accrual and valuation of the benefits and costs associated with avoiding an activity, their prior beliefs regarding the safety of the activity, and their interpretation of tests and studies designed to assess the safety of the activity. Although the model is in most ways a repackaging of the standard decision-analytic model for choice between two alternatives, its expression in this context and the recognition that rational parties may disagree about key model parameters may encourage its use by a broader set of participants in decisions involving a wider range of problems. Explicit consideration of the contribution of the various components of the model to differences in the levels of precaution demanded by the parties to a decision can help to focus and clarify deliberations, and identify possible alternatives for conflict resolution.

The model is *not* a decision-analytic justification of the precautionary principle, but it does illustrate how the traditional decision-analytic method can be used to derive decision thresholds for taking precautionary action to avoid a risky activity. In particular, the threshold given in Equation 5 reflects the relative importance of false positives and false negatives and provides a justifiable standard of proof that is appropriate in such situations. For cases in which this standard of proof is low, precautionary action is more likely to be warranted. Moreover, this approach may be applied to classes of cases when, at least at the outset, there is insufficient evidence to estimate the components of the model separately for each case. These results could serve to legitimate the use of quantitative risk and decision analysis among those supportive of precaution but wary of vaguely defined precautionary approaches that could lead to restriction of almost any activity with unresolved risks. It could also be useful to those already inclined towards risk-based decision analysis but wary of overly narrow, non-representative or biased uses of such analyses.

We intend to explore further the insights gained from this perspective for different problems where the use of precautionary approaches may be indicated. It is also hoped that the proposed framework will motivate further research into the fundamental factors that determine appropriate levels of precaution, and the differences in precaution likely to arise for different types of problems.

Acknowledgements

Support for this research was provided by a seed grant from Carnegie Mellon University, general funding to the Center for the Study and Improvement of Regulation, and a grant from the US Department of Energy Center for Risk Excellence. Special thanks to Margaret MacDonell and Loren Habegger of Argonne National Laboratory for their contribution to this effort. The ideas presented in this paper benefited from discussions with Elizabeth Casman, Hadi Dowlatabadi, Alex Farrell, Baruch Fischhoff, Keith Florig, Benoit Morel, Andrew Solow and Felicia Wu Morris.

Notes

1   The 'if and only if' decision rule need not be applied blindly. As noted earlier, the decision-maker might consider the results of this analysis in conjunction with the distribution of impacts or other difficult-to-value outcomes.
2   If either of these utility differences is not greater than zero, then one alternative dominates the other and there is no need to calculate a decision threshold. One might also consider the case where the magnitudes of B and C are uncertain. In this case, B and C are replaced by their expected values, $E(B)$ and $E(C)$, computed by integrating over the respective

probability distributions for the benefit and cost. We carry forward the simpler case for ease of exposition.

3   Of course, research that provides additional information regarding the benefit or cost (e.g. the value that people place on certain types of environmental damage) is also possible.

4   As noted by a reviewer, the accuracy of the test may not be known before it has been put into place and evaluated. In such cases, one can at least assess the sensitivity of the decision to test accuracy.

5   When there is ignorance about the sample space of possible events, the assignment of probabilities is much more difficult (Walley, 1996; Smithson et al, 2000). Although the decision-maker may be willing to consider unusual or 'surprise' events, formal tools for incorporating such events remain weak (Shlyakhter, 1994; Hammitt and Shlyakhter, 1999; Casman et al, 1999). We maintain the structure of the simple decision model, assuming that more risk-averse (or perhaps more 'realistic', 'humble' or 'chastened-by-experience') decision-makers incorporate the possibility of surprise into their assessments of risk magnitude and probability.

6   Johnson and Slovic (1995) note another case in which mistrust in the honesty and competence of those who conduct and/or report scientific studies are differentiated. Their studies with focus groups suggest that honest, full and open expressions of uncertainty on the part of agency risk managers tend to build citizens' trust in the agency's honesty, but lead them to question the agency's competence. Highly confident scientific assertions by those in charge, indicating little or no uncertainty, tend to build citizens' trust in the agency's competence, but lead them to question the agency's honesty.

7   As noted earlier, non-financial impacts could be incorporated into the utilities of the possible outcomes, or they could be considered later, in conjunction with the results of the financial decision analysis.

8   In general, $U(TP)$ and $U(FP)$ need not be equal: what matters are the utility differences $B = U(TP) - U(FN)$ and $C = U(TN) - U(FP)$. Nonetheless, $U(TP)$ and $U(FN)$ may be equal when avoidance of the activity is completely successful, as assumed here. This assumption may be very realistic for some avoidance decisions (e.g. deciding not to build a new nuclear facility) but very unrealistic for others (e.g. deciding to issue an evacuation order because of a possible hurricane strike).

9   For example, Yosie (2000) reported the results of a Charlton Research Company survey for the American Chemistry Council in June 1999, that focused upon the High Production Volume chemical testing initiative. This study found that 40 per cent of the public believed that research conducted by private industry would reveal what industry wanted it to; that 63 per cent believed that a political agenda is behind many of the conclusions of research conducted by government alone; but that 79 per cent would have a favourable or very favourable view of industry, government and environmental groups working together to obtain scientific information.

10 In a model like the one presented here, the likelihood function would reflect the participant's perceptions of the false positive rate *FPR* and the false negative rate *FNR*.

References

Alhakami, A. S. and Slovic, P. (1994) A psychological study of the inverse relationship between perceived risk and perceived benefit, *Risk Analysis* 14, 1085–96.

Allais, M. (1979) The foundations of a positive theory of choice involving risk and a criticism of the postulates and axioms of the American school, in M. Allais and O. Hagen (eds) *Expected*

Utility Hypotheses and the Allais Paradox: Contemporary Discussions of the Decisions Under Uncertainty with Allais' Rejoinder, pp. 38–145. Dordrecht, the Netherlands: Reidel. (Original work published 1953.)

Andrews, R. N. L. (1997) Risk-based decisionmaking, in N. J. Vig and M. E. Kraft (eds) *Environmental Policy in the 1990s: Reform or Reaction?*, pp. 208–30. Washington, DC: Congressional Quarterly Books.

Apostolakis, G. E. and Pickett, S. E. (1998) Deliberation: integrating analytical results into environmental decision involving multiple stakeholders, *Risk Analysis* 18, 621–47.

Applegate, J. S. (2000) The precautionary preference: an American perspective on the precautionary principle, *Human and Ecological Risk Assessment* 6, 413–43.

Arrow, K. J. and Fisher, A. C. (1974) Environmental preservation, uncertainty, and irreversibility, *Quarterly Journal of Economics* 88, 312–19.

Arrow, K. J., Cropper, M. L., Eads, G. C., Hahn, R. W., Lave, L. B., Noll, R. G., Portney, P. R., Russell, M., Schmalensee, R., Smith, V. K. and Stavins, R. N. (1996) Is there a role for benefit-cost analysis in environmental, health, and safety regulation? *Science* 272, 221–22.

Ashford, N. A. (1999) A conceptual framework for the use of the precautionary principle in law, in C. Raffensperger and J. Tickner (eds) *Protecting Public Health and the Environment: Implementing the Precautionary Principle*, pp. 198–206. Washington, DC: Island Press.

Barrett, K. and Raffensperger, C. (1999) Precautionary science, in C. Raffensperger and J. Tickner (eds) *Protecting Public Health and the Environment: Implementing the Precautionary Principle*, pp. 106–22. Washington, DC: Island Press.

Bodansky, D. (1991) Scientific uncertainty and the precautionary principle, *Environment* 33 (7), 4–5, 43–44.

Boiney, L. G., Kennedy, J. and Nye, P. (1997) Instrumental bias in motivated reasoning: more when more is needed, *Organizational Behavior and Human Decision Processes* 72, 1–24.

Casman, E. A., Morgan, M. G. and Dowlatabadi, H. (1999) Mixed levels of uncertainty in complex policy models, *Risk Analysis* 19, 33–42.

Chaloner, K. M. (1996) The elicitation of prior distributions, in D. A. Berry and D. K. Stangl (eds) *Bayesian Biostatistics*, pp. 141–56. New York: Marcel Dekker.

Clemen, R. T. (1996) *Making Hard Decisions: An Introduction to Decision Analysis* (2nd edn). Belmont, CA: Duxbury Press.

Cohon, J. and Rothley, K. (1997) Multiobjective methods, in C. Revelle and A. E. McGarity (eds) *Design and Operation of Civil and Environmental Engineering Systems*, pp. 513–66. New York: Wiley.

Commission of the European Communities (2000) *Communication from the Commission on the Precautionary Principle*. Brussels, Belgium: CEC.

Connolly, T. (1987) Decision theory, reasonable doubt, and the utility of erroneous acquittals, *Law and Human Behavior* 11, 101–12.

Cullison, A. D. (1969) Probability analysis of judicial fact-finding: a preliminary outline of the subjective approach, *Toledo Law Review* 1969, 538–98.

Cranor, C. F. (1999) Asymmetric information, the precautionary principle, and burdens of proof, in C. Raffensperger and J. Tickner (eds) *Protecting Public Health and the Environment: Implementing the Precautionary Principle*, pp. 74–99. Washington, DC: Island Press.

Cvetkovich, G., Siegrist, M., Murray, R. and Tragresser, S. (2002) New information and social trust: asymmetry and perseverance of attributions about hazard managers, *Risk Analysis* 22, 359–67.

Dakins, M. E., Toll, J. E. and Small, M. J. (1994) Risk-based environmental remediation: decision framework and role of uncertainty, *Environmental Toxicology and Chemistry* 13, 1907–15.

Dakins, M. E., Toll, J. E., Small, M. J. and Brand, K. P. (1996) Risk-based environmental remediation: Bayesian Monte Carlo analysis and the expected value of sample information, *Risk Analysis* 16, 67–79.

DeKay, M. L. (1995) How sure is sure enough? Outcome evaluations and action thresholds in binary decisions (Doctoral dissertation, University of Colorado, Boulder, 1994), *Dissertation Abstracts International-B* **56**(2), 1148, University Microfilms No. AAC 9518612.

DeKay, M. L. (1996) The difference between Blackstone-like error ratios and probabilistic standards of proof, *Law and Social Inquiry* **21**, 95–132.

DeKay, M. L. and Asch, D. A. (1998) Is the defensive use of diagnostic tests good for patients, or bad? *Medical Decision Making* **18**, 19–28.

DeKay, M. L. and McClelland, G. H. (1991) *Setting Decision Thresholds for Dam Failure Warnings: A Practical Theory-Based Approach* (CRJP Report No. 328). Boulder: University of Colorado, Center for Research on Judgment and Policy.

DeKay, M. L. and McClelland, G. H. (1993) Predicting loss of life in cases of dam failure and flash flood, *Risk Analysis* **13**, 193–205.

Dixit, A. K. and Pindyck, R. S. (1994) *Investment Under Uncertainty.* Princeton, NJ: Princeton University Press.

Dumas, L. J. (1999) *Lethal Arrogance: Human Fallibility and Dangerous Technologies.* New York: St. Martin's Press.

Ellsberg, D. (1961) Risk, ambiguity, and the Savage axioms, *Quarterly Journal of Economics* **75**, 643–99.

Fairbrother, A. and Bennett, R. S. (1999) Ecological risk assessment and the precautionary principle, *Human and Ecological Risk Assessment* **5**, 943–49.

Farrow, S. (1998) Environmental equity and sustainability: rejecting the Kaldor-Hicks criteria, *Ecological Economics* **27**, 183–88.

Farrow, S. and Morel, B. (2001) Continuation rights, the precautionary principle, and global change, *Risk Decision and Policy* **6**, 145–55.

Farrow, S. and Toman, M. (1999) Using benefit-cost analysis to improve environmental regulations, *Environment* **41** (2), 12–15, 33–38.

Farrow, R. S., Goldburg, C. B. and Small, M.J. (2000) Economic valuation and the environment: a special issue, *Environmental Science and Technology* **34**, 1381–83.

Finucane, M. L., Alhakami, A., Slovic, P. and Johnson, S. M. (2000) The affect heuristic in judgments of risks and benefits, *Journal of Behavioral Decision Making* **13**, 1–17.

Fischhoff, B. (1991) Value elicitation: is there anything in there? *American Psychologist* **46**, 835–47.

Fischhoff, B. (1998) Communicate unto others ... , *Reliability Engineering and System Safety* **59**, 63–72.

Fischhoff, B. (2000) Informed consent for eliciting environmental values, *Environmental Science and Technology* **34**, 1439–44.

Fischhoff, B., Riley, D., Kovacs, D. C. and Small, M. (1998) What information belongs in a warning? *Psychology and Marketing* **15**, 663–86.

Fredholm, L. (2000) Sweden to get tough on lingering compounds, *Science* **290**, 1663–66.

Freeze, R. A., Massmann, J. W., Smith, L., Sperling, T. and James, B. (1990) Hydrogeological decision analysis, 1. A framework, *Ground Water* **28**, 738–66.

Frewer, L. J., Howard, C. and Shepard, R. (1998) Understanding public attitudes to technology, *Journal of Risk Research* **1**, 221–25.

Funtowicz, S. O. and Ravetz, J. R. (1992) Three types of risk assessment and the emergence of post-normal science, in S. Krimsky and D. Golding (eds) *Social Theories of Risk*, pp. 251–73. Westport, CT: Praeger.

Garthwaite, P. H. and Al-Awadhi, S. A. (2001) Non-conjugate prior distribution assessment for multivariate normal sampling, *Journal of the Royal Statistical Society, Series B* **63**, 95–110.

Graham, J. D. (2001) Decision-analytic refinements of the precautionary principle, *Journal of Risk Research* **4**, 127–41.

Green, D. M. and Swets, J. A. (1966) *Signal Detection Theory and Psychophysics*. New York: Wiley. (Reprinted 1988, Los Altos, CA: Peninsula.)

Gregory, R., Lichtenstein, S. and Slovic, P. (1993) Valuing environmental resources: a constructive approach, *Journal of Risk and Uncertainty* 7, 177–97.

Gregory, R. and Mendelsohn, R. (1993) Perceived risk, dread, and benefits, *Risk Analysis* 13, 259–64.

Hacking, I. (1975) *The Emergence of Probability*. London: Cambridge University Press.

Hammit, J. K. (2000) Global climate change: benefit-cost analysis vs. the precautionary principle, *Human and Ecological Risk Assessment* 6, 387–98.

Hammitt, J. K. and Shlyakhter, A. I. (1999) The expected value of information and the probability of surprise, *Risk Analysis* 19, 135–52.

Hobbs, B. F., Von Patterson, C, Maciejowski, M. E. and Haimes, Y. Y. (1988) Risk analysis of aquifer contamination by brine, *Journal of Water Resources Planning and Management* 114, 667–85.

Institute of Medicine, Committee on Environmental Justice (1999) *Toward Environmental Justice: Research, Education, and Health Policy Needs*. Washington, DC: National Academy Press.

Irwin, A. (1995) *Citizen Science: A Study of People, Expertise, and Sustainable Development*. London: Routledge.

Jasanoff, S. (1993) Bridging the two cultures of risk analysis, *Risk Analysis* 13, 123–29.

Jenkins-Smith, H. and Bassett, G. W., Jr. (1994) Perceived risk and uncertainty of nuclear waste: differences among science, business, and environmental group members, *Risk Analysis* 14, 851–56.

Johnson, B. B. and Slovic, P. (1995) Presenting uncertainty in health risk assessment: initial studies of its effects on risk perception and trust, *Risk Analysis* 15, 485–94.

Kadane, J. B. (1980) Predictive and structural methods for eliciting prior distributions, in A. Zellner (ed) *Bayesian Analysis in Econometrics and Statistics: Essays in Honor of Harold Jeffreys*, pp. 89–93. Amsterdam: North-Holland.

Kadane, J. B. (1992) Healthy skepticism as an expected-utility explanation of the phenomena of Allais and Ellsberg, *Theory and Decision* 32, 57–64.

Kadane, J. B. and Wolfson, L. J. (1998) Experiences in elicitation (with discussion), *Journal of the Royal Statistical Society, Series D* 47, 3–19.

Kadane, J. B., Dickey, J. M., Winkler, R. L., Smith, W. S. and Peters, S. C. (1980) Interactive elicitation of opinion for a normal linear model, *Journal of the American Statistical Association* 75, 845–54.

Kahneman, D. and Tversky, A. (1979) Prospect theory: an analysis of decisions under risk, *Econometrica* 47, 263–91.

Kaplan, J. (1968) Decision theory and the factfinding process, *Stanford Law Review* 20, 1065–92.

Kasperson, R. E, Golding, D. and Tuler, S. (1992) Social distrust as a factor in siting hazardous facilities and communicating risks, *Journal of Social Issues* 48, 161–87.

Katz, R. W. and Murphy, A. H. (1987) Quality/value relationship for imperfect information in the umbrella problem, *American Statistician* 41, 187–89.

Keeney, R. L. (1982) Decision analysis: an overview, *Operations Research* 39, 803–38.

Keeney, R. L. and von Windterfeldt, D. (2001) Appraising the precautionary principle – a decision analysis perspective, *Journal of Risk Research* 4, 191–202.

Keller, L. R. and Sarin, R. K. (1995) Fair processes for societal decisions involving distributional inequalities, *Risk Analysis* 15, 49–59.

Krzysztofowicz, R. (1985) *Choice of Action Based on the Probability of a Flash Flood*. Charlottesville: University of Virginia, School of Engineering and Applied Science, Department of Systems Engineering.

Krzysztofowicz, R. (1993) A theory of flood warning systems, *Water Resources Research* 29, 3981–94.

Kunreuther, H. and Linnerooth, J. (1984) Low probability accidents, *Risk Analysis* 4, 143–52.

Lopes, L. L. (1981) Decision making in the short run, *Journal of Experimental Psychology: Human Learning and Memory* 7, 377–85.

Lichtenstein, S. and Fischhoff, B. (1977) Do those who know more also know more about how much they know? *Organizational Behavior and Human Performance* 20, 159–83.

Macmillan, N. A. and Creelman, C. D. (1991) *Detection Theory: A User's Guide.* New York: Cambridge University Press.

Massman, J. and Freeze, R. A. (1987) Groundwater contamination from waste management: the interaction between risk-based engineering design and regulatory policy, 1. Methodology, *Water Resources Research* 23, 351–67.

Mellers, B. A., Schwartz, A. and Cooke, A. D. J. (1998) Judgment and decision making, *Annual Review of Psychology* 49, 447–77.

Merkofer, M. W. and Keeney, R. L. (1987) A multiattribute utility analysis of alternative sites for the disposal of nuclear waste, *Risk Analysis* 7, 173–94.

Merz, J., Small, M. J. and Fischbeck, P. (1992) Measuring decision sensitivity: a combined Monte Carlo-logistic regression approach, *Medical Decision Making* 12, 189–96.

Michael, M. (1992) Lay discourses of science: science-in-general, science-in-particular, and self, *Science, Technology and Human Values* 17, 313–33.

Miller, D. S., Green, J. J. and Gill, D. A. (1999) Bridging the gap between the reductionist perspective of public policy and the precautionary perspective of communities, *Electronic Green Journal*, Issue 11, http://egj.lib.uidaho.edu/index.php/egj/article/view/2751/2709, accessed 16 September 2008.

Montague, P. (1998) The precautionary principle, *Rachel's Environment and Health News*, Issue 586, www.rachel.org/bulletin/index.cfm?issue_ID=532, accessed 20 June 2002.

Montgomery, H. (1983) Decision rules and the search for a dominance structure: towards a process model of decision making, in P. Humphreys, O. Svenson and A. Vari (eds) *Analysing and Aiding Decision Processes*, pp. 343–69. Amsterdam: North-Holland.

Montgomery, W. D. and Smith, A. E. (2000) Global climate change and the precautionary principle, *Human and Ecological Risk Assessment* 6, 399–412.

Morgan, K. M., DeKay, M. L., Fischbeck, P. S., Fischhoff, B., Morgan, M. G. and Florig, H. K. (2001) A deliberative method for ranking risks (II): evaluation of validity and agreement among risk managers, *Risk Analysis* 21, 923–37.

Morgan, M. G., Fischhoff, B., Bostrom, A. and Atman, C. J. (2002) *Risk Communication: The Mental Models Approach.* New York: Cambridge University Press.

Murphy, A. H. (1977) The value of climatological, categorical and probabilistic forecasts in the cost-loss ratio situation, *Monthly Weather Review* 105, 803–16.

National Research Council, Committee on Risk Perception and Communication (1989) *Improving Risk Communication.* Washington, DC: National Academy Press.

National Research Council, Board on Agriculture and Natural Resources (2000) *Incorporating Science, Economics, and Sociology in Developing Sanitary and Phytosanitary Standards in International Trade: Proceedings of a Conference.* Washington, DC: National Academy Press.

O'Brien, M. (2000) *Making Better Environmental Decisions: An Alternative to Risk Assessment.* Cambridge, MA: MIT Press.

Orr, D. (1992) Pascal's wager and economics in a hotter time, *Ecological Economics* 6, 1–6.

Ozonoff, D. (1999) The precautionary principle as a screening device, in C. Raffensperger and J. Tickner (eds) *Protecting Public Health and the Environment: Implementing the Precautionary Principle*, pp. 100–5. Washington, DC: Island Press.

Page, T. (1978) A generic view of toxic chemicals and similar risks, *Ecology Law Quarterly* 7, 207–44.

Pauker, S. G. and Kassirer, J. P. (1975) Therapeutic decision making: a cost-benefit approach, *New England Journal of Medicine* 293, 229–34.

Pauker, S. G. and Kassirer, J. P. (1980) The threshold approach to clinical decision making, *New England Journal of Medicine* 302, 1109–17.

Payne, J. W., Bettman, J. R. and Schkade, D. A. (1999) Measuring constructed preferences: towards a building code, *Journal of Risk and Uncertainty* 19, 243–70.

Raffensperger, C. and Tickner, J. (eds) (1999) *Protecting Public Health and the Environment: Implementing the Precautionary Principle.* Washington, DC: Island Press.

Raiffa, H. (1968) *Decision Analysis: Introductory Lectures on Choice Under Uncertainty.* Reading, MA: Addison-Wesley.

Riley, D. M., Fischhoff, B., Small, M. J. and Fischbeck, P. (2001) Evaluating the effectiveness of risk-reduction strategies for consumer chemical products, *Risk Analysis* 21, 359–69.

Rothbart, M. and Park, B. (1986) On the confirmability and disconfirmability of trait concepts, *Journal of Personality and Social Psychology* 50, 131–42.

Russo, J. E., Medvec, V. H. and Meloy, M. G. (1996) The distortion of information during decisions, *Organizational Behavior and Human Decision Processes* 66, 102–10.

Russo, J. E., Meloy, M. G. and Medvec, V. H. (1998) Predecisional distortion of product information, *Journal of Marketing Research* 35, 438–52.

Russo, J. E., Meloy, M. G. and Wilks, T. J. (2000) Predecisional distortion of information by auditors and salespersons, *Management Science* 46, 13–27.

Sand, P. H. (2000) The precautionary principle: a European perspective, *Human and Ecological Risk Assessment* 6, 445–58.

Santillo, D. and Johnston, P. (1999) Is there a role for risk assessment within precautionary legislation? *Human and Ecological Risk Assessment* 5, 923–32.

Satterfield, T., Slovic, P. and Gregory, R. (2000) Narrative valuation in a policy judgment context, *Ecological Economics* 34, 315–31.

Sexton, K. (1999) Setting environmental priorities: is comparative risk assessment the answer? in K. Sexton, A. A. Marcu, K. W. Easterand and T. D. Burkhardt (eds) *Better Environmental Decisions: Strategies for Governments, Businesses, and Communities*, pp. 195–219. Washington, DC: Island Press.

Sexton, K. and Zimmerman, R. (1999) The emerging role of environmental justice in decision making, in K. Sexton, A. A. Marcus, K. W. Easterand and T. D. Burkhardt (eds) *Better Environmental Decisions: Strategies for Governments, Businesses, and Communities*, pp. 419–43. Washington, DC: Island Press.

Shapin, S. (1994) *A Social History of Truth.* Chicago: University of Chicago Press.

Shlyakhter, A.I. (1994) Improved framework for uncertainty analysis: accounting for unsuspected errors, *Risk Analysis* 14, 441–47.

Siegrist, M. and Cvetkovich, G. (2000) Perception of hazards: the role of social trust and knowledge, *Risk Analysis* 20, 713–19.

Slovic, P. (1986) Perception of risk, *Science* 236, 280–85.

Slovic, P. (1993) Perceived risk, trust, and democracy, *Risk Analysis* 13, 675–82.

Small, M. J. and Fischbeck, P. S. (1999) False precision in Bayesian updating with incomplete models, *Human and Ecological Risk Assessment* 5, 291–304.

Smithson, M., Bartos, T. and Takemura, K. (2000) Human judgment under sample space ignorance, *Risk Decision and Policy* 5, 135–50.

Soderstrom, E. J., Sorensen, J. H., Copenhaver, E. D. and Carnes, S. A. (1984) Risk perception in an interest group context: an examination of the TMI restart issue, *Risk Analysis* 4, 231–44.

Sox, H. C., Blatt, M. A., Higgins, M. C. and Marton, K. I. (1988) *Medical Decision Making*. Newton, MA: Butterworth-Heinemann.

Stern, P. C. and Fineberg, H. V. (eds) (1996) *Understanding Risk: Informing Decisions in a Democratic Society*. Washington, DC: National Academy Press.

Svenson, O. (1996) Decision making and the search for fundamental psychological regularities: what can be learned from a process perspective? *Organizational Behavior and Human Decision Processes* 65, 252–67.

Swets, J. A. (1992) The science of choosing the right decision threshold in high-stakes diagnostics, *American Psychologist* 47, 522–32.

Swets, J. A., Dawes, R. M. and Monahan, J. (2000) Psychological science can improve diagnostic decisions, *Psychological Science in the Public Interest* 1, 1–26.

Thompson, J. C. (1950) A numerical method for forecasting rainfall in the Los Angeles area, *Monthly Weather Review* 78, 113–24.

Thompson, J. C. and Brier, G. W. (1955) The economic utility of weather forecasts, *Monthly Weather Review* 83, 249–54.

Tickner, J. A. (1999) A map toward precautionary decision making, in C. Raffensperger and J. Tickner (eds), *Protecting Public Health and the Environment: Implementing the Precautionary Principle*, pp. 162–86. Washington, DC: Island Press.

Tversky, A. and Kahneman, D. (1971) Belief in the law of small numbers, *Psychological Bulletin* 2, 105–10.

Tversky, A. and Kahneman, D. (1992) Advances in prospect theory: cumulative representation of uncertainty, *Journal of Risk and Uncertainty* 5, 297–323.

US Environmental Protection Agency (1992) *Environmental Equity: Reducing Risk for All Communities*. Washington, DC: Office of Policy, Planning, and Evaluation.

Walley, P. (1996) Inference from multinomial data: learning about a bag of marbles (with discussion), *Journal of the Royal Statistical Association, Series B* 58, 3–57.

Winkler, R. L. (1980) Prior information, predictive distributions, and Bayesian model-building, in A. Zellner (ed), *Bayesian Analysis in Econometrics and Statistics: Essays in Honor of Harold Jeffreys*, pp. 95–109. Amsterdam: North-Holland.

Winkler, R. L. and Murphy, A. H. (1985) Decision analysis, in A. H. Murphy and R. W. Katz (eds), *Probability, Statistics, and Decision Making in the Atmospheric Sciences*, pp. 493–524. Boulder, CO: Westview Press.

Wolfson, L. J. (1995) Elicitation of Priors and Utilities for Bayesian Analysis. Unpublished doctoral dissertation, Carnegie Mellon University, Pittsburgh, PA.

Wolfson, L. J., Kadane, J. B. and Small, M. J. (1996a) Bayesian environmental policy decisions: two case studies, *Ecological Applications* 6, 1056–66.

Wolfson, L. J., Kadane, J. B. and Small, M. J. (1996b) Expected utility as a policy-making tool, in D. A. Berry and D. K. Stangl (eds) *Bayesian Biostatistics*, pp. 261–77. New York: Marcel Dekker.

Wolfson, L. J., Kadane, J. B. and Small, M. J. (1997) A subjective Bayesian approach to environmental sampling, in C. Gatsonis, J. S. Hodges, R. E. Kass, R. McCulloch, P. Rossiand and N. D. Singpurwalla (eds) *Case Studies in Bayesian Statistics*, Vol. III, pp. 457–68. New York: Springer-Verlag.

Wolpert, R. L. (1989) Eliciting and combining subjective judgments about uncertainty, *International Journal of Technology Assessment in Health Care* 5, 537–57.

Wynne, B. (1987) *Risk Management and Hazardous Wastes: Implementation and the Dialectics of Credibility*. Berlin, Germany: Springer.

Yosie, T. F. (2000, December) *Science-Based Decision Making at the Crossroads: Information, Choices and Values*. Paper presented at the annual meeting of the Society for Risk Analysis, Arlington, VA.

13

Risk Regulation Under Pressure: Problem-Solving or Blame-Shifting?

Christopher Hood and Henry Rothstein

Background: Openness in Risk Regulation Regimes

Openness and transparency in regulation is conventionally regarded as a formula for 'good governance' because of its expected effects in reducing corruption and transaction costs, increasing legitimacy and legality of regulation, and improving policy quality through enhanced intelligence and learning (see, e.g., Bentham, 1931, p410, and 1983, p410; New Zealand Treasury, 1987, p48; Brin, 1998). The aim of this chapter is to assess how widespread demands for increased openness are in risk regulation and how organizations engaged in risk regulation and management respond to such pressures. To what extent or in what conditions do they seek to contain the pressure, alter what they do, or simply roll with the punch?

There are plenty of bar-room anecdotes about the organizational politics of such responses. But research of a more systematic kind is still in its infancy. In a partial attempt to fill the gap, this chapter draws on a detailed study of risk regulation regimes (RRRs) in six different policy domains (see Hood et al, 1999). The aim is to explore how far conventional accounts of organizational responses to environmental disturbance describe institutional behaviour in the face of pressures for increased openness and transparency. The next (second) section defines openness and identifies pressures for openness in the RRR six-pack referred to above. The third section lays out some hypotheses about expected institutional responses and outlines a standard disturbance-response model of institutional behaviour in the face of pressures for increased openness. The fourth section describes observed institutional behaviour in three regimes subject to strong pressures for increasing openness, and the fifth section assesses the fit between observed behaviour and the hypotheses described earlier. The sixth section develops a hybrid form of two of the hypotheses, and the final section discusses what has been learned and its implications for policy.

Defining and Tracking RRR Openness

Increasing openness is defined for this purpose as involving some or all of the following three elements:

1. greater transparency in organizational procedure;
2. wider participation in some or all elements of an RRR; and
3. heightened accountability in the sense of increased obligations on the part of those responsible for regulating and managing risks to explain and justify their behaviour to others.

Indicators of a change in openness as defined above accordingly include changes in information rules (extending access to information) and participation rules (extending the range of players in the decision process) and de facto accountability by decision-makers to public scrutiny. Openness in the sense defined above can be analytically distinguished from social pressures for increased openness in the form of campaigns by media, law courts, business lobbies, politicians or other pressure groups. The extent of media scrutiny overlaps the condition of openness and pressures for greater openness, but pressures for greater openness are here taken to mean specific demands for change in that direction coming from business interests, the media, and other lobby groups.

Some changes in openness in risk regulation and management may go across a whole society or legal jurisdiction (for instance, with freedom of information measures, human rights conventions, or larger cultural shifts). And there is no doubt that some domains of risk regulation, like food safety, health care and nuclear power, have experienced considerable pressures for increased openness over the past decade or two. Nevertheless, social and political pressures to increase openness in RRRs do not seem to be of equal intensity for all types of risk, despite generalizations sometimes offered about risk regulation as a whole being exposed to such pressures (Health and Safety Executive, 1998, p6; Royal Commission on Environmental Pollution, 1998). Appendixes A and B describe changes in the three elements of openness noted above for six selected domains of risk regulation in the United Kingdom. Those domains are as follows: (a) domestic radon – a natural radioactive gas that seeps into homes in some parts of the country; (b) dangerous dogs; (c) road risk regulation, particularly concerning the changing balance of road risks between those in motor vehicles and other road users; (d) benzene – the car exhaust air pollutant and genotoxic carcinogen; (e) the release of paedophile ex-offenders into the community; and (f) pesticide residues in food and drinking water.

Appendix A summarizes the continuing 'openness' characteristics of three RRRs (radon, dangerous dogs and road risks) that do not seem to have been subjected to substantially increasing pressures for openness over the past two decades. Appendix B gives the same information for three other RRRs (benzene, paedophile release and pesticide residues in food and drinking water) where pressures for openness appear to have grown. In each case, we present the salient features of the information rules and conventions operating within the RRR (legal obligations or conventions on reporting, collecting and disclosing information), the participation and scrutiny rules, and the amount of de facto accountability to public or media scrutiny by those regulating or managing the risk. Putting those three elements together enables us to assess the overall level of openness of the RRR, though that assessment is necessarily qualitative. Scoring overall regime openness is certainly not an exact science.

Nevertheless, even from a broad-brush qualitative analysis of a limited set of cases, we can draw at least three general conclusions. First, as noted earlier, RRRs vary considerably both in their point of departure – the status quo level of openness – and also in the degree of change in openness over recent decades. Second, regimes starting from a low base in openness are not necessarily exposed to strong 'catching up' pressures to converge with those starting from a high base. Although the appendixes include at least one case of an RRR (road risks) starting from a relatively high status quo level of openness that shows little change from the status quo level, the reverse does not always apply. The domestic radon case in the United Kingdom shows that in the absence of outside pressure, there can be a low degree of movement from a low status quo level (Leiss et al, 1998).

Third, although all the three 'change cases' described in Appendix A are regimes previously dominated by cohesive professional policy communities, Appendix B shows RRRs can move to greater openness in different ways and in response to different pressures. This finding shows the value of a comparative-regime approach for the analysis of regulatory dynamics and also suggests that a plurality of styles and routes to openness may lead to different policy or institutional consequences, given the conventional expectations about the effects of policy openness as summarized at the outset.

To better understand the consequences of openness pressures, the institutional responses in those regimes experiencing high pressures for change from the status quo need to be examined (given that neither the condition of openness nor pressures for greater openness appear universal or uniform in RRRs). Accordingly, we give a detailed account of institutional changes in the three cases in Appendix B, after considering hypotheses about institutional responses in the next section.

Hypotheses about Responses to Pressures for Openness in RRRs

What institutional responses to pressures for openness might be expected within RRRs? Many scholars have commented on the diversity of institutional theory (e.g. Hall and Taylor, 1997) and some have even questioned whether there is any distinctive institutional approach at all (e.g. John, 1998, p65). But a theme that runs through much institutional analysis is a vision of human organizations and conventions as relatively closed systems that adapt selectively to environmental disturbance (the disturbance in this case being pressures for increased openness). Selective adaptation means that institutions adopt strategies for survival that seek to reconcile their own purposes and imperatives with environmental conditions or external demands. Institutions are thus seen as filters or distorting lenses in their dealings with the outside world – e.g. in Clay and Schaffer's (1984, p10) 'bureaucratic paradox,' in which organizations focus on what is readily doable whether it contributes to some larger purpose or not. Although such ideas are often linked with biological evolutionary-strategy metaphors, they can be derived from independent propositions about individual and social behaviour.

Responses to demands for increased openness in risk regulation offer a particularly good test site for this institutionalist perspective. There are good reasons to expect the filtering or distorting processes that institutionalists emphasize because more transparency, participation and accountability can increase the threat of blame and liability for failures or make regulators' work more stressful and conflict laden. Indeed, one of the reasons institutions limit openness in risk regulation in the first place is to limit or deflect blame and liability (in line with standard advice from lawyers and insurers to 'never admit fault'). So in spite of the policy consequences conventionally expected to flow from increased openness, as discussed at the outset, there are especially strong reasons to expect a filtering response to demands for increased openness in risk regulation, whether in the form of privacy protection (Brin, 1998), official secrecy or commercial confidentiality.

Three hypotheses about institutional responses to demands for more RRR openness were initially examined. None of them imply anything about the desirability or otherwise of organizational adaptation to pressures for change, and all of them were initially examined at the level of individual organizations rather than regimes (we shall return to the regime perspective later). The three hypotheses are as follows:

- *Null hypothesis.* A null hypothesis is one of neutral compliance by organizations to external demands without perceptible filtering or distortion. Full compliance behaviour can be considered a null hypothesis because, by positing that organizational responses to demands for increased openness will be straightforward and unproblematic, it runs against the central tenet of institutionalist analysis.
- *Autopoiesis.* At the opposite extreme, a hypothesis drawn from the idea of autopoiesis (the tendency toward self-closure in the conceptual programmes of bounded systems with rich patterns of 'discourse' that makes it impossible to exert direct control over those systems from outside (Brans and Rossbach, 1997, pp432ff). From an autopoietic perspective, institutions would tend to respond to pressures for greater openness in ways that reproduced their own purposes (particularly over issues of blame shifting and blame avoidance) or modi operandi with minimal disturbance.
- *Staged-response pattern.* Then there is a hypothesis somewhere between the first and the second that posits a staged-response pattern. The idea is that institutions respond to pressures for increased openness in a series of phases or steps that amount to a staged retreat or rearguard action away from some initially preferred position in the face of pressure for abandonment of that position. Style-phase models of such staged-retreat responses are common in institutional theory (see, e.g., Beck Jørgensen, 1985, 1987; Joo, 1999). And it is common to distinguish, following Levy (1986), between first-order and second-order responses by organizations to environmental disturbance. First-order responses involve shifts in managerial arrangements and other organizational systems that leave core value systems or deeper structures unchanged. Second-order responses involve changes in those value systems.

In a well-known development of this general approach, Laughlin (1991; see also Laughlin and Broadbent, 1995) and his colleagues have further differentiated first-order and second-order institutional responses to environmental disturbance. Laughlin divides first-order responses into rebuttal (responses designed to resist the disturbance) and reorientation (responses designed to change an organization without affecting its core values). Similarly, second-order responses, involving changes in core values, are divided into colonization (where new core values have colonized part of the

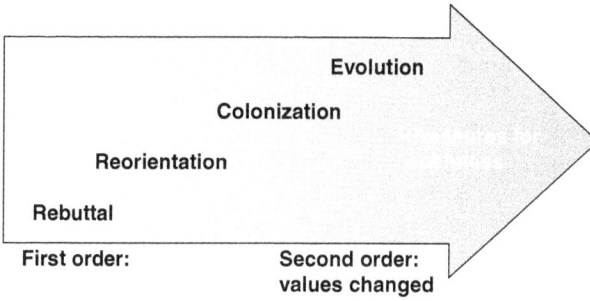

Figure 13.1 *Institutional responses to environmental disturbance: Laughlin's (1991) four types of change conceived as a progressive set of responses*

organization) and evolution (where all stakeholders have absorbed the new core values). Evolution would have a different meaning at the level of regimes rather than single organizations, as we discuss later, but for the moment, the focus is mainly on adaptation at the level of individual organizations.

Laughlin does not present the four responses in style-phase terms, though he argues that the first three are 'progressive' in some sense (Laughlin, 1991, p200). He suggests that evolution will normally be produced by forces different from the other three responses and argues that attempts to produce colonization change in organizations by increasing financial pressure will not always succeed. Nevertheless, for our third hypothesis, we modify Laughlin's approach by representing the four responses as progressive forms of staged retreat, going from the least to the most radical kind of adaptation as outside pressure for change continues. The hypothesis is that in such circumstances, organizations move from first-order to second-order responses following the pathway depicted in Figure 13.1. This hypothesis is a mixture of the null hypothesis and the autopoietic hypothesis in that it leads us to expect first-order responses to new environmental demands that involve some element of autopoiesis, to be followed later by responses that are closer to the null hypothesis.

A Tale of Three RRRs Facing Pressures for Increased Openness

We now examine the relative plausibility of the three hypotheses set out above by analysing the institutional dynamics of the three RRRs that were exposed to continuing pressure for increased openness as outlined in Appendixes A and B. This section gives a brief narrative account of developments in each of those three RRRs, and we assess the hypotheses in the light of these cases in the following section. The focus is on the collection of organizations involved in risk regulation in each regime, comprising both public-sector organizations and third-sector or corporate organizations with a role as intermediaries in regulation (notably in the form of obligations on corporations to operate first-line controls subject to general oversight from regulators).

Regulating the risk of paedophiles released from custody

Increased awareness and public discussion of the sexual abuse of children by adults has been observable in the United Kingdom and many other developed countries over the past decade. Although statistically, the greatest risk to children of murder or sexual abuse comes overwhelmingly from family members, public debate focuses largely on risks from strangers, particularly those with a criminal record for such offences. Several interviewees from the police, probation and social services told us that as recently as 15 years ago, neither these services nor the public saw the risk of child sexual abuse as widespread. The state was not obliged to collect systematic information on the whereabouts and risks of ex-offenders in the community. Such information as existed was limited and ad hoc, rarely shared among the relevant state organizations (police, probation officers, housing and social-services professionals) and never relayed to the general public.

Professional and public concern about the risks from paedophiles in the community grew in the 1990s, in the context of controversial child sexual abuse investigations, releases from prison of high-profile ex-offenders, and cases of infiltration of state education and social welfare organizations by paedophiles. What-to-do debates focused on the information held by the state on offenders, the sharing of that information among police and other public agencies, and its public disclosure. Central to the debate was a risk–risk trade-off issue. Reducing the risk of child sexual abuse by publicly identifying released paedophiles may increase the risk of vigilante activity. The prospect of increased vigilante activity in turn increases incentives for ex-offenders to go underground, out of the reach of support and surveillance services, thus potentially mitigating or confounding the intended goal of risk reduction. Such downside risks of transparency have been much stressed by civil libertarians both in the United States and the United Kingdom.

The UK government response to increased public concern was the 1997 Sex Offenders Act. Paralleling similar developments in the United States, the Act required the police to record the names and addresses of child sex offenders.[1] The UK regime was heavily biased against public disclosure of information on the Sex Offenders Register, however, in contrast to the transparent arrangements adopted by some US states under the 1994 Megan's Law (Brin, 1998, p19). Although the 1997 Act allowed for disclosure in some conditions, the state authorities committed substantial resources to preventing leaks and defending a no-disclosure policy. They avoided the use of court-imposed restrictions on offenders that would reveal identity and fought off pressures for disclosure through the courts.[2]

Even so, the legal requirement that police systematically collect information on ex-offenders potentially increased the 'blamability' of police, probation and other welfare bureaucracies for inept risk management if released paedophiles reoffended. In consequence, there were at least three changes in the institutional management of released offenders.

One strategy was the adoption of more collegial behaviour among the various bureaucracies involved in the management of released offenders. This strategy aided the risk management process by increasing information flow between public agencies and, increasingly, trusted third-sector voluntary organizations. The adoption of collegial risk-management processes, however, also limited the blame potential for any single agency in the event of a tragedy by distributing responsibility among all parties.

Linked to the collegial strategy was the adoption of more formal written procedures or checklists for risk assessment and management of ex-offenders. The ostensible purpose of such protocols was to improve risk decision-making, particularly in allocating scarce resources. But they also served the important purpose (as noted by many of our interviewees) of limiting blame by forming the basis of a procedural defence for officials if registered offenders committed further offences.

A third change, albeit limited, was the classic 'not in my backyard' (NIMBY) response, in the form of a few local authorities refusing to provide public housing for ex-offenders in their communities. In other cases, some local authorities and housing organizations had to shoulder increased burdens because a bias toward conservative risk assessment by local police and probation officials (seeking to protect themselves from blame in the event of reoffence) led to a large number of released offenders being classed as 'high risk'. Local authority reluctance to provide public housing for high-profile offenders led central government to create secure accommodations for a small number of hard-to-place offenders in one of the English prisons, but that move itself encountered substantial local resistance.

Arrangements for control of pesticide residues in food and drinking water

Risks to human health from pesticide residues in food and drinking water have attracted public and lobby-group attention since the early days of the environmental movement in the 1960s and have been identified as a 'dread risk' in the well-known Oregon risk-perception studies (Slovic et al, 1980, p191). But until the 1980s, regulation focused on official approval of pesticides rather than on monitoring or controlling residue levels in food and drinking water. In an era of public-enterprise drinking water supply there was little or no external regulation other than a statutory duty to supply 'wholesome' water. But this concept was not legally defined and it seems to have been assumed that professionalism and public service ethos on the part of water suppliers could be relied on to ensure drinking water was clean and safe (Healey, 1992). Food retailers and suppliers were similarly subject to general safety regulations that implied avoidance of excessive pesticide residue levels, but no specific limits were laid down in law.

That fairly relaxed approach to regulation of pesticide residue levels changed both for food and drinking water in the 1980s, though in different ways. In the case of food, the UK government started to introduce statutory maximum residue levels for some pesticides in 1988. Commercial confidentiality arguments largely prevailed, however, such that food retailers and suppliers were not obliged to disclose pesticide residue levels to consumers, and the same went for the local authorities responsible for enforcement. At central government level, some ad hoc monitoring of pesticide residues was undertaken by the Ministry of Agriculture, Fisheries and Food (MAFF) from 1957, and from 1988 this monitoring developed into a systematic testing programme with aggregated results published annually but sample sources anonymized.

As pressure continued for more openness and transparency, the Pesticides Safety Directorate – the UK government agency responsible for pesticides – responded in two ways. First, it extended participation in debate over pesticide regulation by establishing a Pesticides Forum in 1996, which included a broader group of stakeholders, such as established and trusted consumer and green groups, than the formerly narrow group of insider expert and agribusiness consultees. Second, in 1999 central government decided to move away from the previous aggregated and anonymized residue reporting to a new 'name and shame' approach that identified the retailers and suppliers of food tested (MAFF, 1999). This apparently radical shift toward greater transparency was limited, however, in that annual reporting allowed errant food suppliers to claim that the problems identified had long been remedied, with suppliers notified at least eight weeks in advance of publication. It also led, perhaps predictably, to greater scrutiny of the adequacy of the government's sampling and testing methodologies by supermarkets, putting more pressure on the transparency of those arrangements.

A more substantial shift toward transparency took place in the case of drinking water, which perhaps offers the clearest case of a move from a first-order to a second-order response in the face of demands for more openness. In 1980, levels of pesticide residues in drinking water were limited to a surrogate-zero level of 0.1 parts per billion (ppb) by a much-discussed European Commission (EC) Drinking Water Directive (1980) that epitomized the precautionary doctrine in risk management. The initial response to this directive was far from transparent. At first (according to industry and regulatory officials we interviewed), it was simply assumed that the EC's surrogate-zero threshold was by and large being met, conveniently rendering any extensive monitoring effort unnecessary. Research in the early 1980s, however, revealed that pesticide levels in drinking water in the United Kingdom, and particularly England, exceeded the EC limit in many cases. The UK government responded by invoking scientific advice that most of the breaches did not represent any health hazard and campaigned (unsuccessfully) on several occasions for the replacement of the EC's blanket precautionary limit by generally higher health-based limits for individual pesticides.[3] In the meantime, UK ministers formally advised water companies that they did not have to observe the precautionary limit as long as health-based limits specified by government were met (see Healey and Jones, 1989).

Only a few other European Union (EU) member states undertook any monitoring for pesticide residues in drinking water. Member states' response to EU requests for information tended to be one of delay, meaning that the EC had little information on this subject. Even though monitoring became mandatory across the EU after the renegotiation of the directive in 1998, delay in reporting is likely to be a continuing feature of many member state responses.

A major step toward transparency in the UK regime came with the privatization of drinking water supply in England and Wales in 1989 (Ward et al, 1995). This privatization conveniently removed direct public responsibility for water supply in those parts of the country (specifically England) where pesticide contamination of drinking water was a real issue. Part of the privatization settlement was an enhanced regulatory regime that embodied freedom of information requirements over pesticide residue levels along with mandatory monitoring, such that breaches of the limit were openly established. Water companies had to put forward plans to deal with pesticide residues and because privatization around £2 billion has been spent on compliance, with the costs fully borne by captive consumers because the price control regulatory regime for drinking water allowed full cost pass-through.

Arrangements for control of ambient benzene

Benzene, an air pollutant associated mainly with vehicle exhausts, has been known as a genotoxic carcinogen for almost 30 years. But until the 1990s, little or no information was collected on levels of ambient benzene and there were no legal maximum limits. A similar 'unpolitics' (Crenson, 1971) applied to benzene in other European countries. Indeed, one interviewee claimed that ambient benzene only came onto the risk regulation agenda in the late 1980s when a petrochemical company objected to proposals to reduce levels of lead in petrol on the grounds that benzene emissions would be increased.

The long delay in introducing monitoring or targets for benzene began to change in the 1990s. Systematic monitoring of urban air quality began to develop in the early 1990s, replacing an earlier uneven and ad hoc approach. And, following the line of least resistance, government began publishing the results (on CEEFAX and the Internet) to avoid the need for bespoke responses to green groups and others demanding data under European rules on freedom of access to environmental information (SI 1992 No. 3240). Specific targets for benzene, with a long lead time, began to be introduced from the mid-1990s. In 1997, the UK government set an 'objective' (whether it is a justiciable limit is ambiguous, according to the government's own lawyers) of not more than 5 ppb as an air quality standard, to take effect only in 2004 (SI 2000 No. 928) In a parallel process, the EU set a more stringent European objective of just over 1.5 ppb to be achieved by 2010, accompanied by mandatory monitoring by member states (see Department of Environment, Transport and Regions, 2000). The delay built into both of these targets reflected a calculation that changes in vehicle engine and fuel technology would eventually make the targets achievable without excessive pain to bureaucrats or voter drivers (see Department of Environment, Transport and Regions, 1998a, p7). But even then the long lead time creates the possibility that targets could be altered later if non-achievement seems likely closer to the operative dates.

In setting the benzene objective, the UK government drew on the recommendations of an expert panel (Expert Panel on Air Quality Standards and Department of Environment, 1994) that used a new methodology for assessing risk from genotoxic carcinogens. The objective provoked pressure for more transparency from the petrochemical industry, fearful that its interests might be threatened by the new standards. The department responsible (Department of Environment, Transport and the Regions) responded to such criticism in a review of advisory processes, concluding that full openness might inhibit candid discussion among expert advisers. The proposal was therefore to publish non-verbatim minutes or not attribute remarks to named individuals (Department of Environment, Transport and the Regions, 1998b, p11).

The advent of transparent monitoring and quantified standards for air quality was accompanied by at least two notable institutional changes. One was legislation in 1995 (The Environment Act 1995) that laid on local authorities the responsibility for assessing and reviewing air quality in their areas to meet centrally imposed standards. This legislation could be interpreted as an effort by central government to share or shift blame in the UK context, even though the division of responsibilities between central and local government (for instance, over trunk roads and local roads) create fertile opportunities for mutual blame avoidance.[4] A second development was that if local authorities failed to achieve the UK targets set to take effect in 2004, the preparation of an action plan to reduce benzene levels as part of an Air Quality Management Zone would serve as a procedural defence against legal or regulatory sanctions.[5]

Evaluating the Initial Hypotheses

Table 13.1 summarizes the institutional responses to openness pressures within each of the three 'high-pressure' RRRs described above, identifying responses that are consistent with the three hypotheses set out earlier. It may surprise those who see the first two hypotheses as 'straw men' to find that both of those hypotheses were consistent with several elements of observed organizational behaviour within each of the three high-pressure RRRs. However, neither the null hypothesis (of straightforward responses to demands to openness pressures) nor the autopoietic hypothesis (of closed discourse communities transforming every external demand into 'self-reproduction') can account for all the observed responses on its own. There was a substantial amount of organizational behaviour that fits institutionalist expectations of distortion or filtration, but there were also substantial changes in behaviour or the distribution of power. For instance, water companies and regulators had to get used to a transparency regime that would have been unthinkable 20 years before and new benzene standards set the stage for an attempt by central government to shift at least part of the blame (or glory) over compliance to local authorities.

By a process of elimination, we might conclude that observed organizational behaviour in these three cases fits the staged-response hypothesis more closely than the other two. Recall from Figure 13.1 that Laughlin and Broadbent (1995) divided first-order institutional responses to environmental disturbance into rebuttal and reorientation strategies. Both strategies were readily observable in the three high-pressure RRRs. Problem denial and resistance to demands for transparent operation occurred in some form in all of them, often (but not always) at an early stage of policy development – such as the defensive information-sharing approach developed in the paedophiles regime. Reorientation also figured prominently in institutional behaviour, notably in the redistribution of responsibilities with the aim of reducing blame or liability or the introduction of additional complexity into organizational structures. An example was central government's designation of local authorities as responsible for local air quality with the advent of standards and monitoring, creating a structure in which blame for failure to meet targets is ambiguous.

But little evidence could be found of a clear progression from a first-order of unchanged institutional values to a second-order when those values had changed. Drinking water seemed to be the only fairly clear-cut case of such a progression because it moved from an initial pattern of see-no-evil denial and regulatory collusion over evasion in the public-enterprise era to a substantially transparent regime after privatization. Across much of what was observed in institutional responses, it seems hard to argue that there was a clear shift between what Laughlin (1991) and similar analysts see as first-order institutional responses to disturbances to second-order responses at a later stage.

Table 13.1 *Institutional responses to pressures for increased openness within three risk regulation regimes*

	Risk regulation regime domain		
	Arrangements for release of paedophiles	*Control of pesticide residues*	*Control of ambient benzene*
Degree and type of pressure for openness	Strong public and media pressure for public disclosure over released paedophiles but counter-pressures on privacy from human rights lobbies and institutions	General public and media concern for more information over pesticide residues; business concern with commercial confidentiality and regulatory requirements	General public and green lobby pressure for more information on general air pollution, rather than benzene in particular; strong business pressure for transparency over standards
Features of regulator response			
Fitting null hypothesis	Substantial resources committed by police to collection of information on released ex-offenders	Post-1989 privatized water companies now generally meet European Commission limits after public disclosure at first revealed breaches of those limits	Many local authorities adopted a 'get on with it' approach and central government took line of least resistance in publishing monitoring data under European Union monitoring rules
Fitting autopoietic hypothesis	Alteration of procedures to keep public disclosure to the minimum	Pre-1989 state-owned water suppliers simply ignored EC limits (but on ministerial advice)	Flexible approach to national targets and objectives – goalposts movable in the event of non-compliance

Table 13.1 *Institutional responses to pressures for increased openness within three risk regulation regimes (cont'd)*

	Risk regulation regime domain		
	Arrangements for release of paedophiles	*Control of pesticide residues*	*Control of ambient benzene*
Fitting staged-response hypothesis	Not much more than "first-order" responses discernible (e.g. more resources committed to explaining policy of non-disclosure); alteration of procedures to limit possibility of blame shifting by "hang-together" approaches; extension of checklist approach and written procedures to provide procedural defence against blame; NIMBY approach of refusal to house by a few local authorities	Not much more than "first-order" responses discernible in food (with reorientation of regulators to "control of control" but limited and delayed disclosure policy over noncompliance). Apparently, clearer case of progression to second order in drinking water, with eventual move to "transparent compliance" approach after earlier delay and regulatory collusion over evasion	Not much more than first-order responses discernible, with developing 'inertia compliance' approach of delaying onset of targets until long-term technological changes can be expected to deliver compliance without 'hard choices', linked with reorientation of formal responsibility to make culpability ambiguous in the event of non-compliance

Indeed, the organizational value that seems most consistent with the pattern of responses described in the last section is that of limiting blame and liability. But blame-and-liability limiting considerations had different implications for organizations dependent on their institutional position. In the high-pressure regimes, public-sector regulators adopted reorientation or rebuttal strategies where new standards threatened to increase their exposure to blame or make their jobs more stressful, as in the case of paedophiles. But those public regulators took up different stances where openness could not be expected to have such consequences (as in the case of ambient benzene, where the long delay over implementation against a changing pattern of vehicle and fuel technology meant standards would be likely to be reached by a process of inertia compliance).

Similar variation applied to private-sector organizations where they formed part of the regulatory regimes, notably as intermediaries applying enforced self-regulation (Ayres and Braithwaite, 1992), as in the cases of pesticide residues in food and water. Where such organizations were in competitive markets, as in the case of food and agribusiness companies, blame-and-liability limitation led them to press for greater transparency over regulatory standard setting, but to oppose it over enforcement on grounds of commercial confidentiality. However, private-sector organizations in monopoly positions with pass-through price control regimes, as in the case of the privatized water utilities, had much less reason to adopt such a position. If blame-and-liability limitation was a key consideration in organizational responses to demands for greater openness, it played out differently according to institutional position and type, and it could play out differently at regime and organizational level.

Modifying the Initial Hypotheses

A hypothesis that would fit best with these, admittedly limited, observations seems to be a mixture of the second and third hypotheses (i.e. a weak form of autopoiesis and a staged-response approach dominated by first-order responses at an organizational level). A modified hypothesis of that type, compatible with the behaviour observed, would have the following seven components:

1   The response of individual regulator organizations to demands for increased openness in RRRs is heavily conditioned by the expected implications for blame and liability, but those implications are not the same for all organizations.
2   Where a shift to increased openness and transparency has major expected implications for blame and liability, organizations facing demands for greater openness will tend to engage in blame prevention re-engineering (BPR),[6] seeking to transfer or dissipate the increased blame or liability that increased transparency or new information requirements might bring.
3   The repertoire of BPR responses at the organizational level can be broadly characterized in Laughlin's (1991) terms as variants of rebuttal and reorientation behaviour, but comprised at least six different specific responses, as shown in Table 13.2. Apart from simple rebuttal and reorientation in the ordinary-language sense of these terms, the four other observed responses were as follows:

- *Delay* in responding to demands for greater openness was a feature of observed organizational behaviour in all the high-pressure regimes. Delay is a common bureaucratic response to freedom of information regimes – see, for example, Roberts's (1998, pp3–6) analysis of responses to Canadian freedom of information legislation. The clearest example from the three regimes was the delay by EU member states (in some cases by up to several years) in supplying information to the European Commission on pesticide residue levels in drinking water in the mid-1990s. Variants on the delay theme also included planned obsolescence in reporting violations of standards (pesticide residues in food) and delaying the onset of targets when monitoring information becomes available (ambient benzene). Finally, in the paedophiles regime, the police only disclosed the identity of known offenders to the public as a last resort if nothing else could ensure public safety.
- *Prebuttal* was also an observed BPR response by organizations facing demands for increased openness – attempts by organizations to respond to anticipated criticisms or demands for information before they materialize. At one level, this response involves an increase in organizational sophistication or capacity to cope with a 'goldfish-bowl' existence (more flak-catchers and environmental scanners to get the organization's retaliation in first, which was a notable feature of police responses to the 1997 Sex Offenders Act). The key feature of prebuttal is the manufacture of excuses or alibis in advance, such that attempts to blame an organization in the light of increased transparency will fail to hit their target.
- *Protocolization*, or formalization of organizational operations, was a third observed BPR response, and indeed such behaviour is a standard bureaucratic approach to minimizing blame and liability problems (see Lawton and Parker, 1998). Following transparent rules potentially provides due diligence defences when an organization's risk management comes to be questioned and produces a verifiable audit trail for regulators (see Power, 1997). As the account of the three RRRs indicated, protocolization in some form appeared in all cases and particularly in the paedophile regime, where it was central to the defensive BPR strategy of the public organizations concerned.
- *Service abandonment* – the abandonment of some types of service altogether – was observable as a drastic BPR response to openness pressures in some cases. Such a response is more commonly observable among regulatees (particularly small or marginal operators faced with increasing regulatory burdens) than among regulators or public authorities. But it can occur in the latter case, for instance, when public authorities stop issuing advice or information for fear of blame, legal liability or other adverse reactions. In the three high-pressure regimes, the clearest case of service abandonment was observed in the paedophiles regime. That was the refusal by some local authorities to resettle paedophile ex-offenders classed as high risk by the

Table 13.2 *Six varieties of institutional response*

Institutional response	Risk regulation regime domain		
	Management of paedophile release	*Pesticide residues in food and drinking water*	*Ambient benzene*
Delay	Public disclosure of information about paedophiles only as final resort	Heavy emphasis in drinking water (e.g. delay by some EU member states in reporting levels of pesticide residues in drinking water and built-in delay in 'naming and shaming' policy over food)	Heavy emphasis – 20-year delay in developing monitoring after discovery of benzene as a genotoxic pollutant; delay in EU member states' response to Commission demands for information; delay of onset of targets until technological change makes them likely to be achievable without pain
Simple rebuttal	Rejection and legal contestation of demands for greater public disclosure	Original denial of compliance problem over drinking water, followed by assertion that no health hazard involved in breach of EC precautionary limits; use of commercial confidentiality to limit public disclosure over food	
Organizational reorientation	Pooling information to share blame for management of risks of registered paedophiles	Privatization of water in England and Wales creating greater ambiguity over blame in failure to meet standards	Assignment of management responsibilities to local authorities, creating a structure of studied ambiguity through organizational complexification over blame for non-achievement of targets

Table 13.2 *Six varieties of institutional response (cont'd)*

Institutional response	Risk regulation regime domain		
	Management of paedophile release	*Pesticide residues in food and drinking water*	*Ambient benzene*
Service abandonment	Some local authorities refusing to house registered paedophiles		
Protocolization	Checklist approach as a procedural defence against blame	'Due diligence' checklist defence developed in food after 1990 Food Safety Act, and in water	'Management plan' as potential defence against blame by local authorities not in compliance with targets
Prebuttal	Increasing effort of agencies to explain management of offenders in the community to local residents without disclosing specific information	'Control of control' approach in food to limit regulator exposure to blame	

joint deliberation process described above. That service-abandonment response partly created the need for a national back-stop facility as described earlier.

4   The six types of blame prevention re-engineering responses discussed above and summarized in Table 13.2 will not necessarily succeed in deflecting blame in practice, and need not necessarily follow any fixed or uniform sequence. Although simple rebuttal can often be expected to come at an early stage in the sequence of responses, these cases suggest that rebuttal may precede, follow or accompany a delay response, and rebuttal's 'cousin' prebuttal may come later in the sequence of responses. Service abandonment, protocolization, and reorganization of organizational boundaries, procedures or responsibilities likewise need not take place in any particular order.

5   Many of the six organizational BPR responses observed here are hard to categorize according to the distinction between first- and second-order responses discussed earlier. Many if not all of them could be responses of both types. For example, prebuttal might be a sophisticated first-order response, representing a high point of anticipation and manipulative capacity. But it could also be a second-order response by an organization that has so thoroughly absorbed openness values that its public information base constitutes a way of nipping in the bud demands for more transparency. Protocolization also seems ambiguous in terms of any distinction between first-order and second-order responses because it could either be a symptom of an organization that has adopted new values or simply function as an official shield against prying outsiders, offering a procedural defence that established routines have been followed. Service abandonment too might be an extreme form of first-order response – perhaps the only way to keep underlying values unchanged – or it could be the ultimate expression of change in values.

6   This account of organizational responses to pressures for increased openness in RRRs, represented in Figure 13.2, is a mixture of weak autopoiesis and a less linear form of our initial third (staged-response) hypothesis. It looks less like an evolutionary ladder or stairway than a Catherine wheel (a type of rotating firework). It conceives of a problem space (constituted by demands for increased openness and accountability over risk management) to which organizations within a regime can respond in any of the ways discussed above. If those responses relieve the openness pressure, the system moves out of the problem space. But if the response fails to relieve the pressure, the system returns to the problem space for another iteration. There is no automatic sequence of response and no necessary ladder process. Apart from simple rebuttal (but not prebuttal), each of the organizational responses depicted in Figure 13.2 could be linked with both value change and value stasis.

7   Outcomes for openness at regime level will depend on the combination of individual organizational responses, and on the distribution of power among the various organizations in the regime. Even if some organizations within an RRR adopt a null-hypothesis response to pressures for greater openness, the regime as a whole will not necessarily exhibit greater openness if other organizations adopt autopoietic or first-order responses.

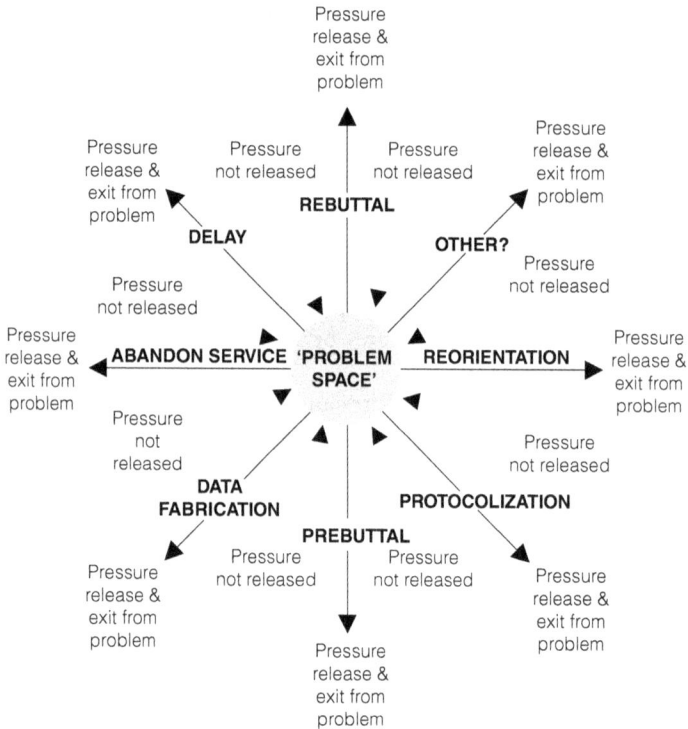

Figure 13.2 *A Catherine wheel approach to institutional blame prevention re-engineering*

Conclusion

The analysis here is based on a limited number of cases, so conclusions are tentative and the repertoire of observed responses by organizations to pressures for increased openness is not likely to be exhaustive. For instance, the response of data falsification, which has been observed in other risk and safety regimes (for example in nuclear safety and chemical safety; see Millstone, 1986, p99; *The Independent*, 1999), was not observed in the three high-pressure regimes examined here, though it is included among the repertoire of possible responses in Figure 13.2. Detailed investigation of more cases and further differentiation of types of pressures for increased openness (distinguishing, for instance, different sources and patterns of incidence over time) is needed for systematic identification of what types of pressures for openness produce what types of BPR responses in what types of organization.

Nevertheless, three fairly clear conclusions can be drawn from this study. First, not all domains of risk regulation are exposed equally – or at all – to long-term pressures for greater transparency and openness. Only half of the cases considered here fell into that category. Second, observation of institutional responses in three RRRs exposed to openness pressures suggests institutional filtering or distortion processes can readily be detected. The null hypothesis was compatible with only a minority of observations, and hence, it seems dangerous to base design of regulatory arrangements on some version of the null hypothesis. Such an assumption may lead to unanticipated 'toothpaste tube' outcomes (in the language of Baldwin and Hawkins, 1984, p582) in which a squeeze at one point in a regime is accompanied by a bulge at another and the net change is problematic. Something closer to an institutional-design equivalent of the well-known precautionary principle would seem a more robust basis for policy.

Third, much of what was observed in the three high-pressure RRRs is compatible with a model of dynamic interaction between organizations and their environment in which inertia is the default response and BPR considerations heavily influence a varied repertoire of further responses. The Catherine wheel schema portrayed by Figure 13.2 summarizes such a model. The implication is that society-wide generalizations about risk regulation based on aggregated conceptions of risk society (Beck, 1992) will have little power to predict or explain the variety (both static and dynamic) of risk regulation regimes. A less aggregated level of analysis, and more attention to institutional filtering, is needed for that purpose.

Three other more tentative and closely related conclusions can also be drawn from this study. One is that what happens over transparency and openness at the regime level of risk regulation can be different from what happens at the level of individual organizations. For example, in some risk domains numerous organizations may move to higher levels of openness, but the regime as a whole remains limitedly open because a key group of players whose information is needed to complete the loop in some way stay at the level of first-order responses. Something approximating to that pattern was exhibited in the pesticide residues in food regime (where enforced self-regulation by food retailers remained largely within the realms of commercial confidentiality). A regime can involve commercial confidentiality as the main bulwark against disclosure even if public institutions become procedurally more open. Alternatively, even if the various regulator organizations within an RRR respond to pressures for openness by increased organizational complexification (as in subcontracting or decoupling of RRRs), the upshot may be a regime that is even harder for ordinary consumers, workers or citizens to understand, hence substantively more opaque even if each component organization is procedurally more open.

Equally, in some domains all that is needed for the regime as a whole to move to greater transparency and openness is for one powerful organizational player to change its position. As we saw, in the case of pesticide residues in water, the UK central government's move to privatize the drinking water supply in England and Wales meant that it no longer had an interest in opacity over pesticide levels, and the result was a regime that was substantially open. To understand regulatory dynamics over openness, a distinction between regime and individual organizational responses and outcomes is crucial.

A further conclusion is that strategies intended to avoid blame will not necessarily achieve that effect in practice (which is why Figure 13.2 incorporates an iterative search) and may still produce effects incorporating some of the policy consequences conventionally associated with increased openness, as noted at the outset. For example, even if the police response to statutory requirements for registration of paedophile ex-offenders is interpreted as dominated by BPR considerations of locking in all the other public-sector players into collective deliberation, the effect of that strategy was nevertheless to enhance intelligence and shared information across the regime. Similarly, even if blame-shifting was a key factor in the UK central government response assigning responsibility to local authorities for ambient benzene in the face of openness pressures, those authorities nevertheless had to compile explicit and locally oriented responses against a background of published benzene monitoring data. Although BPR-dominated responses to pressures for increased openness may in some conditions detract from policy effectiveness through the side-effects they produce (for instance, in service abandonment or goal displacement through protocolization, one of the classic sources of bureaucratic dysfunction identified by Merton, 1960), they can also in some conditions contribute to greater policy capacity and intelligence.

Finally, this analysis shows that regulatory regimes and organizations can respond to openness pressures from different starting points and in different ways. Not all of the responses included in the Catherine Wheel model in Figure 13.2 are necessarily available to all organizations in a regime. And if responses and starting-points are diverse, so are the policy consequences of shifts in openness and transparency. For example, in the paedophile regime, change began from a low level of transparency and took the form of increased internal openness among the professional-bureaucratic players in the field rather than disclosure to the public at large. Given the risk–risk trade-offs involved in increased openness to the public at large in that domain, it is far from indisputable that full public disclosure would lead to an increase in overall policy effectiveness in limiting risk. The same does not apply to risk domains like pesticide residues and ambient benzene.

The purpose of this chapter is primarily descriptive and comparative. The study it describes sought to observe and analyse institutional responses to pressures for increased openness in RRRs, not to follow the many authors who have discussed the inherent desirability or otherwise of increasing openness in risk management (e.g. Shrader-Frechette, 1991) or the much-discussed policy dilemmas associated with such openness.[7] Nevertheless, descriptive and analytic work of this kind has implications for normative questions of policy and institutional design.

Notes

1 As well as some other types of sex offenders.
2 In a 1997 test case, a court upheld the status quo, holding that disclosure should be only on a need-to-know basis, not a matter of general entitlement (R v. Chief Constable for the North Wales Police Area Authority et al, 10 July 1997).
3 A few pesticides present risks to health at residue levels below 0.1 ppb.
4 In a European Union (EU) context, central rather than local government would be answerable to the European Court of Justice over failure to meet standards.

5   By contrast, the EU regime required member states to meet specified targets by 2010, but the even longer implementation lead time creates scope for member states to apply for derogations from the Air Quality Directive (96/62/EC) and its associated directives before the target takes effect.
6   BPR in the language of management science conventionally denotes 'business process re-engineering.' But BPR as blame prevention re-engineering seems equally important in organizational behaviour.
7   Such dilemmas include the danger of increasing public risks through exploitation of information by criminals or terrorists (Sieber, 1981), through panic responses to official information (Partridge, 1988, pp330–343) and through complacency or placation, with reduction in care and alertness.

References

Ayres, I., and Braithwaite, J. (1992). *Responsive regulation*. Cambridge, UK: Cambridge University Press.
Baldwin, R., and Hawkins, K. (1984). Discretionary justice: Davis reconsidered. *Public Law*, 570–599.
Beck, U. (1992). *Risk society*. London: Sage.
Beck Jørgensen, T. (1985). *The management of survival and growth in public organizations*. ECPR Joint Sessions, Barcelona.
Beck Jørgensen, T. (1987). *Models of retrenchment behavior* (Working paper No. 24). Brussels, Belgium: International Institute of Administrative Sciences.
Bentham, J. (1931). *The theory of legislation*. London: Routledge.
Bentham, J. (1983). *Constitutional code*. Oxford, UK: Clarendon.
Brans, M., and Rossbach, S. (1997). The autopoeisis of administrative systems: Niklas Luhmann on public administration and public policy. *Public Administration, 75*, 417–39.
Brin, D. (1998). *The transparent society*. Reading, MA: Addison-Wesley.
Clay, E., and Schaffer, B. (Eds.). (1984). *Room for manoeuvre*. London: Heinemann.
Crenson, M. (1971). *The un-politics of air pollution*. Baltimore: Johns Hopkins University Press.
Department of the Environment, Transport and the Regions. (1998a). *An economic analysis of the NAQS objectives*. London: HMSO.
Department of the Environment, Transport and the Regions. (1998b). *Finance, management and policy review of the expert panel on air quality standards: Final report*. London: Author.
Department of the Environment, Transport and the Regions. (2000). *Amended proposal for a directive of the European parliament and the council on limit values for benzene and carbon monoxide in ambient air* (Explanatory memorandum on European Community legislation 7906/00). London: Author.
Drinking Water Directive 80/778/EEC. (1980, 15 July). *Official Journal of the European Communities, L229*, 11.
Expert Panel on Air Quality Standards and Department of Environment. (1994). *Benzene*. London: HMSO.
Hall, P., and Taylor, R. (1997). Political science and the three new institutionalisms. *Political Studies*, 44(5), 936–957.
Healey, M. (1992, 7–9 September). *Regulating drinking water quality in England and Wales*. Paper presented at the Berzelius Symposium on Water and Public Health, London.

Healey, M., and Jones, A. (1989, 29 September). *Pesticides in water supplies* (Memo to chief executives of water service companies and secretaries of water companies in England and Wales, WP 18). London: Department of Environment, Welsh Office.

Health and Safety Executive. (1998). *Risk assessment and risk management.* Second report prepared by the Interdepartmental Liaison Group on Risk Assessment. London: Author.

Hood, C., Rothstein, H., Baldwin, R., Rees, J., and Spackman, M. (1999). Where risk society meets the regulatory state: Exploring variations in risk regulation regimes. *Risk Management,* 1(1), 21–34.

The Independent. (1999, 14 September). Inspectors sent in as Sellafield admits to serious safety lapses, p. 1.

John, P. (1998). *Analysing public policy.* London: Pinter.

Joo, J. (1999). Dynamics of social policy change: A Korean case study from a comparative perspective. *Governance,* 12(1), 57–80.

Laughlin, R. (1991). Environmental disturbances and organizational transitions and transformations: Some alternative models. *Organization Studies,* 12(2), 209–232.

Laughlin, R., and Broadbent, J. (1995, 2–5 July). *The new public management reforms in schools and GP practices: Professional resistance and the role of absorption and absorbing groups.* Paper presented at the First Asian Pacific Interdisciplinary Perspectives on Accounting Conference, University of New South Wales, Australia.

Lawton, R., and Parker, D. (1998). Procedures and the professional: The case of medicine. *Social Science and Medicine,* 49, 353–361.

Leiss, W., Massey, C., and Walker, L. (1998). Communicating the risks from radon in buildings. In P. Gray, R. Stern, and M. Biocca (Eds.), *Communicating about risks to environment and health in Europe.* Dordrecht, Boston, London: Kluwer.

Levy, A. (1986). Second-order planned change: Definition and conceptualisation. *Organizational Dynamics,* 15(1), 5–23.

MAFF (Ministry of Agriculture, Fisheries and Food), Pesticides Safety Directorate, Health and Safety Executive. (1999). *Annual report of the working party on pesticide residues 1998.* London: Ministry of Agriculture, Fisheries and Food.

Merton, R. (Ed.). (1960). *Reader in bureaucracy* (2nd ed.). New York: Free Press.

Millstone, E. (1986). *Food additives.* New York: Penguin.

New Zealand Treasury. (1987). *Government management* (Vol. 1). Wellington, New Zealand: Author.

Partridge, E. (1988). Ethical issues in emergency management policy. In L. Comfort (Ed.), *Managing disaster.* Durham, NC: Duke University Press.

Power, M. (1997). *The audit society.* Oxford, UK: Oxford University Press.

R. v. Chief Constable for the North Wales Police Area Authority, The Secretary of State for the Home Office, The National Association for the Care and Resettlement of Offenders ex parte: 1) A.B; 2) C.D. 10 July 1997.

Roberts, A. (1998). *Closing the window: Public service restructuring and the weakening of freedom of information law* [Mimeo]. Kingston, Canada: Queen's University School of Policy Studies.

Royal Commission on Environmental Pollution. (1998). *Setting environmental standards. The twenty-first report* (Cm 4053). London: HMSO.

SI 2000 No. 928. The Air Quality (England) Regulations 2000. London: HMSO.

Shrader-Frechette, K. (1991). *Risk and rationality.* Berkeley: University of California Press.

Sieber, S. (1981). *Fatal remedies.* New York: Plenum.

Slovic, P., Fischoff, B., and Lichtenstein, S. (1980). Facts and fears: Understanding perceived risk. In R. Schwing and W. Albers, *Societal risk assessment.* New York: Plenum Press.

Ward, N., Buller, H., and Lowe, P. (1995). *Implementing European environmental policy at the local level: The British experience with water quality directives.* Newcastle upon Tyne, UK: Centre for Rural Economy, University of Newcastle upon Tyne.

Appendix A

Changes in Openness and UK Risk Regulation Regimes: Three Cases With Little General Increase in Pressures for Openness Over 20 Years

Domain	Information rules (a) Reporting/collecting obligations; (b) Publication/disclosure obligations
Radon in homes	(a) No obligation on property owners to undertake tests; no obligation on government to assess radon levels (apart from a 1990 EC recommendation that member states assess radon levels); UK government by convention has conducted a UK-wide survey of radon levels by area (b) *Caveat emptor* rule on disclosure for property vendors: Government by convention publishes radon levels by area but not house by house
Dangerous dogs	(a) No general obligation to register dogs (except for four types specified in 1991 and in North Ireland); no obligation on public reporting of dog attacks and or for state authorities to collect or collate dog accident statistics (except North Ireland) (b) No obligation for dogs to carry ID (by chips/collar tags, etc.) except for four types specified under 1991 Act and no obligation to publish or disclose any risk information
Road accident risks	(a) Statutory obligation to report vehicle accidents and, since 1974, for local authorities to assess and reduce road risks. Vehicle manufacturers obliged to conduct safety tests, and by convention new EU assessments of safety performance of cars (b) By convention national government publishes aggregated road accident data and values of benefits of prevention of road accidents for use in cost – benefit analysis and appraisal of safety projects, and local road accident statistics are disclosed by discretion. Commercial confidentiality over vehicle safety test data but by convention EU publishes results of car safety performance programme

Enduring features		
Participation and scrutiny rules (a) Consultation obligations; (b) Formal public accountability rules	De facto accountability to public scrutiny	Overall openness
(a) Consultation by convention only with international policy community of radon experts and UK radiation professionals (b) Limited formal accountability rules with responsibility located in an expert UK-wide quango relatively detached from government departments	Low – kept within professional sphere	LOW Low salience and "expertized" but with official risk database providing general information
(a) Ministers obliged to consult domestic dog experts but little international consultation (b) Parliamentary scrutiny/questions to ministers; other formal accountability (through local councillors and police)	Variable media and depending on public salience of issue	MEDIUM Occasional high salience but no official risk database
(a) Local authorities obliged to consult local residents for traffic management schemes requiring Road Traffic Orders. Safety standard setting for vehicles expertized. (b) Mainly through local councillors for local road safety engineering but limited by professionalized and "protocolized" nature of road traffic engineering	Medium mainly localized, occasionally higher in response to "big news tragedies"	MEDIUM TO HIGH Mainly localized salience and largely "expertized" but with official risk database providing general information, and slowly increasing information on car safety performance

Appendix B

Changes in Openness and UK Risk Regulation Regimes: Three Cases Subject to Increasing Pressures for Openness Over 20 Years

	Status quo features			
Domain	*Information rules* *(a) Reporting/ collecting obligations;* *(b) Publication/ disclosure obligations*	*Participation and scrutiny rules* *(a) Consultation obligations;* *(b) Formal public accountability rules*	*De facto accountability to public scrutiny*	*Overall openness*
Ambient benzene	(a) No legal obligation to collect information on ambient benzene until 1997	(a) By convention consultation restricted to professionals	Minimal until 1990s	LOW
	(b) No legal obligation to disclose	(b) No defined regulator responsibility apart from general ministerial responsibility		
Paedophiles	(a) No general duty on government to collect information on offenders and no general duty on offenders to report	(a) No obligation to consult and little/no consultation by convention	Low – kept within professional sphere	LOW
	(b) No duty or convention to disclose	(b) Orthodox ministerial and public police accountability		
Pesticide residues	(a) General duty on food and drinking water suppliers to test for fitness for human consumption	(a) No general consultation outside professional community	Low – kept within professional sphere	LOW
	(b) No duty or convention to disclose information until late 1980s for both water and food suppliers	(b) Mix of local authorities and central government for food; minimal for water providers		

Post-status quo features			
Information rules (a) Reporting/ collecting obligations; (b) Publication/ disclosure obligations	*Participation and scrutiny rules (a) Consultation obligations; (b) Formal public accountability rules*	*De facto accountability to public scrutiny*	*Overall openness*
(a) Statutory obligations on local authorities and other bodies to assess and manage ambient air quality (b) Statutory disclosure of ambient benzene levels under EU Freedom of Information rules and public dissemination	(a) Ministers obliged to consult widely on ambient air quality policy. EU consultation with business and public interest groups by convention (b) Overlapping local authority, quango, and central government responsibility	Medium – low specifically for benzene but relatively high media and political engagement on general air pollution	MEDIUM TO HIGH Move to more transparent standards and information on ambient air quality from a low base
(a) Police duty to keep record of released offenders and offenders' duty to report (b) No change on publication/disclosure obligations	(a) Consultation and exchange of information across public agencies by convention including other organizations by discretion (b) No change on formal public accountability rules	Low – kept within professional sphere	LOW Creation of official database and consultation across government but limited or no general disclosure
(a) Obligation on food and drinking water suppliers to test for pesticide residues (b) Water regulators obliged to publish residue data. Food regulators introducing "name and shame" policy by convention	(a) More general; consultation by convention beyond a narrow professional group (except for approvals) (b) No change for food on formal public accountability rules; specific regulators for water since 1988	Medium – increasing media and political engagement	MEDIUM Starting from low base, more transparency on water and to a lesser extent on food

14

What Price Safety? The Precautionary Principle and its Policy Implications

Giandomenico Majone

Introduction

Like the English constitution according to Walter Bagehot, the precautionary approach includes two distinct sets of elements: the 'dignified' parts ('those which bring it force'), and the 'efficient' parts ('those by which it, in fact, works'). In its 'dignified' aspect, the approach purports to provide a legitimate basis for taking protective regulatory measures even when reliable scientific evidence of the causes and/or the scale of potential damage is lacking. Thus it appeals to many Europeans who are increasingly concerned about the 'globalization of risk': the transmission of environmental and health risks through the channels of free trade.

In its 'efficient' aspect, however, the approach tends to expand regulatory discretion at the national and international level – a discretion which can be used for a variety of purposes: to meet legitimate public concerns, but also to practise protectionism, or to reclaim national autonomy in politically sensitive areas of public policy. Even the European Commission (EC), which considers the precautionary principle a key tenet of its policy, admits that the principle may be used as a disguised form of protectionism (Commission, 2000, pp3 and *passim*).

In sum, the precautionary approach is deeply ambiguous, and as we shall see in the following pages, this ambiguity is abetted by a lack of clear definitions and sound logical foundations. In the EC Treaty the precautionary principle appears only in the title on the environment. It is not defined there or anywhere else in the Treaty. Nonetheless, the Commission, pushed by the Council and the European Parliament (see section on The Commission's Communications), is presently engaged in a sustained effort to promote the principle to the status of a 'central plank' of Community policy and, more ambitiously, to the status of a general principle of international economic and environmental law.

However, given the conceptual deficiencies and disturbing policy implications discussed at some length in this chapter, it seems unlikely that the other members of the World Trade Organization (WTO) will accept the precautionary principle, at least in the permissive interpretation advocated by the Commission. In the end the major beneficiaries of this promotional campaign may well be the member states of the

EC/EU, which can use the approach to reclaim significant portions of their regulatory autonomy in the management of environmental and health risks.

There are, in fact, indications that the member states are quickly learning to rely on the principle of precaution as an argument to justify stricter national regulations. In theory, the Commission allows member states to rely on the precautionary principle only when the Community's scientific committees consider that the scientific evidence presented by the member states is justified in light of new evidence, or by a particular national situation. The problem is that member states seem to be increasingly suspicious of the findings of the Community's scientific committees, and increasingly inclined to rely on the determinations of their own regulatory bodies (Scott and Vos, 2001). For example, the precautionary principle has recently been invoked by Denmark as an argument for the annulment of the Commission's refusal to grant that country's derogation request for its stricter national regulations on the use of certain food additives (Scott and Vos, 2001, p22).

The politically significant question is why the Commission is willing to risk international isolation and the segmentation of the European market for the sake of a controversial and ill-understood principle. This chapter offers some suggestions which may help to explain this puzzle, but its focus is on the conceptual problems and policy implications of the principle itself. A full discussion of the politics and the political economy of the precautionary approach would require a separate treatment. At any rate, a useful discussion along such lines presupposes some knowledge of the substantive issues analysed in the following pages.

Regulatory Science and Free Trade

Increasingly, science is playing a significant role in the regulation of international trade. In particular, the WTO agreement on the application of sanitary and phytosanitary (SPS) measures introduces a new science-based regime for disciplining health regulations which may affect international trade in agricultural products and foodstuffs. Annex A to the agreement defines a sanitary or phytosanitary measure as any measure applied to protect human, animal or plant life or health from a variety of risks, including 'risks arising from additives, contaminants, toxins or disease-causing organisms in foods, beverages or feedstuffs'.

Article 2(2) of the agreement states, *inter alia*, that members of the WTO shall ensure that any SPS measure 'is based on scientific principles and is not maintained without sufficient scientific evidence, except as provided for in paragraph 7 of Article 5'. Article 5 deals with risk assessment as a method for determining the appropriate level of health protection. Risk assessment is the standard by which SPS measures are to be judged as necessary and justified. In other words, for such measures to be necessary, based on scientific principles and not maintained without sufficient scientific evidence, they must be supported by a risk assessment conducted according to the criteria, and taking into account the factors mentioned in Article 5. As interpreted by the WTO appellate body in the beef hormones case (see section on The Precautionary and the

WTO: The Beef Hormones Case), this article says that there must be a rational relationship between the SPS measure and the risk assessment.

The exception provided by Article 5(7) applies to cases where relevant scientific evidence is insufficient, in which case a member state may *provisionally* adopt a measure 'on the basis of available pertinent information ... members shall seek to obtain the additional information necessary for a more objective assessment of risk and review the sanitary or phytosanitary measure accordingly *within a reasonable period of time*' (emphasis added).

Article 5(7) is the only reference to a precautionary approach in the entire agreement, and I shall come back to it in a later section. The aim of the immediately following pages is simply to introduce the reader to some of the conceptual and technical complexities surrounding the notions of 'scientific justification' and 'risk assessment' as they apply to regulatory measures.

The process of standard setting is at the core of risk regulation. If we understand the extent of scientific uncertainty in the setting of standards, we are in a good position to appreciate the problems of regulatory science. Extrapolation is a key element in the establishment of environmental and health standards, hence a good part of the uncertainty inherent in standard setting originates in various types of extrapolation processes.

There is, first, the problem of extrapolating from animal experiments. A major issue in regulatory science is the determination of the animal species that best predicts the response in humans. There is little hope that one species could provide the broad range of predictive potential needed to assess the responses of a highly heterogeneous human population to different types of toxic substances. The heterogeneity of human populations leaves the public authorities with an almost impossible regulatory task. In an effort to find a way out of this dilemma, scientists have developed several mathematical models expressing the probability of a lifetime response, P, as a function of dosage D: $P = f(D)$. This is the dose–response function. Different choices of f lead to different models.

Regardless of the choice of model, however, one has always to extrapolate from data points at high doses (the type of data provided by animal experiments) to the low levels relevant to the regulation of risk to humans. However, the same data points are compatible with a variety of extrapolating functions (Calabrese, 1978). Thus, under a threshold (non-linear) dose–response model it would be possible to establish a 'virtually safe' level of exposure, at the numerical value of the threshold, even though high doses produce adverse health effects. Instead, if one uses a linear dose–response relationship, adverse health effects are predicted at every level of exposure, so that there is no obvious point at which a reasonable standard could be set.

It may be argued – as do many advocates of the precautionary principle – that if there is no firm scientific basis for choosing among different dose–response models, then one should prefer the safest or most conservative procedure. One problem with the conservatism argument is that it is not clear where one should stop. A no-threshold model is more conservative than one that admits the existence of thresholds for carcinogenic effects. But within the large class of no-threshold models many degrees of conservatism are possible. Again, in designing a toxicological experiment one could use the most sensitive species, the most sensitive strain within the species, and so on down to the level of the most sensitive animal. In short, it is difficult to be conservative in a consistent manner unless one is prepared to propose a zero level of exposure in each case. This, in a nutshell, is the main conceptual problem with the precautionary principle.

Now, extrapolating from the high doses shown to cause harm in animal experiments or in epidemiological studies, to the much lower exposures normally faced by humans is the essence of quantitative risk assessments. From what has been said above it follows that uncertainty is a pervasive characteristic of regulatory risk assessments. But the technique has been accepted and continues to be used because there are no better alternatives. Thus the United States Supreme Court in *AFL-CIO* v. *American Petroleum Institute* (448 U.S. 607 (1980)) – the landmark benzene case – not only confirmed the legitimacy of quantitative risk assessment; it effectively made reliance on the methodology obligatory for all American agencies engaged in health regulation. In most subsequent disputes over regulatory decisions to protect human health, the question has not been whether a risk assessment was required but whether the assessment offered by the agency was plausible (Mashaw et al, 1998, pp823–825). This historical background may explain US advocacy of science-based risk assessment at the international level, as well as that country's opposition to the precautionary principle as interpreted by the European Union (EU). Today the methodology of risk assessment is used by regulators in all developed countries. Moreover, as mentioned above, risk assessment is the standard by which trade-restricting health regulations are evaluated as necessary and justified. As such, it plays a crucial role in the debate about the application of the precautionary principle at the international level.

An Idea in Search of a Definition

The precautionary principle is an idea (perhaps a state of mind) rather than a clearly defined concept, much less a guide to consistent policy-making. In fact it will be shown below (see the next section) that there are logical reasons for its intrinsic vagueness. Not surprisingly, an authoritative and generally accepted definition is nowhere to be found. The principle is of German origin (*Vorsorge Prinzip*), and has been used in that country since the 1980s in order to justify a number of important developments in environmental law. However, an eminent legal expert has distinguished no fewer than 11 different meanings assigned to the precautionary principle within German policy discourse (Rehbinder, 1991).

The German approach was taken up by other policy elites in Europe, including those who drafted the EC's Fourth Environmental Action Programme, and thus sought to develop an approach to environmental policy that was preventive rather than reactive (Weale, 1992, p80). In the EC Treaty the principle appears only in the title on environment. Article 174 EC (ex Article 130(r)) provides that Community environmental policy 'shall be based on the precautionary principle and on the principles that preventive action should be taken, that environmental damage should as a priority be rectified at the source and that the polluter should pay'. No definition of the precautionary principle is provided in this article or anywhere else in the Treaty. In spite of this, it is argued by the Commission and by some legal scholars that the principle applies beyond EC environmental policy. This is because Article 6 EC provides that the environmental protection requirements be integrated into the definition and implementation of Community policies and activities referred to in Article 3 EC. Insofar as the precautionary principle is one of the core principles of EC environmental policy, it is concluded that it should be integrated, as appropriate, into other Community policies (Scott and Vos, 2001, p4).

As mentioned in the section on Regulatory Science and Free Trade, there is an indirect reference to a precautionary approach (again undefined) in Article 5(7) of the WTO SPS agreement. WTO member states are allowed to take measures unsupported by a risk assessment when the relevant scientific evidence is insufficient, but only provisionally. Perhaps the best-known statement of the precautionary principle is provided by principle 15 of the Declaration of the 1992 UN Conference on Environment and Development (Rio Declaration):

> In order to protect the environment, the precautionary approach shall be widely used by States according to their capabilities. Where there are threats of serious and irreversible damage, lack of full scientific certainty shall not be used as a reason for postponing cost-effective measures to prevent environmental degradation.

It is important to notice that the similarity of different statements of the principle is often more apparent than real. Even when such statements refer more or less explicitly to a situation where the probability and extent of damage are poorly understood, they often differ in the conditions which precautionary measures must satisfy. Thus, according to the SPS agreement, such measures must be provisional, but the European Commission chooses to interpret this condition not in terms of clock time, but of the time necessary to achieve a sufficient level of scientific certainty – a very flexible standard, given the limitations of regulatory science!

Again, the Commission quotes with approval principle 15 of the Rio Declaration, even though the standards set by the drafters of the declaration (a threat of serious and irreversible damage, measures must be cost-effective) are a good deal stricter than the ones the Commission advocates. For example, according to the Commission a precautionary measure may be justified if there are 'reasonable grounds for concern that the potentially dangerous effects on the environment, human, animal or plant health may be *inconsistent with the chosen level of protection*' (Commission, 2000, p10; emphasis added) – a significantly more permissive standard than the threat of serious and irreversible damage.

Since the precautionary principle lends itself to a wide range of interpretations, it would be instructive to see how the European Court of Justice (ECJ) and the Court of First Instance have dealt with it. A detailed discussion of relevant cases is of course beyond the scope of this chapter (a good survey may be found in Scott and Vos, 2001). A general inference from major decisions appears to be that in cases of scientific uncertainty, member states have considerable discretion in deciding to err on the side of caution. They must, however, provide some evidence of scientific uncertainty. They must adduce evidence of a specific, concrete risk and not merely of potential risks based on a general precautionary approach (Scott and Vos, p15). Thus in the famous *German Beer* case (Case 178/84 [1987]), the ECJ refused to allow a ban on additives in beer, based on a generic principle of prevention. The national authorities must come up with more specific scientific evidence than a mere reference to the potential risks posed by the ingestion of additives in general.

The Precautionary Principle and the WTO: The Beef Hormones Case

As already mentioned, the EU is currently engaged in a major effort to have the precautionary principle adopted as a 'key tenet' of Community policy and as a 'full-fledged and general principle' of international law (Commission, 2000). While some progress has been made in the field of international environmental law, the EU's commitment to, and application of, the principle has been repeatedly questioned or opposed by the WTO, the United States, and by other developed and developing countries. Thus, the proposals on the precautionary principle presented by the EU to the Codex Alimentarius Commission (a body advising the Food and Agriculture Organization and the World Health Organization) in April 2000 were opposed by the US and many other third countries, which fear that the principle may be too easily misused for protectionist purposes. Such fears are fed by episodes like the proposed aflatoxin standards, to be briefly discussed below (see section on Political and Social Consequences), and the beef hormones dispute which for years has opposed the EU to some of its major trading partners. In this dispute the European Commission found itself in the same position vis-à-vis the WTO bodies that various EC member states have found themselves in vis-à-vis the Community. The Commission was being sanctioned for introducing a public health and consumer protection measure which was not sufficiently supported by scientific evidence (De Búrca and Scott, 2000, p6).

The Commission argued that the precautionary principle applies across the whole of the SPS agreement as a general principle of international law. The WTO's appellate body specifically rejected this argument and stated that the principle must receive authoritative formulation before it can be raised to the status sought for it by the EU. The same body also observed that the precautionary principle has not been written into Article 5(7) of the SPS agreement as grounds for justifying measures that are otherwise inconsistent with the obligations of the WTO set out in particular provisions of the agreement.

The controversy over the use of growth hormones in cattle raising, which has opposed the EU to the US and Canada in the framework of the WTO's dispute resolution mechanism, has been discussed many times and from a variety of disciplinary and policy perspectives. The historical background of the controversy is not widely known, however. Because of its relevance to the present discussion it will be briefly reviewed here. The immediately following pages rely heavily on work by Christian Joerges (1997, 2001).

The hormones regime in the EC stems from Directive 81/602 on the prohibition of 'certain substances having a hormonal action and of any substances having a thyrostatic action'. This directive was amended in 1985 by Directive 85/358, extended in 1988 and consolidated by Directive 96/22. The 1985 directive – which was adopted by qualified majority on the basis of Article 43 EEC (now Article 37 EC) dealing with the common agricultural policy – prohibited the use of hormones in livestock farming. Even then the prohibition was controversial. The United Kingdom brought a suit against the directive, arguing *inter alia* that in view of its health objectives the directive should have been based on Article 100 (now Article 94) on the approximation of laws. This article requires unanimity and hence would have allowed the UK government to veto the prohibition of growth hormones in cattle raising and meat products.

The effect of the 1985 directive was also to prohibit the importation of American and Canadian beef into the Community, although this point was not addressed in the legal controversy between the UK and the Community. Instead, the UK asserted that, in enacting the directive, the Council should have taken into consideration the scientific report which had been prepared in accordance with Article 8 of Directive 81/602. According to this report, risk assessment had shown that growth hormones used according to good veterinary practice would result in no significant harm. This conclusion of its own scientific experts led the Commission to reconsider the strict prohibition imposed by Community law.

However, both the European Parliament and the Economic and Social Council strongly opposed any such policy change. Because of this opposition the Commission cancelled further meetings of the group of scientific experts (Joerges, 2001, p10). At the same time the European Court of Justice rejected the complaint of the UK government with the flimsy argument that Article 8 of Directive 81/602 imposed an obligation on the Commission only, so that the Council was under no obligation to take the scientific report into consideration.

Opposition to the Commission's willingness to accept the result of the risk assessment and to reconsider the Community's hormones policy accordingly, led to a change in the rationale of that policy from health safety to 'the interests of the consumers in general'. As Advocate General Lenz put it, this type of consumer protection need not be supported by scientific evidence. Once its legitimacy as an objective of agricultural policy in general, and of the hormones directive in particular, is accepted, there is 'really no reason to examine the health problem ... and so the fact that in the preamble to the contested directive the Council did not go into the partial findings of the scientific group ... cannot be regarded as a failure to give reasons' (cited in Joerges, 1997, pp309–310). Without citing any empirical evidence, the Advocate General added that 'it could be seen that meat from animals treated with hormones is widely rejected'.

Some years later the Commission was to take a similar position, and even use some of the same language, at the WTO level. In 1997 the US and Canada filed complaints with the WTO against the EC ban of meat products containing growth hormones, submitting that this measure violates the SPS agreement. This agreement, it will be remembered, allows WTO members to adopt health standards that are stricter than international standards, provided the stricter standards are supported by risk assessment. Unfortunately, the risk assessment conducted by the EC scientific experts had shown that the use of growth hormones according to good veterinary practice posed no significant health risk. Hence the Commission was forced to meet the WTO challenge with arguments similar to those used by the Advocate General in rejecting the UK's complaint against Directive 85/358. In particular, it pointed to various incidents since the early 1980s, when hormones that entered the European food market had allegedly made European consumers wary of beef. The Commission concluded that a ban of beef containing growth hormones was necessary to restore consumer confidence.

The WTO's dispute resolution panel decided against the EC. The panel raised three objections: first, more permissive international standards existed for five of the hormones; second, the EC measure was not based on a risk assessment, as required by Article 5(1) of the SPS agreement; finally, the EC policy was not consistent, hence in violation of the no-discrimination requirement of Article 5(5). The WTO's appellate body agreed with the panel that the EC had failed to base its measure on a risk assessment and decided against the EC essentially for two reasons. First because the scientific evidence of harm produced by the Commission was not 'sufficiently specific to the case at hand' – it took the form of general studies, but did not 'address the particular kind of risk here at stake'. Second, the appellate body endorsed the finding of the dispute resolution panel that 'theoretical uncertainty' arising because 'science can never provide absolute certainty that a given substance will never have adverse health effects' is not the kind of risk to be assessed under Article 5(1) of the SPS agreement. The similarity with some of the older jurisprudence of the ECJ, particularly the *German Beer* case, is remarkable.

The Commission's Communication

As the preceding pages have shown, '[t]he issue of when and how to use the precautionary principle, both within the European Union and internationally, is giving rise to much debate, and to mixed, and sometimes contradictory views' (Commission, 2000, p3). With its communication on the precautionary principle of 2 February 2000, the Commission intends to contribute to the ongoing debate by:

- outlining its own understanding of the principle;
- establishing guidelines for applying it;
- building a common understanding of how to assess and manage risks under conditions of scientific uncertainty; and
- avoiding recourse to the precautionary principle as a disguised form of protectionism.

The document also serves political aims, being a response to pressures originating from the European Parliament (EP) and the Council. In its resolution of 10 March 1998 on the Green Paper on the General Principles of Food Law, the EP had invited the Commission 'to anticipate possible challenges to Community food law by WTO bodies by requesting the scientific committees to present a full set of arguments based on the precautionary principle'.

On 13 April 1999, the Council adopted a resolution urging the Commission, *inter alia*, 'to be in the future ever more determined to be guided by the precautionary principle in preparing proposals for legislation and in its other consumer-related activities and develop as a priority clear and effective guidelines for the application of this principle' (both citations in Commission, 2000, p25).

These political pressures are at least partly responsible for the ambiguity which pervades the document, undermining its intellectual coherence. On the one hand, the Commission is well aware of the danger that the member states of the EU may use the precautionary principle in order to extend their own regulatory autonomy vis-à-vis the Community. Hence the exhortation to 'avoid unwarranted recourse to the precautionary principle as a disguised form of protection' (p3); the insistence that 'the precautionary principle can under no circumstances be used to justify the adoption of arbitrary decisions' (p13); the warning that 'reliance on the precautionary principle is no excuse for derogating from the general principles of risk management' (p18).

On the other hand, there is a strong temptation to use the principle to maximize the EU's regulatory discretion at the international level. Thus on page 3 we read: '[t]he Commission considers that the Community, like other WTO members, has the right to establish the level of protection ... that it deems appropriate. Applying the precautionary principle is a key tenet of its policy, and the choices it makes to this end will continue to affect the views it defends internationally, on how this principle should be applied.'

The same demand for maximum regulatory discretion is repeated, in various forms, throughout the communication: 'a member [of the WTO] may apply measures, including measures based on the precautionary principle, which lead to a higher level of protection than that provided for in the relevant international standards or recommendations' (p11); 'the Community is entitled to prescribe the level of protection, notably as regards the environment and human, animal and plant health, which it considers appropriate' (p12); 'application of the precautionary principle is part of risk management, when scientific uncertainty precludes a full assessment of the risk and *when decision-makers consider that the chosen level of environmental protection or of human, animal and plant health may be in jeopardy*' (p13, emphasis added).

While it strives to achieve broad regulatory discretion at the international level, the Commission insists that the envisioned use of the precautionary principle, 'far from being a way of evading obligations arising from the WTO agreements', in fact complies with these obligations. Now, it is true that under the WTO SPS agreement, if a health measure has a scientific basis, there is little other countries can do to challenge it. However, if a measure lacks an adequate scientific justification, it will be subject to attack. The requirement of a scientific justification, and of risk assessment as a prelude to standard setting, may be seen as a limit on regulatory arbitrariness. But for the requirement to have meaning, there must be the possibility of a dispute panel finding an absence of scientific justification and inadequate risk assessment (Atik, 1996–1997).

As discussed in the preceding section, both the WTO's dispute resolution panel and the appellate body determined that the EC's ban on the importation of American beef was unsupported by scientific evidence and by an adequate risk assessment. One of the undeclared aims of the communication is to prevent similar embarrassments in the future by proposing very elastic interpretations of the requirements of the SPS agreement.

Thus, Article 5(7) of the agreement concedes that when scientific evidence is insufficient, a country may adopt measures on the basis of the available pertinent information, but only provisionally. Moreover, the country must obtain the additional information necessary for a more objective risk assessment, and review the measure accordingly *within a reasonable period of time*. The communication interprets these requirements as follows: '[t]he measures, although provisional, shall be maintained as long as the scientific data remain incomplete, imprecise or inconclusive *and as long as the risk is considered too high to be imposed on society*' (Commission, 2000, p21, emphasis added). It is difficult to see how a dispute resolution panel could apply such subjective standards.

Again, according to the communication, the concept of risk assessment in the SPS agreement 'leaves leeway for interpretation of what could be used as a basis for a precautionary approach'. It need not be confined to purely quantitative scientific data, but could include 'non-quantifiable data of a factual or qualitative nature' (p12). This interpretation, the Commission claims, has been confirmed by the WTO's appellate body which, in the hormones case, rejected the panel's initial interpretation that the risk assessment had to be quantitative and had to establish a minimum degree of risk. However, the opinion of the appellate body does not necessarily coincide with the Commission's permissive interpretation. Between this interpretation and a quantitative risk analysis of the traditional type, there is a wide range of possible analytic approaches. One such approach is *comparative* risk assessment. Even though scientists may be unable to make exact quantitative statements about the low-dose risks of particular substances, they can often rank the risks of various substances at currently experienced doses. For example, scientists might say that a lifetime exposure to x parts per million (ppm) of substance A presents in their judgement a larger risk of cancer to a worker than a lifetime exposure to y ppm of substance B (Graham et al, 1988, p200). It is not necessary to evaluate precisely the risks posed by both substances in order to have a reasonable basis for such a comparison.

The communication insists that the precautionary principle offers no excuse for derogating from the general principles of risk management, including an examination of the benefits and costs of action and inaction. However, cost–benefit analysis should include not only evaluation of the costs 'to the Community', but also non-economic considerations such as acceptability to the public. Who should determine public acceptability remains unclear, unless this determination is seen as part of the right of the Community to establish the level of protection that it deems appropriate at any particular time. An adjustable peg can justify any measure, making cost–benefit or risk analysis superfluous.

We have here another manifestation of the deep ambiguity of the communication. This document is also a public relations exercise 'designed to calm the fears of those who perceive that the precautionary principle serves, in the case of the EU, to legitimate decisions which are irrational other than in terms of their capacity to serve protectionist goals' (Scott and Vos, 2001, p31). Hence the emphasis on the centrality of scientific evaluation and on the generally accepted principles of risk management. However, the exercise is ultimately unpersuasive because all the substantive and procedural constraints on regulatory arbitrariness are relaxed to the point of becoming non-binding.

So far the Commission's communication has been criticized for what it says. In the following pages it will be criticized for what it fails to consider.

The Precautionary Principle and the Logic of Decision-Making

A glaring shortcoming of the communication is the failure to consider the overall implications of adopting the precautionary principle, not as an exceptional temporary measure but as a key tenet of Community policy, a 'guide in preparing proposals for legislation', a 'full-fledged and general principle of international law'. In the present section we examine the principle's implications for the logic of decision-making. In the following section political and social consequences will be discussed.

One important factor the communication does not consider is the opportunity cost of precautionary measures. The attempt to control poorly understood, low-level risks necessarily uses up resources that in many cases could be directed more effectively towards the reduction of well-known, large-scale risks. Thus, one of the unanticipated consequences of the precautionary principle is to raise the issue of a rational setting of regulatory priorities at national and European levels. Since resources are always limited it is impossible to control all actual and potential risks. Even if a society is willing 'to pay a higher cost to protect an interest, such as the environment or health, to which it attaches priority' (Commission, 2000, p20), it is still the case that some environmental or risk regulations might be too expensive. Hence the choice of which risks to regulate and when to regulate them is crucially important for a rational allocation of resources and for consistency in policymaking. Precautionary measures – taken on an ad hoc basis, often in response to political pressures – may distort priorities and compromise the consistency of regulatory policies.

More generally, the precautionary principle appears to be seriously flawed as an aid to rational decision-making under uncertainty. Although a lack of precise definitions makes it difficult to develop a formal critique, the following considerations may help to grasp the principle's main theoretical shortcomings.

To begin with, recall that risk is a compound measure (more precisely, a product) of the probability of harm and its severity. Now, according to the fundamental theorem of decision theory, the only consistent rule for decision-making under uncertainty is to choose the alternative which minimizes the expected loss (or maximizes the expected utility). Consider a situation where there are various possible events (or 'states of nature') $E_1, E_2, ..., E_n$, with probabilities $p_1, p_2, ..., p_n$, alternative actions $A_1, A_2, ..., A_m$, and losses l_{ij} for each combination of alternative A_i and event E_j, $i = 1, 2, ..., m; j = 1, 2, ..., n$. The optimal decision consists in choosing the alternative which minimizes the expected loss, i.e. the sum of the products of the losses by the corresponding probabilities (formally: the alternative which minimizes $\Sigma_j p_j l_{ij}$).

Any good textbook on decision theory (e.g. Lindley, 1971) provides the proof that any other decision rule – and in particular any rule which does not use both the losses and the corresponding probabilities – can lead to inconsistent decisions. One such decision rule is the minimax principle, which in some respects is quite similar to the precautionary principle. The minimax approach to decision-making under uncertainty uses losses but not probabilities, either denying the existence of the latter, or claiming that the method is to be used when they are unknown (here is an important similarity

288 Policy and Regulation

with the precautionary principle). This approach makes sense in special situations – zero-sum games where the uncertainty is 'strategic', i.e. part of the strategy of a rational opponent – but not in the general case, as may be seen from the following examples. Consider first the decision problem described in Table 14.1, where the entries indicate losses, e.g. extra deaths due to exposure to a toxic substance.

Following the minimax rule, for each row (i.e. alternative) we select the maximum loss (10 for A_1 and 1 for A_2), and choose that alternative having the minimum of these values. This is A_2 with value 1. Hence the minimax rule says: always choose A_2. The principle of expected loss would assign probabilities p_1 and p_2 to the uncertain events and choose A_2 if $1 < 10 p_1$, i.e. $p_1 > 1/10$, otherwise A_1 should be selected. To see which of the two rules is more reasonable, suppose that p_1 is quite small (say, $p_1 = 0.01$ or 0.001) so that $10 p_1$ is much less than 1. The minimax rule would still choose A_2, even though it is almost sure that no extra deaths would occur under A_1.

The result is even more striking in Table 14.2, where only the loss corresponding to the pair (A_1, E_1) has been changed.

The minimax rule would still choose A_2, even though the expected loss for A_1 is much smaller for all values of p_1 less than, say, 0.8. In short, the problem with the minimax rule is that it does not take account of all the information available to the decision-maker. The advantage of the expected-loss rule is that it takes account of both losses and probabilities.

As noted above, one defence of the minimax is that it is to be used when probabilities are unknown (and perhaps unknowable). This argument is strongly reminiscent of the distinction made by the American economist Frank Knight in the 1920s between 'risk' (when the events are uncertain, but their probabilities are known) and 'uncertainty' (where the probabilities are unknown). Knight attached great theoretical importance to this distinction, but modern analysis no longer views the two classes of events as different in kind. Probabilities may be known more or less precisely, they may be more or less subjective, but there are some logical difficulties involved in giving meaning to the statement that the probabilities are unknown. If we insist that we are 'completely ignorant' as to which of the events $E_1, ..., E_n$ will occur, it is hard to escape the conclusion that all the events are equally likely to occur. But this implies that

Table 14.1 *Comparing decision rules*

	$E_1(p_1)$	$E_2(p_2)$
A_1	10	0
A_2	1	1

Table 14.2 *The minimax rule as precautionary principle*

	$E_1(p_1)$	$E_2(p_2)$
A_1	1.1	0
A_2	1.0	1

the probabilities are in fact known, and that $P(E_i) = 1/n$ for all i: the well-known uniform distribution!

The point of this digression on decision theory is to identify with more precision than would otherwise be possible the logical problems raised by the application of the precautionary principle. Like the minimax principle, the principle of precaution tends to focus the attention of regulators on some particular events and corresponding losses, rather than on the entire range of possibilities. As a consequence, regulators will base their determinations on worst cases, rather than on the weighted average of all potential losses, i.e. on the expected overall loss. The Commission's communication provides a good example. On page 19 we read that in examining the benefits and costs of different alternatives, '[a] comparison must be made between the *most likely* positive and negative consequences of the envisaged actions and those of inaction ...' (emphasis added). Consistent decision-making under uncertainty requires consideration of all consequences, not just the most (or, for that matter, least) likely ones. Note, too, that if we are truly ignorant of the probability distribution of consequences – a condition which is sometimes invoked in order to justify recourse to the precautionary principle – then it is logically impossible to speak of 'most likely' consequences. The phrase implies a ranking of probabilities, and hence at least an approximate knowledge of the relevant distribution.

The most serious conceptual flaw, however, is the artificial distinction between situations where scientific information is sufficient to permit a formal risk assessment, and those where 'scientific information is insufficient, inconclusive or uncertain'. In reality, these are two points on a knowledge–ignorance continuum rather than two qualitatively distinct situations. The same logic which leads to the rejection of Knight's distinction between risk and uncertainty also applies here. As we saw, by its very nature regulatory science deals with uncertainties. For example, for most toxic substances it is still unknown whether the relevant model for standard setting is a threshold or a linear one. Most scientists favour the latter model, but this only complicates the regulator's problem, since it is unclear where a standard should be set above the zero level. Moreover, the continuous progress of science and technology produces increasingly precise measurements of toxicity (e.g. parts per billion) so that the search for safety becomes ever more elusive.

In short, regulatory problems are not solved but only complicated by appealing to different logics of decision-making, according to the available level of information. Especially in risk regulation, the normal state of affairs is neither scientific certainty nor complete ignorance. For this reason a sensible principle of decision-making is one that uses all the available information, weighted according to its reliability, instead of privileging some particular hypothetical risk.

The prescriptions of decision theory break down in only one case, namely when losses (or utilities) are unbounded. In such a case it is clearly impossible to calculate expected values. An example of potential unbounded loss is the threat of serious and irreversible damage – the situation envisaged by principle 15 of the Rio Declaration (see section on An Idea in Search of a Definition). In this and similar situations, the precautionary principle may be a useful tool of risk management. But to acknowledge such possibilities is to recognize that the principle has a legitimate but quite limited role in risk management.

Political and Social Consequences

Under the political conditions prevailing today, the sustainability of a regime of free trade and market integration depends crucially on international regulatory cooperation and, at least in some areas, on the gradual approximation of national rules and regulations. This dual process of trade liberalization and harmonization has gone furthest in Europe, and for this reason the Community has been able to play a key role in fostering international regulatory cooperation. This is especially evident in the area of technical standardization.

While the United States has very few standards based on world standards, the EC has pursued a policy of close cooperation with international standardization bodies. For example, today more than 70 per cent of European electrotechnical standards are based on world standards. Given this tight cooperation between the European and the international levels, it is quite likely that a world standard will automatically provide access to the large EC market. This provides a very strong incentive for producers from third countries to adopt world standards. The success of the European strategy has convinced the United States that reliance on world standards may be critical to the international competitiveness of American industry (Pelkmans, 1995).

Unfortunately, the situation is quite different in the area of health and safety standards. As we saw above, the Commission would like to interpret the entire SPS agreement in the light of the precautionary principle, in order to be able to conclude that the EC is free to adopt the level of safety that it deems appropriate, regardless of the objections other countries may raise. Thus, just as the US is beginning to appreciate the importance of international regulatory cooperation, the Community seems to be switching to an isolationist stance. By rejecting international risk standards in the name of the precautionary principle, it jeopardizes its role of pioneer in regulatory cooperation.

Finally, we should mention the distributive consequences of measures inspired by this principle. The search for higher and higher levels of safety leads to the promulgation of standards so stringent that the regulatory action ultimately imposes high costs without achieving significant additional safety benefits. Perhaps we should not be too concerned if such costs were felt only by exporters in rich countries like the United States and Canada, and by affluent European consumers. But what if the cost is borne by some of the poorest countries in the world?

The EU and all its member states are deeply committed to assist, financially and otherwise, developing countries, especially African ones. However, World Bank economists have recently estimated the impact on some of the poorest African countries of new and very strict standards for aflatoxins (carcinogens present in peanuts and other farm products) proposed by the Commission in the late 1990s in the name of the precautionary principle. The proposed standards are significantly more stringent than those adopted by the US, Canada and Australia, and also stricter than the international standards established by the Codex Alimentarius Commission. Using trade and regulatory survey data for the member states of the EU and nine African countries between 1989 and 1998, the World Bank economists estimate that the new standards would decrease African exports of cereals, dried fruits and nuts to the EU by 64 per cent, relative to a regulation set at the international standard (Otsuki et al,

2000). This reduction in agricultural exports is equivalent to a loss of about US$700 million a year. Notice that African countries cannot shift their exports to other parts of the world because as former colonies they are heavily dependent on European markets. Again, while middle-income developing countries, such as Brazil, can evade the impact of the precautionary measures by shifting to the export of processed food, poor countries do not have this option.

At about the same time as the World Bank report was published, the Commission, through its president, was advertising its intention of eliminating all tariffs and quantitative restrictions on imports from the poorest countries. Of course, the practical significance of this apparently generous offer is greatly reduced by the fact that some of the major obstacles to international trade today are not tariffs or quantitative restrictions, but non-tariff barriers such as the aflatoxin standards and similar measures inspired by the precautionary principle.

Are the additional costs imposed on African countries justified by the health benefits for EU citizens? According to studies conducted by the Joint Food and Agriculture Organization/World Health Organization Expert Committee on Food Additives, the Community standard of 2 parts per billion (ppb) for B_1 aflatoxin would reduce deaths from liver cancer by 1.4 deaths per billion, i.e. by less than one death per year in the EU. For the purpose of this calculation the Community standard is compared to a standard that follows the international (Codex) guideline of 9 ppb. Since about 33,000 people die from liver cancer every year in the EU, one can see that the health gain produced by the precautionary standard is indeed minuscule. Is saving less than two lives in a billion in Europe worth the misery imposed on African farmers? It is true that, according to the Commission, in examining the potential costs and benefits of action or inaction only the 'overall cost to the Community' need be examined (Commission, 2000, p5). But given the international commitments of the EU – not least in the areas of development aid and environmental protection – this sort of Eurocentrism is, at best, undiplomatic.

Conclusions

To repeat: the precautionary principle has a legitimate but limited role to play in risk regulation – whenever there is an imminent danger of irreversible damage, and/or knowledge of causal processes is too limited to bring about a consensus of scientific opinion. As I have tried to show in the preceding pages, however, the principle lacks a firm logical foundation; it may be misused for protectionist ends; it tends to undermine international regulatory cooperation; and it may have highly undesirable distributive consequences. What is perhaps even more serious is that the principle, as interpreted by the Commission, raises the possibility of a double standard for what is permissible internationally and in intra-Community relations. Indeed, in the area of risk regulation member states are beginning to claim, in their relations with each other and with the EC, the same autonomy which the Commission claims in relation to the international community.

Given so many disturbing implications of a broad use of the precautionary principle, how can we explain the Commission's determination in attributing to it the status of 'a central plank of Community policy'? Part of the explanation has to do with inter-institutional politics. As we saw, the Council and the EP urged the Commission 'to be ... ever more determined to be guided by the precautionary principle in preparing proposals for legislation', and 'to anticipate possible challenges to Community food law by the World Trade Organization and by third countries'. These two European institutions were responding to domestic political pressures, as well as to diffuse concerns about the 'globalization' of risk. In turn, a weakened and demoralized Commission is tempted to see in the promulgation of the internationally strictest safety standards a promising way of improving its legitimacy.

Related to this search for legitimacy is the search for credibility. In other words, the 'dignified parts' of the precautionary principle may also serve to conceal a general reluctance to establish credible regulatory institutions at European level. Many observers have commented on the striking difference in the attitudes of Americans and Europeans concerning technological, environmental and health risks. Cultural factors are often mentioned as explanatory variables, but I believe that the explanation is simpler, having to do with the different credibility of regulatory institutions on the two sides of the Atlantic. From the thalidomide disaster of the 1960s to the recent food scares, Europeans have experienced a series of regulatory failures, largely unknown to Americans. Hence it is not surprising that Americans trust their risk regulators while Europeans do not. To re-establish consumers' and producers' confidence it would be necessary to create independent bodies – European agencies or more likely networks of national and European regulators – not just to conduct scientific studies, but with powers of rule-making and enforcement (Majone, 2000). For different reasons, however, neither the Council nor the Commission nor the Parliament presently favours such a solution. Hence the recent emphasis on the precautionary principle could be interpreted as a strategy to avoid or at least delay difficult institutional choices.

Each of these hypotheses probably contains more than a grain of truth. To test them, however, would require a separate treatment. What the present article does attempt to do is to raise reasoned doubts about the general applicability of the precautionary principle. The Commission's communication does not pretend to be the last word on the subject. Rather, it is meant to be 'a point of departure for a broader study of the conditions in which risks should be assessed, appraised, managed and communicated' (Commission, 2000, p22). This chapter is offered as a contribution to such a study.

References

Atik, J. (1996–1997) 'Science and International Regulatory Convergence'. *Northwestern Journal of International Law and Business*, Vol. 17, No. 2–3, pp. 736–58.

Calabrese, E. J. (1978) *Methodological Approaches to Deriving Environmental and Occupational Health Standards* (New York/London: Wiley-Interscience).

Commission of the European Communities (2000) 'Communication on the Precautionary Principle'. *COM* (2000) 1 (Brussels: CEC).

De Búrca, G. and Scott, J. (2000) 'The Impact of the WTO on EU Decision-making'. Harvard Jean Monnet Working Paper 6/00 (Cambridge, MA: Harvard Law School).

Graham, J. D., Green, L. C. and Roberts, M. J. (1988) *In Search of Safety* (Cambridge, MA: Harvard University Press).

Joerges, C. (1997) 'Scientific Expertise in Social Regulation and the European Court of Justice: Legal Frameworks for Denationalized Governance Structures'. In Joerges, C., Ladeur, K. H. and Vos, E. (eds) *Integrating Scientific Expertise into Regulatory Decision-Making* (Baden-Baden: Nomos).

Joerges, C. (2001) 'Law, Science and the Management of Risks to Health at the National, European and International Level – Stories on Baby Dummies, Mad Cows and Hormones in Beef'. *Columbia Journal of European Law*, Vol. 7, No. 1, pp. 1–19.

Knight, F. H. (1971 [1921]) *Risk, Uncertainty and Profit* (Chicago, IL: University of Chicago Press).

Lindley, D. (1971) *Making Decisions* (New York/London: Wiley-Interscience).

Majone, G. (2000) 'The Credibility Crisis of Community Regulation'. *Journal of Common Market Studies*, Vol. 38, No. 2, pp. 273–302.

Mashaw, J. L., Merrill, R.A. and Shane, P.M. (1998) *Administrative Law*, 4th edn (St. Paul, MN: West Group).

Otsuki, T., Wilson, J. S. and Sewadeh, M. (2000) 'Saving Two in a Billion: A Case Study to Quantify the Trade Effect of European Food Safety Standards on African Exports'. Mimeo (Washington, DC: World Bank).

Pelkmans, J. (1995) 'Comments'. In Sykes, A. O. (ed.) *Product Standards for Internationally Integrated Goods Markets* (Washington, DC: Brookings Institution).

Rehbinder, E. (1991) *Das Vorsorge Prinzip im internationalen Vergleich* (Baden-Baden: Nomos).

Scott, J. and Vos, E. (2001) 'The Juridification of Uncertainty: Observations on the Ambivalence of the Precautionary Principle within the EU and the WTO'. In Dehousse, R. and Joerges, C. (eds) *Good Governance in an Integrated Market* (Oxford: Oxford University Press).

Weale, A. (1992) *The New Politics of Pollution* (Manchester/New York: Manchester University Press).

15

Uncertainty and Environmental Learning: Reconceiving Science and Policy in the Preventive Paradigm

Brian Wynne

One of the most important new goals of environmental and technology policies in the last decade has been the shift towards prevention. This change implies acceptance of the inherent limitations of the anticipatory knowledge on which decisions about environmental discharges are based. We can often find out only when it is too late, or at the very least, awesomely expensive, to clean up.

However, while the preventive paradigm is acknowledged in principle, its practice is extremely tenuous, not least because we cannot know definitively what is an adequate level of investment in technological or social change to prevent environmental harm. The preventive approach requires attention to be shifted, from 'end-of-pipe' to 'upstream' decisions about industrial processes, product design and R&D strategies. Inevitably, this means finding criteria to determine decisions affecting environmental loads, at a point much further removed than conventional pollution control is from the point of immediate environmental discharge, thus from the point(s) of identification of environmental effects.

The usual technical approach to clean production poses the general question, how can we improve the efficiency of industrial processes in terms of resource use and waste outputs? A more difficult broader question is whether environmentally sustainable futures are feasible even if we assume the most efficient systems of production to be universally in place tomorrow. Might not growing consumption and production simply swallow up the advances provided by those imagined technical Utopias? It is striking how effectively environmental policy discourses manage to insulate the technical focus on clean production from the equally material social dimensions of ever-increasing resource use and waste (including discarded product) output.

How do we provide authoritative knowledge for defining how far we need to enforce greater process efficiency and product redesign (in both resource use and waste outputs), let alone control the cultural processes of production and consumption? The uncertainties which pervade attribution of environmental effects to specific environmental discharges are often large enough to sustain chronic conflict and indecision. So how can we face the even greater uncertainties which are exposed by moving attention upstream? The first need is to recognize their existence, and then to understand their complex social character, even within the domain of scientific knowledge.

The scientific burden of proof in environmental regulation has become a matter of intensifying conflict in recent years.[1] This has embodied two linked issues. First, where should that burden be located on the spectrum from complete environmental protection to waiting for obvious damage? Second, what burden can the scientific knowledge actually sustain, or be expected to sustain anyway?[2]

Clearly, shifting the locus of environmental responsibility further upstream in the industrial commitment process exposes more of the uncertainty about eventual downstream environmental effects: the uncertainty was already there, but concealed or 'black-boxed'[3] as if all the upstream system were simply a given.

This enlargement of acknowledged uncertainty is not only in scale. There are at least two fundamentally new *kinds* of uncertainty which are introduced, suggesting that established concepts of risk and uncertainty are no longer adequate.[4] These qualitative changes relate to the ways in which we think of decision-making about environmental discharges and damage, and the way we think of the role of scientific authority in relation to such decisions.

In this chapter I attempt to illustrate and characterize these fundamentally different kinds of uncertainty which the shift to the preventive paradigm allows us to recognize. In particular, I emphasize the key distinction between *indeterminacy* and uncertainty as conventionally described; departing from the idea that indeterminacy (when recognized at all) is simply a larger-scale uncertainty. I argue that indeterminacy underlies the construction of scientific knowledge, as well as the wider social world in which we create environmental effects. The implications of this point are developed.

One particular regulatory principle which is associated with the preventive philosophy, and which gives it practical effect, is the precautionary principle.[5] This was first developed in Germany as a means of justifying regulatory intervention to restrict marine pollution discharges in the absence of agreed proof of environmental harm. Despite being difficult to define in precise terms, it has been taken up in other environmental policy arenas, including even global climate change.[6] The scope of the precautionary principle in terms of shifting the burden of proof onto the polluter is still not clearly defined in relation to the nature of scientific proof and to the preventive philosophy. I will argue that the precautionary approach involves much more than simply shifting the threshold of proof to a different place in the same available body of knowledge. The different social premises which that shift implies also open up the possible reshaping of the natural categories and classifications on which that scientific knowledge is constructed.

Before discussing these kinds of issue, however, it is useful to set the scene by reviewing in outline the evolution of environmental risk assessment as a framework for generating knowledge and authority for environmental decision-making problems.

Risk and Reductionism

Risk assessment as a scientifically disciplined way of analysing risk and safety problems was originally developed for relatively very well-structured mechanical problems, such as chemical or nuclear plants, aircraft and aerospace technologies.[7] In such systems, the technical processes and parameters are well defined, and the reliability of separate components is testable or amenable to actuarial in-service analysis. Indeed, so controlled are the parameters of such systems that risk analysis did not develop *after* design and manufacture, to try to understand the built-in risks; it was an *integral part* of design, influencing criteria and choices in normative fashion, right through the whole process. In should be noted that these systems have often shown themselves to be less well defined than analysts and designers thought, exhibiting surprising properties – such as exploding – which indicate that the system was less determined by controlling forces than the analysts recognized.[8] Nevertheless, the point remains that, relatively speaking, this original cradle of risk analysis allowed its authors to build in assumptions of well-defined and deterministic processes.

These intellectual and methodological origins of risk assessment are important to recall because its role has now grown far beyond these well-defined *intensive* risk systems, to badly structured *extensive* problems, such as toxic waste or pesticides, and thence to environmental systems on a global scale. For these last-mentioned kinds of problem the limitations of available knowledge are potentially more serious because the system in question, not being a technological artefact, cannot be designed, manipulated and reduced to within the boundaries of existing analytical knowledge. In constructing analytic models of environmental systems, externally defined significant end-points, or pragmatic considerations, such as what can actually be measured, frequently dictate the structure of the resulting knowledge. Many important parameters have to be charted at one or more removes, via observation of *surrogate variables*. In addition, variables are often used which combine more than one parameter in complex form. Even something so apparently simple and precise as a single pH measure for a lake is, strictly speaking, such a *composite variable*, because we have to extrapolate and weight sample measurements which are always limited, into the mean value for that variable.

These practices artificially reduce uncertainties and variations, for example by the ways in which averaging, standardization and aggregation are performed. The fact that this is necessary and justified by the need to generate knowledge does not alter the point that it imposes man-made intellectual closure around entities which are more open-ended than the resulting models suggest. Yet these intellectual routines become so familiar to practitioners that their indirect and more provisional relationship to the ultimate parameters of interest is forgotten.

The very considerable amount of scientific work which has gone into the modelling of environmental risk systems over the past few decades cannot, therefore, be taken as reassurance that even the main dimensions of environmental harm from human activities have been comprehended. To understand this requires not only intense and open examination of the scientific evidence and competing interpretations in an area of interest; it also requires reflexive learning at a deeper level, about the nature and inherent limitations in principle of that knowledge, however competently produced.

Key distinctions for this task can be applied as follows:

- *Risk* – Know the odds.
- *Uncertainty* – Don't know the odds: may know the main parameters. May reduce uncertainty but increase ignorance.
- *Ignorance* – Don't know what we don't know, Ignorance increases with increased commitments based on given knowledge.
- *Indeterminacy* – Causal chains or networks open.

In the first place, we can talk authentically about *risk* when the system behaviour is basically well known, and chances of different outcomes can be defined and quantified by structured analysis of mechanisms and probabilities.

Second, if we know the important system parameters but not the probability distributions, we can talk in terms of *uncertainties*. There are several sophisticated methods for estimating them and their effects on outcomes. These uncertainties are recognized, and explicitly included in analysis.

Third, a far more difficult problem is *ignorance*,[9] which by definition escapes recognition. This is not so much a characteristic of knowledge itself as of the linkages between knowledge and commitments based on it – in effect, bets (technological, social, economic) on the completeness and validity of that knowledge.

Since this third distinction is conceptually more elusive, an example is justified. In the aftermath of the Chernobyl nuclear accident, in May 1986 a radioactive cloud passed over the UK. Heavy thunderstorms rained out radiocaesium deposits over upland areas, and, despite reassurances that there would be no lasting effects of the radioactive cloud, six weeks after the accident a sudden ban on hill sheep sales and slaughter was announced. Although this ban was expected to last only three weeks, because the radiocaesium was thought to be chemically immobilized in the soil once washed off vegetation, some hill farms in these areas of Cumbria and North Wales in particular, are still restricted six years later.[10] The scientists made a spectacular mistake in predicting the behaviour of radiocaesium in the environment of interest. It was gradually learned that the reason for the mistake was that the original prediction had been based on the observed behaviour of caesium in alkaline clay soils, whereas those of the areas in question were acid peaty soils. It was assumed by the scientists – wrongly as it turned out – that the previously observed behaviour also prevailed in the conditions which existed in the hill areas. Thus, contrary to the confident expectations of the scientists, the elevated levels of radiocaesium in the sheep from these upland areas did not fall, and restrictions had to be extended indefinitely, severely damaging the credibility of the scientists and institutions concerned. Eventually it was realized that the chemical immobilization which had been assumed took place only in aluminosilicate clays, and that in the upland peaty acid soils caesium remains chemically mobile, hence available for root uptake and recycle via edible vegetation back into the food chain.

It is important to recognize that this highly public scientific mistake actually followed normal scientific practice. Scientists attempted to predict the behaviour of an agent (here radiocaesium) by extrapolating from its observed behaviour under certain conditions, making some inadvertent assumptions about the new conditions. When the new observations did not fit with expected behaviour, the models underlying the predictions were (eventually) re-examined. Through this, certain previously unnoticed but significant differences were identified, and the models were elaborated accordingly.

Had this whole process taken place in the seclusion of the professional community of research scientists, it would have been wholly unremarkable (unless some scientist or another had been too committed to a particular model, in which case a dispute might have erupted, or a reputation could have been tarnished). The point is that scientific knowledge proceeds by *exogenizing* some significant uncertainties, which thus become invisible to it: as Kuhn noted, this is not a pathology of science but a necessary feature of structured investigation.[11] The built-in ignorance of science towards its own limiting commitments and assumptions is a problem only when external commitments are built on it as if such intrinsic limitations did not exist,[12] as happened when scientists and government officials pronounced in June 1986, on the basis of then-sovereign models, that radiocaesium levels would come down within a few weeks.

The above example underlines an important general point about scientific knowledge in public, and one not usually understood. The conventional view is that scientific knowledge and method enthusiastically *embrace* uncertainties and exhaustively pursue them. This is seriously misleading. It is more accurate to say that scientific knowledge gives prominence to a *restricted agenda of defined uncertainties* – ones that are tractable – leaving invisible a range of other uncertainties, especially about the boundary conditions of applicability of the existing framework of knowledge to new situations.

Thus ignorance is endemic to scientific knowledge, which has to reduce the framework of the known to that which is amenable to its own parochial methods and models. This only becomes a problem when (as is usual) scientific knowledge is misunderstood and is institutionalized in policymaking as if this condition did not pervade all competent scientific knowledge.[13] This institutionalized exaggeration of the scope and power of scientific knowledge creates a vacuum in which should exist a vital social discourse about the conditions and boundaries of scientific knowledge in relation to moral and social knowledge.

As the later example demonstrates, social commitments are necessary to define the boundaries of, and to give coherence to, scientific knowledge – not only in the large but in quite specific ways. Whenever events expose the ignorance which always underlies scientific models used in public policy, the dominant response is invariably to focus on improving the scientific model. However, although this is important, it is not enough. A response of at least equal importance ought to examine critically the (often inflated) social commitments built over the existing knowledge, because it is here that ignorance and its corresponding risks are created.[14] Indeterminacy exists in the open-ended question of whether knowledge is adapted to fit the mismatched realities of application situations, or whether those (technical and social) situations are reshaped to 'validate' the knowledge.[15]

A fourth distinction, the important one between uncertainty and *indeterminacy*, will be illustrated later. Here, it is relevant simply to note that conventional risk assessment methods tend to treat all uncertainties as if they were due to incomplete definition of an essentially determinate cause–effect system. In other words, they suggest that the route to better control of risks is more intense scientific knowledge of that system, to narrow the supposed uncertainties and gain more precise definition of it.

I will show that many risk sytems embody genuine indeterminacies which are misrepresented by this approach; but I will develop the further argument that the scientific knowledge which we construct of risk and environmental systems is also pervaded by tacit social judgement which covers indeterminacies in that knowledge itself. Lack of recognition of this distorts public debate and understanding of the proper relationship between expert knowledge and public value-choices in constructing regulatory policies for sustainable environmental technologies. In particular, it limits the scope of conceivable change, including change in social identities and relationships, in response to what are called global environmental 'threats'.

Ravetz and Funtowicz, in their concept of 'second-order science', or 'post-normal science', distinguish between three types of risk science, according to two independent dimensions – the size of the decision stakes, and the scale of the system uncertainties involved in defining the risks.[16] When both are low, applied science is in order and risks are the problem. When both are middle-range, then, they say, technical consultancy is the corresponding form of knowledge and the dominant problem is uncertainty. When both are large, as they see it, uncertainty expands into ignorance and indeterminacy, requiring a new, post-normal or 'second-order' science. Rayner and O'Riordan use this classification with no significant adaptation.[17] The perspective offered here is fundamentally different from their approach; whereas that framework suggests that indeterminacy is simply a larger form of uncertainty, existing beyond the limits of 'normal' uncertainty, my perspective draws from social analysis of scientific knowledge in recognizing that there is indeterminacy underlying scientific knowledge even when 'uncertainty' is small. It is kept at bay by the interlocking social commitments and conventions which constitute scientific paradigms or technological systems.

Thus Ravetz et al imply that uncertainty exists on an objective scale from small (risk) to large (ignorance), whereas I would see risk, uncertainty, ignorance and indeterminacy as overlaid one on the other, being expressed depending on the scale of the social commitments ('decision stakes') which are bet on the knowledge being 'correct'. Science can define a risk, or uncertainties, only by artificially 'freezing' a surrounding context which may or may not be this way in real-life situations. The resultant knowledge is therefore *conditional* knowledge, depending on whether these pre-analytical assumptions might turn out to be valid. But this question is indeterminate – for example, will the high quality of maintenance, inspection, operation, etc., of a risky technology be sustained in future, multiplied over replications, possibly many all over the world?

Hence the indeterminacy is embedded *within* the risk or uncertainty definition, not an extension in scale on the same dimension. As I will show, it pervades even apparently purely technical questions. It is the *unconditional* character that is artificially lent to knowledge which obscures its indeterminacy when applied to new situations. Risk, uncertainty and indeterminacy are therefore not on the same dimension in the way that the characterization of Ravetz and Funtowicz suggests they are. Nor, in my perspective, can the 'decision stakes' and the 'uncertainties' be independent of one another. Indeed, just what the 'decision stakes' are in any case is also indeterminate, and conditional.

To appreciate the full extent of our human responsibilities as they shape the basis of policy options requires us to examine more thoroughly the nature of indeterminacy in the systems we are engaged in changing through our human commitments and activities. This, in turn, requires us to re-exhume and explore the more subtle indeterminacies buried (sometimes as forms of self-confirmation) in our natural knowledge of those systems.

Upstream Decisions about Environmental Effects

The shift of attention upstream has at least two regular implications for the way we think about regulatory policies and processes.

First, explicit responsibility shifts more to the internal processes of industrial R&D, design and production, which introduce a range of complex organizational factors to do with how this behaviour is influenced. It is currently unclear to what extent it should be conceived as a self-contained process subject to external regulatory signals, or as an open-learning system within and between organizations, and in which new understandings and practical environmental criteria may become 'organically' embedded. Most of the research literature and policy thinking about regulation and environmental policy is framed in the former terms.[18] This conventional thinking tends to 'black-box' industrial decision processes and technology generally. To treat upstream challenges, new conceptual approaches are needed which are rooted in the guts of industrial–organizational processes of negotiation and commitment, with a fuller sense of both their constraints and flexibilities.[19]

Second, as the centre of gravity for analysis and decision moves further upstream and more distant from environmental effects, greater levels of uncertainty are obviously exposed in the investigation of possible causal links between decisions and environmental consequences. Less obvious, however, is that new *types* of uncertainty are exposed. This is most easily seen by referring to Figure 15.1, in which various stages of decision from upstream to diverse eventual environmental discharges are schematically portrayed.

The key point is that in trying to draw causal connections between an upstream decision option and downstream consequences of that option, the intervening uncertainties are better characterized as *indeterminacies*. They are not merely lack of definition in a determinate cause–effect system; the relationship between upstream

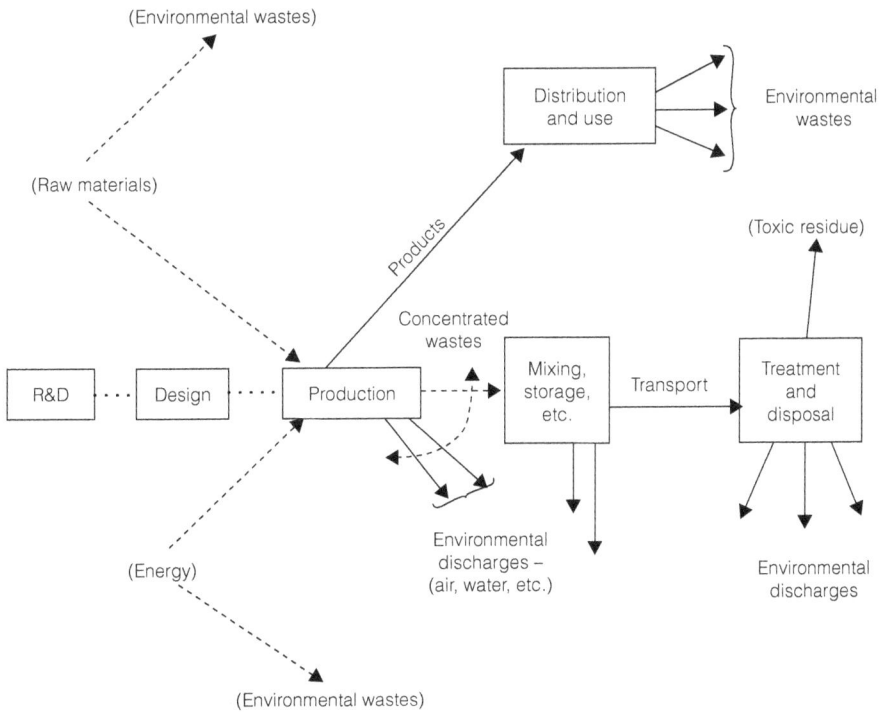

Figure 15.1 *Production–waste–environment system (schematic)*

commitments and downstream outcomes is a combination of genuine constraints which are laid down in determinate fashion, and real open-endedness in the sense that outcomes depend on how intermediate actors will behave. These intermediate actors include managers and workers such as plant operators, waste traders and other commercial agents, consumers, inspectors and other local regulatory actors; in any given case, the significant actors and relationships, and hence the variables affecting environmental outcomes, will be different depending on the system of production, waste generation and disposal, and the regulatory system in question.

By way of illustration, an industrial process generating more or less the same waste streams may present markedly different downstream environmental risks in the US and the UK, because of significant differences in the regulatory cultures of these two countries. Even within the confines of a single system this is also true.[20] Different levels of stringency of allowed discharges from point sources of air or water mean that different waste streams are produced in concentrated form for removal, treatment and disposal. A liquid toxic waste stream, such as an inorganic acid, may under the UK regulations be legally landfill-discharged by co-disposal with municipal garbage. The US regulations rule this out. Even in the same country the same industrial process will vary in the environmental disposition of its wastes depending on many contingent factors, such as where it is produced, which company is involved, which waste disposal company (if any) it deals with, how prices for competing options are changing, and what opportunities exist for maximizing profits by exploiting recovery and recycle possibilities, or alternatively finding cheap disposal outlets in other countries with weak controls.

The distinction between uncertainty and indeterminacy is important because the former enshrines the notion that inadequate control of environmental risks is due only to *inadequate scientific knowledge*, and exclusive attention is focused on intensifying that knowledge, to render it more precise. Very often this extra *technical* precision is a surrogate for more 'precise' control of *social* actors and the indeterminacies they bear. As an aside here, existing interpretations of the potentially revolutionary precautionary principle do not seem basically to change this situation, since they imply placing the decision threshold further into the uncertainties, but on the assumption that this is an early-warning stance, which further scientific knowledge (less imprecision or uncertainty) would later prove correct.

The extra concept of indeterminacy, therefore, introduces the idea that *contingent social behaviour* also has to be explicitly included in the analytical and prescriptive framework. (Of course, behavioural regulation is already implied in technical standards, but the full extent of contingency and indeterminacy, and the implications of this, are not recognized.) This corresponds with the distinction drawn in the risk field between *intrinsic* and *situational* risks from a given toxic waste.[21] The actual risks are a combination of the inherent properties of the chemicals composing the waste, and of the ways various people actually treat it. This contingent 'treatment' also includes how relevant commercial actors *define* the material, since they have some freedom (which varies between regulatory regimes) to define it as 'goods' not 'wastes' (for example, as raw materials for a recycling or energy plant), thus exempting it from regulation.

The type of indeterminacy so far discussed is the open-endedness in the processes of environmental damage due to human interventions. Risk frameworks have found these difficult to treat even for 'the human factor' in well-defined mechanical systems. Almost by definition, analytical knowledge of risks involves the standardization of risk situations, which implies the elaborate control and reorganization of social behaviour so as to conform with the implicit models of social behaviour embedded in the standardized analytical models. Thus an inherent contradiction exists between such standardizing tendencies and the realistic appreciation of the diverse and more open-ended situational forces and factors which defy such reductionist and deterministic treatment. The knowledge used to define risks and justify ensuing regulations is confirmed only if the social world can indeed be reorganized and controlled to reflect the assumption built into that knowledge in the first place. But if the social world does not fit, and wishes greater flexibility, it is an open question whether it should be controlled by determinate discourses from 'nature' or 'technology', or whether socially flexible technologies should be encouraged.

Thus, for example, the UK government's assertion that co-disposal of toxic wastes with municipal garbage is safe is based on studies of several landfills in the 1960s and 1970s. Embedded in that body of risk knowledge is the fact that during those studies great care was taken with respect to the management of the sites and what went into them. The risk knowledge may be valid only if that condition (*inter alia*) is fulfilled. Whether or not it is fulfilled in future cases depends on its being recognized as an indeterminacy in the system, and in the corresponding risk knowledge.[22]

Scientific and Social Indeterminacy

When discussing the burden of proof for environmental decisions it is mistaken to assume that there is an objective level of uncertainty intrinsic to any piece of scientific knowledge at its current state of refinement. The level of recognized uncertainty is itself a function of the perhaps subconscious perceptions of the role(s) of that knowledge.[23]

An illustration is appropriate here. The scientific uncertainties about what happens chemically, physically and biologically in a landfill site are huge, and the opportunities for examining and reducing them extremely limited. Thus the effects of putting a given waste into a site can only be approximately known; and these effects are not in any case determinate, but depend (*inter alia*) on how the site is operated and managed. At which site a waste ends up, and in what condition, also depends on many social unknowns and contingencies. In the US political culture, the scientific uncertainties about what happens to a waste in landfills would be a hostage to fortune for regulators, who would have opponents exposing those uncertainties to insist that landfill was hazardous, that it was irresponsible to sanction it when its safety was so uncertain, and that it should be banned. Thus the *social threat* which exists in the extremely conflictual, mistrustful and adversary US regulatory culture causes a scientific uncertainty to be *accentuated*. The social threat was avoided by the US decision to phase out landfill of toxic wastes. Uncertainty underlying decisions is a social risk because of the *institutionalized mistrust* which pervades the US system. Social discretion is not regarded as an asset, unless of course one can monopolize it.

In the UK political culture, on the other hand, the official attitude towards the same scientific uncertainties has been far more relaxed. The response has been that if things are uncertain they could therefore turn out better – there is no reason to assume the worst. For example, natural bacterial processes in the landfill may detoxify some chemicals so reducing the environmental risks; and if the risks depend upon sound operation and diligent waste handling, optimistic assumptions may be made unless strong evidence to the contrary exists. The point is that this official position has (at least until recently) been possible because the more consensual – and some would say complacent – UK political culture of environmental regulation has not experienced any social threats from opponents exploiting the technical uncertainties which underlie such environmental policy decisions.

Thus uncertainties in the scientific knowledge for environmental protection decisions cannot be properly described as objective shortfalls of knowledge, as most treatments suppose.[24] The extent of uncertainty seen in the scientific knowledge base is itself a subjective function of complex social and cultural factors. Scientific uncertainty can be enlarged by social uncertainties in the context of its practical interpretation, and it can be reduced by opposite social forces.[25]

I would like to give a more detailed example of the deep ways in which indeterminacies pervade the technical structure of scientific knowledge, before attempting to discuss the implications of this for the definition of environmental criteria. It is again drawn from the post-Chernobyl radioactive contamination issue in the UK, but from another aspect of the whole episode.

When monitoring was carried out after the Chernobyl radioactive fallout over the UK, high levels of radiocaesium were discovered. Against scientific predictions, these were found to persist in the fells and hill sheep of Cumbria, downwind and near to the Sellafield nuclear reprocessing plant. People soon began to question whether the government and its scientists had not secretly known all along that there was radioactive contamination in this area dating from well before the Chernobyl accident, either from Sellafield's routine emissions, from the 1957 Windscale reactor accident on the same site, or from atmospheric nuclear weapons testing, or from some combination of these.

Thus the question 'When did they know?' about the long duration of contamination of these hill soils and vegetation with radiocaesium became a highly charged one. Environmental groups critical of government secrecy argued that its scientists had known since the early 1960s that in acid peaty soils radiocaesium persisted and remained available, unlike its behaviour in alkaline clay soils.[26] They pointed to a paper published in *Nature* in 1964 by a team from the Harwell nuclear research establishment as evidence that the scientists had known all along that the radiocaesium was mobile, and would recycle into vegetation from these acid soils.[27]

The *Nature* paper reported measurements of the depth profiles of given surface deposits of radiocaesium after yearly intervals from deposition up to 4.8 years, in six different soil types, including alkaline clays and acid organic peats. Contrary to the assertions of environmentalist critics, it did not conclude that the behaviour of radiocaesium in terms of its depth distribution with time was any different between these soils. Thus it was arguable that the false scientific prediction that high levels of radiocaesium would soon disappear in sheep was based on an innocent, if mistaken, extrapolation from observed behaviour in lowland clay soils to the (peaty) Cumbrian fells. However, further insights can be gained if we look more closely at the research and its relationship to the situation confronted in the post-Chernobyl emergency in the hill-farming areas.

The Harwell measurements of radiocaesium in the different soils were physical depth measurements. The authors observed that the mean depth from several measurements at each interval in each soil type showed no significant differences among the different soils. The only difference was that the peaty soils showed a wider range of variance, but the mean was assumed to be the significant value, and this was the same. Thus in terms of mean physical depth of radiocaesium as the key parameter, these soils were *the same*. On this basis, the mistaken extrapolation on which the false predictions were founded could be said to have been reasonable, and the conclusion reached that the scientists had been wrong, but not conspiratorial – cognitively deficient but at least not morally so.

However, this approach, reasonable as far as it goes, omits a further interesting dimension. The 1964 *Nature* paper was clearly premised on the assumption that the physical depth distribution with time was the main, indeed the only, parameter of interest. This corresponded with the assumption that the significant risks from such deposits of radiocaesium were from an external gamma radiation dose to a person standing on the surface. This kind of dose would be affected mainly by the physical depth distribution of the radiocaesium. Yet in the post-Chernobyl crisis a completely different exposure pathway became the focus of concern; namely, the contamination of grazing sheep and subsequently of humans who ate them. On this different model of the risk situation the central factor was the root uptake of caesium from soil into vegetation, and this depended on its chemical mobility as well as its physical disposition.

In terms of the chemical mobility parameter, the acid peaty soils and alkaline clay soils turned out to be very different, since in the former caesium remains chemically free and mobile, whereas in the latter it adsorbs onto the aluminosilicate molecules of the clays and is thus immobilized except for the relatively much slower processes of physical leaching of host particles. These chemical differences could indeed explain the wider range of variance (observed but not explored in the *Nature* paper) among the measurements in the peaty soil samples.

The example is outlined schematically in Figure 15.2. On the basis of a taken-for-granted social scenario of external gamma exposure as the controlling set of behavioural factors, the scientific knowledge about soils and radiocaesium was constructed on the basis of physical depth measurements, and chemical parameters were not considered. On this taken-for-granted basis, the soils were found to be the same. Yet this was not the only scientific way of defining the question. On the basis of the exposure scenario which unfolded after Chernobyl, the chemical availability of radiocaesium for vegetation uptake became central, without any scientist apparently realizing it at the time. As gradually became clear, on these grounds the soils behaved differently. Sameness had switched to difference, within the same set of scientific observations. The very logic of science had been transformed, not by any new data, but by seeing from a different external perspective, namely a different scenario of human exposure.

This example illustrates how the detailed technical construction of scientific logics about environmental risks is not completely determined by the evidence from nature alone, but is partly open-ended depending on what parameters are treated as the most significant. As several authors have shown in the sociology of scientific knowledge, the construction of 'natural' classes of sameness and difference relations, is never completely determined only by nature, but is open to social commitment.[28] Usually, as with the *Nature* paper, such commitments are made without their authors realizing they have

(a) External γ-dose scenario

Physical depth state parameter
(Soils approximately the same)

(b) Food-chain scenario

Chemical state parameter
(Soils completely different)

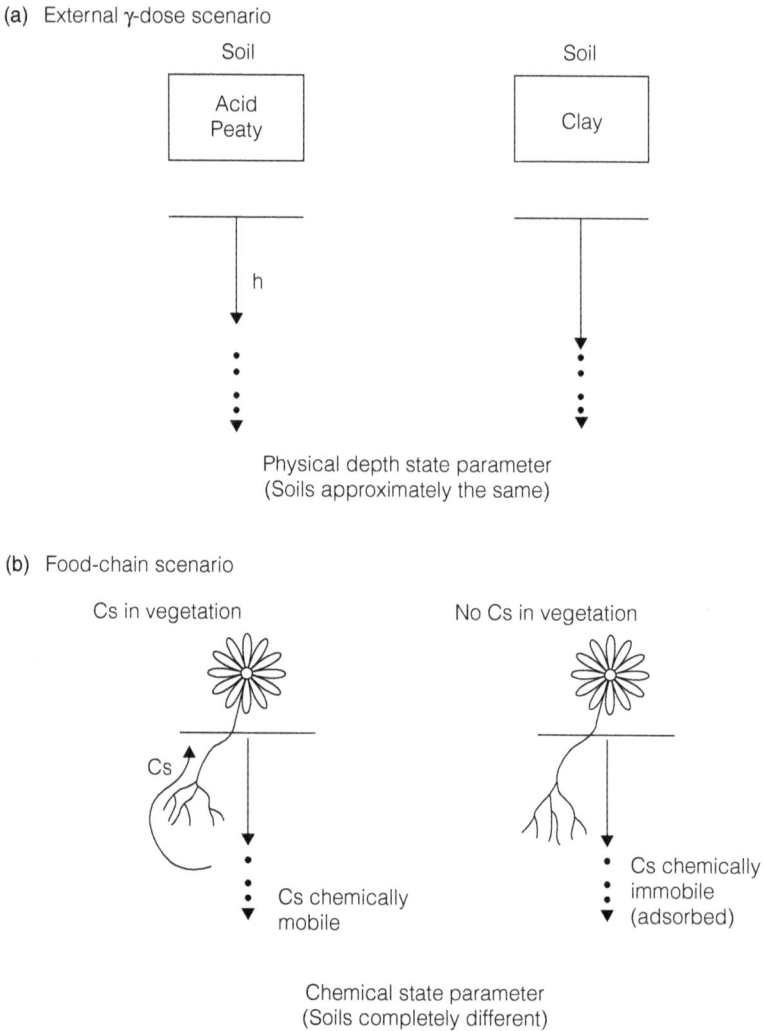

Figure 15.2 *Exposure-scenario dependency of 'natural' scientific categories: (a) external physical γ-dose; (b) food-chain chemical–biological pathway*

effectively made such choices: they are simply part of the culture of the scientific research speciality. Yet the scientific knowledge is not fully determined by 'the facts' – what 'the facts' are has to be actively read into nature to some extent. In other words, social mechanisms of closure around particular logical constructions have to occur in order to complete the otherwise incomplete logical construction. This is a further, more subtle and pervasive sense in which indeterminacies exist in the basis of authoritative natural knowledge about environmental risks.

The implication is that shifting an external policy-driven criterion, such as burden of proof of 'damage', may involve reconstructing the 'natural' architecture of environmental knowledge in reflection of those new moral commitments and identities, not leaving it immune from those currents, as if independently determined.

Retrieving Indeterminacy

I have aimed in this chapter to identify less obvious issues for risk assessment and regulatory knowledge exposed by the policy shift towards preventive, or upstream strategies for integrating environmental criteria into decision-making.

My main argument, that moving attention upstream exposes not just more uncertainty, but fundamentally different *kinds* of uncertainty, especially social indeterminacies even within scientific knowledge, could be used as an argument against upstream regulatory strategies on the grounds of their non-feasibility. My argument seems to imply that we cannot ever expect to find criteria for reasonable decision-making of this kind. However, this misses the main point, which is to treat ignorance and indeterminacy more seriously as potential sources of risk in themselves, and to embrace them in a broader debate about the implications of societal commitment to such production processes.

The policy language of risk, as Donald Schon has noted,[29] falsely reduces the full range of uncertainties to the more comforting illusion of controllable, probabilistic but determinisitic processes. This conceals the dimension of ignorance behind practical policy and technological commitments based on a given body of scientific knowledge. It thus obscures further important questions about the decreasing margins for error, and the social control and manipulation involved in such commitments (in the form of technologies and environmental interventions) become more intensive and extensive in several dimensions at the same time. Thus, in another sense also, scientific uncertainty can be seen to be important not in itself, supposedly measurable on some objective scale, but as a function of (in relation to) the extent of technological or policy commitment riding on the body of knowledge concerned. As such commitments grow larger, we can *tolerate less uncertainty*, ironically as we discover more; the error costs rise alarmingly. Yet conventional risk science is unable to help illuminate these, what we might call 'second-order risks', which incorporate institutional demeanour and forms of social control, among other things. They need to be explicitly included in social and policy debate, but this requires a basic reconceptualization of the relationships between social commitments, moral identities and 'natural' knowledge.[30]

The above could be seen as a philosophical argument for the more radical version of the precautionary principle. However, even precaution involves uncertainties and risks.[31] Thus, as defenders of environmental discharges are fond of saying, if we ban production which cannot meet the zero-discharge standards of strict precautionary principle advocates, what happens if we cannot feed people as a result? Long before that, it would seem, consumers would be marching for pollution.

Bodansky, for example,[32] argues that the precautionary principle would not have captured CFCs, nor DDT, since the existing uncertainty along which the question of scientific proof for regulation was stretched was in each case the wrong question altogether, as we now know. For DDT, uncertainties were recognized only over acute toxicity; chronic toxicity was not even conceived of. For CFCs, the very property thought to bring low risk to biological species, long-term stability, meant it could reach the stratospheric ozone layer – but this was not even considered at that time. However, to conclude against precaution on this basis is to assume only a limited version of uncertainty.

It we take the indeterminacy point seriously, we do not know how far new technologies and social practices can be developed in order to meet new constraints of sustainability, and new opportunities for conviviality. The most important need is surely to develop 'regulatory' cultures which successfully encourage greater public debate on the social benefits, costs and indeterminacies of different products and processes, as well as on conventional environmental strategy questions. This will also mean exposure of and debate on the conditional social assumptions framing, and embedded in, 'natural' knowledges of environmental risks. Only this more rounded approach to the environmental assessment problem can offer the possibility of overcoming what is otherwise a fundamental limitation of the risk-science paradigm, which is its intrinsic inability to recognize ignorance and, thus, second-order risk, underlying present technological commitments and trajectories.

Indeed the dominant risk-science approach is more than a method; it is a misbegotten *culture* which inadvertently but actively conceals that ignorance. It thus blinds us to these more substantial kinds of ignorance and associated risk until they are upon us, and we are forced into remedial modes of operation yet again. Thus we cannot sustain a preventive approach without the reconceptualization which places scientific knowledge within the explicitly social, moral and cultural perspective I have outlined.

All this is relevant to the central issue in criteria for clean production decisions, because it should influence how we treat the issue of scientific burden of proof. With the advent of the precautionary principle, the burden of proof appears to have shifted, but some more basic expectations still remain. Thus, for example, most formulations of the precautionary principle (certainly in the UK) accept the need to stop a discharge in the absence of full scientific proof of harm, if it is *reasonably anticipated* to be irreversibly harmful.[33] However, this still suggests that scientific proof is expected soon for such decisions, which is a limited and mistaken way to view the problem. This conventional view appears to hold that the body of scientific knowledge remains qualitatively the same, while the threshold of acceptable risk is simply moved across the body of knowledge to a different position within that knowledge – as it were, nearer to technology and further from nature (hence further into the uncertainties which exist, *pace* Figure 14.2).

However, the point of the example drawn from radiocaesium-soil research knowledge was to indicate that 'when scientific knowledge knows what?' is more fundamentally open-ended, soft and thus more deeply problematic than this model recognizes, even when it expressly adopts a more precautionary standard. As we shift the normative rule through the body of scientific knowledge in this way, that body of knowledge itself may change. The 'external' normative choices also influence the 'internal' choices of inference options, sameness and difference relations in theoretical models, and what is defined scientifically as problematic or not.

On this point, we can relate the radiocaesium-soils example to the production of competing kinds of environmental scientific knowledge – on the one hand, conventional research recognized under assimilative capacity approaches to marine pollution regulation, and, on the other, that underpinning the precautionary principle.

Dethlefsen has alluded to deeper cultural differences pervading the two competing scientific approaches, in his comment that 'workers who cannot see the correlation between pollution and diseases in their studies are with the exception of Möller from Germany, living on the other side of the North Sea'.[34] But the point is that the scientists involved are not merely looking at the same body of data with different evaluative spectacles, as it were, and then advising policymakers of their policy-related judgements. Their epistemic, theoretical and methodological commitments build up different bodies of 'natural' data or facts, impregnated with incompatible 'natural' logics, well before the policy actors come even to *see*, let alone *exercise*, the normative choices about how strictly to regulate polluting activities. Thus normative responsibilities and commitments are concealed in the 'natural' discourse of the science, indicating the *fundamentally* negotiable definition of the boundary between science and policy.[35] The full range of moral and social issues at stake is *not* adequately described by leaving the 'factual' scientific realm as if it is a separate black box from the normative. It already reflects and reinforces tacit normative boundaries and constraints.

The precautionary scientific idiom from east of the North Sea is much more ready to accept:

- That *composite* variables, such as 'immunocompetence', 'disease' and 'stress', are legitimate components of scientific reasoning. Sindermann identified 18 different factors, some natural, some anthropogenic, which might singly or combined result in stress;[36] and 'disease therefore has to be understood to be an unspecified response towards all kinds of stress'.[37] This idiom thus uses composite variables flexibly, recognizing the possible constituent factors, but not discounting the larger picture just because the precise constituent variables in a composite such as 'stress' may not be defined.
- The scientific legitimacy of *indirect* cause–effect inferences. For example, Dethlefsen reports a study of the possible correlation between diseases and marine contamination.[38] Although no direct correlation was found, bacterial levels in the blood of eels from a contaminated area of the North Sea averaged 80 per cent, compared to 4 per cent in eels from a relatively uncontaminated reference area. This was taken to indicate an indirect effect of pollution, causing reduced immune-system strength in the eels, and thus higher vulnerability to other disorders even if these had not shown at the time of sampling, and even if they might be *finally* induced by a natural factor. Focusing on single-variable direct-cause explanation would in such a case completely miss the damaging role of pollution.
- That, with due caution, *circumstantial* evidence for cause–effect mechanisms is legitimate.

Indeed, on closer inspection, all scientific reasoning is unavoidably circumstantial, as the radiocaesium-soil example also illustrates. The conventional assimilative capacity scientific idiom of marine pollution[39] appears on the face of it to avoid circumstantial reasoning by its reductionist epistemology; but, for example, in the putative connection between fish disease and contamination it defined the observation of high levels of disease away from inshore waters as an anomaly sufficient to 'disprove' the connection, on the general assumption that such offshore water were less contaminated. This conclusion was drawn as a sound scientific fact before measurements which showed the 'offshore is cleaner' assumption to be wrong, at least in this case. The application by assimilative capacity scientists of the general assumption to the specific case was just as much *circumstantial* reasoning as the explicitly accepted circumstantial reasoning sometimes adopted by the 'precautionary' idiom.

Conclusions

There is always an ineradicable element of indeterminacy in deciding whether a new empirical situation is an instance of a class of entities under one theory or model, or another. (Is the soil in the upland sheep areas the same or different from the soil(s) on which the conceptual model of caesium behaviour is constructed? It depends on whether we are concerned about sheep meat contamination, or direct external gamma-ray exposures.) The traces of this endemic indeterminacy are usually already well concealed (even from the scientists involved) by the time it comes to exercising policy responsibilities, even though the way the choices are made at such scientific points may have important policy implications.

We have learned from the detailed analysis of the creation of scientific knowledge over the past 20 years or so, that many of the intellectual commitments which constitute that knowledge are not completely validated, not fully determined by empirical nature.[40] Always central to the process are not just *uncertainties* in the form of imprecision (which, it is assumed, will be narrowed down by more research), but indeterminacies, for example, as to whether things are classified as the same or different, and on what specific properties or *criteria*. The purely technical aspects of such intellectual commitment merge with epistemic questions as to why we are constructing such knowledge anyway. This is always open to social evaluation and negotiation, though that is very far from saying that scientific truth can be subject to social choice.

However, we can see that when scientific knowledge is deployed in the public domain, the social judgements of a relatively private research community which create closure and 'natural validation' around particular constructions of speciality scientific knowledge, need to be reopened (deconstructed) and renegotiated in a wider social circle, possibly one involving different epistemological commitments and expectations, and correspondingly different definitions of the boundaries between nature and culture, or (objective) determinism and (human) responsibility. These too will have to be recognized and renegotiated in some way, as new, more broadly legitimated principles on which scientific knowledge generation can be founded. Unless this element of openness in scientific knowledge can be recognized, we will not be able to see the extent to which existing scientific knowledge 'naturalizes' and limits our moral, cultural and policy horizons.

In this chapter, I have developed the argument that the relationship of knowledge to the world of policy is fundamentally different from dominant notions. Scientific knowledge (in this respect, like any other knowledge) is generated in relation to social worlds, and its validity or invalidity depends not only on its degree of fit with nature (which is negotiable), but also on its correspondence with the social world. To achieve validation, for example in environmental policy, the institutions involved therefore need to control the social world to correspond with that knowledge, as the symbolic currency of their authority. This means *restricting* and controlling the indeterminacies emphasized in this chapter, and which are concealed in scientific discourses.

The proper scope and basis of this attempted restriction should be debated and negotiated in public, as part of environmental policy discourse. This would include our complicity in one of the main fields of such restriction, namely the taking-for-granted of production–consumption technological and cultural systems as determinate and closed, with only marginal room for adjustment. Such a debate cannot be fostered while these dimensions are obscured by the dominant regulatory discourses of scientific knowledge and policy.

The subtle but deep indeterminacies which pervade the constitution of scientific knowledge have a large, but ill-defined domain for which society has responsibility to exercise human values and negotiate moral identities, but which has instead been unconditionally abandoned to the implicit (reductionist and instrumentalist) epistemic commitments of science.

We cannot, therefore, expect to leave the responsibility for defining the criteria of clean technology to environmental science and risk assessment, nor to any such technical disciplines alone. Nor can we even expect them objectively to discover the different risks and benefits, for policy institutions then to exercise societal values and choices. The natural knowledge which those disciplines generate is already partly a reflection of tacit dominant cultural values and identities, ones which may be part of the problem. But this reflection is distorted by the discourse of objective natural determination in which knowledge and persuasion are couched. To confront fully the issues of values and policies will therefore require willingness to wrest open the scientific black boxes and consider their internal reconstruction. The preventive paradigm for environmentally sustainable technology is opening up a more radical shift in our relationship with scientific knowledge, and a correspondingly more radical challenge to society, than has yet been recognized.

Notes and References

1 J. R. Ravetz and S. Funtowicz, *Global Environmental Issues and the Emergence of Second-Order Science*, Council for Science and Society, London, 1990; J. Brown, ed, *Environmental Threats: Analysis, Perception, Management*, Belhaven, London, 1989.

2 S. Jasanoff, *The Fifth Branch: Science Advisers as Policy Makers*, Harvard University Press, Cambridge, MA, 1990; R. Smith and B. Wynne, eds, *Expert Evidence: Interpreting Science in the Law*, Routledge, London and New York, 1989.

3 M. Callon and B. Latour, 'Unscrewing the big Leviathan', in K. Knorr-Cetina and A. Cicourel, eds, *Advances in Social Theory and Methodology*, Routledge and Kegan Paul, London, 1983, pp277–302; B. Latour, *Science in Action*, Open University Press, London, 1986.

4 S. Funtowicz and J. R. Ravetz, *Uncertainty and Quality in Knowledge for Policy*, Kluwer, Dordrecht, 1990; Ravetz and Funtowicz, op cit, Ref 1.

5 K. von Moltke, *The Vorsorgeprinzip in West German Environmental Policy*, Institute for European Environmental Policy, Bonn, London and Brussels, 1987: D. Bodansky,

'Scientific uncertainty and the precautionary principle', *Environment*, Vol 33, No 7, September 1991, pp4–5, 43–44.

6   Ministerial Declaration of the Second World Climate Conference, 7 November 1990, *Environmental Policy and Law*, Vol 20, No 6, 1990, p220.

7   H. Otway, 'Introduction', in H. Otway and M. Peltu, eds, *Risk and Regulation*, Butterworths, London, 1985.

8   B. Wynne, 'Unruly technology: Practical rules, impractical discourses, and public understanding', *Social Studies of Science*, Vol 18, 1988, pp147–167.

9   Ravetz and Funtowicz, op cit, Refs 1 and 4.

10   B. Wynne, 'Sheepfarming after Chernobyl: A case study in communicating scientific information', *Environment*, Vol 31, No 2, March 1989, pp10–15, 33–39.

11   T. S. Kuhn, *The Structure of Scientific Revolutions*, University of Chicago Press, Chicago, IL, 1962.

12   B. Wynne, 'Scientific uncertainty and environmental policy: Towards a new paradigm', paper for UN World Commission on Environment and Development, Geneva, May 1985.

13   Y. Ezrahi, *The Descent of Icarus*, Harvard University Press, Cambridge, MA, 1990.

14   W. Krohn and J. Weyer, 'Die Gesell-schaft als Labor: Die Erzeugung Sociales Risiken durch Experimentale Forschung', *Soziale Welt*, Vol 3, 1989, pp349–373.

15   D. McKenzie, *Inventing Accuracy: A Historical Sociology of Nuclear Missile Guidance*, MIT Press, Cambridge, MA, and London, 1990.

16   Ravetz and Funtowicz, op cit, Ref 4.

17   T. O'Riordan and S. Rayner, 'Risk management for global environmental change', *Global Environmental Change*, Vol 1, No 2, March 1991, pp91–108.

18   J. Schot, 'Constructive technology assessment: The case of clean technology', *Science, Technology and Human Values*, Vol 17, 1992, pp36–56.

19   L. G. Zucker, 'Production of trust: institutional sources of economic structure, 1840–1920', *Research in Organisational Behavior*, Vol 8, 1986, pp53–111.

20   B. Wynne, *Risk Management and Hazardous Wastes*, Springer, London, Berlin and New York, 1987.

21   Ibid.

22   Ibid; B. Wynne, 'Frameworks of rationality in risk management', in J. Brown, ed, *Environmental Threats: Analysis, Perception, Management*, Belhaven, London, 1989.

23   H. Collins, *Changing Order*, Sage, London and Beverley Hills, CA, 1985; B. Latour and S. Woolgar, *Laboratory Life*, Sage, London and Beverley Hills, CA, 1979.

24   UN Conference on Environment and Development, Preparatory Scientific Meeting, Ministerial Declaration of Action for a Common Future, UN Doc A/CONF 151/PC/10, 6 August 1990, Bergen, Norway.

25   N. Gilbert and M. Mulkay, *Opening Pandora's Box: A Sociological Analysis of Scientists' Discourse*, Cambridge University Press, Cambridge, 1985.

26   For example, Jean Emergy (McSorley) of Cumbrians opposed to a Radioactive Environment (CORE), personal communications, during late 1986 and 1987.

27   H. J. Gale, D. L. Humphreys and E. M. Fisher, 'Weathering of Caesium–137 in soils'. *Nature*, No 4916, 18 January 1964, pp257–261.

28   For example, J. Law and P. Lodge, *Science for Social Scientists*, MacMillan, London, 1984; T. Pinch, *Confronting Nature: the Sociology of Solar Neutrino Detection*, Reidel, Dordrecht, 1986; D. Bloor, *Knowledge and Social Imagery*, Routledge and Kegan Paul, London, 1976; S. L. Star, 'Scientific work and uncertainty', *Social Studies of Science*, Vol 15, 1985, pp391–427.

29   D. A. Schon, 'Risk and uncertainty', reprinted in S. B. Barnes and D. O. Edge, eds, *Science in Context*, Open University Press, London, 1982.

30 R. Grove-White, The emerging shape of environmental conflict in the 1990s', *RSA Journal*, June 1991, pp43–51; B. Wynne, 'Risk and social learning: Reification to engagement', in S. Krimsky and D. Golding, eds, *Theories of Risk*, Praeger, New York, 1992.

31 Bodansky, op cit, Ref 5.

32 Ibid.

33 T. Jackson, 'Who needs principles?', background paper to Conference on 'Clean Production: Scientific and Policy Principles', Stockholm Environment Institute, Stockholm, 17–18 April 1991; see also the UK Government White Paper, *This Common Inheritance: Britain's Environmental Strategy*, HMSO, London, 1990.

34 V. Dethlefsen, 'Assessment of data on fish diseases', in P. Newman and A. Agg, eds, *Environmental Protection of the North Sea*, Heinemann, London, pp276–285.

35 S. Jasanoff, 'Contested boundaries in policy-relevant science', *Social Studies of Science*, Vol 16, 1986, pp273–296.

36 C. J. Sindermann, 'Fish and environmental impacts', *Archiven die Fische Wissenschaft*, Vol 35, No 1, 1984, pp125–160.

37 Dethlefsen, op cit, Ref 34, p276.

38 Ibid.

39 T. Jackson and P. Taylor, 'The precautionary principle and the prevention of marine pollution', *Chemistry and Ecology*, special issue on the 1st International Ocean Pollution Symposium, Vol 21, 1991; J. Campbell, 'Assimilative Capacity', paper to 'Conference on Clean Production: Scientific and Policy Principles', Stockholm Environment Institute, Stockholm, 17–18 April 1991.

40 Collins, op cit, Ref 23; Latour and Woolgar, op cit, Ref 23; Law and Lodge, op cit, Ref 28.

Index

For Product Safety Concerns and Information please contact our EU
representative GPSR@taylorandfrancis.com
Taylor & Francis Verlag GmbH, Kaufingerstraße 24, 80331 München, Germany

www.ingramcontent.com/pod-product-compliance
Lightning Source LLC
Chambersburg PA
CBHW070901080426
R18103400001B/R181034PG41932CBX00003B/5

9781844076871